A HOLOCAUST READER

Library of Jewish Studies

EDITOR

Neal Kozodoy

ADVISORY COMMITTEE

Emil L. Fackenheim
Judah Goldin
Isadore Twersky

A HOLOCAUST READER

Edited, with introductions and notes, by

LUCY S. DAWIDOWICZ

BEHRMAN HOUSE, INC. | PUBLISHERS | NEW YORK

ACKNOWLEDGMENTS

The author and publisher thank the following for permission to reprint:

The American Jewish Committee and *Commentary* for "On the Agenda: Death," tr., Milton Himmelfarb, © 1949.

Beacon Press and Nahum N. Glatzer for "Wear the Yellow Badge with Pride," tr., Harry Zohn, in *The Judaic Tradition,* © 1969.

Holt, Rinehart and Winston for illustrations on pp. 113 and 126 from *The War Against the Jews 1933–1945* by Lucy S. Dawidowicz, © 1975 by Lucy S. Dawidowicz; illustrations © 1975 by Holt, Rinehart and Winston.

Yad Vashem; Martyrs' and Heroes' Remembrance Authority for selections from Adam Czerniaków, *Yoman geto varsha;* from *Teudot migeto Lublin;* and from *Darko shel yudenrat: teudot migeto Bialystok.*

YIVO Institute for Jewish Research for selections from the diary of Zelig Kalmanovich, in *YIVO Annual of Jewish Social Science,* vol. 8.

Library of Congress Cataloging in Publication Data
Main entry under title:
A Holocaust reader.
    (Library of Jewish studies)
    Bibliography: p.
    Includes index.
    1. Holocaust, Jewish (1939–1945)—History—
Sources. I. Dawidowicz, Lucy S.
D810.J4H65   940.53'1503'924   75-33740
ISBN 0-87441-219-6
ISBN 0-87441-236-6 pbk.

10 9 8 7 6

In memory of the six million

"History will cherish your memory, people of the ghetto. Your least expression will be studied, your struggle for human dignity will inspire poems. . ."

Zelig Kalmanovich, Vilna Ghetto
December 27, 1942

CONTENTS

PART TWO: THE HOLOCAUST

THIS BOOK is a collection of documents about the Holocaust, a term that has come to signify the destruction and martyrdom of the European Jews under German occupation during the Second World War. These documents are the raw materials, the infrastructure, for the historical narrative of the Holocaust. Although themselves not history, they are indispensable to history, and they provide a unique opportunity to glimpse historical experience in the process of its formation and development. Without such documents there would be no history at all.

The idea for this volume came from Neal Kozodoy and the collection emerged as a by-product of my history, *The War Against the Jews 1933–1945* (Holt, Rinehart and Winston, 1975), to which it can serve most productively as a complement.

All the documents except one are contemporary with the historical events they describe and all reflect the exigencies of the political conditions under which they were composed. (The only noncontemporary document is Kurt Gerstein's deposition, written right after the war's end, while he was imprisoned and being interrogated as a possible war criminal.) Contemporaneity was a determining criterion in my selection of documents, for it guarantees the immediacy of the historical record, testifies to the writer's direct association with the historic events, and minimizes the distortions that arise with the passing of time. Other criteria I applied in the selection of documents were the obvious ones of genuineness and reliability. A document's informativeness and/or its author's perceptiveness was an additional determinative factor. Finally I strove to make the collection as a whole both systematic and comprehensive, to provide documents that would fill out and illustrate the whole historical narrative. Thus the reader and the student who use this book may vicariously experience the events here recorded.

Most of the documents appear in English for the first time. Of the few previously published in English translation, nearly all have been freshly revised. The labors of translation were huge and the translators who worked from German, Yiddish, Polish, French, and Hebrew sources performed their tasks well and sometimes with virtuosity. (Credits for translations appear at the end of the volume.) I wish here to acknowledge my special indebtedness to George Salomon, a translator's translator, from whom I learned much about German style and language.

This volume could not have been completed without the unfailing cooperation of Miss Dina Abramowicz, librarian of the YIVO Institute for Jewish Research, and of Mr. Harry J. Alderman, head of the Blaustein Library of the American Jewish Committee. Grants from several foundations enabled me to undertake this formidable task of translation and I am pleased to acknowledge the assistance of the Atran Foundation, Inc. and its vice-president, Mr. Isaiah M. Minkoff; the Lucius N. Littauer Foundation and its president, Mr. Harry Starr; and the John Slawson Fund for Research, Training and Education and Dr. John Slawson. Dr. Isaiah Trunk and Dr. Lucjan Dobroszycki, both of the YIVO Institute, were consistently helpful in response to my frequent and persistent inquiries. Rose Grundstein typed the manuscript with her customary skill and good humor. Rabbi David Mirsky, Dean of Stern College for Women at Yeshiva University, was a constant source of encouragement.

My husband Szymon, as always, helped me make this book from start to finish. I could not have done so without him.

Lucy S. Dawidowicz
New York, New York

INTRODUCTION:
ON STUDYING HOLOCAUST DOCUMENTS

LIKE ALL DOCUMENTS, Holocaust documents may be classified in two broad categories: official records and private papers. Official records—state papers, government archives, diplomatic reports, institutional files, memoranda, and minutes—are formal and impersonal, dealing with events for the most part in the unimaginative bureaucratic language and characterless style of large institutions. Private papers—memoirs, diaries, letters, "original narratives of eyewitnesses," to use Leopold von Ranke's enumeration—are human expressions of personal feeling and individual perception, imparting the aura and ambience of living reality to the historical record.

I

For the history of the Holocaust, the documentary sources—both official records and private papers—surpass in quantity and comprehensiveness the records of any other historical era. The only nearly comparable period was that of the revolutionary upheavals and the overthrow of governments in the mid-nineteenth century, which led to the opening of the archives of Western Europe; it was then that "the records of dispossessed dynasties" fell into the hands of those who had no interest in preserving their secrecy.[1] Even more sweeping in its effect was the decision of the victorious Western Allies in 1945 to make captured German documents available to the scholarly community. Never before had historians had such total unhindered access to the official records of a state. In fact, the superabundance of captured German documents has presented to the historian a problem nearly as severe and crippling as the lack of documentation altogether, since the behemoth proportions of these seized papers conspire against man's frailty and the limits of his time.[2]

The captured German documents comprise the records of federal, regional, and local government agencies, of military commands and units, as well as of the National Socialist party, its formations, affiliated associations, and supervised organizations, covering a period ranging from 1920 to 1945. After the war they were brought to the United States and housed in a depot at Alexandria, Va., where they were sorted, classified, and microfilmed. They have since been returned to the Federal Republic of Germany. Sixty-seven *Guides to German Records Microfilmed at Alexandria, Va.,* prepared under the direction of the Committee for the Study of War Documents of the American Historical Association, have been published by the National Archives, comprising about 7,500 pages. An average page in a guide covers almost 2,000 frames of film, which means that the captured German documents now available on microfilm from the National Archives total about fifteen million pages.

From the very start, the Allied powers as well as all liberated countries where masses of German documents were seized regarded the German records primarily as legal evidence and documentary proof to be used at the trials of German war criminals. Operating under the exigencies of time, army intelligence personnel, translators, lawyers, scholars, and specialists began to sift the mountainous accumulations of documents for this purpose. The United States teams alone examined about 100,000 documents individually, desig-

---

1. Herbert Butterfield, *Man on His Past: The History of Historical Scholarship* (Boston, 1960), p. 79.
2. Gerhard L. Weinberg has formulated the Malthusian law of documentation in modern times: "As the century progresses arithmetically, the annual increment in records created expands geometrically." In "Nazi Party and Military Records," paper read at the annual meeting of the American Historical Association, December 30, 1958.

nating about 40,000 as valuable. These were then subjected to rigorous screening to search out the most persuasive evidence of war crimes and crimes against humanity committed by the Germans. The documents finally selected became the exhibits presented by the American prosecution at the trial of the twenty-two major war criminals held before the International Military Tribunal at Nuremberg. Great Britain, France, and the Soviet Union, each with its own storehouse of seized German documents, similarly developed exhibits and evidence.

The trial proceedings and the documents admitted in evidence were published—in identical English, French, and German versions—in forty-two volumes, known as the "Blue Series." The United States published its documents under the title *Nazi Conspiracy and Aggression*, in eight volumes and supplements, the "Red Series"; documents not introduced or admitted as evidence were included here.

After the trial of the major war criminals, there were twelve subsequent proceedings before Nuremberg military tribunals in which implicated Germans were tried for a wide range of crimes, including medical crimes, the murders committed by the *Einsatzgruppen*, the complicity of state ministries and armed services in war crimes, and the participation of industrialists in the exploitation of slave labor. A condensed record and selected documents were published in fifteen volumes, the "Green Series."

No one can guess what proportion of the mammoth accumulation of German records refers to the Jews, though clearly the amount must be substantial. Every agency of the German state and of the National Socialist party was involved in one way or another, at one time or another, in anti-Jewish activities, and that involvement was recorded in files, letters, minutes of meetings, reports, memoranda, directives, legislation, speeches, proceedings of conferences, summaries of interdepartmental negotiations, bulletins, statistics, and daily logs. Of the documents brought in evidence at the thirteen trials at Nuremberg, which comprise a very small proportion of all the captured German records, about 3,000 deal with the Jews, their persecution, expropriation, and annihilation.[3]

The overwhelming supply of official records documenting the

3. According to Henry Sachs, compiler of the forthcoming guide to references to Jewish losses—biological, cultural, and property—in the records of the Nuremberg trials, to be published by Yad Vashem/YIVO.

German program to destroy the Jews dwarfs the quantity of personal papers on the subject. These consist, for the most part, of eyewitness accounts prepared as trial evidence or written after the war by Germans seeking to exculpate themselves from involvement in the annihilation of the Jews.

II

The Jewish records of the Holocaust, the documents which provide the foundation for the history of Jewish endurance and suffering, differ altogether in dimension and character from the captured German records. The Jewish documents are far fewer in number and, in contrast to most archival sources, contain a larger proportion of personal papers than of official records. European Jews had no government and no state archives. Under German persecution, even the *Judenräte*—Jewish councils—the only official institutions in the ghettos, maintained records with caution and discretion. Indeed, everywhere among Jews under German occupation, care and circumspection determined what and how much was committed to paper. Nevertheless, the Jews in the ghettos were resolute in their determination to leave a documentary record for posterity, even if they themselves did not expect to survive.

In a collective undertaking without historical parallel, East European Jews generated massive archives and even arranged for their preservation so that evidence might remain of their ordeals and sufferings. All over Europe and especially in Poland, the Jews conspired against their persecutors to keep a historical and documentary record, though the very existence of such a record jeopardized both writer and collector, historian and archivist. That much of this material survived the destruction of the war which the Germans waged against the Jews was not accidental, but was the consequence of conscious Jewish design and policy. The ghetto Jews worked out techniques for safeguarding their documents until after the war and the defeat of the Germans. Some records were buried underground; others were hidden in secure and protected places; still others were transmitted to trustworthy non-Jews. The actual survival of these records was guaranteed, then, by the preparations and sacrificial efforts of the Jews themselves.

The most celebrated of Jewish communal archives was the *Oneg Shabbat* ("Pleasure of the Sabbath"), the code name which

historian Emanuel Ringelblum gave to his conspiratorial undertaking to document Jewish experiences under the German occupation and to preserve a record of the cataclysmic transformations
which the whole Jewish settlement in Poland was undergoing.[4]

As early as October 1939, in the first weeks of the German
occupation of Warsaw, Ringelblum began to keep daily notes of
events.[5] From his vantage point in a self-help welfare organization,
he gathered information brought by friends and clients. Local
people reported developments in Warsaw and visitors told of events
in outlying areas. Refugees and delegations seeking aid for their
uprooted communities came from hundreds of towns and cities
throughout German-occupied Poland and brought firsthand news
about what had happened to them.

At first unsuccessful in involving others in his enterprise,
Ringelblum concluded that a more organized effort was needed.
In May 1940 he gathered a small group of colleagues to engage in
such a collective undertaking. Because the group met on Saturdays,
it chose the name Oneg Shabbat as a cover for its activities. Secretary of the association was Hersh Wasser, a refugee from Lodz,
whose involvement in welfare work brought him into contact with
hundreds of refugees and expelled Jews from all over Poland. He
initiated a project to gather monographic accounts of the fate of
their communities; indeed, a considerable number of such studies,
describing the impact of the war and the German occupation upon
Polish villages, towns, and cities, were written by direct participants,
with firsthand knowledge of the events.

After November 1940, when Warsaw Jews were imprisoned
within the ghetto, Oneg Shabbat expanded its activities. A master
plan was elaborated for documentation and research, and assignments were given out to reliable persons who for the most part
were not trained as historians or journalists. (Ringelblum defended
this practice on the ground that the writing of nonprofessionals

---

4. Emanuel Ringelblum, *Ksovim fun geto*, II, 76–102. His description of the
   origins and development of Oneg Shabbat was written at the end of January
   1943.
5. These notes, written in Yiddish, were published posthumously in Poland by
   the Jewish Historical Institute. The first edition of 1952 bowdlerized Ringelblum's text to conform to the ideological demands of the Communist regime
   at that time. A revised edition, presumably complete and authentic, appeared
   in 1963. The English translation, published in 1958, is unfortunately based
   on the first edition.

would be more immediate and genuine.) Everything that happened to the Jews in Poland was of interest, to be written down, systematized, analyzed. Eventually Ringelblum hoped to use the materials for historical studies and as legal evidence against the Germans. German atrocities, economic conditions, the structure of ghetto institutions, youth activities, forced-labor camps, experiences in prisons and concentration camps, religious life, ghetto folklore (poems, jokes, curses, sayings)—all this and much more fell within the ambitious scope of Oneg Shabbat. Staff members accumulated official German, Polish, and Jewish documents. Copies of the underground Jewish and Polish press were kept at great risk. Letters sent to Warsaw from all over Poland were collected in the thousands, as a rich source of information about local communities. Influential figures in the Jewish community were interviewed, to preserve for the record their ideas on the impact of the ghetto on Jewish morality and morale.

Above all, the ghetto Jews were encouraged to keep diaries, to record the daily events of their existence. To stimulate such activity, Oneg Shabbat, using the cover of the local welfare agency, sponsored contests, offering cash prizes. One Oneg Shabbat co-worker set down his views on this enterprise:

> . . . I regard it as a sacred task . . . for everyone, whether or not he has the ability, to write down everything that he has witnessed or has heard from those who have witnessed—the atrocities which the barbarians committed in every Jewish town. When the time will come—and indeed it will surely come—let the world read and know what the murderers perpetrated. This will be the richest material for the mourner when he writes the elegy for the present time. This will be the most powerful subject matter for the avenger. . . . We are obligated to assist them, to help them, even if we must pay with our own lives, which today are very cheap.[6]

The sense of dedication and sacrificial commitment motivated everyone associated with Oneg Shabbat, regardless of his specific task. A nineteen-year-old youth described his feelings on concealing archives in an underground hiding place in August 1942:

6. M. M. Kon, quoted in Aaron Eisenbach, "Visnshaftlekhe forshungen in varshever geto," *Bleter far geshikhte,* I (January–March 1948), 56.

My work was primitive, consisting of packing and hiding the material. . . . It was perhaps the riskiest, but it was worth doing. We used to say while working: we can die in peace. We have bequeathed and safeguarded our rich heritage. I don't want any thanks. It will be enough for me if the coming generations will recall our times. We were aware of our obligation. We did not fear the risk. We reckoned that we were creating a chapter of history and that was more important than several lives. I can say with assurance that this was the basis, the dynamic of our existence then. What we could not cry out to the world, we buried in the ground. May this treasure be delivered into good hands, may it live to see better times, so that it can alert the world to what happened in the twentieth century.[7]

After the war, a substantial portion of the Oneg Shabbat archives was located and recovered.

Ringelblum's Oneg Shabbat served as a model for the Jews in the Bialystok ghetto. The Bialystok archives, initiated by Mordecai Tenenbaum who had come from Warsaw in November 1942 to organize the resistance movement, enjoyed the support of Ephraim Barash, head of the Bialystok Judenrat, and consequently included most of the minutes, proclamations, reports, and other official documents of the Judenrat and its institutions. (Oneg Shabbat, for security reasons, kept its operations secret from the Warsaw Judenrat.) In addition, a systematic effort was made to gather eyewitness reports and journalistic and historical accounts of the war, the Soviet occupation from 1939 to 1941, and the subsequent German occupation. Ghetto folklore and poetry and the records of the underground Zionist youth movement enriched the collection. In Spring 1943 arrangements were made to have the archives buried in a secure place outside the ghetto. Three metal boxes were constructed to house the documents and were then hermetically sealed to protect them from decay. By May 1943, the boxes were clandestinely transferred out of the ghetto and buried. They were found after the war.[8]

In the Vilna ghetto, a team of writers and intellectuals conspired to create an archive of official Judenrat documents as well as to stimulate people to keep diaries. They even succeeded in remov-

---

7. David Grober, quoted in *ibid.*, p. 57.
8. Bronia Klibanski, "The Underground Archives of the Bialystok Ghetto," *Yad Vashem Studies*, II (1958), 295–329.

ing manuscripts and rare books from the renowned library of the Yiddish Scientific Institute—YIVO, which the Germans had impounded. All these materials, the old and the new, were hidden first from the Germans and then, after their retreat from Vilna, from the Soviet authorities. Eventually, at great personal risk, two Yiddish poets who had organized the whole undertaking, Shmerke Kaczerginsky and Abraham Sutzkever, managed to send about 700 ghetto documents and some prewar materials to the YIVO in New York through clandestine channels.[9]

The most extraordinary archive ever created was buried at Auschwitz. It consisted of eyewitness testimonies written by members of the *Sonderkommando* ("special commando"), a work squad of Jewish prisoners whom the Germans had temporarily spared from the gas chambers. Their task was to remove the dead from the gas chambers and cremate them. In due time the members of the Sonderkommando were themselves gassed and replaced by new workers. In the full realization that they would not survive, some members of the Sonderkommando, under conditions of extreme peril, wrote accounts of the events they had witnessed. They buried their records in the ashes that covered the ground at Auschwitz. These were found after the war, in bad condition, some scarcely decipherable. One testimony began:

> Dear finder, search everywhere, in every inch of ground. Dozens of documents are buried beneath it, mine and those of other persons, which will throw light on everything that happened here. Great quantities of teeth also are buried here. It was we, the commando workers, who deliberately strewed them all over the ground, as many as we could, so that the world should find material traces of the millions of murdered people. We ourselves have lost hope of being able to live to see the moment of liberation.[10]

Most of these Jewish records, buried in, and later exhumed from, Polish soil, remained in Poland. They formed the core of the documentary collections of the Jewish Historical Institute in Warsaw, the central repository in Poland of Holocaust archives.

Aside from these collections, created and preserved by Jewish

9. For more on the Vilna materials and other collections, see *News of the Yivo*, Nos. 22 (Steptember 1947), 24 (December 1947), 27 (June 1948), 33 (June 1949).
10. From a manuscript by Salmen Gradowski, in Jadwiga Bezwińska, ed., *Amidst a Nightmare of Crime: Manuscripts of Members of Sonderkommando* (Oświęcim, 1973), p. 76. The translation has been somewhat altered.

design, a considerable body of official Jewish records survived by accident, having been abandoned by the Jews when they were deported. It was forgotten by the Germans when they later fled from Poland. The official records of the Judenrat of Lodz, for example, survived unharmed. (Part had been spirited away under the eyes of the Germans and hidden.) Scattered records of many other Jewish communities turned up after the war. The records of the official Jewish welfare agency which operated under German auspices in Poland were preserved. Though the material in Poland is not readily available to foreign scholars, much of it has been duplicated and is available, along with countless other records, in the archives of the Yad Vashem, the Martyrs' and Heroes' Memorial Authority, in Jerusalem, and in the archives of the YIVO Institute for Jewish Research in New York, and in other repositories in Israel and Europe.

A new genre of Holocaust records came into being within days after liberation from German rule. As Jewish survivors returned from the kingdom of the dead, emerging from the death camps and the slave-labor installations, from bunkers underground where they had been buried alive, they began to tell the story of their ordeals, to relate the miracle or accident of their survival. Some were determined that their experience become judicial evidence, that their testimony be instrumental in the pursuit of both justice and vengeance. Others, obsessed by their experience, strove to become moral witnesses, to communicate, in whichever literary form they might master, the terror and horror, the anguish and pity that had been their lot. Thousands of survivor accounts thus came into being, dictated, recorded, or written in Yiddish, Polish, German, indeed in all the European languages. Jewish historical committees sprang up in many of the displaced persons' camps in Germany, Austria, and Italy to gather and preserve these accounts. When the camps were disbanded, most of these collections were transferred to the Yad Vashem. The YIVO Institute, too, has over two thousand such survivor accounts.

III

To extract the full value of any document, the historian must first screen it for defects. He must try to establish its genuineness and authenticity. He must verify its credibility, accuracy, and veracity, study the internal evidence of its language, style, and content, and confront it with other, often contradictory, evidence. The documents of the Holocaust should, indeed must, undergo such scrutiny and examination, for they too suffer from the defects spawned by subjectivity and partisanship, bias and prejudice.

Many writers on the Holocaust have failed to apply to Holocaust documents the required rigor of critical scholarship. German documents have all too often been accepted at face value, partly because their thoroughness and precision have been mistaken for truthfulness. Jewish documents, on the other hand, have been received in an attitude of reverence for the dead and respect for the survivors, with the result that critical judgment and analysis have been suspended lest they desecrate the memory of the Holocaust and its victims. But history demands a more astringent approach. There are, as a matter of fact, Holocaust documents that conceal rather than reveal, that are written in language intended to serve ulterior motives or a hidden agenda. There are also Holocaust documents that are outright falsification and some that purvey myth rather than historical fact.

Eyewitnesses to the same event do not give precisely the same account; neither do documents dealing with the same episode describe it the same way. Every document slants the structure of historical events, reflecting its author's unconscious prejudices or his deliberate intent. Writers of documents are committed to their version of events partly because of the "egocentric predicament," the ability to see only through one's own eyes and in the light of one's own experiences, which is the most prevalent form of subjectivity. There is also the writer's own involvement in the events and his partisanship, which may be defined as the subjectivity of self-serving self-interest. Every Holocaust document, whether it is an official record, or a personal account of experience, is an expression of its composer's bias, whether the document be General Stroop's report on the destruction of the Warsaw ghetto, the *Jüdische Rundschau*'s assessment of the Jewish situation in Germany in 1933, or the reports of underground Jewish organizations in the ghettos of Eastern Europe.

Most susceptible of infection by subjectivity and self-interest are the accounts written by Germans who held positions of responsibility in the National Socialist government. Written after the events, in strikingly altered conditions, these records suffer from what Daniel Aaron—speaking of other kinds of memoirs—has characterized as "the treachery of recollection." Their untrustworthiness derives from their authors' involvement in the events described and their "conscious or unconscious motives for selective remembering or forgetting." [11] All abound in attempts at self-vindication. The German participants in the National Socialist government and especially those who collaborated in the Final Solution have, in their writings or testimonies, tried to exonerate themselves, to extricate themselves from responsibility for criminal acts. Without exception their accounts combine self-censored selective recollections with deliberate lies. The task of the historian then must be to distinguish between the historical reality and the self-protective distortion, between the truth and the lie.[12]

Though the genre of Jewish survivor literature in its moral tone and emotional texture in no way resembles the German accounts, nonetheless its defects as historical source material are likewise substantial. These Jewish accounts are often burdened by what has been described as "existential guilt," a sense of remorse for having survived when family and friends did not. Consequently, the accounts tend either to magnify the incidents which the author believes accounted for his survival, or to omit them altogether, thus leaving his survival unexplained. Besides, the survivor's memory is often distorted by hate, sentimentality, and the passage of time. His perspective on external historic events is often skewed by the limits of his personal experience.

Survivor accounts of critical events are typical of all testimony, that is, they are full of discrepancies. About matters both trivial and significant, the evidence is nearly always in dispute.[13] In part the unreliability of these accounts derives from imperfect observation and flawed memory, but in larger part from the circumstance that they are not constructed exclusively on the basis of firsthand experience. In order to present a coherent narrative, the author has likely included a large measure of hearsay, gossip, rumor, assumption, speculation, and hypothesis. Few Jews have survived to tell,

11. Daniel Aaron, "The Treachery of Recollection," in Robert H. Bremner, ed., *Essays in History and Literature* (Ohio State University Press, 1966), p. 19.
12. A characteristic illustration is Albert Speer's autobiography, *Inside the Third Reich* (New York, 1970). See my review (*Commentary*, November 1970) for a critical analysis.
13. A graphic case of disparities in evidence occurs in accounts by four direct participants of a confrontation in the Vilna ghetto between the Judenrat and the resistance organization, published in *YIVO-bleter*, XXX (1947), 188–211.

on the basis of direct knowledge, about the inner operations, the deliberations, and the decision making of the Judenräte or, for that matter, even of the leading underground Jewish organizations. With a few noteworthy exceptions, survivors are individuals who suffered and endured in obscurity, far from the seats of authority and decision. They are somewhat in the position of Fabrizius del Dongo in *The Charterhouse of Parma,* never quite sure that he had been present at the Battle of Waterloo and had seen the Emperor. Their accounts can serve as the raw material for social history, but seldom as testimony to the great events.

Contemporaneous records, too, though free from the distortion of forgetfulness, share the defect of survivor accounts—subjectivity, restricted experience, and feebleness of expression. One ghetto diarist was so obsessed by his hunger that he wrote about practically nothing but food, his vision of life and understanding of his predicament having been constricted along with his stomach. Another ghetto diarist saw events from the perspective of terror, his entries are replete with episodes of violent killings and wholesale slaughter by the Germans which he himself witnessed or heard about. An account by Justina Dawidsohn-Draenger of the Jewish resistance movement in Cracow, in which she played a leading role, is burdened by a vocabulary and style of such exaltation and romanticism that it yields little in hard fact (although it succeeds in transmitting a poignant portrait of the moods and attitudes of the Zionist youth movement). Indeed, many such records are of value precisely as indicators of the way in which participants viewed themselves, rather than as raw materials for the establishment of factual truth.

Some personal records were transformed into documents of a high order because of their author's intellectuality, quality of mind, and dynamic force of personality. Always perceptive, often moving, sometimes powerful and tragic are the diaries of Chaim Kaplan and Zelig Kalmanovich, the fugitive writings of Janusz Korczak, and the interviews with Dr. Israel Milejkowski and Hillel Zeitlin. But the ghetto was no place for creativity, and it is a mistake to think that first-rate literary works could have been produced there. In such conditions no writer could command the discipline and self-control that art demands. The best writing that has survived consists of descriptive essays of ghetto life by journalists like Peretz Opoczynski and Josef Zelkowicz who reached the peak of their careers in the ghetto.

Political bias in both contemporaneous and survivor documents is at once blatant and insidious. Without exception, every official or personal document written during the German occupation or after the war by an active member of a Jewish party or movement is flawed by partisanship. So overpowering in some cases is ideological commitment that even normally sophisticated witnesses fail to perceive how their historical reliability has been impaired. Ringelblum, for instance, a passionate Left Labor Zionist, often forced historical evidence to fit his ideological doctrine.[14]

A less pernicious form of historical falsification is the myth pretending to documentary veracity. In Holocaust history myths are especially abundant about the behavior of pious Jews in circumstances of extreme crisis; this is in fact a genre with many precedents in Jewish history. The most widespread such story is probably that of the ninety-three (more or less) devout girls of a Beth Jacob school in the Cracow ghetto who chose mass suicide over the degradation of a German brothel. It is a fanciful and moving tale of sacrificial piety, a lesson in religious morality, fashioned by people who knew nothing of the Nuremberg Laws which made sexual relations between Germans and Jews illegal, criminal, and subject to severe punishment.

IV

Having searched the documents for subjectivity and bias and tested them for genuineness, the historian must examine their language. Every genre has its own idiom or jargon, and in some cases this diminishes rather than enhances literary quality. Official records are universally encumbered by the language and style of bureaucracy. Their tortuous syntax resembles the convoluted patterns of bureaucratic organization; their abstract and foggy vocabulary

14. Ringelblum is a particularly embarrassing model for the historian. His ideological commitment sometimes distorted his view of the realities of the ghetto. At home or in his office, he heard hundreds of eyewitness accounts of events beyond the range of his own experience and recorded most of them uncritically and without corroboration. From the mass of undigested facts he selected for his own ghetto notes and essays those that were congruent with his political outlook. A recent publication by Yad Vashem of Ringelblum's *Polish-Jewish Relations During the Second World War* (Jerusalem, 1974) illustrates the discrepancies between Ringelblum's eyewitness version of events and subsequent findings of critical history. A long introduction, extensive annotations, and an afterword by the editors, serve to correct, disclaim, and dispute Ringelblum's text.

reflects bureaucratic anonymity and impersonality. Official records written in Yiddish suffer from a particular handicap: Yiddish was seldom spoken in bureaucratic corridors, and was consequently deficient in appropriate terminology. Thus, Yiddish reports of Judenräte and social welfare institutions are often long-winded and awkward, inappropriately grandiloquent, or uncommonly plain, indicating the writer's inexperience with bureaucratic idiom.

The German language of the Nazis had no such deficiency. The syntax and language of German bureaucracy were well developed long before the National Socialists began to fashion the language to conform to their own needs, and they themselves richly contributed to its further development.

Nazi-Deutsch, National Socialist German, dubbed by one of its analysts *LTI, Lingua Tertii Imperii,* "the language of the Third Reich," [15] began to develop in the infancy of the movement and flowered when National Socialist Germany ruled Europe. Nazi-Deutsch embodied the characteristics of totalitarian language which George Orwell described in *1984* as Newspeak, "a medium of expression for the world view and mental habits proper to the devotees" of the ideological movement in power. Like Newspeak, Nazi-Deutsch was designed not to extend, but to reduce, the range of thought, to create a desirable mental attitude by the use of words constructed for political and ideological purposes. It also developed into a language that graphically illustrated the witticism attributed variously to Voltaire and Talleyrand: words were given to man only so that he might conceal his thoughts. Though Nazi-Deutsch was intended as a medium of communication, in the early days primarily among party members and adherents and among all Germans in the days of power, it was a language that concealed more than it communicated, its very structure and vocabulary buffering speaker and listener from reality.

The National Socialists appropriated several familiar and unattractive characteristics of the German language, especially of the language of bureaucracy, and by exploiting and embellishing them, transformed the German language into Nazi-Deutsch. Nazi-

---

15. Victor Klemperer, *Die unbewältigte Sprache: Aus dem Notzibuch eins Philologen "LTI"* (Darmstadt, 1966). The most provocative writing about the debasement of the German language under the National Socialist regime is George Steiner's. See especially his essay, "The Hollow Miracle," in *Language and Silence: Essays on Language, Literature, and the Inhuman* (New York, 1967).

Deutsch abounds, for instance, in verbally weak sentences and favors passive constructions and intransitive verbs with vague, indeterminate meanings.[16] Active sentences with active agents as their subjects are uncharacteristic. The marrow of the sentence is lodged in verbal nouns:

". . . prompt Aryanization is to be sought. . . ."

". . . the planned measures demand the most thorough preparation. . . ."

". . . the handling of the problem will meet with certain difficulties. . . ."

Personal and individual responsibility is disclaimed in Nazi-Deutsch. The structure of the sentence and its syntax convey instead the sense that things happen as a consequence of vast overpowering impersonal forces of a natural or cosmic character, that processes take place—to use a characteristic formula of Nazi-Deutsch—and worlds are moved, all without a sign of a visible agent, as if commanded by a higher power or destined by the onward march of history.

German especially has many nouns with multiple meanings, all of them nonspecific. The National Socialists used these disproportionately, either alone or, in characteristic German fashion, in combination with other nouns. A new vocabulary emerged, consisting of abstract nouns with bland, vague meanings which were intended to camouflage reality, to conceal it from outsiders and to disengage and disembarass the participants. *Aktion,* meaning activity, process, was used to designate mass killing. *Behandlung,* which means treatment, management, was another word for killing. Reports sometimes speak of "appropriate treatment" of Jews, and often of *Sonderbehandlung,* "special treatment." *Einsatz,* which originally had a passive meaning, that which was risked or staked, came into common usage in Nazi-Deutsch through military terminology and was widely employed in combined forms to denote various sorts of action, often with connotations of commitment, dedication, and risk. *Einsatzgruppen* were task forces of the security

16. Cf. the pioneering work of the language field of Nazism, Heinz Paechter, *Nazi-Deutsch: A Glossary of Contemporary German Usage* (New York, 1944), especially pp. 10–15. More recent and very useful is Cornelia Berning, *Vom "Abstammungsnachweis" zum "Zuchtwart": Vokabular des Nationalsozialismus* (Berlin, 1964).

police, assigned to special duties which involved, among other tasks, the mass murder of the Jews.

Euphemisms and code words were intended not only to enshroud the systematic programs of murder in secrecy, but also to make participation in murder palatable to those engaged in it. The clearest case in point is the use of the words "euthanasia" and "mercy killing" to designate the murder of deformed, insane, and incurably sick "Aryan" Germans. After a while, the code name gave way to a code number, further depersonalizing the murders and dehumanizing the murderers. The term "Final Solution" became the code word for the annihilation of the European Jews, the noun imparting a sense of idealism to the participant killers, the adjective investing their killing with an aura of apocalyptic conclusiveness.

V

Like the language of German documents, the language of documents written by Jews under German occupation must also be carefully scrutinized before the historian can conclude that he has properly understood what the writer intended to convey. In the case of Jewish documents the issue is complicated immensely by the obvious yet formidable problem posed by the political circumstances in which the Jews lived. Holocaust documents by Jews were composed under conditions of severe censorship and extreme persecution. Even the most private papers, whose authors never intended them to see publication under German occupation, bear evidence of coercion and terror. One way or another, in tone, style, and vocabulary, nearly every writer had to adapt himself to writing under persecution.

Censorship of forbidden ideas and teachings has been a commonplace of human history, though Americans today, enjoying the widest imaginable latitude in freedom of expression, have scarcely known such restraints. The prohibitions against free speech gave rise even in ancient times to techniques of expression, oral and written, which were intended to circumvent the censor's eye. Ways were found to communicate forbidden ideas and to establish a mutual understanding between speaker or writer and his audience which would not appear subversive or even suspicious to the censorial authorities.

The fable is the oldest such literary form. The technique of putting words into the mouths of animals developed out of a desire to convey ideas about the power-relations between the strong and the weak in a manner that would not incur the disfavor of the strong. Aesop, it was said, was a slave, and his fables amused and comforted the slaves who heard and retold them, giving us today the concept of "Aesopian language" and the "Aesopian method," techniques for transmitting forbidden ideas. If it is not much used in the West, the Aesopian method, according to Anatoly Kuznetsov, is very much alive today in Soviet literature: "At no time in history has the ability to speak or read between the lines, which many Russians learn in their early childhood, been developed to such a fine art as now in the USSR." [17]

The Jews, for the greater part of their existence a powerless people, often forbidden to practice their religion, restricted in their teachings, censored in their spoken and written words, long ago invented devices for esoteric communication, for signaling through a system of allusions and references which they could easily understand but which was beyond the comprehension of the authorities.

One kind of esoteric communication among Jews evolved in the early centuries of the Common Era with the *midrash*, a public sermon or discourse which interpreted, illustrated, and expanded narrative portions of the Bible, for the purpose of moral and ethical teaching. In that period, the Jews, deprived of statehood, lived under conditions of political tyranny and religious persecution. The midrash, itself not an esoteric form, could nevertheless be used by the rabbis in an esoteric manner, to comfort and console by invoking the stories and legends of the past as a commentary on the present. Esau and Haman, for instance, became code names for contemporary tyrants. In the midrash, according to Ernst Simon:

> a persecuted minority created for itself, in its disputes with the outside world, an internal language, which was seldom understood by the enemy but almost always by coreligionists. Thus a sort of cryptic style developed which was interchanged with a smile between speaker and audience, presupposing and nourishing an intimate conspiratorial understanding.[18]

The fable, the midrash, the parable became the mode of public discourse for the Jews in Germany after 1933 when they lived in

17. Martin Dewhirst and Robert Farrell, *The Soviet Censorship* (Metuchen, N.J., 1973), p. 33.
18. Ernst Simon, "Jewish Adult Education in Nazi Germany as Spiritual Resistance," Leo Baeck Institute *Year Book I* (New York: 1956), 92.

precarious instability between freedom and the ghetto, still allowed to congregate and publish, but subject to ever tighter restrictions and severer penalties for transgressing them. Rabbis and preachers who used the Aesopian techniques of fable and midrash were arrested and, if released, forbidden to engage in public speaking. The German secret police attended Jewish religious services, monitored public Jewish meetings, attended Jewish lectures and concerts, sat in at executive sessions of Jewish organizations, studied the Jewish press. Their own early history had made the National Socialists adept in esoteric communication and they were alert to its use among the Jews.

In those days the Jews, in their official dealings with the regime, furthermore, perforce learned to speak in the tongue of their oppressors, sensitive to locutions and circumlocutions the National Socialists would tolerate and those they would punish. Jewish leaders adopted a vocabulary and style that would give the least offense while allowing them to plead the cause of the community. The language of the petitions which German Jewish organizations submitted to the Nazi regime may appear obsequious and submissive, but it served to state their case without bringing disaster upon themselves and the community they spoke for. The Jews had learned the language of accommodation, as all persons do in times of extreme persecution.

As German terror increasingly gripped all Europe, the possibilities of public and even private expression shrank. The Germans allowed official Jewish institutions to publish German decrees and orders but little more. At every level of leadership, Jews feared that whatever they wrote would be regarded by the Germans as punishable. In written communication the techniques of cryptography began to supplant the Aesopian method. Written documents, even letters of plain people, sent from one person to another in the same ghetto or by couriers from one ghetto to another or abroad, were coded to protect the sender, the deliverer, the recipient, and the information itself. First names, only, were used to identify people or places associated with them, as in the Bund report of March 1942. Hebrew words were used to disguise names, institutions, occurrences: "*Mo-vess* [death] visited us." Sometimes the recipients themselves were puzzled, even baffled, by the conundrums posed by these ciphered messages.

Censorship bred self-censorship. The heavy penalties that the Germans levied on the Jews for speaking and writing—enforced silence, imprisonment, torture, even death—soon encouraged a posture of discretion instead of valor. The historian reading the licit Jewish publications issued under German rule will soon perceive that the words have been exsanguinated, that censorship and self-censorship have drained the text's vitality and sometimes even obscured its significance. The Jewish press of Germany between 1933 and 1938, for that reason is an inadequate source of historical evidence, as are also the internal records of Jewish institutions in Germany. Jewish leaders did not discuss matters of communal importance which they did not want the police to know about, nor were such matters recorded in minutes, even when police spies were not present. A member of the executive board of the *Reichsvertretung*, who occasionally went to Paris on business before 1938, used to dictate there a full and true account of the activities of that organization while they were still fresh in his mind. (These records were lost during the war.)

The rigors of censorship and self-censorship utterly fettered the Jews in the ghettos of Eastern Europe. Even diaries kept in secret and written in Yiddish or Hebrew show evidence of disciplined self-control. (Pious Jews, as an additional precaution, did their writing in the margins of religious texts, to give the appearance of commentary.) Diarists seldom referred explicitly to the Germans, preferring the indefinite "they" and "those" or Biblical references to peoples who had oppressed the Jews. Nearly all private writers resorted to cryptic phrases, allusions, and tricks of rhetoric— ellipsis, aposiopesis, periphrasis—that conceal meaning.

Adam Czerniaków, chairman of the Warsaw Judenrat, kept a diary in Polish in which restraint verges on reticence. A Gestapo agent would hardly have found it objectionable. Even in dealing with his own humiliations and the sadism of the Germans, Czerniaków showed a positive talent for self-censorship. Still, notwithstanding the succinctness, indeed the taciturnity of his daily entries, Czerniaków's diary is a document rich in historical evidence, recording in painstaking detail the course he had to steer through the tortuous bureaucratic maze of official German and Polish institutions in the conscientious performance of his duties. To mine the diary's riches the historian must expose each laconic sentence to the light of accumulated knowledge of the Warsaw ghetto and of German policy and then read between and beneath the lines.

Even more difficult exercises in textual analysis are posed by the official records of the Judenräte, whose operations were conducted under extreme duress and the all-seeing vigilance of the SS. These Judenrat records contain no reference to German terror, little mention of Jewish suffering. The minutes of the Lublin Judenrat combine a bureaucratic style with laconism. Informative about the tasks, hardships, and conflicts of Judenrat operations, the minutes nevertheless have a teasing quality, for they leave more unsaid than said. The minutes of the Bialystok Judenrat, by contrast, are almost loquacious—less oblique, more explicit. In its struggle for survival, the Bialystok Judenrat counted on the cooperation of regional officials of the German industrial-military establishment, a confidence expressed in the minutes. Perhaps that confidence extended also to the matter of records and record-keeping.

The problem that bedevils the historian in dealing with Judenrat records is not so much deciphering and understanding what is there as taking into account what is not. There are no records of those awesome decisions involving the life and death of the Jews in the ghettos. There are no records of the arguments for and against armed resistance. There are no records of the relations between the Judenräte and the underground, though in some ghettos those relations were close and supportive. History cannot be constructed out of the silence of the grave, yet when the historian attempts to describe how things really were, he must take that silence into consideration.

VI

The availability of vast quantities of documentary materials, German and Jewish, official records and personal papers, simultaneously simplifies and complicates the task of the historian of the Holocaust. Documents by themselves are no substitute for history, though history cannot be written without them. No documents, of any era, in any culture, in any language, whatever their quantity, comprise the total and true evidence of the historical past. History has always remained full of dark recesses into which the illumination of documents has never penetrated or which can even become distorted and unreal in the sometimes weak and inadequate light cast by documents. There is, noted R. G. Collingwood, only ". . . a strictly limited quantity of evidence concerning any historical question; it is seldom free from grave defects, it is generally tendentious, fragmentary, silent where it ought to be explicit, and detailed where it had better be silent." [19]

Unless the historian treats his documents critically, his work will be nothing more than what Collingwood tagged "scissors-and-paste history," an unselective collage of the past. As raw materials of history, Holocaust documents must be tested and tried for reliability. Witnesses to past events, they need to be subjected to cross-examination to establish their genuineness and credibility. Questions are still to be put to them before the answers of history can be given. Yet they themselves, fascinating, dreary, horrifying, suggest to the careful reader the sorts of questions that should be asked of them, and point the direction in which answers may begin to be found.

19. In Robin W. Winks, ed., *The Historian as Detective: Essays on Evidence* (New York, 1970), p. 514.

PART ONE

THE
FINAL SOLUTION

1 PRECONDITIONS: CONVENTIONAL ANTI-SEMITISM AND ADOLF HITLER

INTRODUCTION

THE FINAL SOLUTION would not have been possible without the pervasive presence and the uninterrupted tradition of anti-Semitism in Germany. The exposure of the German people for generations to conventional anti-Semitism in its manifold forms— political, nationalist, racial, cultural, doctrinal, economic—eventually rendered them insensitive to Hitler's radical and deadly brand of anti-Semitism.

Modern German anti-Semitism abounded in credos, platforms, and declarations whose central thesis was that the Jews were alien to the German nation, its people, culture, and land and that the rights which Jews had or sought should consequently be denied to them. A classic document weaving together the diverse strands of German anti-Semitism was the Anti-Semites' Petition. It was circulated in Germany in 1880–1881 and garnered nearly a quarter of a million signatures. The petition was presented to Reich Chancellor Otto von Bismarck, who merely acknowledged its receipt. An interpellation in the Prussion House of Deputies elicited from the government neither a firm denunciation of anti-Semitism nor a repudiation of the petition's objectives (liberals and progressives had expected the latter), only the mild statement that the government intended to take no action to deprive the Jews of their rights.

The widespread acceptance by the German people of anti-Semitism as a common political dogma paved the way for Hitler's rise to power. Without Adolf Hitler, however, the Final Solution would not have been planned and would not have been carried to its irrevocable end. The idea of destroying the Jews had inhabited the deranged minds of anti-Semites long before Hitler, but only Hitler turned the fantasy into reality. Only Hitler achieved the political power, commanded the economic and technological resources, and maintained the military advantage to carry out that destruction. All his life he was obsessed by the thought of a holy war against the Jews, whom he saw as the Host of the Devil and as the Children of Darkness. He never swerved from his single-minded dedication to the goal of their destruction. The following selections from his speeches and writings, beginning in 1919, when he was thirty years old and still unknown, to his final political testament of April 29, 1945, illustrate his unchanging views on this matter.

In September 1919, a certain Adolf Gemlich addressed an inquiry for enlightenment on anti-Semitism to the Press and Propaganda Office of the Political Department of the District Army Command in Munich, where Hitler was employed. Hitler's superior asked him to reply. The letter, dated September 16, 1919, is the earliest extant document written by Hitler, expressing views that he was later to develop in Mein Kampf. *The selection excerpted here reveals that as early as 1919 Hitler had already evolved a combined short-term and long-term strategy for his anti-Semitic program.*

Just four days before he wrote the letter to Gemlich, Hitler attended his first meeting of the minuscule nationalist Deutsche Arbeiterpartei *(German Workers' Party), and a few days later he joined it. Charged with responsibility for the party's propaganda activity, he began to build up a following by adroit publicity and the appeal of his passionate anti-Semitic oratory. On February 24, 1920, with a capacity audience present at a party meeting, Hitler proposed a new program and a new name for the party—*National-sozialistische Deutsche Arbeiterpartei—*NSDAP (National Socialist German Workers' Party). As the party's most popular speaker, Hitler exploited his favorite subject—the Jews' betrayal of Germany, the Jewish "stab-in-the-back." Portraying the Jews as the eternal antagonists of Germans, he ceaselessly prophesied an ultimate conflict,* *as seen in the extracts from his speeches of August 13, 1920 ("Why Are We Anti-Semites?") and April 12, 1922.*

On November 8, 1923, Hitler and the NSDAP attempted to seize power in Bavaria, but the unsuccessful Putsch ended in his arrest and trial. In prison for nearly a year, he wrote Mein Kampf, part autobiography, part ideological tract, part organizational manual, elaborating in it the ideas and the program to which he would cling fixedly until the end of his life.

Hitler came to power on January 30, 1933, in a time of political paralysis. Within a few months, through terror, violence, and the innovation of concentration camps, he suppressed all political parties, the trade-union movement, the free press, and the political institutions of the Weimar Republic. From 1933 to 1935, he focused attention on consolidating his position within Germany. (For his treatment of the Jews during this period, see Section 2.) In 1936, he turned to foreign affairs and plans for war. His ideology envisaged war as the necessary strategy to destroy world Jewry and Bolshevism and, at the same time, to seize Russian territory to provide the Lebensraum—living space—which, according to his world outlook, Germany required for its existence and deserved because of its racial superiority. In August 1936, Hitler drafted a memorandum outlining a plan which was to make the German army operational and the economy fit for war, within four years' time. The memorandum opened with a lengthy ideological preamble, from which a few passages have been selected here, and concluded with a proposal to expropriate the Jews when Germany was ready for war.

The destruction of the Jews was inextricably associated in Hitler's mind with the war he planned and finally initiated. On January 30, 1939, in his speech to the Reichstag on the anniversary of his accession to power, he prophesied the destruction of the Jews. Having launched the Second World War on September 1, 1939, with his invasion of Poland, he used the upheavals of war to accomplish his objective, as he indicated in his speech on the anniversary of the Putsch on November 8, 1942.

Even after the German government, its army, the Nazi party, and the SS had murdered six million European Jews, and even when the very foundations of Berlin were crumbling under the Russian and Allied assault, the Jews remained uppermost in Hitler's mind, even in the closing paragraphs of his last political testament before his suicide in a Berlin bunker.

ANTI-SEMITES' PETITION, 1880

Your Most Serene Princely Highness,
Most August Reich Chancellor and Prime Minister:

In all regions of Germany the conviction has prevailed that the rank growth of the Jewish element bears within it the most serious dangers to our nationhood. Wherever Christian and Jew enter into social relations, we see the Jew as master, the indigenous Christian population in a subservient position. The Jew takes part only to a negligible extent in the heavy labor of the great mass of our nation; in fields and workshops, in mines or on constructions, in swamps and canals—everywhere only the calloused hand of the Christian is active. But the fruits of his labor are reaped mainly by the Jew. By far the largest part of the capital which national labor produces is concentrated in Jewish hands; along with movable capital, Jewish immovable property increases. Not only do the proudest palaces of our large cities belong to Jewish masters whose fathers and grandfathers, huckstering and peddling, crossed the frontiers into our fatherland, but rural holdings too, that most significant preservative basis of our political structure, fall more and more into the hands of the Jews.

In view of these conditions and of the massive penetration of Semitic elements into all positions which impart power and influence, it certainly does not appear unjustified from either the ethical or the national point of view to ask: What future awaits our fatherland if the Semitic element remains in a position for another generation to make such conquests on our native soil as have been made in the last two decades? If the concept of a fatherland is not to be stripped of its ideal meaning; if the conception that it was our fathers who wrested this soil from the wilderness, who fertilized it in a thousand battles with their blood, is not to be lost to our *Volk;*[1] if the intimate relationship of German custom and German morality with the Christian world view and Christian tradition is to be preserved—then a foreign stock, that has been

1. The German word *Volk*, meaning "people," "nation," was imbued with near-mystical meaning by German nationalists as an innate quality embodying the German "racial" spirit and soul.

accorded visitors' and resident rights by our humane legislation, but whose feeling and thinking is further from us than is that of any people of the whole Aryan world, must never be permitted to rise to dominance on German soil.

The danger to our nationhood is naturally bound to increase to the degree that the Jews succeed not only in atrophying the national and religious consciousness of our nation through the press, but also in attaining public offices whose incumbents are obliged to guard the ideal values of our nation. We are mindful particularly of the professional positions of teachers and judges; until recently both were inaccessible to Jews, and both must again be closed to them if the Volk's concept of authority and its feeling for law and for the fatherland are not to be shaken. Even now the Germanic ideal of personal honor, manly fidelity, genuine piety is starting to be displaced to make room for a cosmopolitan pseudo-ideal.

If our Volk is not to be surrendered to economic slavery under the pressure of Jewish money power, to national decay under the influence of a materialistic world view advocated chiefly by Jewry, then measures that will call a halt to the rank growth of Jewry are indisputably required. Nothing could be farther from our intent than a wish to bring about any renewed oppression of the Jewish people; what we strive for is solely the emancipation of the German Volk from a form of alien domination which it cannot endure for any length of time. Danger is at hand. We therefore permit ourselves to approach Your Highness with the respectful request:

That Your Highness exert his powerful influence in Prussia and Germany to the end that:

(1) the immigration of foreign Jews, if not entirely prevented, at least be restricted;

(2) the Jews be excluded from all governmental (authoritative) positions and that their employment in the administration of justice—particularly as judges sitting alone—undergo an appropriate limitation;

(3) the Christian character of the common school, even when attended by Jewish pupils, be strictly maintained and that only Christian teachers be admitted to it; and that in all other schools Jewish teachers may be appointed, but only in specially motivated, exceptional cases;

(4) resumption of official statistics on the Jewish population be ordered.

With the expression of greatest respect and unshakable confidence, we remain,

[Signatures]

ADOLF HITLER ON THE ANNIHILATION OF THE JEWS

Letter to Adolf Gemlich, September 16, 1919

Anti-Semitism as a political movement should not and cannot be determined by factors of sentiment, but only by the recognition of facts. These are the facts:

To begin with, Jewry is unqualifiedly a racial association and not a religious association. . . . Its influence will bring about the racial tuberculosis of the people.

Hence it follows: Anti-Semitism on purely emotional grounds will find its ultimate expression in the form of pogroms. Rational anti-Semitism, however, must lead to a systematic legal opposition and elimination of the special privileges which Jews hold, in contrast to the other aliens living among us (aliens' legislation). Its final objective must unswervingly be the removal of the Jews altogether. Only a government of national vitality is capable of doing both, and never a government of national impotence.

Speech, NSDAP meeting, August 13, 1920,
"Why Are We Anti-Semites?"

If we wish to carry out these social reforms, then the struggle must go hand in hand against the opponents of every social arrangement: Jewry. Here too we know exactly that scientific understanding can only be a preparation, that after understanding must come organization, which changes over into deed, and the deed remains irrevocably firm: removal of the Jews from our nation, not because we would begrudge them their existence—we congratulate the rest of the world on their company—but because the existence of our own nation is a thousand times more important to us than that of an alien race.

Speech, NSDAP meeting, April 12, 1922

There are only two possibilities in Germany; do not imagine that the people will forever go with the middle party, the party of compromises; one day it will turn to those who have most consistently foretold the coming ruin and have sought to dissociate themselves from it. And that party is either the Left: and then God help us! for it will lead us to complete destruction—to Bolshevism, or else it is a party of the Right which at the last, when the people is in utter despair, when it has lost all its spirit and has no longer any faith in anything, is determined for its part ruthlessly to seize the reins of power—that is the beginning of the resistance of which I spoke a few minutes ago. Here, too, there can be no compromise— there are only two possibilities: either victory of the Aryan or annihilation of the Aryan and the victory of the Jew.

From Mein Kampf

Hence today I believe that I am acting in accordance with the will of the Almighty Creator: *by defending myself against the Jew, I am fighting for the work of the Lord.*[2]

. . . *it is the inexorable Jew who struggles for his domination over the nations.* No nation can remove this hand from its throat except by the sword. Only the assembled and concentrated might of a national passion rearing up in its strength can defy the international enslavement of peoples. Such a process is and remains a bloody one.

In Russian Bolshevism we must see the attempt undertaken by the Jews in the twentieth century to achieve world domination.

The fight against Jewish world Bolshevization requires a clear attitude toward Soviet Russia. You can not drive out the Devil with Beelzebub.

If at the beginning of the War and during the War, twelve or fifteen thousand of these Hebrew corrupters of the people had been held under the poison gas, as happened to hundreds of thousands of our very best German workers in the field, the sacrifice of millions at the front would not have been in vain.

---

2. Italics in this and subsequent passages are in the original German.

From Hitler's memorandum on the Four Year Plan,
  August 1936

Since the outbreak of the French Revolution, the world has been moving with ever increasing speed toward a new conflict, the most extreme solution of which is called Bolshevism, whose essence and aim, however, are solely the elimination of those strata of mankind which have hitherto provided the leadership and their replacement by worldwide Jewry.

No state will be able to withdraw or even remain at a distance from this historical conflict. . . .

It is not the aim of this memorandum to prophesy the time when the untenable situation in Europe will become an open crisis. I only want, in these lines, to set down my conviction that this crisis cannot and will not fail to arrive and that it is Germany's duty to secure her own existence by every means in the face of this catastrophe, and to protect herself against it, and that from this compulsion there arises a series of conclusions relating to the most important tasks that our people have ever been set. *For a victory of Bolshevism over Germany would not lead to a Versailles Treaty but to the final destruction, indeed to the annihilation of the German people.*

. . . I consider it necessary for the Reichstag to pass the following two laws:

1) A law providing the death penalty for economic sabotage, and

2) A law making the whole of Jewry liable for all damage inflicted by individual specimens of this community of criminals upon the German economy, and thus upon the German people.

From Hitler's Reichstag address, January 30, 1939

And one more thing I would like now to state on this day memorable perhaps not only for us Germans. I have often been a prophet in my life and was generally laughed at. During my struggle for power, the Jews primarily received with laughter my prophecies that I would someday assume the leadership of the state and thereby of the entire Volk and then, among many other things, achieve a solution of the Jewish problem. I suppose that meanwhile the then resounding laughter of Jewry in Germany is now choking in their throats.

Today I will be a prophet again. If international finance Jewry within Europe and abroad should succeed once more in plunging the peoples into a world war, then the consequences will be not the Bolshevization of the world and therewith a victory of Jewry, but, on the contrary, the destruction of the Jewish race in Europe.

From Hitler's speech, November 8, 1942

You will recall that meeting of the Reichstag in which I declared: If Jewry perchance imagines that it can bring about an international world war for the annihilation of the European races, then the consequence will be not the annihilation of the European races, but, on the contrary, it will be the annihilation of Jewry in Europe. I was always laughed at as a prophet. Of those who laughed then, countless ones no longer laugh today, and those who still laugh now will perhaps in a while also no longer do so.

From Hitler's last political testament, April 29, 1945

I demand of all Germans, all National Socialists, men, women, and all the men of the Armed Forces, that they be faithful and obedient unto death to the new government and its President.

Above all I charge the leaders of the nation and those under them to scrupulous observance of the laws of race and to merciless opposition to the universal poisoner of all peoples, international Jewry.

Issued in Berlin, this April 29, 1945, 4:00 A.M.
Adolf Hitler

INTRODUCTION

TO RESTORE GERMANY to its former greatness, Hitler believed that the Jews had to be purged from the political and public life of the German nation and removed from all positions of political, social, or cultural influence. The first systematic anti-Jewish acts of the National Socialist government, therefore, deprived the Jews of the equal rights which they had won in the course of the past century.

On March 23, 1933, Hitler had, by a policy of deceit and false assurances, obtained a majority in the Reichstag to pass the Enabling Act, a law authorizing the government to issue legislation on its own responsibility, even if that legislation deviated from the Reich Constitution. Thenceforth, the decrees which were promulgated by the German government adhered to the principles of National Socialist ideology rather than to the rules of law.

The first anti-Jewish decree was issued on April 7, 1933, just two weeks after the passage of the Enabling Act. The Law for the Restoration of the Professional Civil Service, whose very title indicated its nationalist character, provided for the dismissal of "non-

Aryan" civil servants, including clerical employees and workers as well as professionals.War veterans were excepted, an appeal having been made on their behalf by Reich president Field Marshal Paul von Hindenburg. That same day another decree was issued which denied admission to the bar to lawyers of "non-Aryan descent."

On April 11, 1933, an implementing decree appeared, defining "non-Aryan" status: "It is enough for one parent or grandparent to be non-Aryan. This is to be assumed especially if one parent or one grandparent was of the Jewish faith." Thenceforth, proof of "Aryan" origins had to be supplied by all persons in the civil service and eventually for most other positions.

On April 25, 1933, the Law Against the Overcrowding of German Schools and Institutions of Higher Learning established a numerus clausus for students of "non-Aryan descent." An implementing decree issued the same day set the admissible quota of "non-Aryans" at 1.5 percent. By the end of 1933, a spate of pseudolegal legislation had eliminated Jews from public and government positions, bringing about a reversion of status to the pre-Emancipation era.

On September 15, 1935, at the ceremonial session of the Reichstag convened at the annual Nazi party congress in Nuremberg, two new laws were enacted—the Reich Citizenship Law and the Law for the Protection of German Blood and German Honor. The Reich Citizenship Law declared that German citizenship was awarded only to subjects of "German or kindred blood." An implementing decree, issued on November 14, 1935, addressed itself to the unsettled status of offspring of marriages between Jews and "Aryans," designated as Mischlinge *("hybrids"). The law established the racial pedigree of various types of Mischlinge and also removed the exemptions allowed in the 1933 legislation for Jewish civil servants who were war veterans.*

The Law for the Protection of German Blood and German Honor forbade marriage and sexual relations between Jews and those of "German or kindred blood," providing severe penalties for violations. Its first implementing decree further regulated the status of Mischlinge. The enactment of these laws, isolating the Jews from the general population of Germany, marked the end of the first stage of the process disemancipating the Jews in Germany. Hitler hinted, in presenting the Law for the Protection of German Blood and German Honor, at an imminent and ominous change in his anti-Jewish policy. This law, he said, was "an attempt to regulate by law a problem which, in the event of repeated failure, would have to be transferred by law to the National Socialist party for final solution."

The next cycle of anti-Jewish legislation came in 1938 and was synchronized with Hitler's plans for war. The Law Regarding the Legal Status of the Jewish Religious Communities, promulgated on March 28, 1938, withdrew public status from the Gemeinden, *the legally recognized local Jewish communal bodies, putting them under the administrative control of the regime, foreshadowing eventual Gestapo control.*

On April 26, 1938, after the annexation of Austria, the Decree Regarding the Reporting of Jewish Property was issued. Promulgated by Göring, as Plenipotentiary for the Four Year Plan, and by Wilhelm Frick, the Minister of the Interior, this decree ordered every Jew to assess and report the value of his entire domestic and foreign property by June 30, 1938. The first in a series, this law set in motion a process that would lead to the total expropriation of all Jewish property.

On August 17, 1938, the Second Decree for the Implementation of the Law Regarding Changes of Family Names and Given Names was issued. (The original law, issued on January 5, 1938, laconic and mysterious, had merely established the government's authority in the matter of change of name.) Not only were Jews forbidden to take "Aryan" names, in accordance with lists provided, but all Jewish men were now obliged to add the name of Israel to their own names; all Jewish women were to add the name of Sarah. This law presaged the identification of Jews in passports and personal documents, and also by means of Star-of-David armbands and badges, the wearing of which later became obligatory throughout German-ruled Europe.

On November 7, 1938, a Polish Jewish boy by the name of Hershel Grynszpan (Germanized as Grünspan) shot Ernst vom Rath, a member of the German legation in Paris. Two days later, vom Rath died of his wounds. His death, on the anniversary of the Munich Putsch, served as the pretext for a massive pogrom against Jews all over Germany, resulting in enormous destruction of Jewish property. This pogrom became known as Kristallnacht, "night of glass," on account of the large-scale smashing of display windows of Jewish-owned stores. The German government exploited the oc-

casion to accelerate the expropriation of the Jews and the liquidation of their community. On November 12, 1938, Göring, acting as Plenipotentiary for the Four Year Plan, imposed a one-billion-mark penalty payment upon the Jews. Thereafter, in rapid succession, flowed decrees, and orders totally expropriating Jewish property, businesses, and industry, and putting Jews under police surveillance.

LAW FOR THE RESTORATION OF
THE PROFESSIONAL CIVIL SERVICE, APRIL 7, 1933

The Reich Government has enacted the following law, promulgated herewith:

§ 1   (1) To restore a national professional civil service and to simplify administration, civil servants may be dismissed from office in accordance with the regulations that follow, even in the absence of the conditions required therefor under present law.

(2) For the purposes of this law, the following are regarded as civil servants: direct and indirect officials [1] of the Reich, direct and indirect officials of the states and officials of municipalities and confederated municipalities, officials of public corporations as well as of institutions and enterprises of equivalent status (Third Decree of the Reich President for Securing the Economy and Finances, dated October 6, 1931; *Reichsgesetzblatt* I, p. 537—Part 3, Chapter V, Article I, § 15, Paragraph 1). The provisions also apply to functionaries of social-insurance carriers who have the rights and duties of civil servants.

(3) Officials temporarily retired from active service also are civil servants for the purposes of this law.

(4) The Reichsbank and the German Reich Railroad Company are authorized to adopt corresponding regulations.

§ 2   (1) Civil servants who have entered civil-service status

---

1. "Direct and indirect officials" is a technical term dating back to the bureaucracy of Frederick the Great. "Direct" civil servants were employed by government agencies; "indirect" civil servants were employed by public corporations and institutions engaged in public functions.

since November 9, 1918, without having the prescribed or customary training or other qualifications for their careers are to be dismissed from the service. Their previous salaries will be continued for the duration of three months after dismissal.

(2) They are not entitled to half pay, pension, or survivors' benefits, nor to retain their designations of rank, titles, uniforms, or emblems.

(3) In cases of need, especially when they provide for dependents without means, they may be granted annuities, revocable at any time, up to one third of the basic salary of the positions most recently held. No extra insurance under the Reich social-insurance law will be provided.

(4) The provisions of Paragraphs 2 and 3 will be appropriately applied to persons coming under the definitions in Paragraph 1 who retired before this law took effect.

§ 3 (1) Civil servants who are not of Aryan descent are to be retired (§§ 8 ff.); if they are honorary officials, they are to be dismissed from official status.

(2) Paragraph 1 does not apply to civil servants who have been officials since August 1, 1914, or who fought at the front during the World War for the German Reich or her allies, or whose fathers or sons were killed in action in the World War. Further exceptions may be permitted by the Reich Minister of the Interior in agreement with the minister concerned or by the highest state agencies for civil servants working abroad.

§ 4 Civil servants whose political activities to date afford no assurance that they will at any time unreservedly support the national state may be dismissed from the service. Their prevailing salaries will be continued for the duration of three months after dismissal. Thereafter they will receive three-fourths of their pension (§ 8) and corresponding survivors' benefits. . . .

§ 7 (1) Dismissal from office, transfer into another function or retirement will be decreed by the highest Reich or state agency, making a final decision with no right of appeal to the courts. . . .

§ 8 Civil servants retired or dismissed under §§ 3 and 4 will not be granted pensions unless they have completed at least ten years of service. . . .

§ 15   Provisions concerning civil servants will appropriately apply to clerical employees and workers.

Administrative regulations will govern the particulars. . . .

§ 17   (1) The Reich Minister of the Interior, in agreement with the Reich Minister of Finance, will issue the legal decrees and general administrative regulations required for the implementation of this law.

(2) Where necessary, the highest state agencies will issue supplementary regulations. In doing so, they must keep within the framework of the Reich regulations.

§ 18   Upon expiration of the terms designated in this law, the general regulations applying to the professional civil service will regain full effect, without, however, affecting measures taken under this law.

LAW REGARDING ADMISSION TO THE BAR
APRIL 7, 1933

The Reich Government has enacted the following law, promulgated herewith:

§ 1   The admission to the bar of lawyers who, according to the Law for the Restoration of the Professional Civil Service of April 7, 1933 (*Reichsgesetzblatt* I, p. 175), are of non-Aryan descent may be revoked until September 30, 1933.

The provision of Paragraph 1 does not apply to lawyers who were admitted as early as August 1, 1914, or who during the World War fought at the front for the German Reich or its allies, or whose fathers or sons were killed in action in the World War.

§ 2   Persons who, according to the Law for the Restoration of the Professional Civil Service of April 7, 1933 (*RGBl.* I, p. 175), are of non-Aryan descent may be denied admission to the bar, even in the absence of the reasons specified therefor in the Lawyers Code. The same applies to the admission to another court of lawyers designated in § 1, Paragraph 2.

§ 3   Persons who engaged in pro-Communist activities are excluded from admission to the bar. Admissions already granted are to be revoked. . . .

FIRST DECREE FOR IMPLEMENTATION OF
THE LAW FOR THE RESTORATION OF
THE PROFESSIONAL CIVIL SERVICE, APRIL 11, 1933

Pursuant to § 17 of the Law for the Restoration of the Professional Civil Service of April 7, 1933 (*Reichsgesetzblatt* I, p. 175) the following is decreed:

I

To § 2   All civil servants who belong to the Communist Party or to Communist auxiliary or front organizations are unfit. They are accordingly to be dismissed.

II

To § 3   (1)   A person is to be regarded as non-Aryan if he is descended from non-Aryan, especially Jewish, parents or grandparents. It is enough for one parent or grandparent to be non-Aryan. This is to be assumed especially if one parent or one grandparent was of the Jewish faith.

(2)   If a civil servant did not already have civil-service status on August 1, 1914, he must prove that he is of Aryan descent, or that he fought at the front, or that he is the son or father of a man killed in action during the World War. Proof must be given by submission of documents (birth certificate or parents' marriage certificate, military papers).

(3)   If Aryan descent is doubtful, an opinion must be obtained from the expert on racial research attached to the Reich Ministry of the Interior.

III

To § 4   (1)   In determining whether the conditions specified in § 4, Paragraph 1, are present, the civil servant's entire political activity, particularly since November 9, 1918, is to be taken into consideration.

(2)   Each civil servant is required to inform the highest Reich or state authorities (§ 7), upon demand, to which political parties he has heretofore belonged. In the context of this ruling, the *Reichsbanner Schwarz-Rot-Gold*,[2] the Judges' Association for the Republic,[3] and the Human Rights League are also considered political parties.

IV

All transactions, documents, and official certifications required for the implementation of this law are exempt from fees and stamp duties.

§⚜§

LAW AGAINST THE OVERCROWDING OF GERMAN
SCHOOLS AND INSTITUTIONS OF HIGHER LEARNING
APRIL 25, 1933

The Reich Government has enacted the following law, which is promulgated herewith:

§ 1   In all schools except schools providing compulsory education,[4] and in institutions of higher learning, the number of pupils and students is to be limited so as to ensure thorough training and meet professional needs.

§ 2   State governments will determine at the beginning of each school year how many pupils each school may accept and how many new students each university faculty may accept.

§ 3   In those kinds of schools and faculties whose attendance figures are particularly out of proportion to professional needs, the number of pupils and students already admitted is to be re-

---

2. An anti-Nazi paramilitary defense organization, supported by the Social Democrats, the Center, and the Democrats—the original Weimar coalition.
3. An association dedicated to strengthening and preserving the Weimar Republic.
4. All children were required to have eight years of elementary-school education. Hence, the limitations on Jewish enrollment applied to the secondary and higher levels of schooling.

duced during the 1933 school year as far as this can be done without excessive rigor, in order to establish a more acceptable proportion.

§ 4   In new admissions, care is to be taken that the number of Reich Germans who, according to the Law for the Restoration of the Professional Civil Service of April 7, 1933 (*RGBl.* I, p. 175), are of non-Aryan descent, out of the total attending each school and each faculty, does not exceed the proportion of non-Aryans within the Reich German population. The ratio will be determined uniformly for the entire Reich territory.

Likewise, in lowering the number of pupils and students according to § 3, a suitable proportion is to be established between the total number of persons attending and the number of non-Aryans. In doing so, a quota higher than the population ratio may be used as a base.

Paragraph 1 and 2 do not apply to Reich Germans of non-Aryan descent whose fathers fought at the front during the World War for the German Reich or its allies, or to the offspring of marriages concluded before this law took effect, if one parent or two grandparents are of Aryan origin. These also are not to be included in calculating the population ratio and the quota.

§ 5   Obligations incumbent upon Germany as a result of international treaties are not affected by the provisions of this law.

§ 6   Decrees for implementation will be issued by the Reich Minister of the Interior.

§ 7   The law takes effect on the date of promulgation.

FIRST DECREE FOR IMPLEMENTATION OF
THE LAW AGAINST THE OVERCROWDING OF
GERMAN SCHOOLS, APRIL 25, 1933

Pursuant to § 6 of the Law Against the Overcrowding of German Schools and Institutions of Higher Learning of April 25, 1933 (*Reichsgesetzblatt* I, p. 225), the following is decreed:

To § 1

(1)   The law applies equally to public and private schools. To the extent that it is still necessary, the state government will de-

termine to what particular schools and institutions of higher learning the law applies.

(2) The Reich Minister of the Interior may fix general numerical guidelines for limiting the number of pupils and students. . . .

To § 4

(8) The population ratio (§ 4, Paragraph 1) for use in new admissions is set at 1.5 per cent; the quota (§ 4, Paragraph 2) for use in reducing the number of pupils and students is set at a maximum of 5 per cent.

(9) Within university faculties the population ratio is to be maintained among new enrollments.

In each school the population ratio is to be maintained among new admissions for as long as the school is still attended by pupils of non-Aryan descent who remain there within the limits of the quota provided for in § 4, Paragraph 2.

Where the number of new admissions to a particular school is so small that under the population ratio no pupil of non-Aryan descent would be admitted, *one* pupil of non-Aryan descent may be admitted. However, in this case further admission of pupils of non-Aryan descent will be permissible only when the population ratio will not have been reached among the total of new admissions since the effective date of the law.

(10) When a pupil of non-Aryan descent who was newly admitted subsequent to the effective date of the law changes schools, he is to be counted in the population ratio at the school to which he transfers.

(11) Pupils of non-Aryan descent who have newly entered or will newly enter school at the beginning of the 1933 school year will in all cases count as not yet admitted. § 4, Paragraph 1, applies to them.

The same applies analogously to students who have been or will be enrolled for the first time in the 1933 summer semester.

୧୦ଡ଼

REICH CITIZENSHIP LAW, SEPTEMBER 15, 1935

The Reichstag has unanimously enacted the following law, which is promulgated herewith:

§ 1 (1) A subject[5] is anyone who enjoys the protection of the German Reich and for this reason is specifically obligated to it.

(2) Nationality is acquired according to the provisions of the Reich and state nationality law.

§ 2 (1) A Reich citizen is only that subject of German or kindred blood who proves by his conduct that he is willing and suited loyally to serve the German people and the Reich.

(2) Reich citizenship is acquired through the conferment of a certificate of Reich citizenship.

(3) The Reich citizen is the sole bearer of full political rights as provided by the laws.

§ 3 The Reich Minister of the Interior, in agreement with the Deputy of the Führer, will issue the legal and administrative orders required to implement and supplement this law.

Nuremberg: September 15, 1935
at the Reich Party Congress of Freedom

The Führer and Reich Chancellor   *The Reich Minister of the Interior*

FIRST DECREE TO
THE REICH CITIZENSHIP LAW, NOVEMBER 14, 1935

Pursuant to § 3 of the Reich Citizenship Law of September 15, 1935 (*Reichsgesetzblatt* I, p. 1146), the following is decreed:

§ 1 (1) Until further regulations concerning the certificate of Reich citizenship are issued, subjects of German or kindred blood who on the effective date of the Reich Citizenship Law possessed the right to vote in Reichstag elections, or to whom the Reich Minister of the Interior, in agreement with the Deputy of the Führer, granted provisional Reich citizenship, will be provisionally deemed Reich citizens.

(2) The Reich Minister of the Interior, in agreement

---

5. The German term *Staatsangehöriger,* translated as "subject," refers to someone who is under the rule of a government that affords him protection and to which he owes loyalty.

with the Deputy of the Führer, may revoke provisional Reich citizenship.

§ 2   (1)   The provisions of § 1 also apply to subjects who are Jewish *Mischlinge*.

(2)   A Jewish *Mischling* is anyone who is descended from one or two grandparents who are fully Jewish as regards race, unless he is deemed a Jew under § 5, Paragraph 2. A grandparent is deemed fully Jewish without further ado, if he has belonged to the Jewish religious community.

§ 3   Only a Reich citizen, as bearer of full political rights, can exercise the right to vote on political matters, or hold public office. The Reich Minister of the Interior or an agency designated by him may, in the transition period, permit exceptions with regard to admission to public office. The affairs of religious associations are not affected.[6]

§ 4   (1)   A Jew cannot be a Reich citizen. He is not entitled to the right to vote on political matters; he cannot hold public office.

(2)   Jewish civil servants will retire by December 31, 1935. If these civil servants fought at the front during the World War for the German Reich or its allies, they will receive the full pension according to the salary scale for the last position held, until they reach retirement age; they will not, however, be promoted according to seniority. After they reach retirement age, their pension will be newly calculated according to the prevailing salary scales.

(3)   The affairs of religious associations are not affected.

(4)   The conditions of service of teachers in Jewish public schools remain unchanged until the issuance of new regulations for the Jewish school system.

§ 5   (1)   A Jew is anyone descended from at least three grandparents who are fully Jewish as regards race. § 2, Paragraph 2, Sentence 2 applies.

(2)   Also deemed a Jew is a Jewish *Mischling* subject who is descended from two fully Jewish grandparents and
a. who belonged to the Jewish religious

6. The Jewish religious communities *(Gemeinden)* were permitted to retain their legal status as official corporations, that is, having the power and authority of state or municipality, until March 31, 1938. See below, Law Regarding the Legal Status of the Jewish Religious Communities, March 28, 1938.

community when the law was issued or has subsequently been admitted to it;

    b. who was married to a Jew when the law was issued or has subsequently married one;

    c. who is the offspring of a marriage concluded by a Jew, within the meaning of Paragraph 1, after the Law for the Protection of German Blood and German Honor of September 15, 1935 (*RGBl.* I, p. 1146) took effect;

    d. who is the offspring of extramarital intercourse with a Jew, within the meaning of Paragraph 1, and will have been born out of wedlock after July 31, 1936.

§ 6   (1) Requirements regarding purity of blood exceeding those in § 5 that are set in Reich laws or in directives of the National Socialist German Workers Party and its units remain unaffected.

    (2) Other requirements regarding purity of blood that exceed those in § 5 may be set only with the consent of the Reich Minister of the Interior and the Deputy of the Führer. Insofar as requirements of this kind already exist, they will become void as of January 1, 1936, unless approved by the Reich Minister of the Interior in agreement with the Deputy of the Führer. Application for approval is to be made to the Reich Minister of the Interior.

§ 7   The Führer and Reich Chancellor may grant exemptions from provisions of the implementation decree.

            The Führer and Reich Chancellor
The Reich Minister of the Interior   *The Deputy of the Führer*

LAW FOR THE PROTECTION OF
GERMAN BLOOD AND GERMAN HONOR, SEPTEMBER 15, 1935

Imbued with the insight that the purity of German blood is prerequisite for the continued existence of the German people and inspired by the inflexible will to ensure the existence of the German nation for all times, the Reichstag has unanimously adopted the following law, which is hereby promulgated:

§ 1 (1) Marriages between Jews and subjects of German or kindred blood are forbidden. Marriages nevertheless concluded are invalid, even if concluded abroad to circumvent this law.

(2) Only the State Attorney may initiate the annulment suit.

§ 2 Extramarital intercourse between Jews and subjects of German or kindred blood is forbidden.

§ 3 Jews must not employ in their households female subjects of German or kindred blood who are under 45 years old.

§ 4 (1) Jews are forbidden to fly the Reich and national flag and to display the Reich colors.

(2) They are, on the other hand, allowed to display the Jewish colors. The exercise of this right enjoys the protection of the state.

§ 5 (1) Whoever violates the prohibition in § 1 will be punished by penal servitude.

(2) A male who violates the prohibition in § 2 will be punished either by imprisonment or penal servitude.

(3) Whoever violates the provisions of §§ 3 or 4 will be punished by imprisonment up to one year and by a fine, or by either of these penalties.

§ 6 The Reich Minister of the Interior, in agreement with the Deputy of the Führer and the Reich Minister of Justice, will issue the legal and administrative orders required to implement and supplement this law.

§ 7 The law takes effect on the day following promulgation, except for § 3, which goes into force January 1, 1936.

Nuremberg, September 15, 1935
at the Reich Party Congress of Freedom

The Führer and Reich Chancellor   *The Reich Minister of the Interior*
The Reich Minister of Justice   *The Deputy of the Führer*

FIRST DECREE FOR IMPLEMENTATION
NOVEMBER 14, 1935

§ 3 (1) Subjects who are Jewish *Mischlinge* with two fully Jewish grandparents may conclude marriages with subjects of

German or kindred blood, or with subjects who are Jewish *Mischlinge* having only one fully Jewish grandparent, only by permission of the Reich Minister of the Interior and the Deputy of the Führer, or of an agency designated by them.

(2) In making the decision, special attention is to be paid to the physical, psychological, and character attributes of the applicant, the duration of his family's residence in Germany, his own or his father's service in the World War, and other aspects of his family history. . . .

§ 4 No marriage is to be concluded between subjects who are Jewish *Mischlinge* having only one fully Jewish grandparent. . . .

LAW REGARDING THE LEGAL STATUS OF
THE JEWISH RELIGIOUS COMMUNITIES
MARCH 28, 1938

The Reich Government has enacted the following law, which is promulgated herewith:

§ 1 (1) Jewish religious communities and their central organizations shall obtain legal standing through entry in the Register of Associations.

(2) At the end of March 31, 1938, Jewish religious communities and their central organizations will lose the status of official corporations insofar as they possessed it heretofore. From that date on, they will be private associations with legal standing. Entry in the Register of Associations must follow.

§ 2 Officials of the communities and central organizations referred to in § 1, Paragraph 2, will lose their civil-service status at the end of March 31, 1938. At the same time, they will enter into a private-employment relationship with the communities and central organizations, the previous stipulations of their rights and duties being appropriately applied.

§ 3 (1) Approval by the higher administrative authority is required for:

Resolutions of the organs of Jewish religious communities and their central organizations concerning:

a. formation, change, and disbanding of communities and central organizations;

b. disposal of, or substantial changes in, objects of historical, scientific, or artistic value, especially archives or parts of such.

(2) The higher administrative authority may object to the appointment of members of organs of Jewish religious communities and their central organizations.

§ 4   The Reich Minister for Church Affairs may, with the agreement of the Reich Minister of the Interior, issue legal or administrative orders to implement and supplement this law.

§ 5   (1) The law goes into force on January 1, 1938.

(2) On that date, incompatible regulations become invalid.

(3) The enforcement of this law for the land of Austria is reserved.

The Führer and Reich Chancellor
The Reich Minister for Church Affairs
The Reich Minister of the Interior

DECREE REGARDING THE REPORTING OF JEWISH PROPERTY, APRIL 26, 1938

Pursuant to the decree for implementation of the Four Year Plan, of October 18, 1936 (*Reichsgesetzblatt* I, p. 887), the following is decreed:

§ 1   (1) Every Jew (§ 5 of the First Decree to the Reich Citizenship Law of November 14, 1935, *RGBl.* I, p. 1333) must report and assess his entire domestic and foreign property as of the effective date of this decree, in accordance with the regulations that follow. Jews who are foreign subjects must report and assess only their property within this country.

(2) The duty to report and assess property also applies to the non-Jewish spouse of a Jew.

(3) Property must be reported separately for each person required to report.

§ 2   (1) For purposes of this decree, property includes the entire property of the person required to report, regardless of whether or not it is exempt from any or all taxes.

(2) Property does not include movable goods intended solely for the personal use of the person required to report, or household goods, unless they are luxury articles.

§ 3 (1) Each item of property is to be assessed, in reporting, at its common value on the effective date of this decree.

(2) The obligation to report does not apply where the total value of property subject to reporting does not exceed 5,000 Reichsmarks, not figuring liabilities.

§ 4 (1) The report, prepared according to an official form, is to be submitted no later than June 30, 1938, to the higher administrative agency for the place of residence of the person reporting. In individual cases where for special reasons a complete report and assessment of property are not possible by this date, the higher administrative agency may extend the deadline for reporting. In that case, however, the property must be tentatively reported with an estimated value by June 30, 1938, the hindrance being specified. . . .

§ 7 The Plenipotentiary for the Four Year Plan may take measures necessary to ensure that the use made of property subject to reporting will be in keeping with the interests of the German economy.

§ 8 (1) Whoever on purpose or through negligence fails to comply with the obligation to report, assess, or register property according to the above provisions, or complies incorrectly or tardily, or violates an order issued pursuant to § 7, will be punished by imprisonment and a fine or by either of these penalties. In especially grave cases of purposeful violation, the sentence may be penal servitude up to ten years. The perpetrator is also guilty if he commits the act abroad.

(2) Attempted violation is punishable.

(3) In addition to the penalty under Paragraphs 1 and 2, the sentence may specify confiscation of the property insofar as it was the object of the punishable act. When penal servitude is imposed, the sentence must specify confiscation. If no particular individual can be prosecuted or convicted, a sentence of confiscation may also be pronounced separately, provided the other conditions for confiscation are present.

The Plenipotentiary for the Four Year Plan
The Reich Minister of the Interior

SECOND DECREE FOR THE IMPLEMENTATION OF
THE LAW REGARDING CHANGES OF FAMILY NAMES
AUGUST 17, 1938

Pursuant to § 13 of the Law of January 5, 1938, regarding changes of family names and given names (*Reichsgesetzblatt* I, p. 9), the following is decreed:

§ 1   (1)   Jews may be given only such given names as are listed in the Guidelines on the Use of Given Names issued by the Reich Minister of the Interior.

(2)   Paragraph 1 does not apply to Jews who are foreign subjects.

§ 2   (1)   Insofar as Jews have other given names than those which may be given to Jews according to § 1, they are obligated, beginning January 1, 1939, to assume an additional given name, namely, the given name Israel in the case of males, and the given name Sarah in the case of females.

(2)   Whoever, according to Paragraph 1, must assume an additional given name is obligated to give written notice within a month from the date after which he is required to use the additional given name, both to the registrar with whom his birth and his marriage are recorded, and to the local police authorities in his place of residence or usual domicile.

(3)   If the birth or marriage of the person required to give such notice is recorded by a German diplomatic representative or consul or in a German protectorate, the notice required for the registrar is to be directed to the registrar at the Registrar's Office No. 1 in Berlin. If the person required to give the notice resides or is usually domiciled abroad, the notice specified in Paragraph 2, Sentence 1, is to be given to the appropriate German consul in lieu of the local police authorities.

(4)   In the case of incompetent persons and of persons of limited competence, the requirement to give notice rests with the legal representative.

§ 3   Insofar as it is customary to state names in legal and business transactions, Jews must always use at least one of their given names. If they are required under § 2 to assume an additional given name, this given name is also to be used. Regulations regarding the use of names of firms are not affected by this provision.

§ 4   (1)   Whoever willfully violates the provision of § 3 will be punished by imprisonment up to six months. If the violation is due to negligence, the punishment will be imprisonment up to one month.

(2) Whoever willfully or negligently fails to give notice as provided in § 2 will be fined or punished by imprisonment up to one month.

The Reich Minister of the Interior
The Reich Minister of Justice

DECREE ON A PENALTY PAYMENT BY JEWS WHO ARE GERMAN SUBJECTS, NOVEMBER 12, 1938

The hostile attitude of Jewry toward the German Volk and Reich, an attitude which does not shrink even from committing cowardly murder, necessitates determined resistance and harsh penalty.

I, therefore, pursuant to the Decree for the Execution of the Four Year Plan of October 18, 1936 (*Reichsgesetzblatt* I, p. 887), order the following:

§ 1

The payment of a contribution of 1,000,000,000 Reichsmarks to the German Reich is imposed on the Jews who are German subjects.

§ 2

The Reich Minister of Finance issues provisions for implementation in agreement with the Reich Ministers concerned.

Berlin: November 12, 1938   *Plenipotentiary for the Four Year Plan*
Göring, Field Marshal

3 THE INTERIM STAGE: "ALL NECESSARY PREPARATIONS"

INTRODUCTION

THE PLANNING OF the Final Solution was synchronized with plans for the invasion of Poland and then with plans for the invasion of the Soviet Union. Hitler had already decided that the actual mass murder of the Jews would take place on those territories, and had imparted the decision to his closest aides when the German armed forces invaded Poland on September 1, 1939. Preparatory planning had begun even earlier.

Reinhard Heydrich, as chief of the Security Police and Security Service, had primary responsibility for carrying out the Final Solution. Under his command was a paramilitary police force called Einsatzgruppen, *special-duty groups, which he had already used in the annexation of Austria in March 1938 and in the invasion of Czechoslovakia in March 1939 to hunt down opponents of the Nazis. On September 21, 1939, following a meeting held in Berlin with the chiefs of the Einsatzgruppen, to discuss their tasks with regard to the "Jewish question," Heydrich issued written instructions. This document is one of the mileposts in the long-range strategy of the Final Solution.*

According to Heydrich's instructions, the present tasks of the Einsatzgruppen were preparatory to the fulfillment of the "final aim." Their first assignment was to remove the Jews from the areas of occupied Poland that were to be incorporated into Germany, and to concentrate them in the remaining territory, which was later called Generalgouvernement *(General Government). The Jews were to be placed in large settlements, at "as few concentration points as possible," rail junctions or points located along railroad lines, "so as to facilitate subsequent measures."*

The chiefs of the Einsatzgruppen were instructed to see that each Jewish community set up a Council of Jewish Elders, which would be "fully responsible, in the literal sense of the word," for carrying out German orders. The chiefs were cautioned to bear in mind Germany's economic interests and above all the needs of the army. That meant that so long as Jews were required to operate or manage industrial or business enterprises which served German needs, the Jews were to be allowed to function until provisions were made for "Aryans" to take over.

Though the responsibility for carrying out these preparatory tasks with regard to the Final Solution of the Jewish question belonged to the Security Police, the work impinged on most of the military and civil operations of the German government. Consequently, Heydrich sent copies of his instructions to half a dozen different government agencies to apprise them of his plans and activities.

Though the Jews in occupied Poland were under the jurisdiction of the SS and Security Police, the civil government, through the Governor-General Hans Frank, issued a series of decrees which provided a pseudolegal basis for the practices already introduced and enforced by the SS. The four decrees presented here deal with the introduction of forced labor, the obligation of Jews to wear identifying armbands with the Star of David, the establishment of Jewish Councils (Judenräte), and the provision of the death penalty for leaving the ghetto without authorization.

On December 18, 1940, Hitler, as Supreme Commander of the German Armed Forces, issued a directive (No. 21) to prepare for the invasion of the Soviet Union (code name: Operation Barbarossa). The planning of the invasion included preparations for the murder of the Jews in the territory to be wrested from the Russians. On March 13, 1941, Field Marshal Wilhelm Keitel, Chief of the

High Command of the Armed Forces, issued a secret order to top commanders, in implementation of Hitler's directive. One paragraph of this order (2b) authorized Heinrich Himmler, Reichsführer SS, to exercise independent responsibility in the area of army operations, since he had been "entrusted, on behalf of the Führer, with special tasks . . . entailed by the final struggle that will have to be carried out between two opposing political systems." This ideological language was said to have been dictated by Hitler himself for insertion in Keitel's order. It meant that in the territory taken from Russia the Einsatzgruppen had been assigned the task of rounding up and killing the Jews as expeditiously as possible.

Not only the Einsatzgruppen, but German troops, too, were thoroughly indoctrinated to hate the "Jewish-Bolshevist system" and to be prepared to kill its exponents. On October 10, 1941, Field Marshal Walter von Reichenau, Commander-in-Chief of the Sixth Army, operating in Russia, issued a memorandum setting forth the imperative for "pitiless extermination of alien treachery and cruelty." Hitler later called von Reichenau's memorandum "excellent" and ordered it distributed to all German troops in Russian territory.

Meanwhile, as the German Armed Forces swept into Russia, Himmler began to issue orders to his staff to expand the concentration camps and institute facilities for mass killing by means of poison gas, on a larger scale than in the so-called "Euthanasia" program, carried out under Hitler's order, to kill the mentally defective, physically deformed, and the insane. The first annihilation facilities began to be built in the Summer of 1941 on the grounds of the concentration camp at Auschwitz (Polish: Oświęcim).

By midsummer 1941 Germany ruled most of Europe. The time was ready to make "all necessary preparations with regard to organizational, substantive, and financial viewpoints for a total solution of the Jewish question in the German sphere of influence in Europe." In a memorandum of July 31, 1941, Göring charged Heydrich with this responsibility and authorized him to coordinate the activities of all the government agencies to be involved in the enterprise.

While experiments in large-scale gassing were being conducted on Russian prisoners of war at Auschwitz, and the first death camp, using portable gas vans, was being readied for use at Chełmno, Heydrich called an interministerial and interdepartmental confer-

ence to be held on December 8, 1941, "on the final solution of the Jewish question," to deal with matters of coordination, clearance, and scheduling. The bombing of Pearl Harbor and America's subsequent entry into the war forced Heydrich to postpone his meeting, and it was subsequently convened on January 20, 1942, in an elegant villa in suburban Berlin. The participants included second-echelon men from all major state and party agencies. Heydrich chaired the meeting; Adolf Eichmann took the minutes, having also prepared the background information.

Heydrich opened the meeting with a review of the German government's treatment of the Jews heretofore and explained that "evacuation of the Jews to the East" was now "a possible solution" of the Jewish question, "in accordance with previous authorization by the Führer," apparently referring to the Einsatzgruppen killings. But then, referring no doubt to the construction of the death camps and the experiments under way, he said, "even now practical experience is being gathered that is of major significance in view of the coming final solution of the Jewish question."

The discussion turned to statistics, logistics, and schedules for "evacuating" the Jews from the countries in which they lived and the extent of anticipated cooperation or resistance on the part of individual governments. Since the Nuremberg Laws, defining who was a Jew, were the basis for implementing the Final Solution, determinations had to be made about various categories of Mischlinge: which were to be regarded as Jews and which classed with "persons of German blood." The meeting closed with drinks and lunch.

෯෯෯

HEYDRICH'S INSTRUCTIONS TO
   CHIEFS OF EINSATZGRUPPEN, SEPTEMBER 21, 1939

The Chief of the Security Police
SECRET   Berlin: September 21, 1939

To: *Chiefs of all Einsatzgruppen of the Security Police*
Subject: Jewish question in the occupied territory

I refer to the conference held in Berlin today and once more point
out that the *planned overall measures* (i.e., the final aim) are to
be kept *strictly secret.*
Distinction must be made between:
   (1)   The final aim (which will require extended periods of
time), and
   (2)   The stages leading to the fulfillment of this final aim
(which will be carried out in short terms).

The planned measures demand the most thorough preparation in
their technical as well as economic aspects.

It is obvious that the tasks that lie ahead cannot be laid down in
full detail from here. The instructions and guidelines below will at
the same time serve the purpose of urging the chiefs of the Einsatzgruppen to give the matter their practical thought.

I

*For the time being, the first prerequisite for the final aim is the
concentration of the Jews from the countryside into the larger cities.*
This is to be carried out with all speed.
   In doing so, distinction must be made:
   (1)   between the areas of Danzig and West Prussia, Posen,
Eastern Upper Silesia, and
   (2)   the rest of the occupied territories.[1]

1. The areas of Danzig, West Prussia, Posen, and Eastern Upper Silesia were to
   be incorporated into Germany, whereas the rest of the occupied territory of
   Poland would comprise the Generalgouvernement.

As far as possible, the area mentioned (in *item* 1) is to be cleared of Jews; at least the aim should be to establish only a few cities of concentration.

In the areas mentioned in *item* 2, as few concentration points as possible are to be set up, so as to facilitate subsequent measures.

In this connection, it is to be borne in mind that only cities which are rail junctions, or at least are located along railroad lines, are to be designated as concentration points.

On principle, Jewish communities of *fewer* than 500 persons are to be dissolved and to be transferred to the nearest city of concentration.

This decree does not apply to the area of Einsatzgruppe 1, which is situated east of Cracow and is bounded roughly by *Polanico, Jaroslaw*, the new line of demarcation, and the former Slovak-Polish border. Within this area, only an improvised census of Jews is to be carried out. Furthermore, Councils of Jewish Elders, as discussed below, are to be set up.

II

Councils of Jewish Elders [Jüdische Ältestenräte]

(1)   In each Jewish community, a Council of Jewish Elders is to be set up, to be composed, as far as possible, of the remaining influential personalities and rabbis. The council is to comprise up to 24 male Jews (depending on the size of the Jewish community).

The council is to be made *fully responsible,* in the literal sense of the word, for the exact and punctual execution of all directives issued or yet to be issued.

(2)   In case of sabotage of such instructions, the councils are to be warned of the severest measures.

(3)   The Jewish councils are to take an improvised census of the Jews in their local areas—broken down if possible by sex (age groups): a) up to 16 years of age, b) from 16 to 20 years of age, and c) over, as well as by principal occupational groups—and are to report the results in the shortest possible time.

(4)   The Councils of Elders are to be informed of the dates and deadlines for departure, departure facilities, and finally departure routes. They are then to be made personally responsible for the departure of the Jews from the countryside.

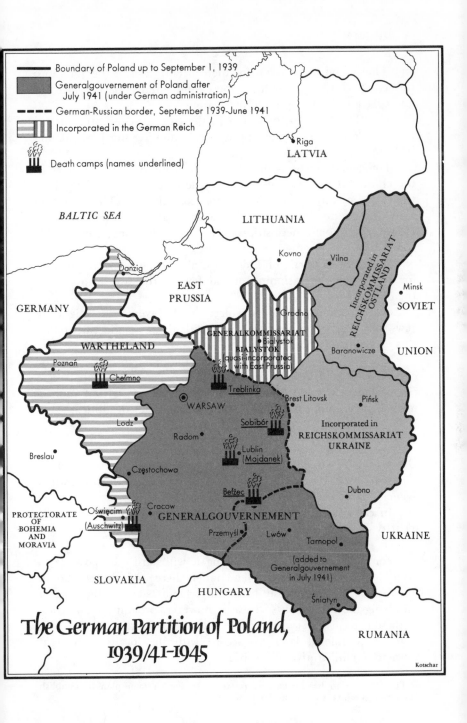

Boundary of Poland up to September 1, 1939

Generalgouvernement of Poland after July 1941 (under German administration)

German-Russian border, September 1939–June 1941

Incorporated in the German Reich

Death camps (names underlined)

LATVIA

Riga

BALTIC SEA

LITHUANIA

Kovno

Danzig

GERMANY

EAST PRUSSIA

Vilna

Minsk

SOVIET

WARTHELAND

Grodno

GENERALKOMMISSARIAT BIALYSTOK (quasi-incorporated with East Prussia)

Baranowicze

Incorporated in REICHSKOMMISSARIAT OSTLAND

UNION

Poznań

Chełmno

Treblinka

WARSAW

Brest Litovsk

Pińsk

Lodz

Sobibór

Radom

Incorporated in REICHSKOMMISSARIAT UKRAINE

Breslau

Lublin (Majdanek)

Częstochowa

Bełżec

Dubno

Oświęcim (Auschwitz)

Cracow

GENERALGOUVERNEMENT

PROTECTORATE OF BOHEMIA AND MORAVIA

Przemyśl

Lwów

Tarnopol

UKRAINE

SLOVAKIA

HUNGARY

(added to Generalgouvernement in July 1941)

Śniatyn

The German Partition of Poland, 1939/41–1945

RUMANIA

Kotschar

The reason to be given for the concentration of the Jews into the cities is that Jews have most influentially participated in guerrilla attacks and plundering actions.

(5)   The Councils of Elders in the cities of concentration are to be made responsible for appropriately housing the Jews moving in from the countryside.

For general reasons of security, the concentration of Jews in the cities will probably necessitate orders altogether barring Jews from certain sections of cities, or, for example, forbidding them to leave the ghetto[2] or go out after a designated evening hour, etc. However, economic necessities are always to be considered in this connection.

(6)   The Councils of Elders are also to be made responsible for appropriate provisioning of the Jews during the transport to the cities.

No objections are to be voiced in the event that migrating Jews take their movable possessions with them, to the extent that this is technically possible.

(7)   Jews who do not comply with the order to move into the cities are to be allowed a short additional period of grace where circumstances warrant. They are to be warned of strictest punishment if they should fail to comply with this latter deadline.

III

On principle, all necessary measures are always to be taken in closest accord and cooperation with the German civil administration agencies and locally competent military authorities.

In carrying them out, care must be taken that the economic security of the occupied territories not be impaired.

(1)   Above all, the needs of the army must be considered.

For example, for the time being it will hardly be possible to avoid leaving behind some Jew traders here and there, who in the absence of other possibilities simply must stay for the sake of supplying the troops. In such cases, however, prompt Aryanization of these enterprises is to be sought and the emigration of the Jews is to be completed later, in accord with the locally competent German administrative authorities.

---

2. This appears to be the earliest reference to the German plan to establish ghettos in which to confine the Jews.

(2) For the preservation of German economic interests in the occupied territories, it is obvious that Jewish-owned essential or war industries and enterprises, as well as those important for the Four Year Plan, must be kept up for the time being.

In these cases also, prompt Aryanization is to be sought, and the emigration of the Jews is to be completed later.

(3) Finally, the food situation in the occupied territories must be taken into consideration. For instance, as far as possible, real estate owned by Jewish settlers is to be provisionally entrusted to the care of neighboring German or even Polish farmers, to be worked by them together with their own, so as to assure harvesting of the crops still in the fields or renewed cultivation.

With regard to this important question, contact is to be made with the agricultural expert of the Chief of the Civil Administration.

(4) In all cases in which the interests of the Security Police on one hand and those of the German Civil Administration on the other cannot be reconciled, I am to be informed in the fastest way before the particular measures in question are carried out, and my decision is to be awaited.

IV

The chiefs of the Einsatzgruppen will report to me continuously on the following matters:

(1) Numerical survey of the Jews present in their territories (broken down as indicated above, if possible). The numbers of Jews who are being evacuated from the countryside and of those who are already in the cities are to be reported separately.

(2) Names of cities which have been designated as concentration points.

(3) Deadlines set for the Jews to migrate to the cities.

(4) Survey of all Jewish-owned essential or war industries and enterprises, as well as those important for the Four Year Plan, within their areas.

If possible, the following should be specified:

    a. Kind of enterprise (also statement on possible conversion into enterprises that are truly essential or war-related, or important for the Four Year Plan);

    b. Which of these enterprises need to be Aryanized most promptly (in order to forestall any kind of loss)?

What kind of Aryanization is suggested? Germans or Poles? (This decision depends on the importance of the enterprise.)

c. How large is the number of Jews working in these enterprises (including leading positions)?

Can the enterprise simply be kept up after the removal of the Jews, or will such continued operation require assignment of German or Polish workers? On what scale?

Insofar as Polish workers have to be introduced, care should be taken that they are mainly brought in from the former German provinces, so as to begin the weeding out of the Polish element there. These questions can be carried out only through involvement and participation of the German labor offices which have been set up.

V

For the attainment of the goals set, I expect total deployment of all forces of the Security Police and the Security Service.

The chiefs of neighboring Einsatzgruppen are to establish contact with each other immediately so that the territories concerned will be covered completely.

VI

The High Command of the Army, the Plenipotentiary for the Four Year Plan (Attention: Secretary of State *Neumann*), the Reich Ministries of the Interior (Attention: Secretary of State *Stuckart*), for Food and for Economy (Attention: Secretary of State *Landfried*), as well as the Chiefs of Civil Administration of the Occupied Territory have received copies of this decree.

[Signed]   *Heydrich*

FOUR DECREES ISSUED IN
   OCCUPIED POLAND, 1939–1941

Decree on the Introduction of Forced Labor for the Jewish Population of the Generalgouvernement
October 26, 1939

Pursuant to § 5, Paragraph 1, of the Decree of the Führer and Reich Chancellor on the Administration of the Occupied Polish Territories, of October 12, 1939, I issue this ordinance:

§ 1

Effective immediately, forced labor is instituted for Jews resident in the Generalgouvernement. For this purpose, the Jews will be concentrated in forced-labor teams.

§ 2

Directives required for the execution of this ordinance will be issued by the Higher SS and Police Leader. He may designate areas east of the Vistula in which the execution of this ordinance is suspended.

Warsaw: October 26, 1939
                                    Governor-General
for the Occupied Polish Territories
Frank

Decree on Identification of Jewish Men and Women in the Generalgouvernement, *November 23, 1939*

Pursuant to § 5, Paragraph 1, of the Decree of the Führer and Reich Chancellor on the Administration of the Occupied Polish Territories, dated October 12, 1939 (*Reichsgesetzblatt* I, p. 2077), I issue this ordinance:

§ 1

All Jewish men and women in the Generalgouvernement who are over ten years of age are obliged, beginning December 1, 1939, to wear a white band, at least 10 centimeters wide, with the Star of David on the right sleeve of their inner and outer clothing.

§ 2

Jewish men and women must themselves procure these arm bands and provide them with the appropriate distinguishing mark.

§ 3

(1)   Violations will be punished by imprisonment.
(2)   The Special Courts will have jurisdiction for judging such cases.

§ 4

Regulations required for execution of this ordinance will be issued by the Chief of the Internal Administration Division in the Generalgouverneur's office.

Cracow: November 23, 1939

> Governor-General
> for the Occupied Polish Territories
> Frank

Decree on Establishing
Jewish Councils (Judenräte), November 28, 1939

Pursuant to § 5, Section 1, of the Decree of the Führer and Reich Chancellor on the Administration of the Occupied Polish Territories, of October 12, 1939 (*Reichgesetzblatt* I, p. 2077), I issue this ordinance:

§ 1

In each municipality a body representing the Jews will be formed.

§ 2

This body representing the Jews will be known as the Jewish Council [*Judenrat*]. In communities with up to 10,000 inhabitants, it will consist of 12 Jews, and in communities with more than 10,000 inhabitants, of 24 Jews, drawn from the resident population. The Judenrat will be elected by the Jews of the community. If a member of the Judenrat ceases to serve, a new member is to be elected immediately.

§ 3

The Judenrat will elect a chairman and a deputy from among its members.

§ 4

(1)   After these elections, which must be completed no later than

December 31, 1939, the Judenrat roster is to be reported to the appropriate senior district official [*Kreishauptmann*], in urban districts to the senior subdivisional district official [*Stadthauptmann*]. (2) The *Kreishauptmann (Stadthauptmann)* will decide whether the Judenrat roster reported to him should be approved. He may direct changes in the roster.

§ 5

The Judenrat is obliged to accept the orders of German agencies, through its chairman or his deputy. It is answerable for conscientious execution of orders to their full extent. The directives it issues to implement these German decrees must be obeyed by all Jewish men and women.

Cracow: November 28, 1939

Governor-General
for the Occupied Polish Territories
Frank

Third Decree on the Restriction of
Residence in the Generalgouvernement, October 15, 1941

Pursuant to § 5, Paragraph 1, of the Führer's Decree of October 12, 1939 (*Reichsgesetzblatt* I, p. 2077), I issue this ordinance:

ARTICLE 1

In the Decree on Restrictions of Residence in the Generalgouvernement September 13, 1940 (*VBlGG* [Verordnungsblatt Generalgouvernement] I, p. 288), as amended by the Second Decree on Limitations of Residence in the Generalgouvernement, of April 29, 1941 (*VBlGG*, p. 274), the following § 4b is inserted after § 4a:

§ 4b

(1) Jews who, without authorization, leave the residential district to which they have been assigned will be punished by death. The same punishment applies to persons who knowingly provide hiding places for such Jews.

(2) Abettors and accomplices will be punished in the same way as the perpetrator, and an attempted act in the same way as an accomplished one. In less serious cases the sentence may be penal servitude, or imprisonment.

(3) Cases will be judged by the Special Courts.

ARTICLE 2

This ordinance takes effect on the day of promulgation.
Warsaw: October 15, 1941

Governor-General
Frank

SECRET ORDER BY
FIELD MARSHAL KEITEL, MARCH 13, 1941

Secret—For Command Only
For Chief Only
Only Through Officer

Führer HQ, March 13, 1941
5 copies; 4th copy

High Command of the Armed Forces
Armed Forces Operational Staff

Secret—For Command Only   For Chief Only
Orders for Special Areas in Connection with Directive No. 21
(Operation Barbarossa)

I   *Area of Operations and Executive Power*
(1) In *East Prussia* and the *Generalgouvernement,* authoriza-
tions to issue orders and regulations regarding supply, valid *within
the Armed Forces* for an area of operations, will be put into effect
no less than four weeks before operations are started by the High
Command of the Armed Forces. A proposal is to be submitted in
time by the High Command of the Army, after agreement with the
Commander of the Air Force is reached.

There is no plan to declare East Prussia and the Generalgouvernement *an area of army operations.* However, in accordance with
the Führer's unpublished decrees of October 19 and 21, 1939, the
Supreme Commander of the Army is authorized to order such
measures as may be necessary for the execution of his military task
and for the safeguarding of the troops. He may transfer this authority to the Supreme Commanders of Army Groups and Armies.
Orders of this kind take precedence over all other obligations and
over directives issued by civilian agencies.

(2) *The Russian territory* to be occupied in the course of operations is to be divided up into states with *governments of their own,* according to special directives, as soon as the progress of military operations permits.

This implies:

a. *The area of Army operations* created by the advance of the Army beyond the frontiers of the Reich and the neighboring states is to be limited in depth as far as possible. The Supreme Commander of the Army is authorized to exercise the executive power in this area and is permitted to transfer it to the Supreme Commanders of Army Groups and Armies.

b. In the area of Army operations the *Reichsführer SS* will be entrusted, on behalf of the Führer, with *special tasks* for the preparation of the *political administration*—tasks entailed by the final struggle that will have to be carried out between two opposing political systems. Within the framework of these tasks, the Reichsführer SS will act independently and on his own responsibility. However, the executive power vested in the Supreme Commander of the Army and in agencies acting under his orders will not be affected by this. The Reichsführer SS is to see that operations are not disturbed by the execution of his tasks. Details are to be worked out directly between the High Command of the Army and the Reichsführer SS.

c. As soon as the area of operations has reached sufficient depth, it will be *limited in the rear.* The newly occupied territory in the rear of the area of operations will receive a *political* administration of its own. For the present it is to be *divided,* according to the ethnic configuration and with a view to the boundaries of the Army Groups, into *North (Baltic countries), Center (White Russia),* and *South (Ukraine).* In these territories *the political administration will be transferred to Reich Commissars* who receive their directives from the Führer.

(3) For the execution of all *military tasks* within the areas under political administration to the rear of the area of operations, *Armed Forces commanders* will be assigned, who will be responsible to the Chief of the High Command of the Armed Forces.

The Armed Forces commander is the *supreme representative of the Armed Forces* in a given area, and exercises the *military sovereign rights.* He has the *tasks of a Territorial Commander* and the authority of a Supreme Army Commander or a Commanding General.

In this capacity he is responsible, above all, for the following tasks:

a. Close cooperation with the Reich Commissar in order to support him in his political task.

b. Utilization of the country and securing of its economic assets for the purposes of the German economy (see item 4).

c. Utilization of the country for supplying the troops according to the requirements of the High Command of the Army.

d. Military security measures for the whole area, especially airports and supply routes and installations, against revolt, sabotage, and enemy paratroops.

e. Regulation of road traffic.

f. Billeting for Armed Forces, police organizations, and for prisoners of war insofar as they remain in the administrative areas.

In his relations with the *civilian* agencies, the Armed Forces commander has the right to issue orders necessary for the execution of military tasks. His orders within this field take precedence over all others, even those of the Reich Commissars. . . .

(6) The behavior of the troops toward the population and the tasks of the *military courts* are to be covered by special regulations and commands. . . .

The Chief of the High Command
of the Armed Forces
Keitel

CRUSHING THE "JEWISH-BOLSHEVIST SYSTEM":
FIELD MARSHAL VON REICHENAU'S ORDERS

Army H.Q., October 10, 1941
Army Command 6

Secret!

Subject: Conduct of the Troops in the Eastern Region.

With respect to the conduct of troops toward the Bolshevist system, vague ideas are still widely prevalent.

The essential aim of the campaign against the Jewish-Bolshevist system is the complete crushing of its means of power and the extermination of Asiatic influence in the European cultural region.

This poses tasks for the troops which go beyond the onesided routine of conventional soldiering. In the Eastern region, the soldier is not merely a fighter according to the rules of the art of war, but also the bearer of an inexorable national idea and the avenger of all bestialities inflicted upon the German people and its racial kin.

Therefore, the soldier must have *full* understanding for the necessity of a severe but just atonement on Jewish sub-humanity. An additional aim is to nip in the bud any revolts in the rear of the army, which, as experience proves, have always been instigated by Jews.

The fight against the enemy behind the front line is not yet being taken seriously enough. Treacherous, cruel *partisans* and unnatural women are still being made prisoners of war; snipers and vagabonds, only partly in uniform or in civilian clothes, are still being treated as decent soldiers and taken to the prisoner-of-war camps. Captured Russian officers actually state, sneeringly, that *Soviet agents* move around unchallenged on the roads and often eat at German field kitchens. Such an attitude on the part of the troops can only be explained by complete thoughtlessness. That being so, it is time for the commanders to awaken an understanding of the present struggle.

The *feeding* at army kitchens of *natives and prisoners of war* who are not working for the armed forces is as mistaken a humanitarian act as giving away cigarettes and bread. Items which the home front must forgo under great self-abnegation and which the leadership brings to the front under the greatest difficulties may not be given to the enemy by the soldier—not even if they originate from booty. They are an indispensable part of our supply.

When retreating, the Soviets have often set buildings on fire. The troops have an interest in extinguishing fires only to the extent that needed billets must be preserved. Other than that, the disappearance of symbols of the former Bolshevist rule, even in the form of buildings, is part of the struggle of destruction. In this context, neither historic nor artistic considerations play any role in the Eastern region. The leadership will issue the necessary directives for preserving raw materials and plants essential for the war economy. Complete *disarming of the population* in the rear of the fighting troops is urgent in view of the long and vulnerable supply lines. Where possible, captured weapons and ammunition are to be stored and guarded. If combat conditions do not permit this, the weapons and ammunition are to be rendered inoperative. If isolated partisans are found to have used weapons in the rear of the army, the situation is to be dealt with by draconian measures. These measures are to extend to those among the male population who would have been in a position to prevent or report the planned ambushes. The indifference of numerous ostensibly anti-Soviet elements, arising from a wait-and-see attitude, must give way to a clear decision to collaborate actively against Bolshevism. Short of this, no one may complain of being evaluated and treated as an adherent of the Soviet system. The dread of German countermeasures must be stronger than the threats of the Bolshevist remnants still wandering about. *Apart from any political consideration of the future,* the soldier has to fulfill two tasks:

(1)   *The total annihilation of the false Bolshevist doctrine, of the Soviet State, and of its armed forces;*

(2)   *The pitiless extermination of alien treachery and cruelty, and thus the protection of the lives of the German forces in Russia.*

Only in this way will we do justice to our historic task *of liberating* the German people, *once and for all,* from the Asiatic-Jewish peril.

The Commander in Chief
[Signed] *von Reichenau*
Field Marshal

GÖRING'S COMMISSION TO HEYDRICH
JULY 31, 1941

Berlin: July 31, 1941

The Reich Marshal of the Greater German Reich
Plenipotentiary for the Four-Year Plan
Chairman of the Ministerial Council for the Defense of the Reich

To: the Chief of the Security Police and the SD,
SS Major General Heydrich, Berlin:

As supplement to the task which was entrusted to you in the decree dated January 24, 1939, to solve the Jewish question by emigration and evacuation in the most favorable way possible, given present conditions, I herewith commission you to carry out all necessary preparations with regard to organizational, substantive, and financial viewpoints for a total solution of the Jewish question in the German sphere of influence in Europe.

Insofar as the competencies of other central organizations are hereby affected, these are to be involved.

I further commission you to submit to me promptly an overall plan showing the preliminary organizational, substantive, and financial measures for the execution of the intended final solution of the Jewish question.

[Signed] GÖRING

MINUTES OF THE WANNSEE CONFERENCE
JANUARY 20, 1942

Secret Reich Business!

Protocol of Conference

I   The following took part in the conference on the final solution of the Jewish question held on January 20, 1942, in Berlin, Am Grossen Wannsee No. 56–58:

Gauleiter Dr. Meyer and Reich Office Director Dr. Leibbrandt	Reich Ministry for the Occupied Eastern Territories
Secretary of State Dr. Stuckart	Reich Ministry of the Interior
Secretary of State Neumann	Plenipotentiary for the Four Year Plan
Secretary of State Dr. Freisler	Reich Ministry of Justice
Secretary of State Dr. Bühler	Office of the Governor General
Undersecretary of State Luther	Foreign Office
SS Oberführer Klopfer	Party Chancellery
Ministerial Director Kritzinger	Reich Chancellery
SS Gruppenführer Hofmann	Race and Settlement Main Office
SS Gruppenführer Müller	Reich Security Main Office
SS Obersturmbannführer Eichmann	
SS Oberführer Dr. Schöngrath, Commander of the Security Police and the SD in the Generalgouvernement	Security Police and SD

SS Sturmbannführer Dr. Lange, Commander of the Security Police and the SD in the General District of Latvia, as representative of the Commander of the Security Police and the SD for the Reich Commissariat for the Ostland

Security Police and SD

II   At the beginning of the meeting the Chief of the Security Police and the SD, SS Obergruppenführer *Heydrich,* announced his appointment by the Reich Marshal, as Plenipotentiary for the Preparation of the Final Solution of the European Jewish Question, and pointed out that this conference had been called to clear up fundamental questions. The Reich Marshal's request to have a draft sent to him on the organizational, substantive, and economic concerns on the final solution of the European Jewish question necessitates prior joint consideration by all central agencies directly concerned with these questions, with a view to keeping policy lines parallel.

Primary responsibility for the handling of the final solution of the Jewish question, the speaker stated, is to lie centrally, regardless of geographic boundaries, with the Reichsführer SS and the Chief of the German Police (Chief of the Security Police and the SD).

The Chief of the Security Police and the SD then gave a brief review of the struggle conducted up to now against this enemy. The most important aspects are:

a. Forcing the Jews out of the various areas of life of the German people;

b. Forcing the Jews out of the living space of the German people.

In carrying out these efforts, acceleration of the emigration of the Jews from Reich territory, being the only possible provisional solution, was undertaken in intensified and systematic fashion.

By decree of the Reich Marshal, a Reich Central Office for Jewish Emigration was set up in January 1939, and its direction was entrusted to the Chief of the Security Police and the SD. In particular, its tasks were:

a. To take all measures toward *preparation* for intensified emigration of the Jews;

     b. To *direct* the stream of emigration;

     c. To expedite emigration *in individual cases.*

The objectives of these tasks was to cleanse the German living space of Jews in a legal way.

The disadvantages entailed by such a forcing of emigration were clear to all the authorities. But in the absence of other possible solutions, they had to be accepted for the time being.

In the ensuing period, the handling of emigration was not only a German problem, but also a problem with which the authorities of the countries of destination or immigration had to deal. Financial difficulties—such as increases decreed by the various foreign governments in the moneys which immigrants were required to have and in landing fees—as well as lack of steamship berths, continually intensified restrictions, or bans on immigration hampered the emigration efforts exceedingly. Despite these difficulties, a total of approximately 537,000 Jews was processed into emigration between the assumption of power and the date of October 31, 1941, consisting of the following:

Since January 30, 1933:	from the Altreich [3]	approx. 360,000
Since March 15, 1938:	from the Ostmark [4]	approx. 147,000
Since March 15, 1939:	from the Protectorate of Bohemia and Moravia	approx. 30,000

Financing of the emigration was handled by the Jews or Jewish political organizations themselves. To avoid a situation where only the proletarianized Jews would remain behind, the principle was followed that well-to-do Jews had to finance the emigration of destitute Jews. To this end, a special assessment or emigration levy, staggered by property levels, was decreed, the proceeds being used to meet financial obligations in connection with the emigration of destitute Jews.

In addition to the funds raised in German marks, foreign currency was needed for the moneys which emigrants were required to have and for landing fees. To conserve the German supply of foreign currencies, Jewish financial institutions abroad were

---

3. *Altreich* was the Nazi term to designate Germany's boundaries prior to March 1938.
4. *Ostmark* was the Nazi term to designate Austria after the Anschluss.

prompted by the Jewish organizations in this country to see to it that appropriate funds in foreign currencies were obtained. Through these foreign Jews, a total of approximately $9,500,000 was made available by way of gifts up to October 30, 1941.

Since then, in view of the dangers of emigration during wartime and in view of the possibilities in the East, the Reichsführer SS and Chief of the German Police has forbidden the emigration of Jews.

III   Emigration has now been replaced by evacuation of the Jews to the East as a further possible solution, in accordance with previous authorization by the Führer.

However, these actions are to be regarded only as provisional options; even now practical experience is being gathered that is of major significance in view of the coming final solution of the Jewish question.

In connection with this final solution of the European Jewish question, approximately 11 million Jews may be presumed to be affected.[5] They are distributed among the individual countries as follows:

	Country	Number
A.	Altreich	131,800
	Ostmark	43,700
	Eastern Territories	420,000
	Generalgouvernement	2,284,000
	Bialystok	400,000
	Protectorate of Bohemia & Moravia	74,200
	Estonia—free of Jews	
	Latvia	3,500
	Lithuania	34,000
	Belgium	43,000
	Denmark	5,600
	France: Occupied territory	165,000
	Unoccupied territory	700,000
	Greece	69,600
	The Netherlands	160,800
	Norway	1,300
B.	Bulgaria	48,000
	England	330,000
	Finland	2,300

5. These statistics, the product of Eichmann's research, are far from correct. The size of the Jewish population of the U.S.S.R., for example, was grossly exaggerated.

Country	Number
Ireland	4,000
Italy, including Sardinia	58,000
Albania	200
Croatia	40,000
Portugal	3,000
Rumania, including Bessarabia	342,000
Sweden	8,000
Switzerland	18,000
Serbia	10,000
Slovakia	88,000
Spain	6,000
Turkey (European part)	55,500
Hungary	742,800
U.S.S.R.	5,000,000

Ukraine	2,994,684
White Russia, excluding Bialystok	446,484

TOTAL   over   11,000,000

However, the numbers of Jews given for the various foreign states reflect only those of Jewish faith, as definitions of Jews according to racial principles are still partly lacking there. The handling of the problem in the individual countries, especially in Hungary and Rumania, will meet with certain difficulties, on account of prevailing attitudes and ideas. To this day, for example, a Jew in Rumania can for money obtain appropriate documents officially confirming him to be of some foreign citizenship.

The influence of the Jews upon all areas in the U.S.S.R. is well known. About five million live in the European area, a scant quarter-million in the Asian territory.

The occupational breakdown of Jews residing in the European area of the U.S.S.R. was about as follows:

In agriculture	9.1%
Urban workers	14.8%
In commerce	20.0%
Employed as government workers	23.4%
In professions—medicine, the press, theater, etc.	32.7% [6]

6. Jewish occupational structure in the U.S.S.R. was actually quite different. About forty percent of the Soviet Jews were industrial workers and fewer than twenty percent were in the professions and government service.

Under appropriate direction, in the course of the final solution, the Jews are now to be suitably assigned to labor in the East. In big labor gangs, with the sexes separated, Jews capable of work will be brought to these areas, employed in roadbuilding, in which task a large part will undoubtedly disappear through natural diminution.

The remnant that may eventually remain, being undoubtedly the part most capable of resistance, will have to be appropriately dealt with, since it represents a natural selection and in the event of release is to be regarded as the germ cell of a new Jewish renewal. (Witness the experience of history.)

In the course of the practical implementation of the final solution, Europe is to be combed through from west to east. The Reich area, including the Protectorate of Bohemia and Moravia, will have to be handled in advance, if only because of the housing problem and other socio-political necessities.

The evacuated Jews will first be brought, group by group, into so-called transit ghettos, to be transported from there farther to the East.

An important prerequisite for the implementation of the evacuation as a whole, SS Obergruppenführer *Heydrich* explained further, is the exact determination of the category of persons that may be affected.

The intent is not to evacuate Jews over 65 years of age, but to assign them to a ghetto for the aged. Theresienstadt is under consideration.[7]

Along with these age groups (of the approximately 280,000 [8] Jews who on October 31, 1941, were in the Altreich and the Ostmark, approximately 30 per cent are over 65 years old), Jews with serious wartime disabilities and Jews with war decorations (Iron Cross, First Class) will be taken into the Jewish old-age ghettos. With this efficient solution, the many interventions [requests for exceptions] will be eliminated at one stroke.

The beginning of each of the larger evacuation actions will depend largely on military developments. With regard to the handling of the final solution in the European areas occupied by

---

7. Theresienstadt served a dual purpose. It was a ghetto for privileged categories of German Jews and at the same time a transit camp for assembling the Czech Jews prior to their deportation to Auschwitz.
8. Likely a typographical error in the original, this figure probably should read "180,000."

us and under our influence, it was proposed that the appropriate specialists in the Foreign Office confer with the competent official of the Security Police and the SD.

In Slovakia and Croatia the undertaking is no longer too difficult, as the most essential problems in this matter have already been brought to a solution there. In Rumania, likewise, the government has by now appointed a Commissioner for Jewish Affairs. For settling the problem in Hungary it will be necessary in the near future to impose upon the Hungarian Government an adviser in Jewish problems.

With regard to beginning preparations for the settling of the problem in Italy, SS Obergruppenführer *Heydrich* considers liaison with the Police Chief appropriate in these matters.

In occupied and unoccupied France, the roundup of the Jews for evacuation can in all probability take place without great difficulties.

On this point, Undersecretary of State *Luther* stated that thorough handling of this problem will occasion difficulties in a few countries, such as the Nordic states, and that it will therefore be advisable to postpone these countries for the time being. In consideration of the small number of Jews presumably affected there, this postponement does not constitute an appreciable curtailment in any case.

On the other hand, the Foreign Office sees no great difficulties with respect to the Southeast and West of Europe.

SS Gruppenführer *Hofmann* intends to have a specialist of the Race and Settlement Main Office sent along to Hungary for general orientation when the matter is taken in hand there by the Chief of the Security Police and the SD. It was decided that this specialist of the Race and Settlement Main Office, who is not to be active, should temporarily be assigned the official capacity of assistant to the Police Attaché.

IV   In the implementation of the final-solution program, the Nuremberg Laws are to form the basis, as it were; and in this context, a solution of the questions concerning mixed marriages and *Mischlinge* is a precondition for complete settlement of the problem.

In connection with a letter from the Chief of the Reich Chancellery, the Chief of the Security Police and the SD discusses the following points—theoretically, for the time being:

(1) *Treatment of first-degree Mischlinge*

As far as the final solution of the Jewish question is concerned, first-degree *Mischlinge* are deemed equal to Jews.

The following will be exempt from this treatment:

a. First-degree *Mischlinge* married to persons of German blood from whose marriages children (second-degree *Mischlinge*) have been born. These second-degree *Mischlinge* are deemed essentially equal to Germans.

b. First-degree *Mischlinge* for whom exceptions with respect to any area of life have been granted prior to the present time by the highest authorities of the Party and the State.

Each individual case must be re-examined, and the possibility is not ruled out that the decision may again be in the *Mischling's* disfavor.

The basis for granting an exception must always be the fundamental merits of the particular *Mischling himself* (not the merits of the parents or spouse of German blood).

The first-degree *Mischling* who is to be exempted from evacuation is to be sterilized, in order to prevent any offspring and to settle the *Mischling* problem once and for all. Sterilization takes place on a voluntary basis. It is, however, the condition for remaining in the Reich. The sterilized *Mischling* is thereafter freed from all restrictive regulations to which he was previously subject.

(2) *Treatment of second-degree Mischlinge*

Second-degree *Mischlinge* are normally classed with persons of German blood, *with the exception of the following cases,* in which second-degree *Mischlinge* are deemed equal to Jews:

a. Descent of the second-degree *Mischling* from a bastard marriage (both spouses being *Mischlinge*).

b. Especially unfavorable appearance in racial terms, such as will put the second-degree *Mischling* with the Jews on the strength of his exterior alone.

c. Especially bad police and political rating of the second-degree *Mischling*, indicating that he feels and conducts himself like a Jew.

Even in these cases, however, exceptions are not to be made if the second-degree *Mischling* is married to a person of German blood.

(3) *Marriages between full Jews and persons of German blood*

In such instances it must be decided from case to case whether the Jewish spouse is to be evacuated or whether, in consideration of the effect of such a measure on the German relatives of the mixed couple, he or she is to be assigned to an old-age ghetto.

(4)   *Marriages between first-degree Mischlinge and persons of German blood*
a. Without children.

If no children have been born of the marriage, the first-degree *Mischling* is evacuated or assigned to an old-age ghetto. (The same treatment as in the case of marriages between full Jews and persons of German blood, item 3.)
b. With children.

If children have been born of the marriage (second-degree *Mischlinge*), they are to be evacuated or assigned to a ghetto, together with the first-degree *Mischlinge, provided they are deemed equal to Jews.* Insofar as such children *are deemed equal to Germans* (routine cases), they are to be exempted from evacuation, and also therewith the first-degree *Mischling.*

(5)   *Marriages between first-degree Mischlinge and first-degree Mischlinge or Jews*

In the case of such marriages (including children), all parties are treated like Jews and accordingly evacuated or assigned to an old-age ghetto.

(6)   *Marriages between first-degree Mischlinge and second-degree Mischlinge*

Both spouses, regardless of whether there are children or not, are evacuated or assigned to an old-age ghetto, since any children of such marriages normally show a greater share of Jewish blood in their racial makeup than do second-degree Jewish *Mischlinge.*

SS Gruppenführer *Hofmann* takes the position that extensive use must be made of sterilization, particularly since the *Mischling,* when confronted with the choice of being evacuated or sterilized, would prefer to submit to sterilization.

Secretary of State Dr. *Stuckart* states that the practical implementation of the possible solutions just communicated for settling the problems of mixed marriages and those of the *Mischling* would entail endless administrative labor in their present form. Thus, in order to take biological realities fully into account, Secretary of State Dr. *Stuckart* suggested that compulsory sterilization be undertaken.

Also, he stated, to simplify the mixed-marriage problem, further possibilities must be considered to the effect that the legislator will say something like: "These marriages *are* dissolved."

As to the question of the effect the evacuation of Jews may have on economic life, Secretary of State *Neumann* stated that the Jews employed in essential war industries could not be evacuated for the present, as long as no replacements were available.[9]

SS Obergruppenführer *Heydrich* pointed out that those Jews would not be evacuated anyway, according to the directives approved by him for the implementation of current evacuation actions.

Secretary of State Dr. *Bühler* stated that the Generalgouvernement would welcome it if the final solution of this problem *were begun in the Generalgouvernement,* because here the transport problem plays no major role and considerations of labor supply would not hinder the course of this action. Jews needed to be removed as quickly as possible from the territory of the Generalgouvernement, he said, because here particularly the Jew constitutes a marked danger as a carrier of epidemics, and also because by his constant black-market operations he throws the economic structure of the country into disorder. Furthermore, of the approximately two-and-one-half million Jews here in question, the majority of cases were *unfit for work,* he added.

Secretary of State Dr. *Bühler* further states that the solution of the Jewish question in the Generalgouvernement is primarily the responsibility of the Chief of the Security Police and the SD and that his work would be supported by the agencies of the Generalgouvernement. He had only one request, he said: that the Jewish question in this territory be solved as quickly as possible.

In conclusion, the various kinds of possible solutions were discussed, and here both Gauleiter Dr. *Meyer* and Secretary of State Dr. *Bühler* took the position that certain preparatory tasks connected with the final solution should be performed right in the territories concerned, but that, in doing so, any alarm among the population must be avoided.

With a request by the Chief of the Security Police and the SD to the conference participants that they afford him appropriate support in carrying out the tasks connected with the solution, the conference was concluded.

---

9. For more on how the Germans resolved the conflict between economic considerations and the ideological objectives of the Final Solution, see Section 4, below.

4 THE FINAL STAGE: MASS KILLINGS, "RESETTLEMENT," DEATH CAMPS

INTRODUCTION

THE CONCLUDING STAGE of the Final Solution was inaugurated by four Einsatzgruppen of about 3,000 men and officers, following hard upon the German armed forces invading Soviet-held territory, with instructions to destroy the Jews. Everywhere, from the Baltic in the North to the Crimea in the South, the Einsatzgruppen adhered to a master strategy. First they incited indigenous anti-Semitic groups to riot against the Jews. These pogroms, photographed and filmed, were designed to demonstrate that all peoples, not just the German people, regarded the Jews as their enemy and took appropriate "defense" measures. During the pogroms, the German Security Police remained in the background.

Thereafter, the chiefs of the Einsatzgruppen began to organize the systematic annihilation of the Jews. Security Police commandos, units of the Einsatzgruppen, took charge, reinforced by auxiliary battalions of indigenous collaborators. By apposite applications of chicanery and terror, the Security Police rounded up the Jews, who were ordered to appear at designated places and times to be "resettled" for work. Those who did not report, the orders warned, would be shot. Once assembled, the Jews were marched off or taken by truck to an outlying area where they were forced to dig trenches or pits. The Einsatzkommandos stripped the Jews of their posses-

sions and even clothing, lined them up at the edge of the trenches, and machinegunned them en masse.

According to the Operations Situation Report of Einsatzgruppe C of October 7, 1941, 33,771 Jews of Kiev were "executed" on September 29 and 30, a rate of killing that far exceeded the daily maximum operational capacity of the gas chambers at Auschwitz. The locus for the murder of the Jews of Kiev was Babi Yar, a desolate ravine on the outskirts of the city. In the Baltic, units of Einsatzgruppe A were equally diligent. According to their chief's round-up report of October 15, 1941, they killed about 120,000 Jews in Lithuania, Latvia, Estonia, and White Russia.

In all, it is estimated that the Einsatzgruppen, aided by both the German armed forces and collaborators, murdered about two million Jews.

At the end of 1941, when the Einsatzgruppen were bringing the first cycle of their mass killings to a halt, the death camp at Chełmno began functioning. Then Auschwitz, Bełžec, Sobibór, Majdanek, and Treblinka were successively put into operation. Everywhere using the stratagem that the Jews were being "resettled for work in the East," the Germans began transporting them to the death camps. On July 19, 1942, Himmler issued an order to the effect that by December 31, 1942, no Jews were to remain in the Generalgouvernement, except for those assigned to specified forced-labor camps.

Three days later, on July 22, 1942, immediately upon completion of the gassing facilities at Treblinka, SS Hauptsturmführer (Captain) Hans Höfle, euphemistically titled Commissioner for Resettlement of the Warsaw Ghetto, issued orders and instructions to the Judenrat for "resettling" the Warsaw Jews "in the East." All Jews to be resettled were permitted to take with them fifteen kilograms of personal luggage as well as valuables. Those exempted from "resettlement" were Jews employed by German industrial enterprises and by the Judenrat. The penalty for disobeying Höfle's orders was shooting. Compliance on the part of the Judenrat was enforced by the habitual German practice of taking hostages who would be shot in the event German orders were not "carried out 100 percent."

In his undeviating commitment to the annihilation of the Jews, Himmler made only minimal, short-term concessions to the needs of the German war industry, summarily ordering Jewish manpower to be replaced by Poles and Ukrainians. But the German armaments authorities could not speedily obtain efficient substitute workers among the non-Jewish peasant populations. In the Generalgouvernement top military officers became convinced that the elimination of the Jews would harm Germany's military potential. Consequently, on September 18, 1942, General Kurt Freiherr von Gienanth, Commander of the Generalgouvernement Military District, addressed a memorandum to General Alfred Jodl, Chief of the Army's Operations Staff, setting forth the manpower difficulties and requesting permission to handle matters in a way that would not hinder the war effort. "The principle should be," he declared, "to eliminate the Jews as promptly as possible without impairing essential war work."

The records yield no reply from Jodl, but on September 30 Gienanth was relieved of his post, no doubt on account of an outraged Himmler's intervention. On October 9, 1942, Himmler issued a memorandum reiterating his order of July 19, and, as Reichsführer SS, assuming the responsibility for uninterrupted delivery of needed supplies to the German Armed Forces. Furthermore, in a scathing reference to Gienanth's proposal, he instructed "that steps be ruthlessly taken against all those who think it their business to intervene in the alleged interests of war industry, but who in reality want only to support the Jews and their businesses." In conclusion, he made it clear that those few Jewish forced-labor concentration camps that he permitted to continue in operation were merely a temporary expedient, for "even from there the Jews are some day to disappear, in accordance with the Führer's wishes."

Everywhere in Europe the Jews began to disappear. Six death camps operated on the territory that once had been Poland, and at each the procedure was the same. The Jews, disembarking from freight cars with the remnants of their possessions, were herded along a ramp or passageway to barracks where they were told to check their clothing before entering a bathhouse or shower room. Then, completely nude, prodded by Balt or Ukrainian auxiliary police with bayonets and whips, the Jews were driven into the gas chambers. In Auschwitz and Majdanek, where the SS maintained large industrial enterprises operating on forced labor, a small proportion of physically fit Jews was assigned to slave labor. After a short while, their vigor spent, they too were dispatched to the gas chambers.

The only witnesses to the death agony of the Jews in the gas chambers were German observers who watched through a peep-hole—either technicians checking on the speed and effectiveness of the poison gases or visiting dignitaries. Aside from the technical description by Rudolf Höss, commandant at Auschwitz, only one testimony has survived of the final Jewish ordeal. It was written at war's end by Kurt Gerstein (1905–1945), a man of mysterious contradictions, who committed suicide while under arrest in a French military prison as a war criminal.

Jews who escaped the death camps and their slave-labor adjuncts brought back harrowing tales of German barbarism and Jewish suffering and provided detailed descriptions of the physical installations in the killing centers and of the procedures before and after the gassings. The most authoritative report on Auschwitz was compiled in the spring of 1944 by two young Jews, Rudolf Vrba and Alfred Weczler, who escaped and returned to their native Slovakia, where they recounted their experiences to Jewish leaders. Their report reached the War Refugee Board in Washington some months later and was released under American government auspices. The statistics which Vrba compiled on the basis of daily records confirmed previous reports of the gigantic dimensions of the Final Solution.

In the mass deportations from the Warsaw ghetto that began on July 22 and ended eight weeks later on September 12, 1942, about 300,000 Jews were deported to their deaths at Treblinka. Only 50,000 remained when, on April 19, 1943, the Germans began the final liquidation of the ghetto. At that point instead of obeying German orders to assemble for resettlement, the Jews resisted. The SS responded not only with habitual terror, but also with massive military force. SS and Police Leader Jürgen Stroop (1895–1951; hanged in Warsaw) led units of the SS, the Security Police, and other SS police forces, the German army, and Ukrainian militia in a major military effort to suppress Jewish resistance and destroy the ghetto.

On April 23, when it became apparent that Jewish resistance would not easily crumble, Himmler issued an order to comb out the ghetto "with the greatest severity and ruthless tenacity." Stroop undertook to destroy the ghetto totally by burning down all the buildings, including even those attached to the armaments factories. Those Jews who were not murdered by shootings, fires, and explosions were ultimately taken to Treblinka. On May 16, when the resistance had been quelled, Stroop wrote a lengthy report on his liquidation of the Warsaw ghetto, which he submitted to his superior, the top SS officer in the Generalgouvernement, Higher SS and Police Leader Krüger. On July 18, 1943, Field Marshal Keitel, in the name of the Führer, rewarded Stroop with the Iron Cross, First Class.

By October 1943, over five million Jews had been murdered. At a meeting of top SS officers in Poznań on October 4, Himmler, in a long, rambling speech which touched on subjects ranging from the military situation to the organization and ethos of the SS, openly spoke of the annihilation of the Jews. "All in all," he maintained, "we have carried out this heaviest of our tasks in a spirit of love for our people." In summing up "this really grave matter," a subject, he said, not again to be spoken of in public, he exulted: "In our history, this is an unwritten and never-to-be-written page of glory."

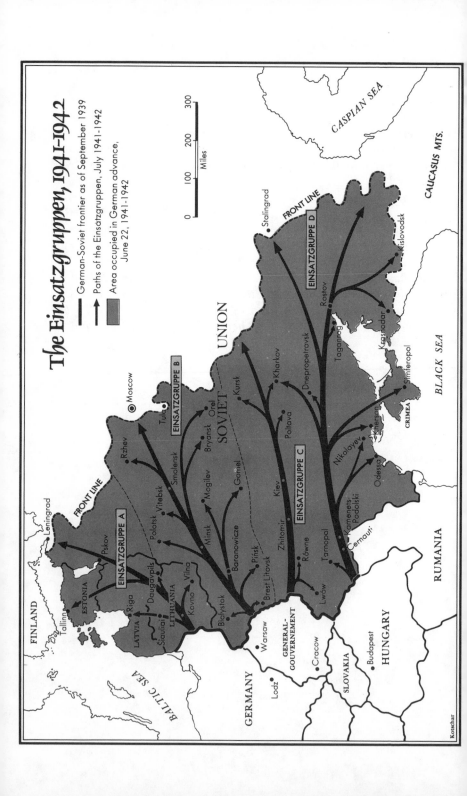

The Einsatzgruppen, 1941–1942

— German-Soviet frontier as of September 1939

→ Paths of the Einsatzgruppen, July 1941–1942

▨ Area occupied in German advance,
June 22, 1941–1942

0 100 200 300
Miles

FINLAND

BALTIC SEA

CASPIAN SEA

CAUCASUS MTS.

BLACK SEA

Tallinn
Leningrad
Pskov
ESTONIA
Riga
Daugavpils
LATVIA
Šiauliai
LITHUANIA
Kovno
Vilna
FRONT LINE
EINSATZGRUPPE A
Rzhev
Polotsk
Vitebsk
Moscow
Tula
EINSATZGRUPPE B
Smolensk
Orel
Bryansk
Bialystok
Minsk
Mogilev
Gomel
Kursk
SOVIET UNION
Baranowicze
Pinsk
Brest Litovsk
Warsaw
Kharkov
**GENERAL-
GOUVERNEMENT**
Zhitomir
Kiev
Poltava
Dnepropetrovsk
Stalingrad
FRONT LINE
Lwów
Rowne
Tarnopol
EINSATZGRUPPE C
EINSATZGRUPPE D
Rostov
Cracow
Kamenets-
Podolski
Cernauti
Nikolayev
Kherson
Taganrog
Krasnodar
Kislovodsk
Lodz
GERMANY
Budapest
Odessa
Simferopol
CRIMEA
SLOVAKIA
HUNGARY
RUMANIA

Kotschar

FIELD REPORTS FROM CHIEFS OF EINSATZGRUPPEN

Operations Situation Report, Einsatzgruppe C
October 7, 1941

I

KIEV

An advance commando of the *Sonderkommando* [1] 4a, led by SS
Obersturmführer Häfner and Janssen, 50 men strong, arrived on
September 19, 1941, with the fighting troops in Kiev. The main
commando of the Sonderkommando 4a reached Kiev on September
25, 1941, after SS Standartenführer Blobel had already been in Kiev
on September 21 and 22. The advance commando of the Einsatzgruppe staff, Police Captain Krumme, SS Obersturmführer Dr.
Krieger and Breun and SS Oberscharführer Braun, arrived in Kiev
on September 21, 1941. The Einsatzgruppe staff followed on September 25, 1941. . . .

The Army first of all systematically secured public buildings,
factories, and stocks of the scarcest goods, so that no large-scale
plunder occurred either by members of the Army or by the population. Reports on mines and other explosive material in public
buildings and apartment houses were made by the population in
great numbers from the very first day of the occupation of Kiev. On
September 20, 1941, a delayed-action mine exploded in the citadel
where Artillery Headquarters were located. . . . On September 24,
1941, an explosion occurred in the offices of the Rear Area German
Military Headquarters and developed during the day into a large
fire, especially because of the lack of water. A large part of the city
center and several large buildings in the suburbs were destroyed by
further explosions and resulting fires. In order to control the fire,
the Army was forced to blow up more buildings to prevent the fire
from spreading to other districts. As a result of these necessary
explosions, the offices of the Einsatzgruppe headquarters and of the
Sonderkommando 4a had to be evacuated. . . .

1. *Sonderkommando* (special commando) was a special detachment of SS troops
assigned to police and political tasks, apparently differentiated from the
Einsatzkommando, special-duty units, several of which constituted an Einsatzgruppe. Personnel of both Sonderkommandos and Einsatzgruppen were
drawn from the Security Police and Security Service (Sipo and SD).

II
EXECUTIONS AND OTHER MEASURES

Public feeling against the Jews was very strong, partly because of the better economic situation of the Jews under the Bolshevist regime and their activities as NKVD [2] informers and agents, partly because of the explosions and the resulting fires (which deprived about 25,000 people of shelter). As an added factor, it was proved that the Jews participated in the arson. The population expected appropriate retaliatory measures by the German authorities. Consequently, all Jews of Kiev were ordered, in agreement with the city commander, to appear on Monday, September 29, by 8 a.m., at a designated place. These announcements were posted throughout the city by members of the Ukrainian militia. At the same time it was announced orally that all Jews were to be resettled. In collaboration with the Einsatzgruppe staff and 2 commandos of the Police Regiment South, the Sonderkommando 4a executed 33,771 Jews on September 29 and 30. Money, valuables, underwear, and clothing were confiscated and placed in part at the disposal of the NSV[3] for the use of *Volksdeutsche* [4] and in part given to the city's administrative authorities for the use of the needy population.

It was accomplished without interference. No incidents occurred. The "resettlement measure" against the Jews was approved throughout by the population. The fact that in reality the Jews were liquidated was hardly known until now; in the light of the latest experiences, however, there would scarcely have been objections. The measures were also approved by the Army. The Jews who were not caught before, as well as those who returned to the city little by little after their flight, were in each case treated appropriately.

Round-up Report of Einsatzgruppe A
to October 15, 1941

Einsatzgruppe A, after preparing their vehicles for action, proceeded to their area of concentration, as ordered, on June 23, 1941, the second day of the campaign in the East. Army Group North, consisting of the 16th and 18th Armies and Tank Group 4, had begun

---

2. NKVD = People's Commissariat of Internal Affairs, the Soviet secret police.
3. NSV = *Nationalsozialistische Volkswohlfahrt,* National Socialist People's Welfare.
4. *Volksdeutsche* = ethnic Germans living outside the borders of the German Reich, but loyal to it because of a sense of "racial" and cultural identity.

their advance the day before. Our task was, with all dispatch, to establish personal contact with the commanders of the Armies and with the Commander of the Army of the rear area. It must be stressed that cooperation with the Armed Forces was from the start generally good; in some cases, for instance, with Tank Group 4 under General Höpner, it was very close, almost cordial. Misunderstandings with some authorities which cropped up in the first days were settled principally through personal discussions. . . .

For the Security Police it appeared, at the start of the Eastern campaign, that its special work had to be done not only in rear areas, as was provided for in the original agreements with the High Command of the Army,[5] but also in the combat areas, and this, on the one hand, because the consolidation of the rear area of the armies was delayed because of the quick advance and, on the other hand, because the subversive Communist activity and the fight against partisans took place intensively within the areas of actual warfare. . . .

To carry out the tasks of the Security Police, it was desirable to enter into the larger towns together with the Armed Forces. We had our first experiences in this direction when a small advance squad under my command entered Kovno together with the advance units of the Armed Forces on June 25, 1941. When the other larger towns, specifically Libau, Mitau, Riga, Dorpat, Reval, and the larger suburbs of Leningrad were captured, a Security Police commando was always with the first troop units. Above all, Communist functionaries and Communist documentary material had to be seized, and the Armed Forces themselves had to be safeguarded against surprise attacks inside the towns; the troops themselves were usually not able to take care of that because of their small numbers. For this purpose the Security Police, immediately after entry, set up volunteer formations of trustworthy indigenous residents of all three Baltic provinces who successfully performed their duties under our command. . . .

Similarly, in the first hours after our entry, even under considerable hardships, native anti-Semitic elements were induced to start pogroms against Jews. In conformity with orders, the Security Police was determined to solve the Jewish question with all means and full decisiveness. It was, however, desirable that the Security

---

5. A reference to Field Marshall Keitel's directive of March 13, 1941. See Section 3 for the text.

Police should not be visible, at least in the beginning, since the extraordinarily harsh measures would attract attention even in German circles. It had to be demonstrated to the world that the native population itself took the first measures by way of natural reaction against decades-long suppression by the Jews and against the terror exercised by the Communists in the preceding period.

After reaching the Dvina River and therewith Riga, the Einsatzgruppe, to begin with, detached itself from the further advance of the Army Group North, and concentrated its forces on the pacification of the Lithuanian and Latvian area. . . .

A. THE BALTIC AREA

I   *Organization Measures*
   (1) Formation of auxiliary police and police troops:
   In view of the extensiveness of the area of operations and the great number of Security Police tasks, it was intended from the very start to obtain the cooperation of the trustworthy population for the fight against the vermin in their land—that is, particularly the Jews and Communists. While directing the first spontaneous self-purging actions, which will be reported about elsewhere, care had to be taken that trustworthy elements should be harnessed to the purging job and assigned to regular auxiliary organs of the Security Police. . . .

In Lithuania, at the start of the Eastern campaign, activist nationalist elements formed so-called partisan units [6] in order to take part in the struggle against Bolshevism. . . .

II   *Mopping-up and Security of the Area of Operations*
   (1) Instigation of self-purging operations:
   Considering that the people of the Baltic countries had suffered very heavily under the dominion of Bolshevism and Jewry during the period they were incorporated in the U.S.S.R., it was to be expected that after liberation from foreign rule they would render harmless most of the enemies left behind after the retreat of the Red Army. The task of the Security Police was to set these self-purging aspirations in motion and to direct them into the

6. The word "partisan" is usually associated with irregular pro-Soviet forces fighting the Germans behind the lines. But when the Einsatzgruppe commander designated the pro-German Lithuanian and Lettish auxiliary forces as their "partisans," the pro-Soviet partisan movement had not yet come into existence.

proper channels in order to accomplish the purpose of the mopping-up operations as quickly as possible. It was no less important,
for the time to come, to adduce the well-established and demon-
strable fact that the liberated populace itself took the severest
measures against the Bolshevist and Jewish enemy on its own, and
hence no instructions by German authorities should be discernible.

In Lithuania this was achieved for the first time by the readiness of the partisans in Kovno. Surprisingly, it was not easy at first
to set in motion a pogrom against the Jews on a large scale. Klimatis,
the leader of the partisan unit mentioned above, who was used
primarily for this purpose, succeeded in initiating a pogrom on
the basis of instructions given to him by a small advance unit
operating in Kovno. He worked in such a way that no German order
or German instigation was discernible. During the first pogrom on
the night of June 25 to 26, the Lithuanian partisans eliminated
over 1,000 Jews, set fire to several synagogues or otherwise destroyed
them, and burned down a Jewish quarter of about 60 buildings. On
subsequent nights, about 2,300 Jews were made harmless in a
similar way. In other parts of Lithuania similar actions followed
the example of Kovno, though on a smaller scale, and extended to
the Communists who had been left behind.

These self-purging operations went smoothly because the Army
authorities, who had been apprised, were understanding of this
procedure. From the beginning it was obvious that only the first
days after the occupation would offer the opportunity for carrying
out pogroms. After the disarmament of the partisans, the self-
purging operations automatically ceased.

It proved much more difficult to set in motion similar mopping-up operations and pogroms in Latvia. Essentially, this was
because the entire stratum of national leadership, especially in Riga,
had been murdered or deported by the Soviets. Nevertheless,
through appropriate influence, the Latvian auxiliary police did set
in motion a pogrom against the Jews in Riga, in the course of which
all synagogues were destroyed and about 400 Jews were killed. As
the population of Riga quietened quickly, further pogroms were not
feasible.

So far as possible, both in Kovno and in Riga, motion-picture
films and still photographs showed that the first spontaneous executions of Jews and Communists were carried out by Lithuanians
and Latvians. . . .

(2)   Combating Communism:

The fight against Communism and Jewry stood in the forefront of Security Police work in all parts of the area of operations. . . .

(3)   The fight against Jewry:

It was to be expected from the first that the Jewish problem in the East could not be solved by pogroms alone. On the other hand, in accordance with the basic orders,[7] the mopping-up work of the Security Police had as its goal the annihilation, as comprehensive as possible, of the Jews. Sonderkommandos reinforced by selected units—partisan detachments in Lithuania, units of the Lettish auxiliary police in Latvia—therefore carried out extensive executions both in the towns and in the countryside. The operations of the execution commandos were performed without trouble. In assigning Lithuanian and Lettish forces to the execution commandos, men were chosen whose relatives had been murdered or deported by the Russians.

Especially severe and comprehensive measures became necessary in Lithuania. In some places—especially in Kovno—the Jews had armed themselves and participated actively in guerrilla warfare and committed arson. Besides, the Jews in Lithuania had worked hand in hand most actively with the Soviets.

The sum total of Jews liquidated in Lithuania amounts to 71,105.

In the pogroms in Kovno, 3,800 Jews were eliminated; in the smaller towns about 1,200 Jews.

Also in Latvia the Jews participated in acts of sabotage and arson after the entry of the German Armed Forces. In Dvinsk so many fires were started by Jews that a large part of the town was lost. The electric power station was burned out. The streets which were mainly inhabited by Jews remained unscathed.

In Latvia up to now a total of 30,000 Jews was executed. Five hundred were rendered harmless by pogroms in Riga.

Of the 4,500 Jews living in Estonia at the beginning of the Eastern campaign, most fled with the retreating Red Army. About 2,000 stayed behind. About 1,000 Jews lived in Reval alone.

The arrest of all male Jews over 16 years of age is nearly

---

7. No documents have come to light which contain the "basic orders" given to the Einsatzgruppen to annihilate the Jews. These may have been communicated orally at the Einsatzgruppen training centers prior to the invasion of Russia.

finished. With the exception of the doctors and the Elders of the Jews who were appointed by the Sonderkommandos, they were executed by the Estonian Home Guard under the supervision of Sonderkommando 1a. In Reval and Pernau able-bodied female Jews from 16 to 60 years of age were arrested and put to peat-cutting or other required labor.

At present a camp is being constructed in Harku, in which all Estonian Jews are to be assembled, so that Estonia will shortly be free of Jews.

After the first larger executions in Lithuania and Latvia, it soon became apparent that an absolute annihilation of the Jews was not feasible, at least not at the present moment. Since handicrafts in Lithuania and Latvia are for the most part in Jewish hands and many occupations (especially glaziers, plumbers, stove-fitters, shoe-makers) consist almost exclusively of Jews, a large number of Jewish craftsmen is indispensable at present for repairing installations of vital importance, for the reconstruction of destroyed towns, and for work of military importance. Although employers aim to replace Jewish labor with Lithuanian or Lettish labor, it is not yet possible to replace all employed Jews, especially not in the larger towns. In cooperation with the labor offices, however, all Jews who are no longer fit for work are being arrested and will be executed in small batches.

In this connection it should be mentioned that some author-ities in the Civil Administration offered resistance, at times quite considerable, to carrying out executions of large scope. Such re-sistance was countered by calling attention to the fact that basic orders were involved. . . .[8]

8. The reference is apparently to the correspondence between a top official called Trampedach in the Reich Commissariat Ostland, stationed in Riga, and Berlin headquarters. Explaining his previous action in forbidding "the wild executions of Jews in Libau," Trampedach addressed a memorandum on November 15, 1941, to his superiors in Berlin, asking whether all Jews in the East were to be liquidated: "Is this to take place without regard to age and sex and economic interests (e.g., the Wehrmacht's in skilled workers in arma-ment plants)? Of course, purging the East of Jews is an urgent task; its solu-tion, however, must be harmonized with the necessities of the war economy." The answer from Berlin, December 18, 1941, was tersely peremptory: "On the Jewish question, clarification should by now have been achieved through oral discussions. As a matter of principle, economic considerations should be overlooked in the solution of the problem. As for questions that may arise, it is requested that they be settled directly with the Higher SS and Police Leader."

APPENDIX 8

[Round-up Report of Einsatzgruppe A, to October 15, 1941]

SURVEY OF THE NUMBER OF EXECUTIONS CARRIED OUT TO DATE

SURVEY OF THE NUMBER OF EXECUTED PERSONS

	Jews	Communists	Together
Lithuania			
Kovno area			
town and countryside	31,914	80	31,994
Shavli area	41,382	763	42,145
Vilna area	7,015	17	7,032
	80,311	860	81,171

	Jews	Communists	Together
Latvia			
Riga area			
town and countryside			6,378
Mitau area			3,576
Libau area			11,860
Wolmar area			209
Dvinsk area	9,256	589	9,845
	30,025	1,843	31,868

	Jews	Communists	Together
Estonia	474	684	1,158
White Russia	7,620		7,620

TOTAL			
Lithuania	80,311	860	81,171
Latvia	30,025	1,843	31,868
Estonia	474	684	1,158
White Russia	7,620	—	7,620
	118,430	3,387	121,817

"A TOTAL CLEANUP":
HIMMLER'S ORDER, JULY 19, 1942

I order that the resettlement of the entire Jewish population of the Generalgouvernement be carried out and completed by December 31, 1942.

By December 31, 1942, no persons of Jewish extraction are to be found in the Generalgouvernement, except if they are in the assembly camps [9] of Warsaw, Cracow, Częstochowa, Radom, Lublin. All other work projects employing Jewish labor must be completed by then or, if completion is not possible, must be transferred to one of the assembly camps.

These measures are necessary for the ethnic separation of races and peoples required in the context of the New Order of Europe, as well as in the interest of the security and purity of the German Reich and the spheres of its interest. Any breach in this proceeding constitutes a threat to peace and order in the entire sphere of German interest, a starting point for the resistance movement, and a center of moral and physical contagion.

For all these reasons, a total cleanup is necessary and is accordingly to be carried out. Anticipated delays beyond the deadline are to be reported to me in time for early remedial measures. All requests from other agencies for alterations or for permission to make exceptions are to be submitted to me personally.

Heil Hitler!
[Signed]
H. Himmler

9. The German word is *Sammellager,* designating tightly closed forced-labor installations. Himmler regarded these merely as a temporary concession in the interest of the German war economy.

"RESETTLEMENT" ORDER FOR
THE WARSAW GHETTO, JULY 22, 1942

Orders and Instructions for the Judenrat

The Judenrat is informed of the following:

(1)   All Jewish persons, regardless of age and sex, living in Warsaw, will be resettled in the East.

(2)   Exempt from resettlement are:

a.   All Jewish persons who are employed by German authorities or workshops and can submit proof to that effect.

b.   All Jewish persons who are members or employees of the Judenrat (as of the day of promulgation of this ordinance).

c.   All Jewish persons who are employed by firms headquartered in the German Reich and can submit proof to that effect.

d.   All Jews able to work who have not to date been assigned in the employment process. These are to be segregated in the Jewish quarter.

e.   All Jewish persons belonging to the staff of the Jewish hospitals; also the members of the Jewish decontamination squad.

f.   All Jewish persons who are members of the Jewish police.[10]

g.   All Jewish persons belonging to the immediate families of persons listed in a through f.

h.   All Jewish persons who on the first day of resettlement are confined to one of the Jewish hospitals and are not fit to be discharged. Fitness for discharge will be determined by a physician to be named by the Judenrat.

(3)   Each Jew to be resettled may take with him as luggage 15 kilograms of personal property. All valuables (gold, jewelry, money, etc.) may be taken along. Provisions for three days should be taken.

(4)   The start of the resettlement is on July 22, 1942, at 11:00 a.m.

---

10. The German word is *Ordnungsdienst,* "order service." It has been translated throughout as "Jewish police."

I   In connection with the resettlement, the Judenrat is charged with the following duties, for the precise observance of which the Judenrat members will be held answerable with their lives:

The Judenrat will receive orders having to do with resettlement solely from the Commissioner for Resettlement or from his deputy. For the period of resettlement, the Judenrat may elect a special Resettlement Committee, whose chairman must be the president of the Judenrat, and whose deputy chairman must be the commandant of the Jewish police.

II   The Judenrat is responsible for providing the Jews for shipment each day. For the execution of this task, the Judenrat will utilize the Jewish police (1,000 men). The Judenrat will see to it that each day, beginning July 22, 1942, 6,000 Jews report to the point of assembly by 4:00 p.m. The point of assembly during the entire period of evacuation will be the Jewish Hospital on Stawki Street. On July 22 the 6,000 Jews will report directly to the staging area next to the *Transferstelle*.[11] Initially, the Judenrat may take the required daily contingents of Jews from the population as a whole; later the Judenrat will receive definite instructions, according to which specific streets or blocks of houses are to be cleared.

III   On July 22, 1942, the Judenrat is to clear the Stawki Street Jewish Hospital and to move the inmates and equipment into another suitable building within the ghetto, so that on the evening of July 23, 1942, the hospital will be free to receive the Jews arriving for resettlement each day.

IV   The Judenrat, furthermore, is to see to it that objects and valuable property left behind by the resettled Jews, insofar as they are not contaminated, are gathered and inventoried at collection points still to be determined. For this purpose, the Judenrat will make use of the Jewish police and a sufficient quantity of Jewish manpower. This activity will be supervised by the Security Police, which will give the Judenrat special instructions on the

---

11. *Transferstelle* was the German agency which regulated the flow of goods in and out of the Warsaw ghetto.

matter. Unlawful acquisition of objects or valuable property in the course of this activity will be punished by death.

V   The Judenrat, furthermore, will see that during the period of resettlement Jews working in German enterprises or for German interests will attend to this work. To ensure compliance with this order, it will issue an appropriate announcement to the Jewish population, threatening the severest penalties. The Judenrat must also see to it that enough Jewish food-supply enterprises operate undisturbed in order to secure the food supply both of the Jews at the assembly point and of those remaining behind.

VI   In addition, the Judenrat is responsible for seeing that Jews who die during the period of resettlement are buried the same day.

VII   The Judenrat will immediately, by posters, make the following announcement to the Jewish population of Warsaw:

> "Upon order by the German authorities, all Jewish persons, regardless . . . (etc., from items, 1 through 4).[12]

VIII   Penalties:
> a. Any Jewish person who leaves the ghetto after the start of resettlement not belonging to the categories of persons enumerated in numbers 2a and c, and not hitherto entitled to do so, will be shot.
> b. Any Jewish person who commits an act intended to evade or interfere with the resettlement measures will be shot.
> c. All Jews who are found in Warsaw after conclusion of the resettlement not belonging to the categories of persons enumerated under 2a through 2h will be shot.

The Judenrat is notified that if the orders and instructions given to it are not carried out 100 percent, an appropriate number of hostages, who will meanwhile have been taken, will be shot in each instance.

Dictated by the Commissioner for Resettlement

12. That very day, July 22, 1942, the Judenrat of Warsaw issued the announcement as specified by the Germans.

CONFLICT OF INTERESTS:
THE FINAL SOLUTION VS. MANPOWER NEEDS

General Gienanth to General Jodl
September 18, 1942

I   To date, the regulations for the Generalgouvernement have provided:

(1) Polish and Ukrainian workers will be replaced by Jewish workers, so that the former can be released into the Reich. To this end, camps will be set up for Jews assigned to industrial enterprises.

(2) In order to utilize Jewish labor fully for the war effort, wholly Jewish enterprises or divisions of enterprises will be formed.

The removal of the Jews, initiated without giving notice to the majority of Army agencies, has caused major difficulties in personnel replacement and delays in urgent war production. Work for the SS with winter priorities cannot be completed within the deadline.

II   Unskilled workers can be replaced in part if the General Plenipotentiary for Labor Allocations [13] will forgo the consignment of 140,000 Poles to the Reich, which was to have been carried out by the end of this year, and if it proves possible to obtain police cooperation. In view of previous experiences, this is to be doubted.

On a small scale, students currently being trained in the government vocational schools can be employed as semi-skilled workers.

Skilled workers must first be trained. The training of manpower, most of which will have to be taken from agriculture, re-

13. The Plenipotentiary for Labor Allocations, Fritz Sauckel, functioned in the Office for the Four Year Plan. He headed the operation of a forced-labor system involving millions of European workers, most of whom were deported from their countries to perform heavy labor in Germany's war economy. Sauckel was sentenced to death by the International Military Tribunal at Nuremberg and hanged in 1946.

quires from several months to a year, and even more time in the case of some workers and craftsmen who will require especially high qualifications.

Whether the solution of this particularly difficult problem—upon which maintenance of the Generalgouvernement's efficiency in the war economy chiefly depends—can be expedited by consigning skilled workers from the Reich is beyond my competence to judge.

III   According to the data of the Government—Main Labor Office, the total number of workers in industry comes to slightly more than one million, of which over 300,000 are Jews. Of these, about 100,000 are skilled workers.

Within the various enterprises that work for the Wehrmacht, the number of Jews among the skilled workers ranges from 25 to 100 percent; in the textile factories producing winter clothing, it amounts to 100 percent. In other enterprises—for example, in the important manufacture of vehicles of the Fuhrmann and Pleskau types—the key men, i.e., the wheelwrights, are mainly Jews. Harness makers, with few exceptions, are Jews.

A total of 27,000 workers are at present employed in repairing uniforms in private firms. Of these, 22,000 (97 percent) are Jews; among them, approximately 16,000 skilled workers in textile and leather plants.

One wholly Jewish enterprise, with 168 employees, produces metal harness parts. The entire harness production in the Generalgouvernement, the Ukraine, and, to some extent, in the Reich depends on this operation.

IV   Immediate removal of the Jews would cause the Reich's war potential to be considerably reduced, and supplies to the front as well as to the troops in the Generalgouvernement would be at least momentarily halted.

(1)   In the armaments industry, serious drops in production, from 25 to 100 percent, would occur.

(2)   In motor-vehicle repair shops, an average productivity decrease of about 25 percent would occur; i.e., 2,500 fewer motor vehicles would be repaired each month, on the average.

(3)   Replacement units would have to be deployed to maintain the supply operation.

V   Unless essential war work is to suffer, Jews can be released after their replacements have been trained, i.e., unit for unit. This task can only be carried out locally, but must be centrally directed by one agency in cooperation with the Higher SS and the Police Leader.

Permission is requested to handle this priority decree in this way. In this connection, the principle should be to eliminate the Jews as promptly as possible without impairing essential war work.

VI   As has now been established, war-essential requisitions of the highest priority, particularly for winter requirements, have been placed in the Generalgouvernement by the most varied Army agencies in the Reich without the knowledge of the Armament Inspectorate or of the Commander of the Military District in the Generalgouvernement. Prompt completion of this work has been made impossible by the removal of the Jews.

To deal systematically with all such enterprises will require some time.

It is requested that the removal of Jews working in industrial enterprises be suspended until then.

Commander of the Military District,
Generalgouvernement
[*General Kurt Freiherr von Gienanth*]

CIRCULAR MEMORANDUM OF
REICHSFÜHRER SS HIMMLER: OCTOBER 9, 1942

With reference to the memorandum from the Commander of the Military District in the Generalgouvernement to the High Command of the Army, concerning replacement of Jewish labor by Poles, I have the following comments to make:

(1)   I have ordered all so-called armament workers who are actually employed in tailoring, fur, and shoemaking workshops to be assembled in concentration camps on the spot, i.e., in Warsaw, Lublin, under the direction of SS Obergruppenführer Krüger and

SS Obergruppenführer Pohl.[14] The Army is to convey its requisitions to us, and we guarantee uninterrupted delivery of the clothing called for. I have issued instructions, however, that steps be ruthlessly taken against all those who think it their business to intervene in the alleged interests of war industry, but who in reality want only to support the Jews and their businesses.

(2) Jews in real war industries, i.e., in armament plants, automotive plants, etc.—are to be detached unit by unit. As a first step they are to be concentrated in isolated workrooms in the factories. As a second step in this procedure, the labor forces in these isolated workrooms are to be combined, by means of exchange, into closed enterprises where feasible, so that we will then have only a few closed concentration-camp industries in the Generalgouvernement.

(3) Our endeavor then will be to replace this Jewish labor force with Poles and to consolidate the majority of these Jewish concentration-camp enterprises into a few large Jewish concentration-camp enterprises—in the eastern part of the Generalgouvernement, if possible. Even from there, however, the Jews are someday to disappear, in accordance with the Führer's wishes.

H. Himmler

DEATHWATCH AT BEŁŻEC:
KURT GERSTEIN'S DEPOSITION

. . . In January 1942, I was appointed head of the Department of Sanitation Techniques and at the same time to the parallel position for the same sector of the SS and Police Medical Office. In this capacity I took over the entire technical service of disinfection, including disinfection with highly toxic gases. On June 8, 1942,

14. Friedrich Wilhelm Krüger (1894–1945) became Obergruppenführer in the SS (equivalent to rank of general) and General of the Police in January 1935. From 1939 to 1943 he was Higher SS and Police Leader in the Generalgouvernement, the top-ranking SS officer in Poland. He committed suicide in Russia. Oswald Pohl (1892–1951), holding the same rank in the SS, headed the SS *Wirtschafts- und Verwaltungshauptamt*—WVHA (Economic and Administrative Main Office), which managed the SS's economic enterprises in the forced-labor and concentration camps. Pohl was hung as a war criminal.

SS Sturmbannführer Günther of the *Reichssicherheitshauptamt*,[15] dressed in civilian clothes, walked into my office. He was unknown to me. He ordered me to obtain for him, for a top secret mission, 100 kilos of prussic acid and to take it to a place known only to the truck driver. A few weeks later, we set out for the potash plant near Kolin (Prague).

I understood little of the nature of my mission. But I accepted. To this day, I believe that it was luck, strangely resembling Providence, that gave me the opportunity to see what I was trying to find out. Out of hundreds of other possible assignments, I was put in charge of that post which was closest to the area that interested me. . . .

On the way to Kolin, we were accompanied by SS Obersturmbannführer and M.D., Professor Pfannenstiel, Professor of Hygiene at the University of Marburg/Lahn.

From my deliberately bizarre technical questions, the people at the Kolin prussic acid plant could understand that the acid was going to be used to kill human beings. I did this in order to spread rumors among the population.

We then set off with the truck for Lublin (Poland). SS Gruppenführer Globocnik [16] was waiting for us. He told us: "This is one of our most secret matters, indeed the most secret. Anyone who talks about it will be shot. Only yesterday two babblers were shot." He then explained to us: "At present"—this was August 17, 1942—"there are three installations":

(1) Bełżec, on the Lublin-Lwów road. Maximum per day: 15,000 persons (seen)!
(2) Sobibór, I don't know exactly where: not seen: 20,000 persons per day.
(3) Treblinka, 120 km. northeast of Warsaw: 25,000 persons per day; seen.
(4) Majdanek, near Lublin; seen in preparation.

Except for the last one, I made a thorough inspection of all these

15. The *Reichssicherheitshauptamt*—RSHA (Reich Security Main Office), established in 1939, amalgamated the Security Police with the *Sicherheitsdienst*—SD, which, under Reinhard Heydrich, became the chief apparatus for terror in the National Socialist regime. Rolf Günther was Adolf Eichmann's deputy in the RSHA's IV B 4, the section dealing with the Jews.
16. Odilo Globocnik (1904–1945), SS Gruppenführer and Lieutenant-General of the Police, was SS and Police Leader in the Lublin District 1939–1943, directly responsible to Krüger. Globocnik was in charge of the death camps in the Lublin area.

camps, accompanied by Police Chief Wirth, the head of all these death factories.[17] Wirth had earlier been put in charge by Hitler and Himmler of the murder of the insane at Hadamar, Grafeneck, and various other places.

Globocnik said: "You will have to disinfect large quantities of clothing ten or twenty times, the whole textile accumulation. It is only being done to conceal that the source of clothing is Jews, Poles, Czechs, etc. Your other duty will be to improve the service in our gas chambers, which function on diesel engine exhaust. We need gas which is more toxic and works faster, such as prussic acid. The Führer and Himmler—they were here on August 15, the day before yesterday—instructed me to accompany personally all those who have to see these installations." Then Professor Pfannenstiel: "But what did the Führer say?" Globocnik replied: "The Führer ordered all action speeded up! Dr. Herbert Lindner,[18] who was with us yesterday, asked me: 'But wouldn't it be wiser to cremate the corpses instead of burying them? Another generation may perhaps judge these things differently!' I replied: 'Gentlemen, if there were ever, after us, a generation so cowardly and so soft that they could not understand our work which is so good, so necessary, then, gentlemen, all of National Socialism will have been in vain. We ought, on the contrary, to bury bronze tablets stating that it was we who had the courage to carry out this gigantic task!' The Führer then said: 'Yes, my good Globocnik, you are right!' "

Nevertheless, Dr. Lindner's opinion subsequently prevailed; even the corpses already buried were burned in gasoline or oil, on grates improvised on rails. The office for these factories is at the Julius Schreck barracks in Lublin. The following day I was introduced to the men who worked there.

We left for Bełżec two days later. A small special station with two platforms was set up on a yellow sand hill, immediately to the

17. Christian Wirth, SS Sturmbannführer, equivalent to the rank of major, had been Criminal Police Chief in Stuttgart, later employed at the "euthanasia" killing station at Brandenburg in Germany. In 1941 he was transferred to Globocnik and became one of his top aides assisting in the construction and operation of the gassing facilities at the death camps.
18. Most likely Dr. Herbert Linden, a medical officer of the Ministry of Interior, who headed one of the institutions of the "euthanasia" program, the euphemistically entitled *Gemeinnützige Krankentransportgesellschaft* (Public-Benefit Patient Transportation Society), which transported the adult insane from their institutions to one of six killing centers in Germany.

north of the Lublin-Lwów railway. To the south, near the road, were some service buildings and a notice: "Sonderkommando of the Waffen-SS in Bełżec." Globocnik presented me to SS Hauptsturm- führer Obermeyer of Pirmasens, who showed great reserve when taking me over the installations. We saw no dead that day, but a pestilential odor blanketed the whole region and millions of flies were everywhere. Alongside the station was a large barrack marked "Cloak Room," with a ticket window inside marked "Valuables." Further on, a room with about a hundred chairs, "Barber." Then a passageway about 150 meters long, in the open, barbed wire on both sides, and notices: "To Baths and Inhalators." In front of us was a building of the bathhouse type, with large pots of geraniums and other flowers. Then stairs and then left and right 3 enclosures 5 meters square, 1.90 meters high, with wooden doors like garages. At the rear wall, not properly visible in the darkness, large wooden platform doors. On the roof, a copper Star of David. On the build- ing, the inscription: "Heckenholt Foundation." That afternoon I saw nothing else.

Next morning, a few minutes before seven, I was told: "In ten minutes the first train will arrive!" Indeed, a few minutes later a train arrived from Lemberg, with 45 cars holding 6,700 people, of whom 1,450 were already dead on arrival. Behind the small barbed- wire window, children, young ones, frightened to death, women, men. The train pulled in: 200 Ukrainians detailed for the task tore open the doors and with their leather whips drove the Jews out of the cars. A loudspeaker issued instructions: to remove all clothing, even artificial limbs and eyeglasses; to tie their shoes together with small pieces of string handed out by a little Jewish boy; to turn in all valuables, all money at the ticket window "Valuables," without voucher, without receipt. Women and girls were to have their hair cut off in the "Barber's" barrack. (An SS sergeant on duty told me: "That's to make something special for submarine crews.")

Then the march began. To the left and right, barbed wire; behind, two dozen Ukrainians, guns in hand.

They approached. Wirth and I, we were standing on the ramp in front of the death chambers. Completely nude, men, women, young girls, children, babies, cripples, filed by. At the corner stood a heavy SS man, who told the poor people, in a pastoral voice: "No harm will come to you! You just have to breathe very deeply, that strengthens the lungs, inhaling is a means of preventing contagious diseases. It's a good disinfection!" They asked what was going to happen to them. He told them: "The men will have to work, building roads and houses. But the women won't be obliged to do so; they'll do housework, cooking." For some of these poor creatures, this was a last small hope, enough to carry them, unresisting, as far as the death chambers. Most of them knew all, the odor confirmed it! They walked up the small wooden flight of stairs and entered the death chambers, most without a word, pushed forward by those behind them. One Jewish woman of about forty, her eyes flaming torches, cursed the murderers; after several whiplashes by Captain Wirth in person, she disappeared into the gas chamber. Many people pray, while others ask: "Who will give us water for washing the dead?" [19] . . .

Inside the chambers, SS men crowd the people. "Fill them up well," Wirth had ordered, "700–800 of them to every 25 square meters." The doors are shut. Meanwhile, the rest of the people from the train, naked, wait. I am told: "Naked even in winter!" "But they may catch their death!" "But that's what they're here for!" was the reply. At that moment, I understand the reason for the inscription "Heckenholt." Heckenholt was the driver of the diesel truck whose exhaust gases were to be used to kill these unfortunates. SS Unterscharführer Heckenholt was making great efforts to get the engine running. But it doesn't go. Captain Wirth comes up. I can see he is afraid because I am present at a disaster. Yes, I see it all and I wait. My stop watch showed it all, 50 minutes, 70 minutes, and the diesel did not start! The people wait inside the gas chambers. In vain. They can be heard weeping, "like in the synagogue," says Professor Pfannenstiel, his eyes glued to a window in the wooden door. Furious, Captain Wirth lashes the Ukrainian assisting Heckenholt 12, 13 times, in the face. After two hours and 49 minutes—the stop watch recorded it all—the diesel started. Up to that moment, the people shut up in those four crowded chambers were still alive, four times 750 persons in four times 45 cubic meters! Another 25 minutes elapsed. Many were already dead, that could be seen through the small window because an electric lamp inside lit up the chamber for a few moments. After 28 minutes, only a few were still alive. Finally, after 32 minutes, all were dead.

19. A reference to *taharah,* the traditional Jewish rite of washing the dead body before burial.

On the far side members of the work commando opened the wooden doors. They—themselves Jews—were promised their lives and a small percentage of the valuables and money collected for this terrible service. Like pillars of basalt, the dead were still erect, not having any space to fall, or to lean. Even in death, families could be seen still holding hands. It is hard to separate them as the chambers are emptied to make way for the next load; corpses were tossed out, blue, wet with sweat and urine, the legs covered with faeces and menstrual blood. Two dozen workers were busy checking the mouths of the dead, which they opened with iron hooks. "Gold to the left, without gold to the right!" Others inspected anuses and genital organs, searching for money, diamonds, gold, etc. Dentists hammered out gold teeth, bridges and crowns. In the midst of them stood Captain Wirth. He was in his element, and showing me a large can full of teeth, he said: "See for yourself the weight of that gold! It's only from yesterday and the day before. You can't imagine what we find every day—dollars, diamonds, gold! You'll see yourself!" . . .

Then the bodies were flung into large trenches, each 100 × 20 × 12 meters, located near the gas chambers. After a few days the corpses swelled, because of the gases which formed inside them, and everything rose from two to three meters. A few days later, when the swelling subsided, the bodies settled. Subsequently, I was told, the bodies were piled on train rails and burned in diesel oil so that they would disappear. . . .

The next day we drove in Captain Wirth's car to Treblinka about 120 km. northeast of Warsaw. The equipment in that place of death was almost the same as at Bełżec, but even larger. Eight gas chambers and veritable mountains of clothing and underwear, about 35–40 meters high. Then, in our honor, a banquet was held for all those employed at the establishment. Obersturmbannführer Professor Doctor Pfannenstiel, Professor of Hygiene at the University of Marburg/Lahn, made a speech: "Your work is a great work and a very useful and very necessary duty." To me, he spoke of the establishment as "a kindness and a humanitarian thing." To all present, he said: "When one sees the bodies of the Jews, one understands the greatness of your work!"

꧁ ◆ ꧂

AUSCHWITZ OBSERVED:
REPORT OF TWO ESCAPED EYEWITNESSES

On April 13, 1942, our group of 1,000 men was loaded onto railroad cars at the assembly camp at Sered. The doors were sealed, so that nothing would reveal the direction of the journey. When they were opened after a long while, we realized that we had crossed the Slovak frontier and were in Zwardoń.[20] Until then the train had been guarded by Hlinka men,[21] but it was now taken over by SS guards. After a few cars had been uncoupled from our convoy, we continued on our way, arriving at night at Auschwitz, where we stopped at a siding. . . . Upon arrival, we were counted off in rows of five. There were 643 of us. After a walk of about twenty minutes with our heavy packs—we had left Slovakia well equipped—we reached the concentration camp of Auschwitz.

We were led at once into a huge barracks, where we had to deposit all our luggage on one side and on the other undress completely, leaving our clothes and valuables behind. Naked, we then proceeded to an adjoining barracks, where our heads and bodies were shaved and disinfected. At the exit, every man was given a number, beginning with 28,600. With this number in hand, we were then herded to a third barracks, where so-called registration took place. Here the numbers we received in the second barracks were tattooed on the left side of our chests. The extreme brutality with which this was done made many of us faint. The particulars of our identity were also recorded. Then we were led by hundreds into a cellar and later to a barracks, where we were issued striped prisoners' clothes and wooden clogs. This lasted until 10 a.m. In the afternoon our prisoners' outfits were taken away from us and replaced by the ragged and dirty remains of Russian uniforms. Thus equipped, we were marched off to Birkenau.

20. Zwardoń was on the Polish side of the Polish-Czech frontier.
21. These were members of the Hlinka Guard, the paramilitary arm of the Hlinka People's party, a right-wing Catholic nationalist party, the only legal party in Slovakia after March 1939. The Hlinka Guard collaborated with the SS.

Auschwitz is a concentration camp for political prisoners under so-called "protective custody." At the time of my arrival, that is, April 1942, about 15,000 prisoners were in the camp, the majority Poles, Germans, and civilian Russians under protective custody. A small number of prisoners came under the categories of criminals and "work-shirkers."

Auschwitz camp headquarters also controls the labor camp of Birkenau as well as the farm-labor camp of Harmense. All the prisoners arrive first at Auschwitz, where they are provided with prisoners' registration numbers and then are kept there, or are sent either to Birkenau or, in very small numbers, to Harmense. . . .

There are several factories on the grounds of the camp of Auschwitz: a war production plant of *Deutsche Ausrüstungswerke* (DAW), a factory belonging to the Krupp works, and one to the Siemens concern. Outside the camp's boundary is a tremendous plant covering several square kilometers named Buna.[22] The prisoners work in all the aforementioned factories.

The prisoners' actual living quarters, if such a term is at all appropriate, covers an area approximately 500 by 300 meters, surrounded by a double row of concrete posts about three meters high, interconnected, inside and out, by a dense netting of high-tension wires fixed into the posts by insulators. Between these two rows of posts, at intervals of 150 meters, there are five-meter-high watchtowers, equipped with machine guns and searchlights. The inner high-tension ring is encircled by an ordinary wire fence. Merely to touch this fence is to draw a stream of bullets from the watchtowers. This system is called the "small" or "inner ring of sentry posts."

The camp itself is composed of three rows of houses. The camp thoroughfare lies between the first and second row. A wall used to stand between the second and third row. Up to mid-August 1942, the over 7,000 Jewish girls deported from Slovakia in March and April 1942, lived in the houses separated by this wall. After these girls had been removed to Birkenau, the wall was removed. The road into the camp bisects the row of houses. Over

22. *Deutsche Ausrüstungswerke* (German Armament Works) was an SS enterprise founded in 1939. It was administered by the WVHA (see Note 14). Krupp and Siemens were among Germany's largest industrial manufacturers, with plants all over Europe. The Buna plant at Auschwitz, part of the vast network of I.G. Farben industrial enterprises, produced synthetic rubber.

the entrance gate, always, of course, heavily guarded, stands the ironic inscription: "Work brings freedom."

At a radius of some 2,000 meters, the whole camp is encircled by a second ring called the "big" or "outer ring of sentry posts," also with watchtowers every 150 meters. Between the inner- and outer-ring sentry posts are the factories and other workshops. The towers of the inner ring are manned only at night when the high-tension current is switched into the double row of wires. During the day the garrison of the inner-ring sentry posts is withdrawn, and the men take up duty in the outer ring. Escape—and many attempts have been made—through these sentry posts is practically impossible. Getting through the inner-ring posts at night is completely impossible, and the towers of the outer ring are so close to one another that it is out of the question to pass unnoticed. The guards shoot without warning. The garrison of the outer ring is withdrawn at twilight, but only after all the prisoners have been ascertained to be within the inner ring. If the roll call uncovers a missing prisoner, sirens immediately sound the alarm.

The men in the outer ring remain in their towers on the look-out, the inner ring is manned, and hundreds of SS guards and bloodhounds begin a systematic search. The siren brings the whole surrounding countryside to a state of alarm, so that if by miracle the escaping man has succeeded in getting through the outer ring, he is almost certain to be caught by one of the numerous German police and SS patrols. The escapee is furthermore handicapped by his clean-shaven head, his striped prisoner's outfit or red patches sewn on his clothing, and the passiveness of the thoroughly intimi-dated population. The mere failure to give information on the whereabouts of a prisoner, not to speak of extending help, is pun-ished by death. If the prisoner has not been caught sooner, the garrison of the outer-ring sentry posts remains on the watch for three days and nights, after which it is presumed that the fugitive succeeded in breaking through the double ring. The following night the outer guard is withdrawn. If the fugitive is caught alive, he is hanged in the presence of the whole camp. If he is found dead, his body—wherever it may have been located—is returned to camp (it is easily identifiable by the tattooed number) and seated at the entrance gate, a small notice clasped in his hands, reading: "Here I am." During our two years' imprisonment, many attempts at escape were made, but except for two or three, all were brought back dead or alive. It is not known whether those two or three actually managed to get away. It can, however, be asserted that among the Jews who were deported from Slovakia to Auschwitz or Birkenau, we are the only two who were lucky enough to save ourselves.

As stated previously, we were transferred from Auschwitz to Birkenau on the day of our arrival. Actually there is no such district as Birkenau. Even the word Birkenau is new in that it has been adapted from the nearby Brzezinki.[23] The existing camp center of Birkenau lies four kilometers from Auschwitz, though the outer borders of Birkenau and Auschwitz adjoin. . . .

When we arrived in Birkenau, we found only one huge kitchen there for 15,000 people and three stone buildings, two already completed and one under construction. The buildings were encircled by an ordinary barbed-wire fence. The prisoners were housed in these buildings and in others later constructed. . . . All are built according to a standard model. Each house is about 30 meters long and 8 to 10 meters wide, [divided into tiny cubicles] . . . too narrow for a man to lie stretched out and not high enough for him to sit upright. There is no question of having enough space to stand upright. Thus, some 400–500 people are accommodated in one house or "block.". . .

After three days I was ordered, together with 200 other Slovak Jews, to work in the German armament factories at Auschwitz, but we continued to be housed in Birkenau. We left early in the morning, returning at night, and worked in the carpentry shop as well as on road construction. Our food consisted of one liter of turnip soup at midday and 300 grams of bad bread in the evening. Working conditions were inconceivably hard, so that the majority of us, weakened by starvation and the inedible food, could not endure. The mortality was so high that our group of 200 had 30–35 dead every day. Many were simply beaten to death by the overseers—the *Kapos*[24]—during work, without the slightest provocation. The gaps in our ranks caused by these deaths were replaced daily by prisoners

23. "Birch tree" in Polish is *brzezina*; in German, *Birke. Brzezinki* is the plural diminutive, hence, a wood of small birches; the German equivalent was Birkenwald.

24. *Kapo* (sometimes *Capo*) was concentration-camp slang for a foreman of a labor gang, who was himself a camp inmate. The origin of the word is obscure. It may be an abbreviated form of the French *caporal,* a term used in the German army during the Second World War. *Kapo* was also used long before the war among carpenters as a German slang word for a foreman. Another hypothesis is that *Kapo* is a borrowing from the Italian *capo,* "head" or "chief."

from Birkenau. Our return at night was extremely painful and dangerous, as we had to drag, over a distance of five kilometers, our tools, firewood, heavy cauldrons, and the bodies of those who had died or had been killed during the working day. With these heavy loads we had to maintain a brisk pace, and anyone incurring the displeasure of one of the Kapos was cruelly knocked down, if not beaten to death. Until the arrival of the second group of Slovak men some fourteen days later, our original number had dwindled to 150. At night we were counted, the bodies of the dead were piled up on flat, narrow-gauge cars or in a truck and brought to Brzezinki, where they were burned in a trench several meters deep and about fifteen meters long. . . .

Until the middle of May 1942, a total of four convoys of Jewish men from Slovakia arrived at Birkenau and all were given treatment similar to ours.

From the first two transports 120 men—90 Slovak and 30 French Jews—were chosen, including myself, and placed at the disposal of the administration of the camp of Auschwitz, which needed doctors, dentists, intellectuals, and clerks. As I had in the meantime managed to work my way up to a good position in Birkenau—being in command of a group of fifty men, which had brought me considerable advantage—I at first felt reluctant to leave for Auschwitz. However, I was finally persuaded to go. After eight days, eighteen doctors and attendants as well as three other persons were selected from this group of 120. The doctors were used in the so-called *Krankenbau* ("patients building," infirmary) at Auschwitz. . . . The remaining 99 persons were sent to work in the gravel pits where they all died within a short time.

Shortly thereafter a Krankenbau was set up. It was destined to become the much dreaded Block 7, where I was first chief attendant and later administrator. The "infirmary" chief was a Pole. This building actually was nothing but an assembly center of candidates for death. All prisoners incapable of working were sent there. There was no question of any medical attention or care. We had some 150 dead daily and their bodies were sent for cremation to Auschwitz.

At the same time, the so-called "selections" were introduced. Twice weekly, Mondays and Thursdays, the camp doctor indicated the number of prisoners who were to be gassed and then burned. Those selected were loaded onto trucks and brought to Brzezinki.

Those still alive upon arrival were gassed in a big barracks erected near the trench used for burning the bodies. The weekly contingent of dead from Block 7 was about 2,000, 1,200 of whom died a "natural death" and about 800 by "selection." For those who had not been "selected," a death certificate was issued and sent to the central administration at Oranienburg, whereas a special list was kept of the "selectees" with the indication "S.B." (*Sonderbehandlung*—special treatment). Until January 15, 1943, up to which time I was administrator of Block 7 and therefore in a position directly to observe the events, some 50,000 prisoners died of "natural death" or by "selection."

As previously described, the prisoners were numbered consecutively, so that we can reconstruct fairly clearly their order of succession and the fate which befell each individual convoy on arrival.

The first transport of Jewish men reaching Auschwitz for Birkenau was composed, as mentioned, of 1,320 naturalized French Jews bearing approximately the following numbers: 27,400–28,000

28,600–29,600	In April 1942 the first convoy of Slovak Jews (our convoy).
29,600–29,700	100 men (Aryans) from various concentration camps.
29,700–32,700	3 complete convoys of Slovak Jews.
32,700–33,100	400 professional criminals (Aryans) from Warsaw prisons.
33,100–35,000	1,900 Jews from Cracow.
35,000–36,000	1,000 Poles (Aryans)—political prisoners.
36,000–37,300	In May 1942—1,300 Slovak Jews from Lublin-Majdanek.
37,300–37,900	600 Poles (Aryans) from Radom, a few Jews among them.
37,900–38,000	100 Poles from the concentration camp of Dachau.
38,000–38,400	400 naturalized French Jews with their families.

This whole convoy consisted of about 1,600 individuals, of whom approximately 200 girls and 400 men were admitted to the camp, while the remaining 1,000 persons (women, old people, children, as well as men) were sent without further procedure from the railroad siding directly to Brzezinki, and there gassed and burned. From this moment on, all Jewish convoys were dealt with in the same way. Approximately ten percent of the men and five percent of the women were assigned to the camps and the remaining members were immediately gassed. This process of annihilation had already been applied earlier to the Polish Jews. During long months, without interruption, trucks brought thousands of Jews from the various ghettos directly to the pit in Birkenwald. . . .

48,300–48,620	320 Jews from Slovakia. About 70 girls were transferred to the women's camp, the remainder, some 650 people, gassed in Birkenwald. This convoy included about 80 people who had been transferred by the Hungarian police to the camp at Sered. . . .
49,000–64,800	15,000 naturalized French, Belgian, and Dutch Jews. This figure certainly represents less than ten percent of the total convoy. This was between July 1 and September 15, 1942. Large family convoys arrived from various European countries and were at once directed to Birkenwald. The Sonderkommando, employed for gassing and burning, worked day and night shifts. Hundreds of thousands of Jews were gassed during this period.
64,800–65,000	200 Slovak Jews. Of this transport, about 100 women were admitted to the camp, the rest were gassed and burned. . . .
65,000–68,000	Naturalized French, Belgian, and Dutch Jews. Not more than 1,000 women were "selected" and sent to the camp. The others, 30,000, at the least, were gassed.
71,000–80,000	Naturalized French, Belgian, and Dutch Jews. The prisoners brought to the camp hardly represented ten percent of the total transport. A conservative estimate would be that approximately 65,000 to 70,000 persons were gassed. . . .

Number 80,000 marks the beginning of the systematic annihilation of the Polish ghettos.

80,000–85,000	Approximately 5,000 Jews from various ghettos in Mława, Maków, Ciechanów, Lomża, Grodno, Bialystok. For fully thirty days truck convoys arrived without interruption. Only 5,000 persons were sent to the concentration camp; all the others were gassed at once. The Sonderkommando worked in two shifts, twenty-four hours daily, and was scarcely able to cope with the gassing and burning. Without exaggeration, it may be said that some 80,000–90,000 of these convoys received Sonderbehandlung. These transports also brought in a considerable amount of money, valuables, and precious stones.
85,000–92,000	6,000 Jews from Grodno, Bialystok, and Cracow, as well as 1,000 Aryan Poles. The majority of the Jewish convoys were directly gassed and about 4,000 Jews daily were driven into the gas chambers. During mid-January 1943, three convoys of 2,000 persons each from Theresienstadt arrived. . . . Only 600 men and 300 women of these 6,000 persons were admitted to the camp. The remainder were gassed.
99,000–100,000	End of January 1943, large convoys of French and Dutch Jews arrived; only a small proportion reached the camp.
100,000–102,000	In February 1943, 2,000 Aryan Poles, mostly intellectuals.
102,000–103,000	700 Czech Aryans. Later, those still alive were sent to Buchenwald.
103,000–108,000	3,000 French and Dutch Jews and 2,000 Poles (Aryans). During the month of February 1943, two contingents arrived daily. They included Polish, French, and Dutch Jews who, in the main, were sent to the gas chambers. The number gassed during this month can be estimated at no smaller than 90,000.

At the end of February 1943, a new modern crematorium and gassing plant were inaugurated at Birkenau. The gassing and burning of the bodies in Birkenwald were discontinued, the whole job being taken over by the four specially built crematoria. The large ditch was filled in, the ground levelled, and the ashes used, as before, for fertilizer at the farm labor camp of Harmense, so that today it is almost impossible to find traces of the dreadful mass murder which took place.

At present four crematoria are in operation at Birkenau, two large ones, I and II, and two smaller ones, III and IV. Those of type I and II consist of three parts, i.e.: the furnace room, the large hall, and the gas chamber. A huge chimney rises from the furnace room around which are grouped nine furnaces, each having four openings. Each opening can take three normal corpses at once, after an hour and a half the bodies are completely burned. Thus, the daily capacity is about 2,000 bodies. A large "reception hall" adjoins, so as to give the impression of the antechamber of a bathing establishment. It holds 2,000 people and apparently there is a similar waiting room on the floor below. From there, a door and a few stairs down lead into the very long and narrow gas chamber. The walls of this chamber are also camouflaged with simulated entries to shower rooms in order to mislead the victims. The roof is fitted with three traps which can be hermetically closed from the outside. A track leads from the gas chamber to the furnace room.

The gassing takes place as follows: the unfortunate victims are brought into the reception hall where they are told to undress. To complete the fiction that they are going to bathe, each person receives a towel and a small piece of soap issued by two men in white coats. Then they are crowded into the gas chamber in such numbers that there is, of course, only standing room. To compress this crowd into the narrow space, shots are often fired to induce those already at the far end to huddle still closer together. When everybody is inside, the heavy doors are closed. Then there is a short pause, presumably to allow the room temperature to rise to a certain level, after which SS men with gas masks climb on the roof, open the traps, and shake down a preparation in powder form out of tin cans labelled "Zyklon—For use against vermin," manufactured by a Hamburg concern. It is presumed that this is a cyanide mixture of some sort which turns into gas at a certain temperature. After three minutes everyone in the chamber is dead. No one is known to have survived this ordeal, although it was not uncommon to discover signs of life after the primitive measures employed in Birkenwald. The chamber is then opened, aired, and the Sonderkommando carts the bodies on flat trucks to the furnace rooms where the burning takes place. Crematoria III and IV work on nearly the same principle, but their capacity is only half as large. Thus the total capacity of the four gassing and cremating plants at Birkenau amounts to about 6,000 daily.

On principle only Jews are gassed; Aryans very seldom, as they are usually given Sonderbehandlung by shooting. Before the crematoria were put into service, the shooting took place in Birkenwald and the bodies were burned in the long trench; later, however, executions took place in the large hall of one of the crematoria which has been provided with a special installation for this purpose.

Prominent guests from Berlin were present at the inauguration of the first crematorium in March 1943. The "program" consisted of the gassing and burning of 8,000 Cracow Jews. The guests, both officers and civilians, were extremely satisfied with the results and the special peephole fitted into the door of the gas chamber was in constant use. They were lavish in their praise of this newly erected installation.

At the beginning of 1943, the political section of Auschwitz received 500,000 discharge certificates. We thought, with ill-concealed joy, that at least a few of us would be liberated. But the forms were simply filled out with the names of those gassed and filed away in the archives. . . .

Cautious estimate of the number of Jews gassed
in Birkenau between April 1942 and April 1944,
by country of origin

Poland (transported by truck)	ca.	300,000
" (" " train)	"	600,000
Holland	"	100,000
Greece	"	45,000
France	"	150,000
Belgium	"	50,000
Germany	"	60,000
Yugoslavia, Italy, and Norway	"	50,000
Lithuania	"	50,000
Bohemia, Moravia, and Austria	"	30,000
Slovakia	"	30,000
Various camps for foreign Jews in Poland	"	300,000
	ca.	1,765,000

"THE WARSAW JEWISH QUARTER IS NO MORE!"
GENERAL STROOP'S REPORT: MAY 16, 1943

THE WARSAW JEWISH QUARTER IS NO MORE!

I

*For the Führer
and for their country*

the following were killed in action during the destruction of Jews
and bandits in the former Jewish quarter in Warsaw [15 names
with date of birth and rank, arranged by date of death]. In addition,
the Polish Police Sergeant Julian Zieliński, born November 13,
1891, 14th Commissariat, was killed on April 19, 1943, while carrying
out his duties.

They ventured their utmost, their lives. We shall never forget
them. . . .

Units Used in the Action	*Average Number of Personnel* [25] *Used per Day*
SS Staff and Police Leaders	6/5
Waffen-SS	
SS Armored Grenadier Training and Reserve Battalion No. 3, Warsaw	4/440
SS Cavalry Training and Reserve Unit, Warsaw	5/381
Police	
SS Police Regiment 22, 1st Battalion	3/94
3rd Battalion	3/134
Engineering Emergency Service	1/6
Polish Police	4/363

25. Officers and men are shown separately; 4/440 means four officers, 440 men.

Units Used in the Action	Average Number of Personnel Used per Day
Polish Fire Brigade	166
Security Police	3/32
Army	
Light Anti-Aircraft Alarm Battery III/8, Warsaw	2/22
Engineers Detachment of Railway Armored Trains Reserve Unit, Rembertow	2/42
Engineers Reserve Battalion 14, Gora-Kalwaria	1/34
Foreign Guard Units	
1 Battalion Trawniki men	2/335 [26]

II

. . . Security considerations made it necessary to remove the Jews entirely from the city of Warsaw. The first large resettlement action took place in the period from July 22 to October 3, 1942. In this action, 310,322 Jews were removed for resettlement. In January 1943, a second resettlement action was carried out, comprising 6,500 Jews in all.

In January 1943, the Reichsführer SS, on the occasion of his visit to Warsaw, ordered the SS and Police Leader in the District of Warsaw [27] *to transfer to Lublin the armament factories and other enterprises of military importance installed within the ghetto, including their personnel and machines.*[28] The execution of this order proved to be quite difficult, since both the managers and the Jews resisted the transfer in every conceivable way. The SS and Police Leader therefore decided to effect the transfer of the enterprises by

26. Totals: 36 officers, 2054 men.
27. Ferdinand von Sammern-Frankenegg (1897–1944) was for a short while SS and Police Leader in the Warsaw District. He was replaced by General Stroop on April 19, 1943.
28. On January 9, 1943, Himmler, astonished that his orders (of July 19 and October 9, 1942), to clear the Generalgouvernement of Jews by the end of 1942 had not yet been complied with, gave Sammern-Frankenegg until February 15 to do so and to transfer the industrial enterprises to Lublin.

force, in a large-scale action to be carried out in three days. My predecessor had attended to the preparation and orders for this large-scale action. I myself arrived in Warsaw on April 17, 1943, and took over the command of the large-scale action on April 19, 1943, at 0800 hours, the action itself having started the same day at 0600 hours.

Before this large-scale action began, the boundaries of the former Jewish quarter had been blocked by an exterior cordon to prevent the Jews from breaking out. This cordon was continually maintained from the start to the end of the action and was especially reinforced at night.

When the ghetto was first invaded, the Jews and the Polish bandits, by a well-prepared concentration of fire, succeeded in repelling the participating units, including tanks and armored cars. In the second attack, at about 0800 hours, I deployed the forces separately through previously defined fighting zones, so as to have the whole ghetto combed out by the different units. Although the firing was repeated, the blocks were now successfully combed out according to plan. The enemy was forced to retreat from roofs and elevated bases to basements, bunkers, and sewers. To prevent escapes into the sewers, the sewer system beneath the Jewish quarter was promptly closed off and filled with water, but this move was for the most part frustrated by the Jews, who blew up the turn-off valves. Late the first day, rather heavy resistance was encountered, but was quickly broken by a specially assigned raiding party. Further operations succeeded in expelling the Jews from their prepared resistance bases, sniper holes, etc., and, during April 20 and 21, in gaining control of most of the so-called residual ghetto, to the extent that resistance within these blocks could no longer be called major or considerable.

The main Jewish fighting group, which was mixed with Polish bandits,[29] retreated as early as the first and second day to the so-called Muranowski Square. There it had been reinforced by a considerable number of Polish bandits. Its plan was to maintain itself in the ghetto by every means in order to prevent us from invading it. Jewish and Polish flags were hoisted on top of a concrete building as a call to arms against us. These two flags, however,

29. No non-Jews participated in the fighting in the ghetto. By predicating a Polish presence, Stroop could portray the Jews as cowards, unable to fight without outside help.

were captured as early as the second day of the action by a special raiding party. In this skirmish with the bandits, SS Untersturm-führer Dehmke was killed when a grenade he was holding in his hand was hit by the enemy and exploded, injuring him fatally.

After the first few days, I realized that the original plan had no prospect of success, unless the armament factories and other enter-prises of military importance scattered throughout the ghetto were dissolved.[30] It was therefore necessary to require these enterprises to evacuate their quarters and move immediately, within an appropri-ate deadline. One enterprise after another was dealt with in this way, and thus in minimal time the Jews and bandits were deprived of the opportunity to take refuge, again and again, in these enter-prises, which were under the supervision of the Army. Thorough inspections were necessary to decide in what length of time these enterprises could be evacuated. The conditions observed in the course of these inspections are indescribable. I cannot imagine that greater chaos could have existed anywhere than existed in the Warsaw ghetto. The Jews had control of everything, from chemical substances for manufacturing explosives to Army clothing and equipment. The managers knew so little of their own enterprises that the Jews were able to produce arms of every kind, especially hand grenades, Molotov cocktails, etc., inside these shops.

Moreover, the Jews had managed to set up resistance bases in these enterprises. One such resistance base, in an enterprise serving the Army Quartermaster's Office, had to be combatted as early as the second day by deploying an engineers' unit with flame throwers and by artillery fire. The Jews had installed themselves so firmly in this enterprise that it proved impossible to induce them to leave the shop voluntarily. I therefore resolved to destroy the enterprise by fire on the next day.

The managers of these enterprises, even though usually super-vised by an Army officer, were in nearly all cases unable to provide concrete information about their stocks or the locations where stocks were stored. The statements they made as to the number of Jews employed by them did not check out in a single case. Again and again it was found that rich Jews, under cover as "armament

30. Most of the units of the Jewish Combat Organization were based in the fac-tories, where both fighters and civilians worked and slept. For a Jewish de-scription of the resistance, see Section 9, Yitzhak Zuckerman, "The Creation and Development of ŻOB."

workers," had found accommodations for themselves and their families in the labyrinths of buildings attached to the armament concerns as residential blocks, and were leading cushy lives there. Despite all orders to make the Jews leave those enterprises, it was repeatedly found that managers shut the Jews in, expecting that the action would last only a few days and that they then would go on working with the Jews remaining to them. According to statements by arrested Jews, owners of businesses arranged drinking parties with Jews. In these, women were said to have played a prominent part. The Jews reportedly endeavored to maintain good relations with Army officers and men. Carousals are said to have been frequent; and, in their course, business deals allegedly were concluded between Germans and Jews.

The number of Jews taken out of the houses and apprehended during the first few days was relatively small. It turned out that the Jews were hiding in the sewers and in specially constructed bunkers. Whereas it had been assumed during the first days that there were only isolated bunkers, it appeared in the course of the large-scale action that the whole ghetto had been systematically equipped with cellars, bunkers, and passageways. In every case these passageways and bunkers had access to the sewer system. Thus, undisturbed subterranean traffic among the Jews was possible. The Jews also used this sewer network to escape underground into the Aryan part of the city of Warsaw. Continually, reports were received of Jews attempting to escape through the sewer holes. Under the pretext of building air-raid shelters, the bunkers had been constructed in this former Jewish quarter since the late fall of 1942. They were intended to house all Jews during the new resettlement action, which had long been expected, and the resistance against the task forces was to be organized from here. Through posters, handbills, and whispering campaigns, the Communist resistance movement [31] in the former Jewish quarter had in fact managed to have the bunkers occupied as soon as the new large-scale action started. How far the Jews' precautions went was demonstrated by many instances of bunkers skillfully laid out with accommodations for entire families, washing and bathing facilities, toilets, arms and munition-storage bins, and ample food supplies for several months. . . . To discover the individual bunkers was extremely difficult

---

31. The Jewish resistance movement was in fact Zionist and Bundist, with the Jewish Communists playing only a modest role.

for the task forces, due to camouflage, and in many cases was possible only through betrayal on the part of Jews.

After only a few days it was clear that the Jews no longer had any intention to resettle voluntarily, but were determined to fight back by every means and with the weapons at their disposal. Under Polish Bolshevik leadership,[32] so-called combat groups had been formed; they were armed and paid any price asked for available arms.

During the large-scale action it was possible to capture some Jews who had already been evacuated to Lublin or Treblinka, but had broken out from there and returned to the ghetto, equipped with arms and ammunition. Time and again Polish bandits found refuge in the ghetto and remained there virtually undisturbed, since no forces were on hand to penetrate this maze. Whereas at first it had been possible to capture the Jews, who normally are cowards, in considerable numbers, apprehending bandits and Jews became increasingly difficult during the second half of the large-scale action. Again and again, battle groups of 20 to 30 or more Jewish youths, 18 to 25 years of age, accompanied by corresponding numbers of females, kindled new resistance. These battle groups were under orders to put up armed resistance to the last and, if necessary, to escape capture by suicide.

One such battle group managed to climb from a sewer basin in the so-called Prosta [33] onto a truck and to escape with it (about 30–35 bandits). One bandit, who had arrived with this truck, exploded two hand grenades, which was the signal for the bandits waiting in the sewer to climb out of the basin. The bandits and Jews—there frequently were Polish bandits among them, armed with carbines, small arms, and one with a light machine gun—climbed on the truck and drove away in an unknown direction.[34] The last member of this gang, who was on guard in the sewer and was assigned to close the sewer-hole cover, was captured. He gave the above information. The search for the truck unfortunately proved fruitless.

During the armed resistance, the females belonging to the bat-

---

32. Stroop falsely attributed Polish, that is non-Jewish, and Communist initiative to the organization of Jewish resistance.
33. A street that ran from inside the ghetto to beyond its confines.
34. In this case, a few members of the Communist Polish (non-Jewish) underground cooperated with the Jewish combatants, picking up, by truck, those who had managed to escape through the sewers and taking them to safety.

tle groups were armed in the same way as the men; some were members of the *halutzim* movement. Not infrequently, these females fired pistols with both hands. Time and again it happened that they kept pistols and hand grenades (Polish "pineapple" hand grenades) concealed in their drawers up to the last moment, to use them against the men of the Waffen-SS, Police, or Army.

The resistance put up by the Jews and bandits could be broken only through energetic, indefatigable deployment of the patrols day and night. *On April 23, 1943, through the Higher SS and Police Leader for the East, at Cracow, the Reichsführer SS issued an order to effect the combing of the ghetto in Warsaw with the greatest severity and ruthless tenacity.* I therefore decided to carry out the total destruction of the Jewish quarter by burning down all residential blocks, including the blocks attached to the armament factories. One enterprise after the other was systematically evacuated and immediately destroyed by fire. Nearly always the Jews then came out of their hiding places and bunkers. Not infrequently, the Jews stayed in the burning houses until, because of the heat and the fear of being burned to death, they chose to jump from the upper floors after having thrown mattresses and other upholstered articles from the burning houses into the street. With bones broken, they still would try to crawl across the street into blocks of houses which were not yet in flames, or only partly so. Often, too, Jews changed their hiding places during the night, by moving into the ruins of buildings already burned out and taking refuge there until they were found by the individual patrols. Their stay in the sewers also ceased to be pleasant after the first week. Frequently, loud voices, coming through the sewer shafts, could be heard in the street. The men of the Waffen-SS or Police or Army engineers would then courageously climb down the shafts to bring out the Jews, and not infrequently they stumbled over Jews already dead, or were shot at. It was always necessary to use smoke candles to drive out the Jews. Thus, one day 193 sewer entrance holes were opened and at a fixed time smoke candles were lowered into them, with the result that the bandits, fleeing from what they believed to be gas, assembled in the center of the former Jewish quarter and could be pulled out of the sewer holes there. Numerous Jews, who could not be counted, were taken care of by explosions in sewers and bunkers.

The longer the resistance lasted, the tougher the men of the Waffen-SS, Police, and Army became; here as always, they tackled their duties indefatigably, in faithful comradeship, and constantly held their own in model, exemplary fashion. Their duty often lasted from early morning until late at night. At night, search patrols with rags wound around their feet remained at the heels of the Jews and kept up the pressure on them without interruption. Not infrequently, Jews who used the night for supplementing their stores of victuals from abandoned bunkers or for making contact or exchanging information with neighboring groups were apprehended and taken care of.

Considering that the men of the Waffen-SS for the most part had had only three to four weeks' training before being assigned to this action, the mettle, courage, and devotion to duty which they showed deserves special recognition. It may be stated that the Army engineers, too, executed their work of blowing up bunkers, sewers, and concrete buildings with indefatigable devotion to duty. Officers and men of the Police, a large part of whom already had front-line experience, again proved themselves through exemplary daring.

Only the continuous and untiring deployment of all forces made it possible to apprehend or verifiably destroy a total of 56,065 Jews. To this figure should be added those Jews who lost their lives in explosions, fires, etc., but whose numbers could not be ascertained.

Even while the large-scale action was going on, the Aryan population was informed by posters that entering the former Jewish quarter was strictly forbidden, and that anybody found in the former Jewish quarter without a valid permit would be shot. At the same time, the Aryan population was once more instructed by these posters that anybody who knowingly gave refuge to a Jew, especially anyone who housed, fed, or concealed a Jew outside the Jewish quarter, would be punished by death.

The Polish police were authorized to turn over to any Polish policeman who arrested a Jew in the Aryan part of the city of Warsaw one third of the Jew's cash property. This measure has already produced results.

The Polish population by and large welcomed the measures taken against the Jews. Toward the end of the large-scale action, the Governor [35] addressed a special proclamation, which was submitted to the undersigned for approval before publication, to the

35. Governor Hans Frank.

Polish population, enlightening the Poles about the reasons for destroying the former Jewish quarter and calling them to battle against Communist agents, with reference to the assassinations lately carried out in the territory of the city of Warsaw and to the mass graves in Katyn.[36]

The large-scale action was terminated on May 16, 1943, with the blowing up of the Warsaw synagogue at 2015 hours.

At this time, there no longer are any industrial enterprises in the former Jewish quarter. All objects of value, raw materials, and machines there have been moved and stored elsewhere. Whatever buildings, etc., existed have been destroyed. The only exception is the so-called Dzielna Prison[37] of the Security Police, which was exempted from destruction.

III

Inasmuch as one must reckon with the possibility, even after completion of the large-scale action, that a few Jews still remain among the ruins of the former Jewish quarter, this area must remain firmly shut off from the Aryan quarter during the near future, and must be guarded. Police Battalion III/23 has been assigned to this duty. This Police Battalion has instructions to keep watch over the former Jewish quarter, particularly to see that no one enters the former ghetto, and immediately to shoot anybody found there without authorization. The Commander of the Police Battalion will continue to receive further instructions directly from the SS and Police Leader. In this way, the small remnants of Jews, if any, must be kept under constant pressure and destroyed. By the destruction of all buildings and hiding places and the cutting off of the water supply, the remaining Jews and bandits must be deprived of any further chance of existence.

It is suggested that the Dzielna Prison be made into a concentration camp and that the inmates be used to salvage the millions of bricks, scrap iron, and other materials, collect them and make them available for reuse.

36. A reference to the mass graves of 4,250 Polish officers found in 1943 in a forest near the village of Katyn in the Soviet Union. The Germans charged that the Russians had captured the Polish officers during the Russian invasion and occupation of Eastern Poland in 1939 and had subsequently murdered them.
37. The prison was more commonly known as Pawiak, because it was located on Pawia street, with its main entrance on Dzielna.

IV

Of the total of 56,065 Jews apprehended, about 7,000 were destroyed within the former ghetto in the course of the large-scale action, and 6,929 by transporting them to T. II,[38] which means that altogether 14,000 Jews were destroyed. Beyond the number of 56,065 Jews, an estimated 5,000 to 6,000 were killed by explosions or in fires.

The number of destroyed bunkers amounts to 631.

BOOTY:

7 Polish rifles, 1 Russian rifle, 1 German rifle

59 pistols of various calibers

Several hundred hand grenades, including Polish and homemade ones

Several hundred incendiary bottles

Homemade explosives

Infernal machines with fuses

A large amount of explosives, ammunition for weapons of all calibers, including some machine-gun ammunition.

Regarding the booty of arms, it must be taken into consideration that the arms themselves could in most cases not be captured, as the bandits and Jews would, before being arrested, throw them into hiding places or holes which could not be ascertained or discovered. The smoking out of the bunkers by our men also often made the search for arms impossible. As the bunkers had to be blown up at once, a search later on was out of the question.

The captured hand grenades, ammunition, and incendiary bottles were at once reused by us against the bandits.

FURTHER BOOTY TAKEN:

1,240 used military tunics (part of them with medal ribbons—Iron Cross and East Medal)

600 pairs of used trousers

Other equipment and German steel helmets

108 horses, 4 of them still in the former ghetto (hearse).

38. A code for the death camp of Treblinka.

Up to May 23 [*sic*], 1943, we had counted:

> 4.4 million zloty; furthermore, about 5–6 million zloty not yet counted, a large amount of foreign currency, among others, $14,300 in paper money and $9,200 in gold, besides jewelry (rings, necklaces, watches, etc.) in large quantities.

State of the ghetto at the termination of the large-scale action:

> Apart from 8 buildings (police barracks, hospital, and accommodations for housing the factory police), the former ghetto is completely destroyed. Only fireproof walls are left standing where no explosions were carried out. But the ruins still contain a vast amount of stones and scrap material which could be used.

Warsaw: May 16, 1943

> *The SS and Police Leader in the District of Warsaw*
> [Signed]   *Stroop*
> *SS Brigadeführer and Major General of Police*

HIMMLER'S SUMMATION, OCTOBER 4, 1943

. . . In 1941 the Führer attacked Russia. That was, as we probably can assert now, shortly—perhaps three to six months—before Stalin was winding up for his great push into Central and Western Europe.[39] I can sketch this first year in a very few lines. The attack cut through. The Russian army was herded together in great pockets, ground down, captured. At that time we did not value this human mass the way we value it today, as raw material, as labor. In the long run, viewed in terms of generations, it is no loss, but today, because of the loss of manpower, it is regrettable that the prisoners died by the tens and hundreds of thousands of exhaustion, of hunger. . . .

Good Nature in the Wrong Place

It is a basic mistake for us to infuse our inoffensive soul and feeling, our good nature, our idealism, into alien peoples. This has been

39. There was never any evidence that Josef Stalin, dictator of the U.S.S.R., planned to attack Germany.

true since the time of Herder, who must have written *Stimmen der Völker* in a boozy hour,[40] and who thereby brought such immeasurable sorrow and misery on us later generations. This has been true since the case of the Czechs and Slovenes, to whom, after all, we gave their sense of nationality. They themselves were not capable of achieving it; we invented it for them.

One basic principle must be absolute for the SS man: we must be honest, decent, loyal, and comradely to members of our own blood and to nobody else. What happens to the Russians, what happens to the Czechs, is a matter of total indifference to me. What there is among the nations in the way of good blood of our kind, we will take for ourselves—if necessary, by kidnapping their children and raising them among us. Whether the other nations live in prosperity or croak from hunger interests me only insofar as we need them as slaves for our culture; otherwise, it does not interest me. Whether 10,000 Russian females drop from exhaustion while building an anti-tank ditch interests me only insofar as the anti-tank ditch gets finished for Germany's sake. We shall never be brutal and heartless where it is not necessary—obviously not. We Germans, the only people in the world who have a decent attitude toward animals, will also take a decent attitude toward these human animals. But it is a crime against our own blood to worry about them and to give them ideals that will make it still harder for our sons and grandsons to cope with them. If someone were to come to me and say, "I cannot build the anti-tank ditch with women or children; it is inhuman, they will die in the process," then I would have to say, "You are a murderer of your own blood, for if the anti-tank ditch is not built, German soldiers will die, and they are sons of German mothers. They are our own blood." This is what I want to instill into the SS and what I believe I have instilled into them as one of the most sacred laws of the future: Our concern, our duty is to our people and our blood; it is for them that we have to provide and to plan, to work and to fight, and for nothing else. Toward anything else we can be indifferent. I wish the SS to take this attitude in confronting the problem of all alien, non-Germanic peoples, especially the Russians. All else is just soap bubbles, is a fraud

40. Johann Gottfried von Herder (1744–1803), German philosopher and poet, has been called the father of German nationalism. As a champion of the idea of nationalism, he published an anthology of folk songs of various peoples called *Stimmen der Völker* (Voices of the Peoples).

against our own nation and an obstacle to the earlier winning of
the war. . . .

Foreigners in the Reich

We must also realize that we have between six and seven million
foreigners in Germany, perhaps even eight million by now. We have
prisoners in Germany. They are none of them dangerous so long as
we hit them hard at the smallest trifle. Shooting ten Poles today is
a mere nothing when compared with the fact that we might later
have to shoot tens of thousands in their place, and that the shooting
of these tens of thousands would also cost German blood. Every
little fire will immediately be stamped out and quenched and extinguished; otherwise—as with a real conflagration—a political and
psychological fire may break out among the people.

The Communists in the Reich

I do not believe the Communists could risk any action, for their
leading elements, like most criminals, are in our concentration
camps. Here something needs saying: After the war it will be possible to see what a blessing it was for Germany that, regardless of
all humanitarian sentimentality, we imprisoned this whole criminal
substratum of the German people in the concentration camps; and
for this I claim the credit. If these people were going about free, we
would be having a harder time of it. For then the subhumans would
have their NCO's and commanding officers, they would have their
workers' and soldiers' councils. As it is, they are locked up, and are
making shells or projectile cases or other important things, and are
very useful members of human society. . . .

The Evacuation of the Jews

I also want to make reference before you here, in complete frank-
ness, to a really grave matter. Among ourselves, this once, it shall
be uttered quite frankly; but in public we will never speak of it.
Just as we did not hesitate on June 30, 1934, to do our duty as
ordered, to stand up against the wall comrades who had transgressed,
and shoot them,[41] so we have never talked about this and never will.

---

41. A reference to the purge of the SA and the murder of its top leaders by SS
officers and men.

It was the tact which I am glad to say is a matter of course to us that made us never discuss it among ourselves, never talk about it. Each of us shuddered, and yet each one knew that he would do it again if it were ordered and if it were necessary.

I am referring to the evacuation of the Jews, the annihilation of the Jewish people. This is one of those things that are easily said. "The Jewish people is going to be annihilated," says every party member. "Sure, it's in our program, elimination of the Jews, annihilation—we'll take care of it." And then they all come trudging, 80 million worthy Germans, and each one has his one decent Jew. Sure, the others are swine, but this one is an A-1 Jew. Of all those who talk this way, not one has seen it happen, not one has been through it. Most of you must know what it means to see a hundred corpses lie side by side, or five hundred, or a thousand. To have stuck this out and—excepting cases of human weakness—to have kept our integrity, that is what has made us hard. In our history, this is an unwritten and never-to-be-written page of glory, for we know how difficult we would have made it for ourselves if today —amid the bombing raids, the hardships and the deprivations of war—we still had the Jews in every city as secret saboteurs, agitators, and demagogues. If the Jews were still ensconced in the body of the German nation, we probably would have reached the 1916–17 stage by now.[42]

The wealth they had we have taken from them. I have issued a strict order, carried out by SS-Obergruppenführer Pohl, that this wealth in its entirety is to be turned over to the Reich as a matter of course. We have taken none of it for ourselves. Individuals who transgress will be punished in accordance with an order I issued at the beginning, threatening that whoever takes so much as a mark of it for himself is a dead man. A number of SS men—not very many—have transgressed, and they will die, without mercy. We had the moral right, we had the duty toward our people, to kill this people which wanted to kill us. But we do not have the right to enrich ourselves with so much as a fur, a watch, a mark, or a cigarette or anything else. Having exterminated a germ, we do not want, in the end, to be infected by the germ, and die of it. I will

42. The reference is to the time when the tide of the First World War began to turn against Germany. German nationalists and rightists then attributed Germany's losses and ultimate defeat to the *Dolchstoss,* the "stab in the back" by the Jews.

not stand by and let even a small rotten spot develop or take hold. Wherever it may form, we together will cauterize it. All in all, however, we can say that we have carried out this heaviest of our tasks in a spirit of love for our people. And our inward being, our soul, our character has not suffered injury from it.

The Bearing of the SS Man

In giving, I might almost say, an accounting before and on behalf of all of us of what we have done this year, there is one thing I must not overlook or pass over: the significance of the SS man's bearing. . . .

We have come into being through the law of selection. We have made our selection from a cross section of our people. This people came into being by the throw of the dice of fate and of history—eons ago, through generations and centuries. Alien peoples swept over this people and left their heritage behind them. Alien bloodlines merged into this people; yet, in spite of the most terrible hardships and the most terrible blows of fate, this people in the essence of its blood has had the strength to win through. Thus this whole people is permeated and held together by Nordic-Falic-Germanic blood, so that one could and can, after all, still speak of a German people. From this people, multifariously mixed in its hereditary tendencies, as it emerged from the collapse after the years of the fight for freedom, we have consciously tried to select the Nordic-Germanic blood, for we could most fully expect this portion of our blood to be the bearer of the creative and heroic, the life-preserving qualities of our people. We have gone partly by outward appearance, and for the rest have verified this outward appearance through constantly renewed demands, constantly renewed tests—physical and mental— of the character and the psyche. Again and again we have sifted out and cast aside what was unfit, what did not belong with us. As long as we have the strength to do so, this brotherhood [43] will be healthy. If we were to forget for one moment the law of our basis as a people and the law of selection and of severity toward ourselves, in that moment we would have the seed of death in us; in that moment we would perish just as every human organization, just as every

43. The German is *Orden,* a monastic or military order. Himmler tried to organize the SS along the line of a medieval religious/military order.

blossom in this world perishes at some time. To make this blossoming and bearing of fruit as beneficial as possible for our people, to make it continue as long as possible, even—don't be alarmed—for thousands of years if possible, must be our endeavor, our inner law. That is why, whenever we meet and whatever we do, we are obligated to be mindful of our guiding principle: blood, selection, severity. The law of nature, after all, is this: What is hard is good; what is vigorous is good; whatever wins through in the struggle of life, physically or in terms of the will or the spirit, that is what is good—always taking the long view. Of course, occasionally (and this has often happened in history) someone may get to the top by fraud and deceit. To nature, to the fate of the earth, to the fate of the world this makes no difference. After some time, reckoned not in generations of man but in historical eras, reality (that is, nature) and fate depose the imposter. Never to deceive ourselves but always to remain genuine, that must be our endeavor; that is what we must continually preach and instill into ourselves and into every boy and each of our subordinates. . . .

The Virtues of the SS Man

I will speak now of the most important virtues which I began years ago to preach to, and impress on, this brotherhood, this whole General SS [44]—for they are the basis of the brotherhood and just now, in the fifth year of the war, are of such decisive significance and importance.

(1) Loyalty

So far, I am glad to say, we have not had a single case in our ranks of a prominent SS man becoming disloyal. Let this be your guideline: If within your purview anyone should ever be disloyal to the Führer or the Reich, even if only in thought, it is up to you to see to it that this man departs from the brotherhood, and we will see to it that he departs this life. For anything—I have said this before, and I repeat it today—anything can be forgiven in this world, but one thing cannot be forgiven among us Germanic

44. The *Allgemeine SS* (General SS) denoted the general body of SS members, as distinct from special groups within the SS, like the *Totenkopfverbände* (Death's-Head units), assigned to the concentration camps, or the *Waffen-SS*, fully militarized combat formations that participated in military campaigns alongside the Armed Forces.

people, and that is disloyalty. It would be unforgivable and *is* unforgivable. Cases like the Badoglio [45] case in Italy must not and will not occur in Germany. In the future, the name Badoglio will be the name for bad dogs, the epithet for four-legged mongrel curs, just as in antiquity the name Thersites was the epithet for traitors. We can say only this and preach it constantly: Let the German people as embodied in each of its men and each of its women, show by means of matchless and unconditional loyalty that it was worthy to live in the time of Adolf Hitler, and to have this leader arise for its sake, who has dedicated his life of care, of responsibility, of toil, to our German, Germanic people.

(2) *Obedience*

In the soldier's life, obedience is demanded and given, morning, noon, and night. And the man of low rank obeys all or most of the time. If he does not obey, he is locked up. The question of obedience is more difficult where it concerns higher-ranking officials in the state, the party and the armed forces, and here and there in the SS as well. I would like here to state clearly and unequivocally: It is a matter of course that the man in the ranks must obey; it is even more a matter of course that all high-ranking leaders of the SS—the whole Gruppenführer corps,[46] that is—are models of unconditional obedience. If someone believes that an order rests on a misconception on the part of his superior, or on a false basis, it goes without saying that he—that is, each of you—has the duty and responsibility to bring the matter up for discussion, and also to state his reasons truthfully, like a man, if he is convinced that such reasons speak against the order. But once the superior concerned or the Reichsführer SS—it will be he in most cases where the Gruppenführer corps is concerned—or the Führer himself has made a decision and given the order, it must be carried out, not only according to the word and the letter, but also in spirit. Whoever executes the order must do so as a faithful steward, as a faithful representative of the authority that gives the command. If you thought initially that something was the right thing to do, and something else was not right, or was actually ill-advised, then there are two alternatives. If a man believes he cannot take on the re-

45. Field Marshall Pietro Badoglio (1871–1956) took over the leadership of the Italian government, formed in July 1943, after the overthrow of Mussolini. He later joined the Allies in the war against Germany.
46. The ranks of lieutenant-general and above.

sponsibility for obeying an order, he must candidly state: "I cannot take the responsibility; I beg to be excused." Probably in most cases, an order will then come through, saying: "You must carry it out anyway." Alternately, one may think: "His nerves are shot, he's weak." In that case, one can say, "Very well, retire on a pension." But orders must be sacred. When generals obey, armies obey automatically. This sacredness of orders applies the more, the larger our territory grows. To enforce an order in our little Germany was not difficult at all. To enforce an order once we have—and I am convinced that we will have—garrisons in the Urals, that's a bit more difficult. There it will not always be possible to verify whether the order has been carried out. With us, the verifications must not, must never be left to a commissar, as it is in Russia. The only commissar we have must be our own conscience, devotion to duty, loyalty, obedience. If you lead the way with this example, gentlemen, every subordinate will follow. But you will never be able to demand obedience of your men if you do not give the same obedience to the authority above you, and give it unconditionally and without reservation.

(3) *Bravery*

Bravery, I think, requires the least exhortation among us, for our leaders and our men *are* brave. . . .

Within our ranks we live by our Germanic laws, among which a particularly beautiful one reads: "Honor is compulsion enough." To the alien people we will apply Asiatic laws. We will never confuse this issue. When we are dealing with someone of our own blood, a Norwegian or Netherlander of good race, we can win his allegiance only by way of our—that is, his and our—pan-Germanic laws. When we are dealing with a Russian or with someone who, in terms of blood, is a Slav, we will never apply our sacred laws to him, but will use the proven Russian laws of the commissars. . . .

(4) *Truthfulness*

I now come to a fourth virtue, which is very rare in Germany: truthfulness. One of the greatest evils that have spread during the war is untruthfulness in information, reports, and statements which subordinate agencies in civilian life, in the state, the party, and the armed services send to the agencies above them. The information, the report, is the basis of every decision. It is a fact that during the present war one can assume in many spheres that 95 out of 100 messages are lies, or only half true or partly correct. . . .

While on the subject of truthfulness, I come to another matter. In war and in peace—in peacetime especially this will be an educational task—we SS men must get to the point where we will no longer conclude written agreements; where among us, as was customary in former days, a man's word and handshake constitute a contract, and where the handshake of one SS man will, if necessary, be binding for a million or more. We must get to where the handshake or the word of an SS man is proverbially more reliable than a mortgage on someone else's most valuable property. That's how it must be.

If we enter contracts, we must keep them. If I enter a contract with an agent, even with a disreputable type, I keep the contract. I take my stand unconditionally on this point of view. When I announce in the Generalgouvernement that anyone informing against a Jew who has sought shelter and gone into hiding is to have a third of the Jew's property,[47] it very often happens that some Secretary Huber[48] or Untersturmführer Huber—who takes illegal trips when he can, who orders a new telephone or new pencils without a moment's thought, in short, who never saves—suddenly begins to save for the German Reich. He will say, for instance: "This Jew has 12,000 Reichmarks. Why, that means I'd have to pay out 4,000 RM to the Pole who denounced him. I'd rather save that for Germany. The Pole will get only 400." In this way, a little man goes and breaks the promise of a whole organization. That sort of thing should be impossible. . . .

The Future

. . . When peace has become definitive, we will be in a position to tackle our great work for the future. We will colonize. We will indoctrinate the younger people with the laws of the SS brotherhood. I consider it inescapably necessary for the life of our people that we teach the concepts of ancestry, posterity, and the future not just in a superficial way, but feel them to be part of our being. Without any talk about it, without our having to make use of prizes or suchlike material things, it must be a matter of course that we have children. It must be a matter of course that the most numerous progeny comes from this brotherhood, this racial top stratum of the

---

47. Cf. Stroop's report, part II.
48. The average man, "Huber" is the German equivalent of "John Doe."

Germanic people. Twenty to thirty years from now, we actually must be able to supply the leading echelon for all of Europe. If the SS together with the farmers—we with our friend Backe [49]—will then carry on the colonization in the East, on a grand scale, without any inhibition, without any concern about traditional ways, with elan and revolutionary impetus, we will within twenty years push the ethnic boundary 500 kilometers eastward.

I requested of the Führer today that the SS—provided we fulfill our task and our duty up to the end of the war—be granted the privilege of holding Germany's extreme eastern frontier as a defense frontier. I believe this is the only privilege for which we have no competitors. I believe not one person will dispute our claim to this privilege. Out there, we will be in a position to give each year's crop of young men practical training in the use of arms. We will force our laws upon the East. We will charge ahead and push our way forward, little by little, to the Urals. I hope our generation can still succeed in having each year's age group fight in the East, and in having each of our divisions spend a winter in the East every second or third year. If so, we will never grow soft; we will never have wearers of our uniform who join us only because it is classy and because the black coat naturally will be very attractive in peacetime. Each one will know: "If I join the SS, there is the possibility that I might be shot dead." He has it in writing that every other year he will not be dancing in Berlin or celebrating the carnival in Munich, but will be stationed on the Eastern frontier in an icy winter. In this way, we will have a healthy elite for all time. With it we will create the conditions under which the whole Germanic people and the whole of Europe—guided, organized and led by us, the Germanic people—will be able to prevail generations hence in its fateful struggles with an Asia that is sure to surge forward again. We do not know when that will be. When that human mass lines up on the other side with 1 or 1½ billion, then the Germanic people, numbering, I hope, 240 to 300 million, together with the other European peoples, making a total of 600 to 700 million—and with an outpost area stretching as far as the Urals or, a hundred years from now, beyond the Urals—will have to prevail in its struggle for

---

49. SS Obergruppenführer (General) Herbert Backe (1896–1947) had been the Secretary of State in the Reich Ministry of Food and Agriculture and, since 1943, Reich Minister of Food and Reich Peasant Leader.

existence against Asia. Woe betide if the Germanic people were not to prevail! It would be the end of beauty and civilization, of the creative power of this earth. That is the distant future. It is for this that we fight, pledged to hand down the heritage of our ancestors.

We look into the distance because we know what it will be. That is why we are doing our duty more fanatically than ever, more devoutly than ever, more bravely, obediently, and honorably than ever. We want to be worthy of having been permitted to be the first SS men of the Führer, Adolf Hitler, in the long history of the Germanic people which stretches before us.

We now direct our thoughts to the Führer, our Führer, Adolf Hitler, who will create the Germanic Reich and will lead us into the Germanic future.

To our Führer Adolf Hitler:
Sieg Heil!
Sieg Heil!
Sieg Heil!

PART TWO

THE HOLOCAUST

INTRODUCTION

THE NATIONAL SOCIALIST accession to power confronted the half million Jews in Germany with unprecedented trials and imponderable dilemmas. Though many reacted in panic and despair, most German Jews held steadfast, with faith in Germany's return to political sanity and a determined will to hold out against terror and persecution. For the most part, German Jews responded on two levels. While they maintained their right to continue to live in Germany, they also reaffirmed their identity as Jews.

On the occasion of the boycott of Jewish businesses which the Nazis launched on April 1, 1933, and in reply to the hatred and contempt spewed forth against the Jews, the Jüdische Rundschau, *organ of the Zionist Federation of Germany, published a stirring editorial, "Wear the Yellow Badge with Pride!" by Robert Weltsch, the paper's editor-in-chief. The editorial called for pride in Jewishness, rejection of assimilation, and support of Zionism; its impact—especially on German Jewish youth—was electrifying. (Years later, in retrospect, Weltsch expressed remorse for having underestimated the character and intentions of the enemy.)*

In the early months of the German dictatorship, Jewish leaders believed that it would be possible to negotiate with the regime to clarify the position of the Jews, regulate their situation lawfully, and ensure a basis for their continued eixstence in Germany. One of the first organizations to approach the new German state was the Zionist Federation of Germany, which submitted a memorandum on June 21, 1933, in which it tried to formulate a theoretical case for allowing the Jewish community a sphere of honorable existence and fruitful activity. Besides asking for government assistance for Jewish emigration to Palestine, the Zionist Federation requested the status of a protected national minority for the Jews in Germany within the framework of the racial state. (The regime never responded to this memorandum.)

The Zionist approach was not shared by most German Jews, who continued to insist on their full and equal rights. At this time the major national Jewish organizations in Germany and the large Gemeinde (community) associations were negotiating among themselves to form one central body to represent the Jewish community in dealings with the government. That body came into existence on September 17, 1933, as the Reichsvertretung der deutschen Juden— *Federal Representation of German Jews—with Leo Baeck, the most prestigious rabbi and scholar of German Jewry, as its chairman.*

On January 23, 1934, the Reichsvertretung submitted to each member of the Reich cabinet a memorandum in defense of the Jews and their rights. With three appendices of documentation to buttress its case, the memorandum concentrated on four areas. The first concerned the ouster of Jews from employment; the Reichsvertretung petitioned for a halt in the discriminatory treatment being accorded Jews and for an end to the economic pressure against them. The next area was efforts by the Jewish community toward "occupational restructuring," diverting Jews from business and the professions into physical work, farming and manual trades; pointing to exclusionary practices in these fields with regard to training and employment, the Reichsvertretung requested that restrictions against Jews be lifted. The memorandum then set forth the need for a systematic preparation of emigrants for their life in a new country and for government aid in a regulated procedure to facilitate emigration. Finally, in a petition both daring and quixotic, the Reichsvertretung called on the government to discontinue the defamation of Jews and Judaism. (This memorandum, too, never elicited a response from any official quarter.)

Though the Reichsvertretung found few occasions to negotiate with the National Socialist regime, it had many opportunities, per-

haps more than it had foreseen, to develop new programs for the Jewish community. In reaction to their rejection from Germany, the German Jews turned inward, and began to rediscover their ancestral traditions and neglected cultural treasures, both religious and secular. Judaism, Jewish culture, and Jewish solidarity offered solace and self-esteem. The most outspoken and provocative summoner to Jewish authenticity and self-renewal was Martin Buber, philosopher and religious thinker.

When Jewish children were forced from the public schools, the Reichsvertretung undertook to organize an extensive network of elementary and secondary schools. In May 1933 Buber submitted his proposal to the Reichsvertretung for a program of Jewish education. Its central postulate, Buber held, was that the effort be "not only formally but intrinsically Jewish," that "it should not merely remedy an external state of distress, but should also fill a great internal void." In any event, the educational policy adopted by the Reichsvertretung was based not on this principle but on the dual Jewish/German experience of the child. Buber proved more successful in his proposal for adult Jewish education. In May 1934, the Reichsvertretung established as one of its divisions the Mittelstelle für jüdische Erwachsenenbildung—Central Office for Jewish Adult Education—with Buber as its head. In his address at the founding conference Buber declared that in present circumstances the objective of adult Jewish education was "no longer the equipment with knowledge, but the mobilization for existence." Indeed, in the few short years of its existence, the Mittelstelle became a bulwark of spiritual resistance for the German Jews.

Though Jews, and especially the young, were migrating in substantial numbers from Germany, the feeling was nevertheless widespread that eventually the German dictatorship would reach some modus vivendi *with the Jews, that continued Jewish existence would somehow or other be possible. But the enactment of the Nuremberg Laws on September 15, 1935, demonstrated to most German Jews that the Jewish community no longer had a future in Germany.*

Late September 1935 the Reichsvertretung published a new program, its future directions defined by the changed status of the Jews. The urgent tasks now, according to this program, were: the Jewish educational system; emigration, to Palestine above all; care for the needy, sick, and aged; and economic aid. Instead of the affirmations which had characterized past statements about the rightful place of Jews in Germany, this program stressed the ties of the Jews in Germany to Palestine. The appeal for governmental recognition of "an autonomous Jewish management," for the conduct of Jewish affairs to be left in the hands of the Reichsvertretung, was not a petition for national-minority status, but an oblique protest against the intrusion of the Gestapo into Jewish affairs.

Also at the end of 1935, the Central-Verein—*Central Association—the most representative organization of the German Jews, issued a revised set of bylaws and statement of purpose. The Central-Verein had defended Jewish belonging in Germany and the rights of Jews not only to political equality but also to full participation in German culture and society; its new policy statement reflected the deeply and decisively altered conditions under which it functioned. The statement was an attempt to render an accounting of the accomplishments and failures of the non-Zionist ideology for which the Central-Verein had stood, a statement describing the capitulation of Jewish Emancipation to National Socialism.*

Thereafter the Jewish community in Germany began in earnest the process of its dissolution. The high morale of the first years under National Socialism dissipated as the youngest, strongest, and most energetic among the Jews left Germany and as the noose of SS terror tightened around the necks of those remaining. In a few years the once prosperous community was reduced to some 300,000 impoverished and aging Jews. By the start of 1938, even the stubbornest advocates of a Jewish presence in Germany conceded defeat, and Kristallnacht in November of that year wrote an end to what was left of the autonomous community. Thenceforth, the Jews in Germany became hostages of the SS, which would soon preside over their liquidation.

WEAR THE YELLOW BADGE WITH PRIDE!

The first of April, 1933, will remain an important date in the history of German Jewry—indeed, in the history of the entire Jewish people. The events of that day have not only political and economic aspects, but moral and psychological ones as well. The political and economic implications have been widely discussed in the newspapers, although the requirements of agitation have frequently obscured an objective understanding of them. To speak about the moral aspects is our task. For no matter how often the Jewish question is discussed these days, we ourselves are the only ones who can express what is going on in the hearts of German Jews, what can be said about events from the Jewish point of view. Today Jews can speak only as Jews; anything else is utterly senseless. . . .

The first of April, 1933, can be a day of Jewish awakening and Jewish rebirth—*if the Jews want it to be;* if the Jews are ripe for it and possess inner greatness; if the Jews are not as they are depicted by their adversaries.

Having been attacked, Jewry must avow its faith in itself.

Even on this day of extreme excitement, when the most tempestuous emotions fill our hearts in the face of the unprecedented phenomenon of the entire Jewish population of a great civilized country being universally outlawed, the one thing we must preserve is our composure. Even though we are staggered by the events of recent days, we must not be dismayed, but must take stock without self-deception. What should be recommended at this time is that the work which witnessed the infancy of Zionism, Theodor Herzl's *The Jewish State,* be disseminated among Jews and non-Jews in hundreds of thousands of copies. If there is still left any feeling for greatness and nobility, gallantry and justice, then every National Socialist who looks into this book is bound to shudder at his own blind actions. Every Jew who reads it would also begin to understand and would be consoled and uplifted by it. Page after page of this booklet, which first appeared in 1896, would have to be copied to show that Theodor Herzl was the first Jew dispassionate enough to examine anti-Semitism in connection with the Jewish question. And he recognized that an improvement cannot be effected by ostrich-like behavior, but only by dealing with facts frankly and in full view of the world. . . .

We Jews who have been raised in Theodor Herzl's spirit want to ask ourselves what our own guilt is, what sins we have committed. At times of crisis throughout its history, the Jewish people has faced the question of its own guilt. Our most important prayer says, "We were expelled from our country because of our sins." Only if we are critical toward ourselves shall we be just toward others.

Jewry bears a great guilt because it failed to heed Theodor Herzl's call and even mocked it in some instances. The Jews refused to acknowledge that "the Jewish question still exists." They thought the only important thing was not to be recognized as Jews. Today we are being reproached with having betrayed the German people; the National Socialist press calls us the "enemies of the nation," and there is nothing we can do about it. It is not true that the Jews have betrayed Germany. If they have betrayed anything, they have betrayed themselves and Judaism.

Because the Jews did not display their Jewishness with pride, because they wanted to shirk the Jewish question, they must share the blame for the degradation of Jewry. . . .

The leaders of the boycott gave orders that signs "with a yellow badge against a black background" be affixed to the boycotted stores. Here is a powerful symbol. This measure is intended as an act of stigmatization, of disparagement. We accept it and propose to turn it into a badge of honor.

Many Jews had a shattering experience last Saturday. Suddenly they were Jews—not out of inner conviction, nor out of pride in a magnificent heritage and contribution to mankind, but through the affixing of a red slip and a yellow badge. The squads went from house to house, pasting them on store fronts and business signs and painting them on windows; for twenty-four hours German Jews were in a pillory, as it were. In addition to other marks and inscriptions one frequently saw on the shopwindows a large *Magen David,* the Shield of King David. This was supposed to be a disgrace. Jews, pick up the Shield of David and wear it honorably!

For—and this is the first task of our spiritual stock-taking—if today this shield is stained, it has not been entirely the work of our enemies. There have been many Jews whose undignified self-mockery knew no bounds. Judaism was regarded as something outmoded;

people did not give it their serious attention; they wanted to free themselves of its tragic aspects by smiling. However, today there is a new type: the new, free Jew, a kind as yet unknown to the non-Jewish world. If today the National Socialist and German patriotic newspapers frequently refer to the type of the Jewish scribbler and the so-called Jewish press, if Jewry is held responsible for these factors, it must be pointed out again and again that they are not representative of Jewry, but at most have tried to derive a financial profit from the Jews. At a time of middle-class self-righteousness, these elements could expect acclamation from Jewish audiences if they lampooned and made light of Jews and Judaism. Quite frequently these circles preached to us, nationally oriented Jews, the ideals of an abstract cosmopolitanism in an effort to destroy all deeper values of Judaism. Upright Jews have always been indignant at the raillery and the caricature directed by Jewish buffoons against Jews to the same extent, or even a greater extent, than they aimed them at Germans and others. Jewish audiences applauded their own degradation, and many attempted to create an alibi for themselves by joining in the mockery. . . .

As recently as thirty years ago it was considered objectionable in educated circles to discuss the Jewish question. In those days the Zionists were regarded as trouble-makers with an *idée fixe*. Now the Jewish question is so timely that every small child, every schoolboy as well as the man in the street has no other topic of conversation. All Jews throughout Germany were branded with the word "Jew" on April first. If there is a renewed boycott, the new directives of the boycott committee provide for a uniform designation of all shops: "German business" in the case of non-Jews, the simple word "Jew" for Jewish places. They know who is a Jew. There no longer is any evading or hiding it. The Jewish answer is clear. It is the brief sentence spoken by the prophet Jonah: *Ivri anokhi*, I am a Hebrew. Yes, a Jew. The affirmation of our Jewishness—this is the moral significance of what is happening today. The times are too turbulent to use arguments in the discussion. Let us hope that a more tranquil time will come and that a movement which considers it a matter of pride to be recognized as the pacemaker of the national uprising will no longer derive pleasure from degrading others, even though it might feel that it must fight them. As for us Jews, we can defend our honor. We remember all those who were called Jews, stigmatized as Jews, over a period of five thousand years. We are being reminded that we are Jews. We affirm this and bear it with pride.

THE ZIONIST FEDERATION OF GERMANY ADDRESSES THE NEW GERMAN STATE

I

The situation of the Jews in Germany has, through the events and through the legislation of the most recent time, undergone a development which makes a fundamental clarification of the problem desirable and necessary. We consider it an obligation of the Jews to assist in the untangling of the problem. May we therefore be permitted to present our views, which, in our opinion, make possible a solution in keeping with the principles of the new German State of National Awakening and which at the same time might signify for Jews a new ordering of the conditions of their existence.

These views are based on an interpretation of the historical development of the position of the Jews in Germany, which, by way of introduction, may be briefly outlined here.

II

Historical Summary

The emancipation of the Jews, begun at the end of the 18th, beginning of the 19th century, was based on the idea that the Jewish question could be solved by having the nation-state absorb the Jews living in its midst. This view, deriving from the ideas of the French Revolution, discerned only the individual, the single human being freely suspended in space, without regarding the ties of blood and history or spiritual distinctiveness. Accordingly, the liberal state demanded of the Jews assimilation into the non-Jewish environment. Baptism and mixed marriage were encouraged in political and economic life. Thus it happened that innumerable persons of Jewish origin had the chance to occupy important positions and to come forward as representatives of German culture and German life, without having their belonging to Jewry become visible.

Thus arose a state of affairs which in political discussion today is termed "debasement of Germandom" or "Jewification."

The Jews at first did not even recognize this difficulty, because they believed in an individualistic and legalistic solution of the Jewish question. Zionism (since 1897) was the first to disclose to the Jews the *nature of the Jewish question*. Zionist insight also enabled Jews to understand *anti-Semitism,* which they had fought until then only apologetically. The unsolved Jewish question was recognized as the basic cause of anti-Semitism; hence, a constructive solution of the Jewish question had to be found. To this end the *benevolent support* of the non-Jewish world was sought.

Zionism

Zionism has no illusions about the difficulty of the Jewish condition, which consists above all in an abnormal occupational pattern and in the fault of an intellectual and moral posture not rooted in one's own tradition. Zionism recognized decades ago that as a result of the assimilationist trend, symptoms of deterioration were bound to appear, which it seeks to overcome by carrying out its challenge to transform Jewish life completely.

It is our opinion that an answer to the Jewish question truly satisfying to the national state can be brought about only with the collaboration of the Jewish movement that aims at a social, cultural, and moral renewal of Jewry—indeed, that such a national renewal must first create the decisive social and spiritual premises for all solutions.

Zionism believes that a rebirth of national life, such as is occurring in German life through adhesion to Christian and national values, must also take place in the Jewish national group. For the Jew, too, origin, religion, community of fate and group consciousness must be of decisive significance in the shaping of his life. This means that the egotistic individualism which arose in the liberal era must be overcome by public spiritedness and by willingness to accept responsibility.

III

Proposals

Our conception of the nature of Jewry and of our true position among the European peoples allows us to frame proposals on the regulation of the situation of the Jews in the new German state which are not considerations based on accidental constellations of interests, but which pave the way for a real solution of the Jewish question that will satisfy the German state. In this we are not concerned with the interests of individual Jews who have lost their economic and social positions as a result of Germany's profound transformation. What we are concerned with is the creation of an opportunity for the existence for the whole group, while preserving our honor, which is our most precious possession. On the foundation of the new state, which has established the principle of race, we wish so to fit our community into the total structure so that for us too, in the sphere assigned to us, fruitful activity for the Fatherland is possible.

We believe it is precisely the new Germany that can, through bold resoluteness in the handling of the Jewish question, take a decisive step toward overcoming a problem which, in truth, will have to be dealt with by most European peoples—including those whose foreign-policy statements today deny the existence of any such problem in their own midst.

Relationship to the German People

Our acknowledgment of Jewish nationality provides for a clear and sincere relationship to the German people and its national and racial realities. Precisely because we do not wish to falsify these fundamentals, because we, too, are against mixed marriage and are for maintaining the purity of the Jewish group and reject any trespasses of the cultural domain, we—having been brought up in the German language and German culture—can show an interest in the works and values of German culture with admiration and internal sympathy. Only fidelity to their own kind and their own culture gives Jews the inner strength that prevents insult to the respect for the national sentiments and the imponderables of German nationality; and rootedness in one's own spirituality protects the Jew from becoming the rootless critic of the national foundations of German essence. The national distancing which the state desires would thus be brought about easily as the result of an organic development.

Thus, a self-conscious Jewry here described, in whose name we speak, can find a place in the structure of the German state, because

it is inwardly unembarrassed, free from the resentment which assimilated Jews must feel at the determination that they belong to
Jewry, to the Jewish race and past. We believe in the possibility of
an honest relationship of loyalty between a group-conscious Jewry
and the German state.

IV

Emigration

This presentation would be incomplete, were we not to add some
remarks on the important problem of Jewish emigration. The
situation of the Jews among the nations and their recurrent elimination from professional categories and economic means of livelihood, as well as desire for a normalization of living conditions, force
many Jews to emigrate.

Zionism wishes to shape Jewish emigration to Palestine in such
a way that a *reduction of pressure on the Jewish position in Germany* will result.

Zionism has not been satisfied merely to set forth a theoretical
conception of the Jewish question, but at the practical level has
initiated a normalization of Jewish life through the founding of a
new national settlement of Jews in Palestine, their ancient homeland. There about 230,000 Jews have already to date been settled
in a normally stratified community. The basis of Jewish settlement is
agriculture. All kinds of labor—in agriculture, manual trades, and
industry—are performed by Jewish workers, who are inspired by a
new, idealistic work ethic. The Palestine movement has always been
encouraged by the German Government; it is a fact that the significance of Palestine for German Jewry is constantly growing.

For its practical aims, Zionism hopes to be able to win the collaboration even of a government fundamentally hostile to Jews,
because in dealing with the Jewish question not sentimentalities are
involved but a real problem whose solution interests all peoples,
and at the present moment especially the German people.

The realization of Zionism could only be hurt by resentment
of Jews abroad against the German development. Boycott propaganda—such as is currently being carried on against Germany in
many ways—is in essence un-Zionist, because Zionism wants not to
do battle but to convince and to build.

V

Foreign Policy Consequences

We believe that the proposed regulation of the Jewish question suggested here would entail important advantages for the German people, which would be felt also beyond German borders. The *idea of nationhood,* so important for the German people scattered through the whole world (Germandom abroad), would undergo a decisive deepening and strengthening by a statesmanlike action on the part of the new Germany.

Millions of Jews live as *national minorities* in various countries. During the negotiations about the protection of minorities, at the end of the war, formulas and arguments prepared by Jewish national movements were widely accepted by all states; [1] they led to provisions on the basis of which German minorities, like others, assert their rights today. If consideration is given to the strong community of interests among national minorities, which has repeatedly found expression and which certainly would figure in quite another way if the position of the Jews in Germany is to be regulated through recognition of their special character, the political situation of a portion of the German people all over the world can arrive at an emphatic advancement. This advancement would consist not only of ideological reinforcement of the validity of the principles of nationality proclaimed by the Reich Chancellor in his address of May 17,[2] but could also take the form of direct cooperation among minorities in different countries.

We are not blind to the fact that a Jewish question exists and will continue to exist. From the abnormal situation of the Jews severe disadvantages result for them, but also scarcely tolerable

1. During the peace negotiations after the First World War, regarding the formation of new European states, Jewish delegations convinced European political leaders that the rights of racial, religious, and linguistic minorities would best be protected by a formal obligation embodied in the individual peace treaties of the new states. Consequently, provisions guaranteeing minority, or group, cultural rights, in addition to individual civic rights, were incorporated into the treaties with Austria, Bulgaria, Czechoslovakia, Estonia, Finland, Greece, Hungary, Latvia, Lithuania, Poland, Rumania, and Yugoslavia.
2. The reference is to a passage in Hitler's "Peace" speech in the Reichstag on May 17, 1933, in which he said: "Our boundless love for and loyalty to our own national traditions make us respect the national claims of others."

conditions for other peoples. Our observations, presented herewith, rest on the conviction that, in solving the Jewish problem according to its own lights, the German Government will have full understanding for a candid and clear Jewish posture that harmonizes with the interests of the state.

THE REICHSVERTRETUNG ADDRESSES
THE REICH GOVERNMENT

While the whole German people is being summoned by the Reich government to the renewal of the fatherland, spiritual and material distress burdens the German Jews—who are rooted in Germany and German culture. Jewish origin and group association, which generation upon generation avowed in inherited pride, are being disparaged and reviled. Jewish persons whose conduct is impugned by no one are being dismissed from public office, from profession and occupation, and only too often deep economic misery comes to the families thus afflicted. To the extent that a sacrifice might be imposed upon the German Jews for reasons of state, patriotic dedication and Jewish dignity might prompt them to keep silent. But speaking out becomes a duty when the existence of Jewry is concerned, when a foundation of our religious communities threatens to collapse, when measures are taken against the German Jews which are not only against them but also against the welfare of Germany.

Therefore, the Reichsvertretung der deutschen Juden, which comprises the Jewish communities and their state federations, and which is supported by the confidence of the major organizations of German Jewry,[3] submits the following to the Reich government:

I

Through the legislation of the present year, Jews, apart from the well-known exceptions, have been systematically removed from the

---

3. Central-Verein of German Citizens of Jewish Faith, Federal Union of Jewish War Veterans, Zionist Federation for Germany.

administration of justice and from public offices in the Reich, the states, the municipalities, and other public bodies. The reason given has been that in a Reich to be reconstructed on a racial basis Jews could not exercise sovereign power. Beyond that, the share of Jews in all academic professions has been substantially reduced or even eliminated. In the business sphere, on the other hand, the Reich government, striving to bolster and reassure the German economy, has not applied the Aryan principle in its legislation. The extension of this principle to the economic sphere would not only deprive the German Jews of any basis for existence; in addition, assets of the German economy, valuable domestic and foreign trade relations that depend on individuals, would be gravely impaired. Yet numerous regulations by national and state agencies, by Party circles and municipalities, by professional organizations at all levels, again and again create difficulties for Jews in their *economic activity as employees and employers,* and make such activity almost impossible in some parts of the country and some branches of business. In Appendix I we submit some documents in evidence. They are only a small selection from recent months, but even so they give a clear picture. They show how the German Jews, already largely deprived of their places through legislation, are being boycotted where they have been allowed to remain in the professions, and how attempts are now being made also to dislodge them or exclude them from commerce and industry, manual trades and agriculture.

Pauperization, not just impoverishment, must be the consequence of this interference with the economy. This development has unmistakably already begun. The taxpaying ability of the German Jews is dwindling. The Jewish communities directly affected can hardly cope with their responsibilities of religious, social, and cultural welfare, which today increasingly confront them; if no change occurs, their breakdown can hardly be prevented.

Since this cannot serve the intention or the interest of the new Reich, we apply to the Reich government for redress. It can succeed in reconciling the needs of the new state with the means of livelihood of the German Jews. A premise for this is:

> That differential treatment of Aryan and Jewish employed be discontinued in the future; that any pressure to displace or oust Jewish employees be checked, no matter from what quarters it may emanate.

II

Closely connected with the issue just discussed is the additional question of what occupation Jews already presently unemployed should pursue. Apart from those out of work because of the economic crisis, two groups chiefly come into consideration. First, those employed who were removed from their professions or from their positions through legislation or private boycott, and second, the young people who, the more they are denied attendance at institutions of higher education, the more they currently demand prompt job training. We are aware that the occupational structure of the German Jews to date, their preponderance in academic professions and in the metropolitan centers, was unhealthy. Out of this awareness, Jewish youth has sought for years to correct this undesirable state of affairs, which was in part determined by historical development. Considerable preliminary studies have been guiding a comprehensive *occupational restructuring* of the German Jews. The will of Jewish youth to do physical work, of every kind, is there. But it must also be possible to count on readiness to accept them in occupational groups in which they were previously underrepresented, according to their ratio in the population. For this, too, we request the aid of the government. We submit Appendix II, which shows how the artisans' guilds and agricultural organizations are trying to block the access of Jewish persons to training and admission. Notwithstanding all our educational effort, Jewish youth would fall into despair without the hope of future work. We accordingly anticipate:

> That as a matter of principle no occupation be closed to Jews; that within the corporate state's reconstruction of manual trades and labor, agriculture and forestry, Jews, too, be afforded training and admission.

III

Even if this is done, as we hope it will be, the present situation will compel many Jewish persons to emigrate.

To be sure, the Jewish ratio in the population of the German Reich has been declining for a century. The two largest states may serve as examples: In Prussia in 1816, 1.2 percent of the population were Jews, in 1925 only 1.06 percent; in Bavaria there were in 1818 still 1.45 percent Jews, in 1925 the figure was 0.66 percent. Even in the metropolitan centers, things are no different: Berlin in 1895 had 5.14 percent Jews, in 1925 4.29 percent; Hamburg in 1866 4.4 percent, in 1925 only 1.73 percent. Since then the number of Jews has declined further.

Nevertheless, it must be taken into account that many German Jews will find no living space in Germany and will have to emigrate. German as well as Jewish prestige demands that this *emigration be systematically prepared and regulated*. This requires that appropriate occupational training be provided in the old home country and that, with the aid of domestic authorities and Jewish organizations, emigration be channeled to those countries that are willing to accept and are in need of workers appropriately trained. If this is done, the emigrant in his new place will retain an attachment to the country where his parents and forebears lived and where he himself received his education and training. Family and cultural ties will then also create valuable economic connections with the old homeland. If the emigrant knows his trade, respect for German ability will increase abroad. If, on the other hand, he becomes a burden on migrant aid, then contempt for the beggar will only too easily be paired with a scornful antipathy for the country from which he came. We, therefore, request the Reich government:

In the area of emigration, to support the work that we and competent organizations are doing for emigration to Palestine and other countries.

IV

Weighing even more heavily on us than all economic hardships is spiritual oppression. The racial premises on which the National Socialist state is built presuppose the alienness of its Jewish component. But the charge of inferiority cannot be accepted by any community that values its honor and dignity. We German Jews have had to live through the experience in Germany of efforts to defame us. In Appendix III, only a few examples are assembled, but everyone knows many. We know that government agencies and high-level Party agencies have disapproved of and condemn the brutal and insulting form of such utterances. What we German Jews feel on such occasions, above all for our children's sake, our self-respect forbids us to express in detail. We will, however, point to one fact, because it is also of political significance: There are Jews living in the countries Germany must confront in the struggle for her place in the world. No atrocity propaganda makes such an impression on these Jews as does this fact: That defamation of their own cherished people and faith becomes known to them from German newspapers and manifestations. This hurt is doubly deep when the matter at issue is not some incidental slips in the heat of an election campaign, but premeditated and repeated utterances made at a time when the society appears stable, and within a state which controls the means of harnessing and directing public opinion.

From whatever point of view this question may be considered, we feel that we may express the hope:

That in the future every defamation of Jewish group association and origin be discontinued.

In submitting these statements, we are fully aware of the multitude of tasks that now occupies the Reich government. We, therefore, have limited ourselves to those matters whose regulation seems to us pressing even in the interest of the German state. To point to these is our duty not only vis-à-vis our own communities, but equally vis-à-vis the Reich government. By doing so we firmly believe we are serving the German fatherland.

January 1934   *Reichsvertretung der deutschen Juden*

MARTIN BUBER ON
JEWISH EDUCATION IN GERMANY

A Proposal for a Jewish Education Office

The Education Office of the German Jews has for its task to coordinate, strengthen, and advance the fruitfulness of all efforts and endeavors for the creation of a genuine Jewish education for our generations now growing up in Germany. In doing so, it will give serious consideration to the diversity of local and regional circumstances on the one hand, of different group circumstances on the other, and also to what has already been accomplished or begun in some places; but for all that, it will at the same time draw attention to the fundamental truth that in so extraordinary and unstable a situation a great communal work can succeed only if carried out in a spirit of unity and under united leadership. Where something is already built, the Education Office will advise on expanding what exists; where only foundations have been laid, it will see to it that the work goes on in keeping with the overall idea; and where nothing exists as yet, it will stimulate, supply basic plans, challenge, and encourage.

At a time when necessity demands that schools for Jewish children be provided, the Education Office should put through the central postulate that this educational effort be not only formally but intrinsically Jewish, that is, that it should not merely remedy an external state of distress, but should also fill a great internal void in German Jewry by providing our youth with the firm stability of being united with the eternity of Judaism. The ancestral power of the Hebrew language, the classic literature of Israel, the strength and suffering of Jewish history, the supreme values of this unique people of faith must enter into the living substance of the new generations. But also instruction in non-Jewish subjects should be informed, as far as possible inwardly and outwardly, with a fundamentally Jewish spirit.

The activities of the Office will basically have to include all levels of upbringing, instruction and early education, from kindergarten to college courses. Thereby, because of both existing conditions and of our special educational aim, it will be necessary to establish new types of schools—a new kind of primary school, a new kind of trade school, etc.—that will fashion according to our inner needs what the law allows us. The point will always be to bring up a type of person who will be able to hold his own in the struggle for existence, under even the hardest conditions, through his own highly skilled work, through outstanding achievements in manual crafts, industry, agriculture, commerce. (At the same time, access to higher education will have to be opened up in whatever way proves possible for an elite, which is to be furthered regardless of social status or property.) And these people are to be Jewish-minded, imbued with Jewish values, inspired by a will for a greater Jewry and with readiness to participate actively in it.

In conjunction with these aims, the Education Office will continuously examine and review the legal bases for its work and will at all times carry on whatever negotiations with federal and state agencies which the work requires.

Defining Jewish Adult Education

The concept of "Jewish adult education" might have been understood, even a short time ago, to mean "elements of education" or "cultural values" that were to be transmitted to those growing up and to the grownup—for example, giving a smattering of higher "education" to those who had not enjoyed it, or initiating those not well versed in Jewish subjects into some general acquaintance with the community. When we gave this name to our newly founded venture, we obviously meant something else. The point is no longer equipment with knowledge, but mobilization for existence. Persons, Jewish persons, are to be shaped, persons who will not only "hold out" but will uphold something substantive; who will have not only morale, but moral fiber, and so will also give moral fiber to others; persons who so live that the spark will not be extinguished. Because our concern is for the spark, we work for "education." What we strive to do through the grooming of persons is to groom a community that will stand firm, that will prevail, that will guard the spark.

This aim determines the what and the how of this education, its substance and its method, for those growing up and for the grownup. It must not be intellectual, for its task is to comprehend the totality of man. But neither can it rely on instincts, on "vitality," for it is the spirit which it is to serve. It wishes to serve this living, life-encompassing spirit, wishes to raise the whole incarnate person to its service. Such education must not be individualistic, for it is to put the individual into direct association with his fellows and to let communality sprout in even the smallest circle. But it cannot have as its purpose a collective, which has its existence only in the fusion of its members, not in the authentic relation of one to another. Its concern is for real persons, to whom, precisely as such, it is given to experience what it means to exist for one another and thereby for the communality. And finally this education must not be of the universalizing type that disdains the special strengths of kind and tradition and ventures to obliterate the stamp of history. Yet it cannot find its ultimate and sovereign end in ethnic variety, for it knows the unity of the power created through nature and stamped by history, and the unity of the deed to which the one power commands the multiplicity of tasks. Jewish adult education is integration of the existential elements of the world around us and the world within us into the particularity of Jewish duty toward the world.

THE REICHSVERTRETUNG PROGRAM
AFTER THE NUREMBERG LAWS

The laws passed by the Reichstag at Nuremberg have affected the Jews in Germany most severely. They are, nevertheless, intended to create a basis on which a tolerable relationship between the German and the Jewish peoples will be possible.[4] The Reichsvertretung der Juden in Deutschland is ready to contribute to this end with all its energy. A prerequisite for a tolerable relationship is the hope that the Jews and the Jewish communities of Germany will be allowed the moral and economic means of existence by the halting of defamation and boycott.

The regulation of the life of the Jews in Germany requires governmental recognition of an autonomous Jewish management. The Reichsvertretung der Juden in Deutschland is the agency competent for this. Behind it stand, with few exceptions, the whole of Jewry and the Jewish communities, particularly all state federations and all metropolitan communities, as well as the unaffiliated Jewish organizations:

> Zionist Federation of Germany, Central Association of Jews in Germany, Federal Union of Jewish War Veterans, Association for Liberal Judaism, the Organized Orthodox Community, Union of Jewish Women, Federal Commission of Jewish Youth Organizations.[5]

4. These were Hitler's words when he presented the Nuremberg Laws to the Reichstag at the Nazi party rally on September 15, 1935.
5. All state federations of Gemeinden, all major-city Gemeinden, and these national organizations signed this program.

The most urgent tasks of the Reichsvertretung, which it will pursue with full commitment, energetically following the avenues it has previously taken, are:

(1) Our own Jewish educational system must serve to train the young to become religiously secure, upright Jews. It must be a source of strength for meeting the heavy demands life will make of them due to conscious adherence to the Jewish community, due to work for the Jewish present and faith in the Jewish future. Beyond the transmission of knowledge, the Jewish school must also serve in the systematic preparation for future occupations. With regard to fitness for emigration, particularly to Palestine, the main emphasis will be placed on guidance toward manual occupations and on the study of the Hebrew language. Education and vocational training of girls must be directed to preparing them for fulfilling their responsibilities as upholders of the family and mothers of the next generation.

An independent cultural reconstruction must provide opportunities for the participation of artistically and culturally creative Jews and must serve the cultural autonomy of the Jews in Germany.

(2) The intensified need for emigration is to be accorded large-scale planning, particularly as it applies to youth, and will embrace Palestine above all but will also include all other countries that may come into consideration. To this planning belong the solicitude for augmenting emigration opportunities; training for occupations appropriate for emigration, particularly agriculture and manual trades; the creation of opportunities for mobilizing and liquidating the property of financially independent persons; expansion of existing transfer opportunities and creation of new ones.

(3) Support and care of the needy, the sick, and the aged, must be assured through further systematic expansion of the Jewish welfare services provided by the communities, supplementing government social services.

(4) An impoverished community cannot cope with these varied and difficult tasks. The Reichsvertretung will try by every means to safeguard the economic capability of Jews by seeing that the existing means of livelihood remain. The economically disabled are to be strengthened through further development of measures for economic aid, such as employment referral, economic consultation, and personal or mortgage loans.

(5) The spirited progress in the upbuilding of Jewish Palestine gives us strength in the present and hope for the future. To involve Jewry in Germany even more closely with this development than

heretofore, the Reichsvertretung as a body will join the Palestine Foundation Fund (*Keren Hayesod*),[6] and emphatically urges Jewish communities and organizations to follow its example. The Reichsvertretung stands ready to establish organizational links between the institutions of Jewry in Germany and the Foundation Fund in Palestine.

In full awareness of the magnitude of the responsibility and of the gravity of the task, the Reichsvertretung summons all Jewish men and women and all of Jewish youth to unity, to a Jewish morale, to strictest self-discipline, and to the highest selflessness.

Pursuant to a motion made in the Reichsvertretung's executive board, the Reichsvertretung itself, the state federations, and the communities are requested to undertake, promptly and in close co-operation, such organizational and personnel measures as are required within Jewish organizations to assure vigorous and consistent execution of the new program by all Jewish agencies.

THE CENTRAL-VEREIN BALANCE SHEET, 1935

On October 21, 1935, the plenary assembly of the Central-Verein adopted a change in name and bylaws. . . .[7]

The Verein's new name may—indeed, must—now be used. The old one belongs to the past, to history. This change of name was an external and internal necessity. Realities had to be taken into account, and the necessary conclusions had to be drawn from them. What has now become part of the Verein's bylaws over and above the change of name, merely represents a codification, the legal mooring, of what has already occurred. The legal procedure is the formal conclusion of previous development.

The Central-Verein's political activity, which before January 30, 1933, was in the forefront, has been completely halted. Its continuation would have been merely quixotic.

6. The Palestine Foundation Fund was the major fund-raising arm of the Zionist movement for the purchase of land in Palestine.

7. The full name of the organization, from the time of its founding in 1893, had been *Central-Verein deutscher Staatsbürger jüdischen Glaubens*—Central Association of German Citizens of Jewish Faith. In consequence of the Nuremberg Laws, the Jews were no longer permitted to describe themselves as Germans.

Our relations with the German world around us have changed deeply. We have been eliminated from many important areas of life. What is more, the attitude toward us has decisively altered. These realities have redefined our thoughts, feelings, and behavior. It would be undignified and foolish if we were not to comprehend this experience in its full significance.

The slogan of "assimilationism," once formulated in the Jewish camp and, surprisingly, still surviving, has always been off the mark. Since its foundation, the Central-Verein has been a zealous fighter against any apostasy, any desertion, against self-surrendering assimilation. It has always called for preservation of our individuality, deep-going knowledge of our past, ties with our ancestral heritage— in short, Jewish consciousness, pride in our unique history, and the will to shape a Jewish future.

The nineteenth century—long before the founding of the Central-Verein—brought about among Jews in Germany a union of Jewishness and European culture. This historical synthesis has, in the course of many generations, grown organically and struck deep roots. All Jewish ideologies acknowledge this. Nor is there any disagreement that Jewish content was slighted in this process. More and more vigorously over the years, the Central-Verein has championed its enrichment.

Internal Jewish differences revolve around altogether other questions. What is at issue is the meaning and content of Judaism and Jewish existence. The Central-Verein denies that the nature and purpose of the Jewish community are analogous to those of all the other peoples, or should parallel them. The Central-Verein cannot concede that the Jews constitute a nation among the nations, or that they must strive for normalization. It maintains that Jews, by their natural gifts, their world view, and their fate, constitute a community of a distinctive type. We Jews have always stood in the cold draft of world history. For thousands of years we have lived in the Diaspora. And thanks to this fact Judaism and Jewry have neither died out nor atrophied. We have no nomadic inclinations. Not on our own impulse did we time and again take up the wanderer's staff. Historic causes forced us to part from our chosen homes.

The controversy about this question is of fundamental importance. Its significance is not to be underrated. Neither should it be overrated, particularly as regards the tasks of the present. For there is unanimous agreement on the following:

(1) Our living space in Germany has narrowed. It does not suffice even for our numbers reduced by over 100,000 persons through emigration and excess of deaths. Whoever cannot find any means of existence in Germany and can hope to build a modest existence abroad or even hope just to get by, will emigrate.

These prerequisites will apply mainly to young people.

(2) Emigration has to be carried out systematically and after careful preparation. Adequate linguistic knowledge is indispensable. Good occupational training for one's future surroundings is extremely desirable.

(3) The task thus set for us can be constructively solved only through systematic cooperation among all Jewish agencies and assocations.

We are deeply indebted to the English and American Jews who founded the Council for German Jewry. They have undertaken to raise three million pounds, an amount which will enable an additional 100,000 Jews to emigrate from Germany over a period of five years. In addition, gratitude and appreciation are due the Jewish aid groups abroad, first and foremost the American Joint Distribution Committee, the Central British Fund, and the Jewish Colonization Association, to name the best known.

(4) Palestine itself cannot possibly absorb this stream of migrants. In distributing immigration certificates for Palestine, the situation of the Jews in Germany has been given exceptional consideration. It is to be expected that nothing will change in this. But the Jewish Agency cannot distribute more certificates than it received from the Mandatory Power. It must take into account that in oher countries as well, spiritual and economic needs are driving Jews to emigrate. The number of those seeking a new home under compulsion is frighteningly large. For many, Palestine is in the foreground of their range of vision. What percentage of these will be admitted into Palestine may be variously estimated. Certainly only a modest proportion of the applicants can count on having their hopes fulfilled.

The necessity for planning outside the borders of Palestine and creating new settlements in the Diaspora is thus beyond controversy. Differences arise about the extent of this necessity. Here views are quite varied and differ widely. To present all their shadings is hardly possible as well as unnecessary. Suffice it simply to juxtapose the extreme antitheses. Briefly put, they come to this: Is the inevitable resettlement of Jews in all continents, outside Palestine, an unavoidable evil, to be accepted with regret and resignation? Or is

this a promising solution of present difficulties, from a Jewish viewpoint, and therefore to be welcomed?

For countries whose Jewish population is declining by emigration, this question is of no significance whatsoever. Their concern
is only that the Jewish sector diminish. For the future of Judaism
and Jewry, the problem is basic.

In the purely Jewish aspects of this conflict of opinion, the
Central-Verein stands for the idea of the Diaspora. It by no means
fails to appreciate that Palestine holds a special place among the
countries of immigration. Palestine has strengthened Jewry and is
an essential factor in its survival. The Central-Verein follows with
warmest interest every advance in the building of Jewish Palestine.
The concerns for the Jewish future in Palestine weigh also upon
us. . . . The Central-Verein is gratified that there are, and will be,
in the Palestinian crucible in which the immigrants will be recast
many Jews who used to live in Germany. It hopes that the spirit
and character, the abilities and knowledge of these Jews will be
given their due in the fusion process. . . .

Affirmation of the Diaspora idea does not conflict with this.
Notwithstanding all our confidence in the energy, discipline, and
achievement of the present and future Yishuv and in the British
Mandatory Power's faithfulness to its task, it does not seem de-
fensible to stake everything on one card.

Hypothetical aspects weigh even more heavily. It is not true
that only in Palestine can Jews escape superficiality, unproductivity,
assimilation, and finally apostasy. Were there even a grain of truth
in this, there would be neither Jews nor Judaism after seventy
generations of living in the Diaspora. In reality, in the vast span of
2,000 years neither the vitality nor the will to live has flagged among
Jews. Can and do the Jewish champions of the contrary view seriously maintain that seventy earlier generations have produced
nothing lasting, nothing valuable? History, that great teacher, re-
turns a different verdict. Blunderings in the nineteenth century
have been incorrectly regarded as inevitable. Instead of investigating
and examining if and how they can be avoided in the future, consideration is given only a radical cure. The baby is to be thrown
out with the bath water.

It has often been stated that in the era of our rise in the larger
society we neglected our Judaism. There were laments that for all

too many our sacred books, our beautiful old customs, even our history remained unknown or were no longer meaningful—that only for a few was Jewry still a creative force, an affirmative destiny. There were summonses for self-examination and concentration, appeals to recover the firm support of our Jewishness.

This appeal did not remain unheard. That can be confirmed, even though the effect is not measurable or assessable. At least since the moment when we were denied the right to continue to regard the land we had loved since earliest childhood as our own world, the turning back has been unmistakable. The much maligned Age of Emancipation is not exhaustively judged by stating that serious mistakes were committed on the Jewish side. If light and shade are to be apportioned fairly, we must also recognize the positive significance that the last 150 years have had for us. This, too, has often been discussed in the *Central-Verein-Zeitung*. Three points in particular should be stressed:

(1) The "Wissenschaft vom Judentum" in Germany in this epoch became the center of Jewish scholarship everywhere.[8]

(2) Those who resisted the attractions of modernity and remained faithful to the old banner acquired resistance against hard knocks through the union of their Jewish values with eagerly absorbed German education and culture, a posture of which they surely need not be ashamed.

(3) Living and working, learning and creating in the German, in the European, world have not only strengthened character but also widened perspectives and increased insight. In free competition, to which we were admitted in a lesser or greater degree, our abilities grew, our capacities in all directions rose.

In the accounting of this era, the loss of Jewish content is balanced by a very valuable gain. This insight, too, prompts us to support a continuation of the historical Diaspora line but not at the expense and to the detriment of Palestine, to whose building we wish to contribute according to our means. Rather, it is our desire to further both streams of migration. . . .

The following considerations guide us: Whoever imbues young people with the idea that Palestine alone must be their goal, that in

---

8. Usually *Wissenschaft des Judentums*, "the science of Judaism." The scientific study of Jewish history and literature originated with the *Verein für Kultur und Wissenschaft der Juden* (Society for the Culture and Science of the Jews), founded by Leopold Zunz and a circle of his friends in Berlin in 1819.

any other country they cannot escape superficiality, unproductivity, assimilation, and apostasy, bears a heavy responsibility. He deprives those, for whom the gates of Palestine will not open, of the strength and ability to adjust to another place. Having tasted of this draught, they will spend their lives lamenting the lost paradise. Again, is it right to pronounce a moral death sentence upon those not fit or not young enough to take part in the upbuilding of Palestine? And, finally, there is no escaping this question: Shall the emigrants consider the country that receives them now a way station, looking upon their sojourn there as an episode which it is their dearest wish to keep as brief as possible? Whoever brings this about, even thoughtlessly, takes heavy responsibility on himself. Economically and spiritually only those will succeed who are determined to settle—as Jews—in their newly chosen homes, to strike roots there.

If this is not their attitude, if they feel that they are guests for a time, with their eyes and their hearts set on goals elsewhere, then any wind will blow them away, then they will be regarded, wherever segregation of peoples is not the norm, as an undesirable accretion. And rightly so. For the meaning of the Diaspora lies in living, not next to one another, but with one another.

The gigantic plan of the Council for German Jewry proposes to help 100,000 Jews emigrate from Germany over five years. This goal can be reached only if the necessary funds are raised and if sufficient opportunities for immigration are opened up. Both conditions must be met. The immense sum of £3,000,000, by far the largest ever provided for a Jewish purpose, is to be raised within Jewish circles. We hope and expect that this difficult task will be solved. But whether it will also be possible to obtain the needed opportunities for settlement is an open question. The whole planet is being systematically surveyed. There is no lack of effort. Connections are being utilized wherever they exist. Yet any prediction is risky. Only this much is certain: To go beyond fulfillment of the Council's plan is a practical impossibility. That means: Even if the plan is fully realized, a substantial portion of the Jews now residing in the territory of the Reich will have to remain here. No one familiar with conditions can deny this.

The Reichsvertretung program, which the Central-Verein has approved and signed, enumerates the manifold difficult tasks which fate has posed for the greatly reduced and still dwindling Jewish community in Germany. The Reichsvertretung proceeded on the understanding that the laws enacted in Nuremberg by the Reichstag, which have hit us Jews exceedingly hard, "are to create a basis on which a tolerable relationship between the German and the Jewish peoples will be possible." As a prerequisite, the Reichsvrtretung expressed the hope "that the Jews in Germany will be allowed the moral and economic means of existence." Also it rightly stressed the necessity "of ensuring the economic capability of the Jews by seeing that the existing means of livelihood remain."

This important area has been assigned to the Central-Verein. Its function is to provide legal, economic, and moral aid for Jews living in Germany, for all, without distinction, whether or not they are Verein members. Its duty is to advise, to support, and to help. This field of endeavor must be painstakingly cultivated, with unremitting industry.

Uncounted cases of greatly varying significance have to be taken care of. This motley changing life keeps producing new problems of vital importance for large circles. To this must be added many, many needs that are tangential to our community but central for the persons concerned.

We must do justice to all. Not one must be given short shrift. Our staff members are ever conscious of the ties that unite us with every Jew seeking our advice. In last year's Rosh Hashana greeting, the basic attitude of the Central-Verein loyalists is briefly and aptly summarized: "Your experiences are also our experiences, your suffering is our suffering, your strength is our strength." That is how we shall keep it. Our name has changed; our loyalty, our readiness continue unaltered. . . .

For us Jews in Germany, life has become hard. How we bear this fate depends on ourselves. If we succeed in remaining eager to live and open to life, then we will pass the test. Then we will be able to rekindle the flame in our hearts. Only then can we face the future with truly Jewish confidence.

6 THE ORDEALS OF
THE GHETTOS IN EASTERN EUROPE

INTRODUCTION

WHEN THE GERMANS invaded Poland on September 1, 1939, two million Jews came under their authority. The German assault on the Soviet Union that began in June 1941 brought another three million Jews under German rule. Everywhere German occupation policies, reinforced by the age-old anti-Semitism of the indigenous populations, singled out the Jews for mockery, misery, and misfortune, torture and torment. Jews everywhere were starved and robbed, seized for forced labor and prevented from healing their sick, beaten and killed in random acts of violence.

Jewish fate became the subject of plaintive and lugubrious songs which coursed through the ghettos and labor camps. The anonymous song of the Chełm ghetto, drawing upon verses from Psalms, epitomized the powerlessness and piteousness of the Jews whose only hope for rescue was the God of Israel. In contrast, the song of the Bialystok ghetto, where thousands of Jews sweated and slaved in factories to produce goods for the German war economy, rang a more modern and optimistic note, turning for deliverance to the Red Army.

Still, the Jews themselves were never passive. To provide food, shelter, and care, to alleviate the desolation and despair brought on by the Germans, Jews everywhere created, or recreated, institutions that would strengthen and bolster the community. The Judenrat (Jewish council) which every community formed under German orders, as prescribed by Heydrich on September 21, 1939, was regarded by the Jewish population as the successor to the traditional kehilla, *the autonomous Jewish association that had for centuries regulated the internal affairs of Jewish communities in Central and Eastern Europe. From the start, the Jewish communal leaders who directed the Judenräte regarded their chief tasks as the protection of the Jewish community and the care of its sick and needy.*

Everywhere Jewish self-help institutions came into being, growing out of the prewar welfare and philanthropic societies. The most extensive network was in the Generalgouvernement, known as Żydowska Samopomoc Społeczna—ŻSS *(Jewish communal self-help). From its nucleus in besieged Warsaw in 1939, the ŻSS grew to over 400 branches in 1941; the largest and most effective was in Warsaw, called* Żydowskie Towarzystwo Opieki Społecznej—ŻTOS *(Jewish society for social welfare).*

The Judenräte and the ŻSS, in joint or supplementary programs, spent the bulk of their energies and meager resources trying to mitigate the misery that had become universal among the Jews. The most unfortunate were the refugees, uprooted by the Germans from thousands of villages and small towns and sometimes even large cities. Cast out of their homes, stripped of their worldly goods, over 300,000 Jews—one tenth of Polish Jewry—became refugees in alien ghettos, dependent for bread and shelter upon the charitable good will of strangers. Every ghetto tried to bring comfort to the refugees and provide them with the bare necessities of existence, but their swelling numbers overtaxed local resources and facilities. Housed in large enclosures—one-time schools or unused theaters—without heat or adequate plumbing, the refugees expired at rates that staggered the statisticians of mortality. No commentary is needed on the terse ŻTOS report on refugee care in a Warsaw ghetto precinct for January 1942.

In the Vilna ghetto, where the Jewish population was relatively small—cut down from over 60,000 to barely 12,000 during the first six months of the murderous German occupation—and where hunger was never so desperate as in Warsaw or Lodz, health and social welfare nevertheless were the central concerns of the Judenrat and of private charitable agencies. The monthly reports of the Vilna Judenrat's Health Department for September 1942 and of its Social Welfare Department for April 1943 show how the traditional communal responsibilities in these fields had extended to far-reaching municipal obligations.

The Jewish child, the embodiment of the Jewish future, was in the forefront of all health and welfare work. In the General-gouvernement, with about 1,600,000 Jews, children amounted to one fourth of the population. Warsaw alone had some 100,000 children under 15, most of whom needed some form of welfare assistance. Of the dozens of child-care institutions and boarding homes, the most famous was the Dom Sierot *(Orphans' home), directed by Dr. Janusz Korczak (1878?–1942). Pediatrician, educator, writer, Korczak had won fame beyond Poland itself; his prewar radio broadcasts in Warsaw as "The Old Doctor of the Radio" had made him a household name among the populace. Despite the risks and hardships of the German occupation, Korczak was indefatigable in his efforts to provide for the children under his care. In the elliptical and allusive staccato style that characterized his writing and gave it a distinctive flavor, Korczak appealed to the public at large for help —for money, for food, for clothing. But his protective guardianship could not forestall the Germans from liquidating the Dom Sierot in August 1942, when they were putting an end to all children's institutions. Korczak stayed with his children until the very end, maintaining their courage as he led the procession to the "resettlement" trains.*

Hunger ravaged the ghettos. It was deliberate German policy to kill as many Jews as possible by "natural" means. In all ghettos the rabbis were lenient in their halachic rulings on permitted foods in view of the danger to life posed by the German policy. Everywhere Jewish law was relaxed so as to preserve life. Such decisions were rarely rendered in writing, lest a published sanction to suspend religious law, even under dire circumstances, be abused—hence the careful wording of the decision by the rabbinical council in the Lodz ghetto to permit pregnant women or people in a weakened condition to eat non-kosher meat. The fact that the rabbis issued this decision in written form was indicative of the extent of rampant hunger in the ghetto and the threat it posed to life.

Only the illegal smuggling of food into the ghettos spared most Jews from starvation. The professional smugglers—tough, daring, ingenious, taking immense risks for immense profits—provided the ghetto not just with supplementary food for subsistence, but also with delicacies and luxuries which the ghetto's better-off consumed without thought for the morrow. Peretz Opoczynski (1892–1943), a Warsaw journalist whose contemporaneous reports on ghetto life are vignettes of social history, in an account of smuggling written in 1941, described the organization and mechanics of large-scale food smuggling, with vivid portraits of the smugglers drawn against the backdrop of hunger and death.

Besides the professionals, young children—even five-year olds—constituted a large segment of the smuggler-class. Small and nimble, they squeezed through holes in the ghetto wall or under the barbed-wire entanglements to bring back potatoes and onions to feed their families or sell on the ghetto streets. Henryka Lazawert, a young poet murdered in Treblinka, July 1942, celebrated these child smugglers in a poem, "The Little Smuggler," which was frequently recited at literary entertainments in the ghetto.

Entertainment, recreation, cultural activities, ranging from sports and vaudeville to high culture, helped the ghetto Jews transcend the miseries of their prison environment. In all ghettos the Jewish community rallied to preserve the fundamental institutions of civilized existence. The religious, educational, and cultural activities of the ghetto Jews were permitted in some places, forbidden in others, tolerated at some times and persecuted at other times. Nevertheless, the Jews continued as best they could to maintain their institutions, even in a clandestine way, even in skeletal form. Secular and traditional education was provided for the children, even though in many ghettos in the Generalgouvernement the Germans forbade schooling for Jewish children altogether. Theatrical productions, concerts, art exhibits, literary readings, circulating libraries gave the ghetto Jews surcease from the dreadfulness of everyday living and transported them to other worlds, other times. The report of the Vilna Judenrat's Culture Department shows how tenaciously the Vilna Jews clung to their cultural traditions despite the upheavals in their existence.

A particularly hazardous undertaking was the attempt on the part of the prewar Jewish political parties to maintain their organizations. In independent Poland these parties, from the Aguda and the Revisionists on the right to the Jewish Labor Bund and the Labor Zionists on the left, had been the defenders of the Jewish populace. With the German occupation they became outlawed. The leftist parties particularly were under relentless German harassment, with the police constantly on the lookout for Jewish socialist leaders. Nevertheless, the parties tried to preserve at least nuclei of their organizations, to protect and care for their leaders and active members, and to continue to propagate their beliefs and principles. Most successful in this regard were the left-wing parties whose oppositional stance in prewar Poland had prepared them to function illegally and clandestinely. The Jewish Labor Bund, a mass-based Socialist party which before the war had won pluralities in municipal and kehilla elections in major Polish cities, continued some of its activities underground, but its major endeavor was to extend help to its inner circle of activists. The Bund maintained contact with the Polish underground and was represented in the Polish Parliament-in-Exile in London. At opportune times the Bund sent reports through underground channels to its fraternal parties abroad. The letter of March 16, 1942, starkly portrays the German atrocities and mass killings, and also the structure of the party's underground organization and activities, its desperate problems, its relation with other Jewish political parties and with the Polish underground.

The ghetto became a proving ground of ethical standards and religious absolutes. In 1941, Oneg Shabbat, the clandestine archival society founded by Emanuel Ringelblum, Jewish historian and Left Labor Zionist leader (1900–1944), sent out a questionnaire to leading Jewish personalities, probing their views on ghetto life and morality. The respondents included Hillel Zeitlin (1872–1942), Orthodox writer and philosopher, and Dr. Israel Milejkowski (d. January 1943), then head of the public-health and hospital departments of the Warsaw ghetto Judenrat. Each discussed the ghetto in terms of his own moral and religious values, praising and condemning Jewish behavior in adversity.

Daily familiarity with suffering and the immediacy of the terror under which most Jews lived limited the perspective from which they viewed their experiences. A few Jewish intellectuals, however, saw Jewish fate in the light of millennial Jewish history and under the aspect of eternity. One of these was Zelig Kalmanovich (1881–1943), a Jewish scholar with wide-ranging interests, from ancient Jewish history to modern linguistics, one of the guiding lights of the Yiddish Scientific Institute (YIVO) in Vilna since

1929. In the Vilna ghetto he kept a diary in which he recorded the events of the time and his reflections on their significance. In one entry he wrote: "To be sure, history rages now, a war is waged against the Jews, but the war is not only against one member of the triad but against the entire one: against the Torah and God, against the moral law and the Creator. Can anyone still doubt which side is the stronger?"

A SONG OF THE CHEŁM GHETTO [1]

O look from heaven and behold,[2]
Look down from the skies and see!
For we have become a derision,
A derision among the nations.
We are surely a laughingstock to them.
We are accounted as sheep to the slaughter.
O Creator, how can You look upon this?
Indeed, we never were at ease,
We were always to the slaughter.

> *Refrain*
> Therefore we plead with You ever:
> Help us now, Guardian of Israel,
> Take notice now of our tears,
> For still do we proclaim "Hear O Israel!"
> O, take notice, Guardian of this nation.
> Show all the peoples that You are our God,
> We have indeed none other, just You alone,
> Whose Name is One.

Strangers say there is no salvation.
The nations say that for us
There is no hope.
We may be driven,
We may be tormented.
We have no one to whom
We can complain.
But we surely know
That You are in heaven!
Of You the Bible says:

1. Variants of this song were sung throughout Eastern Europe. One version was recorded as a children's song in Rumania.
2. The italicized lines indicate Biblical verses cited in Hebrew in the Yiddish text.

He doth neither slumber nor sleep.
You must surely protect
Your children.
Therefore we know
That You are in heaven—
With miracles and wonders.

    Refrain
    Spare us O Lord,
    Surrender us not to their hand.
Have pity, do not yield us
Into their hands.
Wherefore should the nations say:
'Where is their God?'
That is always their cry.
O my Jews, my Jews, what are you doing here?
Gather your packs and take ye to Zion!
We would have fled
But the way is not open.
Why do You let them treat us thus?

    Refrain

A SONG OF THE BIALYSTOK GHETTO

In the ghetto factories we slave,
We make shoes and we produce,
We knit and sew and weave.
And for that we earn a pass
For a ride to Treblinka, alas.

Alas, how bitter are the times,
But deliverance is on its way;
It's not so far away.
The Red Army will come to free us,
It's not so far away.

※

REFUGEE CARE IN THE WARSAW GHETTO
    JANUARY 1942

January 1942 was the hardest month for the refugees generally and especially for the residents of the locale at Dzika and Niska Streets. There is no misfortune and illness which they did not experience in the time they have spent in Warsaw.

Hunger, sickness, and want are their constant companions and death is the only visitor in their homes.

In the last months of the past year the typhus epidemic raged there, not bypassing child or adult; hundreds of families were shattered—fathers and mothers passed away, children's lives were cut down, and the last Mohicans among the aged are expiring most hideously.

This January there were only isolated cases of typhus in the locales mentioned, yet the refugees fell like flies from cold and exhaustion, the mortality reached 539, or 18 percent of their number.

Now the newly organized body for refugee care is working in the locales, trying to alleviate the poverty and improve the sorrowful plight of the unfortunate refugees.

The most serious affliction now in the locales is dysentery and its accompanying rash.

The number of refugees declines from day to day. Now, as of the end of January, there are 2,977 refugees in the locales. The locales at Dzika 7, 9, and 11 have been liquidated. A large children's residential center is being organized at No. 9.

If help for the refugee locale is not increased, if the sanitary-hygienic conditions are not improved, if the indifference on the part of the Warsaw Jewish community to the expiring refugees is not combatted and the mortality is not halted, this locale, which is dubbed a "refugee town," will become a "refugee village."

The situation at the end of the month is as follows:
9 Stawki Street
The total number of refugees at the end of the month—1,100; rooms —170. The rooms are generally not heated. There is no heated room

at all in the locale. No running water, and toilets are not working. Typhus—isolated cases. As of now, there are among the refugees 200 who are not exempt from the meal charges. The number of deaths in this locale was 280, the mortality here the highest: 25 *percent of all residents.* . . .

The highest mortality turns out to be among children. The next highest is the age group 20–40. Refugees of advanced age are rare cases.

The deceased refugees come from: Rawa, Łowicz, Zakroczym, Lipno, Skierniewice, Nowy Dwór, Bieżuń, Warka, Góra-Kalwaria, Sokołów, Cracow, Aleksandrów, Głowno, Sierpce, Żyrardów, Kałuszyn, Mszczonów, Błonie, Drobin, Kowal, Wyszków, Kutno, Częstochowa, Leszno, Raciąż, Słupce, Błędów, Grójec, Płońsk, Otwock, Tarczyn, Stryków, Zgierz.

3 Dzika Street
Number of residents—1,613; rooms—153. Only the orphans' rooms and children's club room are heated. No running water, and toilets are not working. About 10 percent are exempt from meal charges. The locale has a diverse population (employable, beggars, and ordinary criminals), as the locale directors remark, because of poor nutrition, lack of occupation, and low cultural standard. . . .

Unfortunately for the locale, persons stricken with dysentery remain here and even persons with broken limbs are not sent to the hospital. The locale still lacks plank beds. The refugees are in rags and tatters. Some are completely naked.

The number of deceased during the month was 183. The mortality rate is 11.5 percent. . . .

9 Dzika Street
The locale at 9 Dzika is being transformed into a large children's residence. The building is dirty, corridors and stairs with mud and excrement. The upper stories are being prepared for the children. Meantime the children are in the most horrible sanitary conditions. Nutrition is inadequate, but tolerable in comparison to living conditions in the locales.

The number of children is 191. During the month 87 children were admitted. The children come from the following cities: Poznań, Zgierz, Lodz, Brzeziny, Żuromin, Stryków, Aleksandrów,

Sierpce, and Kałuszyn, Besides the cities mentioned, there are also a small number of children from Warsaw.

No running water, and toilets are not working. Dysentery stalks the children's center. A large number of children suffer from rashes. The children are naked and barefoot. Several children sleep on one plank bed.

During the month 63 children died.

The mortality among children has reached 33 percent of the total.

The children still do not get supplementary food rations from the management.

19 Dzika Street
The locale holds 136 refugees. Rooms—8. The rooms are unheated. Running water works partially. One toilet is in operation. There have been no typhus cases, but, in contrast, there have been three cases of dysentery. There are also cases where the refugee does not get a midday meal, because some are not exempt from meal charges.

Only the children's club room is heated.

There were 13 deaths, among them five children, 10 percent of all. . . .

Some comments on conclusions to be drawn:

a. Births: O. In December, one birth—a stillborn child.
b. Deaths: Children up to 14 years—42 percent.
c. Deaths are doubtless the result of harsh living and sanitary-hygienic conditions in the above-mentioned locales.

HEALTH CARE IN THE VILNA GHETTO
SEPTEMBER 1942

I   *Public Health-Epidemiology Section*
    (1) The Public Health Inspectorate intensified its activity in September [1942], mainly in the area of public-health supervision of the nutrition agencies and institutions. This was done because of the danger of a rise in stomach and intestinal diseases usually occur-

ring in the fall. With three fewer working days than in August, the number of public-health inspections was the same as in the previous month. The number of public-health reports was twice as large (643 instead of 348).

(2) The *Vaccination Center* renewed its campaign to vaccinate against stomach-typhus persons employed in institutions handling food and hitherto not vaccinated. This campaign embraced nearly 500 persons.

(3) The *Disinfection Center*, beside carrying out disinfections inside the ghetto, also carried out large-scale disinfection of articles sent by a municipal agency outside the ghetto.

(4) The *School Medical Center* continued its work, examining children of school age who do not attend school. Because of possible contagion (scarlet fever), the child-care agencies, the library, reading room, sport club, and children's club were closed.

(5) The *Skin Diseases Center* had significantly less work in September because scabies in the ghetto has been virtually eradicated, and the only sick who were treated were almost exclusively from the outside labor camps. The staff has been cut to one nurse.

(6) Attendance at the *Public Health Stations* [baths and delousing] was low at the beginning of the month, but at the approach of the deadline for the issuance of bread cards for October, because of the announced sanctions that bread cards would be withheld from those who did not have a receipt for a bath visit, the office of the Public Health Stations was besieged and the baths began to operate full time. It is expected that in October required bath visits will be carried out regularly and thoroughly.

(7) The *laundry* washed 406 kg. more loads than had been expected.[3] Despite difficult local and hygienic conditions, the laundry, beginning September 16 (in the course of the last ten days), washed 46 loads of 10–12 kg. each. For this, 3–4 washerwomen were employed. Steps have been taken to open a second large laundry. Suitable premises have been found at Disna and Yatkeva Streets, and the Technical Department is in charge of renovations.

(8) The *epidemiology program* consisted mainly of halting the incidence of diphtheria and scarlet fever. The number of

---

3. Originally set up to wash and disinfect the laundry of the sick and their families, the communal laundry was later expanded to serve the entire ghetto population.

diphtheria cases is now minimal and the number of scarlet-fever cases is constantly decreasing. Dysentery and infectious gastroenteritis were practically nonexistent. The commission appointed by the Ghetto Chief [4] to take the necessary public-health epidemiological measures in the Jewish camps outside the ghetto has prepared the necessary instructions, questionnaires, and statistical tables. The commission will shortly visit the labor camps at their sites.

II   *Health Institutions*

(1) *Hospital*   Current renovation projects have been continued. Because of difficulties on the part of the Technical Department, renovations in the new premises of the laboratory remained in the initial stage. For the same reason, the planned renovation of the pharmacy could not be started.

Partially completed already is the work of preparing the hospital building for the winter. The windows for the most part have been taken care of. Blackout of the windows has been completed. Some of the ovens have been repaired. The roof has been checked and repaired. The cooking vessels in the kitchen have been recoated. Various minor plumbing repairs were made. Because of dampness in the food storage area, a partial transfer was made to other premises.

(2) *Clinic*   Renovation of the additional two new rooms on the ground floor has been partially completed.

Inventory was supplemented with a number of new instruments: forceps, probes, scissors, drains, and others. Received also were several new hospital gowns, table covers, window shades, and the like.

Blackout of the windows has been partially completed.

An exact inventory of the household and medical equipment has been made.

III   *Child Care*

(1) *Children's Consultation*   The prophylactic campaign to combat skin diseases which this agency conducted among the children under its supervision brought positive results: only two scabies cases were noted in September. In contrast, doctors visiting sick children in their homes found several cases of contagious chil-

4. Jacob Gens, a Revisionist from Kovno, was appointed commandant of the Jewish police when the Vilna ghetto was set up in September 1941. He later usurped authority from the Judenrat. He was usually designated as Ghetto Chief.

dren's diseases, like diphtheria (1 case), scarlet fever (5 cases), chicken pox (14 cases).

The Consultation distributes cards for milk and dairy products to the children, according to which the dairy kitchen issues milk and dairy products especially allocated for children. All children are also examined by the doctors and taken under the supervision of the Consultation.

During September this program was carried on only by the normal staff of the institution; for that reason, the number of outpatient visits made was smaller than in the previous month.

The work of the Consultation has been made difficult because of the stifling gases which get into the premises from the workshops of the Technical Department, above which the Children's Consultation is located. For this reason the quarters of the Children's Consultation must be moved.

(2) *Children's Home*   In September there was one case of death in the institution, a child eleven months old died of rachitis. Two problem children were transferred to the institution at 4 Straszun Street.

In the report period two cases of contagious diseases occurred: one of diphtheria and one of scarlet fever. Because of the scarlet-fever case a strict quarantine was observed in the institution for ten days.

The older children are being established gradually in vocational trades. In addition to the two boys who have been working since last month, two more have been placed: one works in the shoemaking workshop and the other in the Technical Department's tinsmith shop. Two older girls are waiting for the opening of the new tailoring shop, where they are listed as applicants.

(3) *Day Care Center*   The institution was opened September 1 this year. It is intended for 100 children from 6 months to 6 years old. The children are admitted into the institution in stages: in the first week of the month 30 children were admitted; by the 15th there were 50 children, and by October 1 there were 70 (12 infants and 58 older children).

The children are mostly half-orphaned and of working mothers. The charge is 1.50 RM per day. The fee for most children is paid by the Department for Social Welfare. Only a small percentage of the children pay the entire fee.

The children remain in the institution from 7 a.m. to 6 p.m.

They are fed three times a day, according to a specially calculated ration. After the midday meal the children rest for two hours.

The children are divided by age into three groups: a) infants—from 6 months to 2 years; b) from 2 years to 3 years, and c) from 3 years to 6 years. Educational work with the children is appropriate to their age. During the first month of the institution's existence, pedagogical work with the older children was conducted with a view to their participating in the organization of the institution: decorating the rooms, appointing monitors in the rooms, helping the smaller children, self-registration, etc.

Great stress is laid on the children's cleanliness. The doctor and the nurse check the children's cleanliness daily.

The internal work of the Day Care Center is closely linked with the work outside. The nurse visits the children's homes. Not only are the children examined, but also the closest members of the family, to prevent infectious diseases as far as possible.

IV *Vitamin Laboratory*
The production of vitamin products has been moved to new quarters on 1 Szpitalna Street.

A popularizing propaganda campaign was conducted among the population with the aid of special posters, announcements, and items in *Geto-yedies* and *Folksgezunt*.[5]

The distribution of vitamin products among the population markedly increased during September. . . .

PROGRAM OF INNOVATIONS PLANNED FOR OCTOBER

(1) *Public Health-Epidemiology Section*   To conduct public-health inspections in the labor camps outside the ghetto, with a view to organizing a public-health and disinfection program.

To open a medical control center for workers and employees in agencies handling food, children's institutions, kindergartens, laundry, baths, and the like. The purpose of this control center is to prevent the spread of communicable diseases by employees of the enumerated institutions.

5. *Geto yedies* ("Ghetto News") was a weekly mimeographed news bulletin issued by the Judenrat. *Folksgezunt* ("People's Health"), a popular prewar journal on medicine and public health, published by the OSE, national Jewish health organization in Poland, continued to appear from time to time in the Vilna ghetto in mimeographed form, eighteen issues in all.

To continue the organizational projects with regard to the new laundry.

To open a seventh teahouse at 6 Umianski Street to supply the newly added ghetto district with hot and boiled water.

(2) *Hospital*   To continue the current renovations (painting of the halls).

To complete repairs of the new quarters of the analytical laboratory.

To complete the work of preparing the buildings of the hospital for the winter (checking the stoves, taking care of the windows and doors, and completing the blackout arrangements).

(3) *Clinic*   To finish renovations of the two new rooms on the ground floor.

To see to the windows, doors, stoves and blackout for the winter. To place small iron stoves in several rooms.

(4) *Children's Consultation*   Because of the stifling gases that rise from the workshops below into the Consultation, to transfer the agency to other quarters.

(5) *Children's Home*   Because the main hall of the agency is unsuitable (cold) for the winter, to obtain for the Children's Home an adjoining apartment (already approved by the Housing Department) and make the necessary repairs there.

(6) *Day Care Center*   To bring the number of children in the institution to the level originally planned, i.e., to 100.

To supply the institution with more bunk beds for the children's afternoon rest period. The children now sleep on blankets on the floor.

(7) *Vitamin Laboratory*   To organize the production and sale of vitamin D: to produce yeast-vitamin wafers treated with ultra-violet rays.

To conduct further researches in the use of hops for the production of toilet soap, hair ointment, wine, and other items.

October 5, 1942   [Signed]   S. Milkanowicki [6]
                                        Head of the Health Department

---

6. Dr. Uri Shabbetai Milkanowicki, Zionist for many years, vice-chairman of the Vilna Kehilla. An official of the Judenrat, he was active also in the underground resistance organization. He was deported to Estonia and from there to several labor camps. He died April 1945.

SOCIAL WELFARE IN THE VILNA GHETTO
APRIL 1943

April [1943] was one of the busiest months in the Department's activity. There was an increase both in the number of persons receiving the Department's assistance and in the amount of aid distributed. And this was related not only to the natural process of increasing impoverishment in the second year of the ghetto, but also because of the arrival in the Vilna ghetto of many Jews from the provincial ghettos and the camps at Rzesza, Waka,[7] etc.

In these circumstances, the Department was given the responsibility of providing emergency aid to all those who, from the first day of their arrival in the ghetto, were forced to apply for help. And in this way to relieve, as much as possible, the indigence of newcomers.

The activity of the Department showed itself in the assistance issued as follows:

1. Food distribution; 2. medical aid (hospital, clinic, pharmacy, baths); 3. rent assistance; 4. cash assistance; 5. assistance to camps; 6. assistance to the Day Care Center; 7. distribution of supplies; 8. child care; 9. miscellaneous aid.

FOOD DISTRIBUTION

The number of midday and evening meals dispensed during the month greatly exceeded 80,000. For many people who could not benefit from the midday meals because they work outside the ghetto, evening meals were substituted for midday meals. During the month over 12,000 evening meals were issued. In principle, either midday or evening meals were issued; in exceptional cases, both. Midday meals were issued in all ghetto kitchens (except at 13 Rudnicka Street). Children receive midday meals in the special children's kitchen at 12 Straszun Street. During the month over 18,000 midday meals were issued by the children's kitchen, i.e., 600 children benefit daily from the midday meals in the children's kitchens at the expense of the Department. Special assistance is also received by the students

---

7. Both were peat-digging labor camps, about fifteen kilometers from Vilna.

of the technical courses; besides regular assistance, they receive in addition coffee and bread.[8]

MEDICAL AID

The determination of the kind, the amount, the duration of medical assistance to be given is supervised by the doctor of the Department.

HOSPITAL

Every patient who is sent to the hospital or is already in the hospital under the auspices of the Social Welfare Department is examined by the doctor. After familiarizing himself with the patient's medical condition, the doctor determines the necessity and the duration of hospital treatment, eventually issues orders to discharge the patient when hospital treatment is no longer absolutely necessary and out-patient clinic treatment will do. The issuance of patent medicines and high-priced treatments is decided upon after joint consideration by the doctor of the Department and the duty doctor of the hospital. For this purpose a special regulation was worked out by the hospital director and the Director of the Department about the manner of admitting and treating patients who are sent for hospital treatment by the Social Welfare Department.

During the month 265 patients (not patients under observation) were treated at the expense of the Social Welfare Department. 52 patients were given X-ray treatments (X-ray diagnosis and X-ray therapy); besides that, 77 patients (not hospital patients) were treated with X-rays. The number of hospital days amounted to 4,675.

A special category of patients are those under observation, who are often hospitalized by force.[9] The costs for treating these patients are automatically charged to the account of Social Welfare. After the patients are discharged, a bill is submitted to the Department, which, after investigating the patient's economic situation, determines if it is possible to ask for reimbursement. Payments are collected by the Department.

8. The department also operated "teahouses," which provided hot boiled water cheaply by glass, kettle, or barrel.
9. The department for infectious diseases was called "Observation Department." To keep the Germans from knowing about the presence of patients with typhus and other infectious diseases in order to avert harsh German measures, the doctors officially diagnosed typhus as *"status febrilis"* (feverish condition).

CLINIC

The number of patients benefitting from medical assistance in the clinic was 649. The Department continued to hold to the principle of issuing the maximum medical aid to the needy.

In principle, an order is issued for one visit to the clinic. After the patient brings a statement from the clinic doctor specifying the length of time for which medical help is needed, an order is given for a period of medical treatment in the clinic. Beside usual treatment, such as visits by a doctor in the clinic or at home, other treatments are also given, like various methods of electrotherapy (diathermy, sweat baths, faradization, and the like).

PHARMACY

The number of prescriptions issued by the ghetto pharmacy at the expense of the Social Welfare Department increased. The number of prescriptions issued came to 760, in the amount of 1,844.10 RM. All prescriptions are checked by the doctor, who tries to substitute for the more expensive preparations, cheaper ones with the same curative properties.

BATH

Every month clients receive free bath tickets for the whole family. In the past months about 1000–1500 bath tickets were issued monthly. Issuance of bath tickets was halted to those persons who receive special tickets from the Sanitation Police.

RENT ASSISTANCE

An important item in the Department's budget is the issuance of assistance for payment of rent. The number of clients who submitted requests for reductions in rent increased considerably in the last month. In the past month about 1,850 requests were submitted regarding reductions in rent for 4,500 persons. In general, about 7,500 RM was distributed for this purpose. Requests are submitted through the building managers, who confirm exactly the number of persons and, as far as possible, also comment on the financial status of the clients.

CASH ASSISTANCE

Also during April cash assistance was given to clients of the Department of Social Welfare. The number of applicants in this month, in connection with the arrival of Jews from the provinces, increased. The total sum of cash assistance dispensed in April amounted to 6,388 RM.

CAMPS IN THE GHETTO

After their arrival in the Vilna ghetto, the Jews from the provinces were settled in closed camps, [and the Department undertook the] task of supervising sanitation in the camps, providing food, and generally concerning itself with the inmates. Within its capacity, the Department distributed soup twice daily, coffee once (in the morning), and bread. Beside that, they also received a larger amount of free medical care, which they very much needed. The Social Welfare Department also provided the camps with fuel, which enabled them to cook their own midday meals. The camps were supplied with an appropriate inventory, and small renovations were made (installing cooking stoves, bringing in electricity, and blackout, etc.). At the same time, plank beds were set up in all camps. . . .

CAMPS

Beside the above, assistance was distributed to other camps in the form of cash, supplies, and medicines. This aid is expected to increase in the future.

DAY CARE CENTER

Also in April assistance was distributed for the support of the children in the Day Care Center. The maximum assistance given is 1 RM per child per day.

There are now 130 children in the Day Care Center receiving assistance from the Social Welfare Department. The majority receives maximum aid (1 RM daily), a smaller number received 0.75 RM daily, and only a minimal number 0.50 RM.

SUPPLY DISTRIBUTION CENTER

The activity of the Supply Distribution Center increased enormously during the month. Most of the credits that had been expected to be used to purchase supplies were not used because of the receipt of a large quantity of supplies from outside the ghetto. A ramified program began in the second half of the month, after the supplies were received. In this connection, the Ghetto Chief appointed a special director for the center, and the staff, as well as the quarters, were enlarged.

The supplies received from the segregation points,[10] after being inventoried, are distributed to clients. The number that applied was very large. The distribution of supplies is conducted with the greatest possible speed. And the number of applications rises steadily. The principle in distributing supplies is to make possible and increase distribution to those working outside the ghetto and also to children. For this reason the need to distribute supplies to these workers is determined in agreement with the Brigadiers Council [11] and finally with the Labor Office.

The distribution of supplies to the workers within the ghetto occurs with the consent of the directors of the departments. In special cases investigations are made.

In the second half of the month, 509 requests were filled. Requests include not only individuals, but often whole families, institutions, camps. It should be stressed that in connection with the completed repairs, the acivity of the program increased and now 140 requests are being filled daily.

MISCELLANEOUS AID

During April parched buckwheat was distributed by the dairy kitchen to a larger number of children. The buckwheat is issued on the basis of permits submitted by the Children's Consultation.

During the month assistance was disbursed for buying plank beds, bandages, artificial limbs, eyeglasses, etc.

THE ACTIVITY OF CHILDREN'S INSTITUTIONS "YELODIM" [12]

The activity of the children's institutions "Yelodim" expanded in April and was marked by growth in respect to both quarters and number of children.

Increasing the number of children in the institutions is an urgent

---

10. Belongings of deported Jews were sorted on Gestapo premises; items of good quality were usually sent to Germany; the rest sometimes were given to the Social Welfare Department.
11. Administrators and column leaders of labor brigades working outside the ghetto.
12. *Yelodim* (Heb. "children") were residential centers for orphaned boys and girls providing not only custodial care and general education, but also vocational training and rehabilitation. Set up under private charitable auspices, they were funded mainly by the Judenrat. The Yelodim institutions also included a Transport Brigade, consisting of older children who worked all day at hauling and carting and who studied in the evenings.

need, demanded by children's poverty, their lack of supervision, and tendencies toward illegal and often even criminal behavior.

In cooperation with the institution's board, close to 100 requests were considered in April, which were in part fulfilled and in part referred to the board, which will take over the supervision of the children in the future.

Children admitted were, in the first place, those left without parents, both residents and new arrivals; next, the children whose environment is harmful to their morale and state of mind, and, re- gardless of any priority, the children who have been referred by the Criminal Police.

The system of admitting children is as follows:

Our Department investigates every application submitted and the application is then transferred to the institution's board to allow it to investigate the matter from its point of view and then the child and its guardian are called for a personal interview with the representative of our Department and the institution's chairman, who decide finally on the request.

One of the important and troublesome problems of the institu- tions is still the question of supplying clothing and footwear. The 55 pairs of clogs [13] distributed in March have not solved the problem, and therefore our Department is making efforts to provide the children with footwear as soon as possible, especially the Transport Brigade, where many children simply go barefoot.

Very little clothing was acquired in April, and therefore our Department is now distributing underwear, clothing, and bed linens for the children in the institutions.

Provisions for the children meet expected standards. During April the quality and quantity of food improved a little, because of the foods—especially fats—which were provided by the commissions to distribute the supplies.

With regard to Passover, besides a larger quantity of food from this commission, a sum of 3,500 RM for the Ghetto Chief was dis- tributed to the institutions for matzos, and in this way the children each had 55 decagrams [20 oz.] of matzo for Passover.

Each institution arranged one festivity—a seder or a party on the seventh day of Passover—with invited guests, which took place with great success and left a good impression in all respects. . . .

With regard to pedagogy, the institutions are under the super- vision of the private charity; no changes were introduced during April.

13. **Ghetto workshops produced wooden shoes to meet the needs for footwear. The clogs soon became widely used.**

At present the most important problems to be solved are:
(1) Providing the children with clothing and footwear
(2) Continuing admission
(3) Vocational training and productivization
(4) Planning and carrying out a specific educational program
in the various institutions. . . .

JANUSZ KORCZAK'S APPEALS FOR CHILD CARE
1939–1942

To the Jews!

Whosoever flees from history will be pursued by history.

Exceptional circumstances demand exceptional efforts of thought, feelings, and action. The Dom Sierot has lived through tragic weeks in dignity. Seven bombings. Two attempts at looting. No time to elaborate. Past. The Lord saved. We are expiring from the lack of immediate aid. I require:

A loan of 2,000 zlotys.

We will repay sooner than you think.

The fourth war, the third revolution—not only do I witness, but I experience. I can read war maps.

We bear a solidary responsibility not just for the Dom Sierot, but for the tradition of aid for the child. Ignoble if we refuse, wretched if we evade, foul if we besmirch it—the 2,000-year-old tradition.

Preserve dignity in adversity!

I myself will come for the answer. I will tell about Count B.— the magnate of Kiev. The title: "A thousand rubles and a bowl of soup." Please read this appeal a few times. Please think it over— don't refuse. I don't threaten, but I warn. If you yourself don't want to, even if you can, advise a cleverer man—in order to appraise the value of insurance!

I write this appeal in my own name and on my own responsibility.

November 1939

* * *

I assert with joy that with a few exceptions man is a creature of understanding and goodness.

Not just 100, but 150 are in the Dom Sierot.

February 1940   *Director, Dom Sierot, 92 Krochmalna St.*
                                          Society to Aid Orphans
                        [Signed]   *Dr. Henryk Goldszmit*
                        [Signed]   *Janusz Korczak*
                              The Old Doctor of the Radio

Appeal

Heavily, rationally, amply, finely flow the weeks.

When a bomb struck the Dom Sierot, the children went without panic down the three flights from dormitory to shelter. Only one broke out of the orderly file; there were one hundred children. When later a security-alarm test was ordered in case of an assault (the neighborhood is not safe, the times unsettled), the children also then passed the text exemplarily. Now there are already more of them—one hundred and fifty.

The latest child who was admitted here after quarantine in hospital: his father disappeared without trace; his mother and his sister were killed by a bomb before his eyes. The injury to his foot has not yet healed. With the one eye that remains to him after the explosion he will view the world. We coax a smile upon his tormented face. Peaceably they run about and play, the children who came recently with wounds on their frozen fingers and toes, abused, hungry, hunted.

The children assist in the educational work of the staff: a circle for useful recreation, a circle for self-improvement, a doll house, a self-study circle, a health committee, a reading room, a self-governing circle, a small newspaper, a court of peers.[14]

Expressions of appreciation for those who do not hinder our arduous work, honor and gratitude to the many who have helped and continue to help. Gone the resentment against that single one

14. Korczak was one of the first educators to advance the idea of the rights of the child. He held that the child, like the adult, had a right to be respected and to be himself. The institutions here listed were his innovations long before the German invasion.

whose rude refusal to help resounded: "There are many to take and few to give." He refused to give part of what still remained with him: he was forced to give up everything—but I already have nothing—not for the children, victims of the cruel present. I ask for:

(1) Cash assistance
(2) Contributions in kind (everything is useful)
(3) Addresses of well-to-do acquaintances
(4) Accept and fill out the enclosed forms. I will come in the next few days to collect them and get an answer.

Director, Dom Sierot, 92 Krochmalna St.
Society to Aid Orphans
[Signed]   *Dr. Henryk Goldszmit*
[Signed]   *Janusz Korczak*
The Old Doctor of the Radio

March 1940

JANUSZ KORCZAK TO THE EDITOR OF
GAZETA ŻYDOWSKA, JANUARY 7, 1942

Dear Editor:

Thank you for the favorable evaluation of the work of Dom Sierot. Nevertheless . . . "Dear is Plato, but dearer still the truth."

The Dom Sierot was not, is not, and will not be Korczak's Dom Sierot. Too small, too weak, too poor, and too foolish, to select, clothe, assemble nearly two hundred children, feed, warm, encircle them with care, and induct them into life. This great work was achieved by a general effort of a few hundred people with an enlightened understanding for the cause of the child—the orphan. Among these are many fine names, many without names—their work, help, guidance, experience—materially and spiritually constructed the worth of the establishment and of the rich enterprise. Wilczyńska, Pozówna,[15] Korczak (if names are needed)—these are the officials and administrators of this significant treasure.

Moderately provided with the needs for their personal life, they

---

15. Stefania Wilczyńska (1886–1942) worked all her life with Korczak in the Dom Sierot. No information is available about Miss Pozówna.

try—as much as they understand, know, and can—correctly and appropriately to carry out the terms of the agreement with the management of the Society to Aid Orphans and, through this management, with the community. The debits and assets of the institution consist of the virtues and deficiencies of the whole Jewish quarter, of all its members. The merit of the children, of their families, of teachers past and present, as also the closest and furthest in heart and memory, is what has given the Dom Sierot possession of good will and confidence, a good name and the possibility of a continued existence.

I would not have taken the time, the attention, and the paper to correct an unimportant mistake, if a misunderstanding would not have the general tenor of identifying the scope, techniques, efficiency, and the results of the work with the person of one official who was entrusted to carry it out.

[Signed]   *J. Korczak*

RABBINICAL SANCTION IN THE CASE OF ENDANGERED LIFE, 1941

Rabbinical Collegium of the Elder of the
Jews in Litzmannstadt [16]

No. 25/41: With
God's help

To the Elder of the Jews in Litzmannstadt:

At its plenary session of Sunday, 26 Shevat, 5701 (February 23, 1941), the Rabbinate decided to formulate its opinion on the subject of eating meat, as follows:

(1) Pregnant women, before and after giving birth, who, in their doctors' opinion, are required to have meat, are obligated to do so without restraint.

(2) People who feel a great enfeeblement of their vigor should apply to a doctor for examination and afterwards apply for a ruling

16. The Germans named the Lodz ghetto after one of their First World War heroes, General Karl Litzmann (1850–1936).

to the Rabbinate (at the Office of the Rabbinate, 4 Miodowa Street, between noon and 3 p.m.) or to an individual rabbi.

At the same time we request the Honorable Chairman to call to the doctors' attention the gravity of their decision in these matters, which should be issued only in cases involving the eventual endangering of life and with all due professional seriousness!

With great respect,
[Fifteen undersigned rabbis]

PERETZ OPOCZYNSKI:
SMUGGLING IN THE WARSAW GHETTO, 1941

Koźla Alley

The ghetto wall cuts across Franciszkańska Street right at Koźla Alley. From the distance you don't see it; only when you stand at the corner of the alley does it become visible, and then in its entirety, as it is. It is an alley, narrow and small, with odd old-fashioned[?] [17] and antiquated buildings, courtyards[?], twisting entryways, and tumbledown stairways. Here and there, a narrow many-windowed five-story house shoots up between two antiquated buildings, a sign that small flats had been here, working people, artisans, and street-vendors.

These forlorn, uprearing buildings, squeezed in between the antiquated little houses, destroy the symmetry of the alley and give an impression of something chaotic, untrammeled[?] neglected and disregarded even before the war. . . .

In front of every house is a dense mass of fruit and vegetable carts and food stands. The food stands are small. On a chair or a small table a woman sets out a few small sacks of two or three kilograms of rye, coarse, and "ration" flour; or groats, millet, and barley. Other types of food, like beans and white flour, are not usually seen[?] on these stands, but can be had in the stores. The prices here are of course a little cheaper than in other streets; after all, it is

17. Illegible portions of the original are indicated by a bracketed question mark, reconstructions in brackets.

Koźla Alley. Still, they are dear enough for a great part of Warsaw Jews, whom the ghetto has robbed of their livelihood and left with idle, useless hands and whose only possibility for sustaining a bare existence is by selling, little by little, their clothes and household effects at the poor man's flea market.

The booths, stands, and carts block the street. Every booth is besieged not so much by customers as by those who want to buy, but don't have the wherewithal. The volume of business is large, but negligible in weight. Rare the housewife who buys a whole kilo of potatoes, beets, or carrots. People buy ten decagrams or less. People buy a single apple, and anyone who buys a quarter kilogram is a super housekeeper.[?] People come to find out how high the market stands today, if prices have fallen. They swallow their mortification and leave with a searing pain of shame that they are penniless. . . .

The traffic of the rickshaws, the distinctive means of locomotion of the Warsaw ghetto, which . . . [?] was taken from as far away as the Japanese and Chinese. The rickshaw is a big help in Koźla Alley, not so much because now there are no droshkies and wagons, since the Germans confiscated the Jewish drivers' horses—that would still not be intolerable. The Warsaw Jewish porter, you may be sure, can carry a fine load of flour on his back. But what's the use if you don't dare do it in the open? For the Gestapo agent's eye is on the lookout. With the rickshaw, it's another story. The Jews have perfected the rickshaw in ways the Chinese never dreamed of. Under the seat is a space where you can stow a few bundles of flour, and sit up there on the plush seat as innocent as you please: I'm just taking a little ride.

But not everyone who carries food from Koźla Alley uses a rickshaw. Most go on foot, and indeed these are the mainstay of Koźla, the receivers and their helpers, the "strollers." They can't afford rickshaws; their rickshaws are their own backs onto which they often load three or four bags of flour, groats, and other sorts of food at one time. A bag may weigh fifteen kilograms, yet off they go.

The market at the corner of Koźla Alley, the congestion among the vegetable buyers, and the rickshaws block the way for the "stroller" and other buyers at Koźla. Each stride brings curses from the crowd. [The "stroller" who hears these curses] hurries. He sweats and pants and tries [to get rid] of his bundles as soon as possible, because a Gestapo agent [is around] and has terrified him.

The movement and the danger [are] not so great all through the day, for the smuggler doesn't want to and can't keep the goods in storage; he must get the goods off his hands as quickly as possible. Just as feverishly and hurriedly as it is smuggled into his house, so quickly must he get it out. Only then can he relax, with no evidence to incriminate him.

Nighttime Smuggling

Nighttime smuggling supplies the smugglers' shops with plenty of everything: vegetables and fruit, groceries, meat and poultry[?], honey, and whatever one's heart desires. Even good drink, too. The city needs to eat in the morning, the "strollers" need a whole day for their work. At five o'clock summer mornings you can see them hauling bags of food, sacks of potatoes, cans of milk. Their faces fresh, washed by the morning, these people have the spirit of working people who eat their fill, and the feeling of assurance and of strength—amid the swarm of swollen feet.

Nighttime smuggling is only a part of all the [smuggling], and cannot supply the ghetto with everything it requires in the few night hours, especially in summer, when the smuggler never gets the goods he ordered at the specified time. When you ask the smuggler if he will have such and such provision later, he will always answer: I don't know, if they get it over to me, I'll have it. Everything depends on when they can pass it over from there.

Nighttime the smuggling goes by way of the rooftops, through tight openings, through cellars, and even over the ghetto wall itself. In short: wherever possible. Daytime, in contrast, it goes much more simply, although not without dodges and very often with inventiveness, a Jewish head. As the Mishna has it: "He who sees a place where miracles happened to Israel. . . ."

Koźla Alley has several even-numbered houses in which non-Jews live, but whose entrances and gates have been walled up. Their entrances are on the other side, on Freta Street, that is, outside the ghetto. Only the windows of some apartments look out on Koźla. This is indeed a blessing not only for the few non-Jews who occupy these apartments, but also for the Jews. And, let's be honest, not only for the Jews of Koźla Alley, for the smugglers, but for all the

Jews in Warsaw. Smuggling, to be sure, is basically a dirty business, a noose on the neck of the hunger-swollen consumer, but, nevertheless, under the terrible conditions of the great prison into which Warsaw Jews have been corralled, the ghetto walls, it is the only salvation for the surviving remnants. Who knows, some day perhaps we ought to erect a monument to the smuggler for his risks, because consequently he thereby saved a good part of Jewish Warsaw from starving to death.

Grated Windows

The windows of the non-Jewish apartments were secured from top to bottom with wire grating, supposedly to fence the building off from the Jewish street. Actually the gratings are a good way to bring off the smuggling. Inside, right at the grates, the Gentile inserts a wooden trough, the kind you see in the mills. The trough reaches[?] through the grating, and when the Gentile pours a sack of rye into it, the rye drains through the grating right into the sack in the hands of the Jewish smuggler of Koźla Alley. In a wink the sack is full, and Meyer Bomke, the tall porter, with shoulders like a Russian peasant, whisks it on his back like a feather and vanishes, as he must.

Cereal, millet, granulated sugar,[?] and other foods are smuggled the same way. Only flour is smuggled in paper bags . . . through upstairs windows. From above, the Polish smuggler lowers a rope to the sidewalk. There the Jewish smuggler ties the paper bags to the rope. The Pole hoists the rope with the paper bags, fills them with flour, then lowers the rope with single bags of flour, which are [promptly] seized by the smugglers who spirit them away. In order not to cut his hands, the Pole wears heavy cotton gloves, through which the rope slides smoothly.

When the time comes to lower the merchandise, the ground-floor windows are besieged. Around the smugglers are their wives, their sons and daughters, porters[?] talking to the Poles. But only those can buy who are entitled, according to the smugglers.

Often you can hear one smuggler arguing with another at the "non-Jewish" window: "Jakie, rat! You stinker! The devil take you! You won't get near that window again! I swear, I'll fix you good!"

"Meyer, shove off! Hurry up. Look how he works."

"Mendel, blazes take you, why are you standing there![?] Here, take this to the market."

. . . People scramble for merchandise and the smuggled goods are quickly removed. A heave, a shove, a yank, and the merchandise is stowed away in the half-closed dark stores. . . . Broad-shouldered women, red-cheeked, with calloused hands[?] wink nervously, keeping a lookout to the end of the alley, where it meets Franciszkańska, to see if someone is coming, driving, riding. And suddenly the air is pierced by a hoarse warning scream: "Passover!" [18]

The warning is picked up on all sides and [all] doors are slammed shut and bolted. Padlocks are hung up outside. Some of the smugglers remain inside, others go out to keep watch. They lean against the store, as if to say they have nothing better to do. The Poles above speedily hoist up the ropes, and Kożla becomes quiet. The atmosphere grows more[?] in tense anticipation. The smuggling routine has ground to a halt.

For it is "Passover." Some non-Jew with a briefcase has turned up. No one knows who he is, but probably he is a police agent. So they wait. When the Pole upstairs, too impatient to wait, has the nerve to lower the rope again, shouting to the Jews below: "There is no more Passover," they send up a warning with the contemptuous manner of the more experienced: "Hold on, Passover is still around."

The Poles deliver milk to Kożla Alley at about seven in the morning, elsewhere still earlier. Large tin cans of standard liter capacity are set outside the windows of the ground-floor apartments. A thick hose equipped with a measuring device is passed through the wire mesh of the grates. One turn of the faucet and out pours a white stream of rich milk, diffusing the aroma of cow sheds, and quickly fills the cans. Even more quickly it is dispatched from the window into the stores, where milkmen and women are already waiting with containers to deliver the milk home to their customers.

Berl the Souse

The Jewish smugglers, receivers of the milk, are provided with tasters to see if the milk is pure, unadulterated, but that is only for themselves. They don't care if the customers are fooled, in fact they

18. One of dozens of code words of warning, usually Hebrew, used by the Jews in the ghettos and labor camps.

manage to somehow, because, after all, it's not a matter of justice, but a matter of profit[?], a plump drumstick or gizzard, and a drink, which a man like Mr. Berl must have. Indeed, this Mr. Berl has prepared the cans in his place in such a way that they contain a goodly quantity of water mixed with a sort of white froth, and that's the way he does business. When a woman comes to the window and insists on buying the milk as it flows directly from the Pole's hose, to be sure of its purity, he argues that it will cost her six zlotys. But just let her hesitate a moment, and the hose will fill Berl's can. Then he says, "Now, you can have it for five zlotys."

The accounting is quite simple.

Actually we've run ahead of ourselves. The work plan or, more accurately, the daily smuggling plan begins not with milk, but with vegetables. Not everybody can buy bread, but a beet, on the other hand, a potato, or carrot, are precious foods in wartime, much in demand.

Solly the Skirt, a squat man with round red cheeks like Simhat Torah apples, and doughy hands stuck in his pants pockets, starts selling at dawn: smuggled potatoes, greens, and also eggs, creamery butter, honey, and sometimes also non-kosher fats. His wife, Rosie, with a big backside, fleshy lips, and puffy beringed fingers, stands at the scales; time and again she lifts a bag of flour and asks this one and that one what he's buying, how much he pays, and giddap—we're off again. If she doesn't like the price, she shouts in her mannish voice: "Beat it, phonies, we'll send [a delivery boy] to your house[?]. Too bad you can't do with less than pure white flour."

Solly stands nearby on his stumpy legs, frowns, his squinty eyes with his whitish brows dusted with flour summon up the sleepiness of a baker. He keeps his hands in his pants pockets; the watch chain over his well-filled vest gleams sumptuously, as if to say: Damn your hides, you paupers! The hell I'll give you such flour for that price. Solly the Skirt knows what flour is. After all, he was a baker before the war.

One of his six or eight partners, Izzy the Face, who is two heads taller but has the same oaken shoulders, also stands around with his hands in the pockets of his lumber jacket and does nothing. He just watches to see if the "capital" is growing. His people sit at the counter, adding, figuring, and taking in money. The young man at the till keeps track, and, at each transaction, he opens the drawer crammed with paper money and closes it. The Polish money which the Germans issued, with reproductions of the Chopin monument and Piast's portrait,[19] lies piled up in heaps like greasy trash piles. Hundreds, five hundreds, and fifties, fifties, fifties—mountains. The young fellow, with the shiny boots and the expensive cigarette in his mouth after a good breakfast, shows contempt both for the money and those who provide it. So much money is piled before him, so much inflated paper, that he imagines he's not short of money. Indeed he too has forgotten what people without money look like, and he waits impatiently for the paupers to pay up, so he can grab it fast.

Izzy the Face has nothing to do. He hangs around the shop, his floury visored cap down over his eyes, looking like a ferocious dog. Also the third, fourth, and fifth partners are in the store. Once they were well-to-do truckers, soft-drink producers, tanners. Now they are smugglers. One of them sits with one leg propped up on the counter, munching a drumstick, a pickle for dessert, loftily eyeing the customers. . . .

Only the women, the partners' wives, are nimble. They are experts on eggs, butter, and all the other foods, and they are dying for that big take. One complains to the other that for thirty zlotys she cannot get anything for her children to eat, but of course she's lying. She wants to make herself out to be a poor slob. Both women know very well that this is said only for the customers, so they won't envy her. Look, upon my word, even the top smugglers of the Kozla can't afford to spend more than thirty zlotys for breakfast. But of course it's not true, because nowadays a kilo loaf of bread costs twenty zlotys, and what about butter and milk and cheese and indeed a fresh egg, which a smuggler's child simply must have for breakfast—things that hundreds of thousands of Jewish children in town see only in their delirious dreams. The twenty-zloty loaf is a sure guarantee that the smuggler's children will have all those good things. It also ensures Solly's peace of mind and that of his partners, as well as the nervous helter-skelter of their wives.

Meanwhile, we're still at the start of the day, at the sale of potatoes. Right away the sale of other foods will begin and then comes the real hullaballoo. You can never know, two hours later a miracle can happen—someone will start a rumor that the Germans are invading Russia. At dawn troops were seen marching over the

19. The legendary peasant ancestor of the first dynasty of Polish dukes and kings.

bridge to Praga.[20] That's enough. The Gentile smugglers understand such sensational news as well as their Jewish counterparts, and prices suddenly soar. That's all they need. When prices soar, things get brisk in Koźla. There is a scramble for the merchandise. Every bag of food lowered from the Polish windows is instantly seized in the pincer-like grip of the strong iron paws of the tough Jewish porters, who grab the goods for the rich traders in the markets. No one can compete with them.

Hundreds of Jews then throng the street, as on festivals in front of the synagogue, portly, well-fed. They make deals and talk politics. The sidewalk is thickly littered with cigarette butts and stubs, at a time when a cigarette costs 60 groszy, about ten to twelve times the prewar price.

Peddlers circulate in the crowd with little boxes of cakes, shouting, "Come on, let's go, who'll take a chance?" Numbers are drawn from a small sack; some lose and some even win a pastry. A couple of smuggler lads besiege the cake peddlers and devour the cakes with such insolent gusto, it is sickening to look at their greasy faces. Street singers and players drop in here in the hope of earning something in this land of plenty, but who appreciates them? The fiddle screeches, the singer sings: "I don't wanna give away my ration card, I wanna live a little more." But it has no effect. This street comes alive, starts to move and surge only when the whisper spreads: "Another quarter, half a zloty . . . two . . . rye flour 24½. . . ." That's the prettiest music in the alley.

Who cares about the corpse, or rather the dying man who has chosen to lie down right in front of Solly's place and plans to die right under the smugglers' feet? On Ostrowska, Wołyńska, even on Franciszkańska, and the Nalewki, the dead lie in the streets as though they were at home. Jews arise in the morning, go out and know they will find dead bodies there—one, two, five, ten; corpses of famine, the bloated dead who hungered through the war and, hungering, attained death, desired yet hated. But here in Koźla Alley? A squashed fly or a louse—who pays it heed?

The smugglers are in shiny boots and fine jackets. The cool September sun gilds their pampered faces. They nibble on the caramels and pastries which the sweets-peddlers bring them, and they never even hear the whir of the death-bullet as it whizzes by.

20. Suburb of Warsaw, on the east bank of the Vistula.

"Hey, boy, lookit! Auntie's coming!"

He means Basha, a red-head, one of the "strollers." It is nine, ten o'clock in the morning. The food smuggling is in full swing. The strollers stuff their knapsacks with the plenty of Koźla Alley and carry it to the bakers. The strollers earn twenty, at most thirty, groszy on each kilo of food, and they have to lug many loads. Some make dozens of trips daily to the alley for fresh food supplies. They have wives and children, they work hard, walk a lot, carry many loads, want to eat, indeed, must eat. For bread and potatoes alone they need fifty zlotys a day, if not a whole hundred. Without them [the smuggler would be] helpless. The smuggler knows it, but he likes to make a living too, no less than anyone else who has hired hands.

Basha, a tall girl with big feet, strides like a boy, and zips across the street with the sacks of flour like a demon. One-two and she's there and back with an empty knapsack and a handful of paper money. Before you look around, she's out and back inside again and so on continuously. Not slower than Basha is old Zelig, a man in his seventies, from childhood accustomed to lugging loads. . . . He also comes to the alley sometimes twenty times a day.

Not all strollers have the same luck. There are some women strollers who can barely manage to drag their swollen legs. They have to plead for eight or ten kilos of flour at one time, and the smugglers regard them as nuisances they can't get rid of. They do them a favor and throw them a few kilos of flour, as though it were a despised handout to these pesky recipients, but this is just for appearances' sake. At bottom they know how to appreciate the value of every stroller[?] because he helps them quickly to unload the forbidden fruit, to avoid tangling with a stray gendarme, a Polish policeman or a Junak.[21]

Yesterday there was a pretty piece of business. Right after a good deal on all sides, the Germans appeared unexpectedly at night—different Germans who had not been "fixed," and they did a real piece of mischief. They confiscated food worth tens of thousands of zlotys and, besides, it cost a fortune to get off with only the losses. During the tumult three boundary guards fell from the roof and were killed on the spot. Well, after all, they do live from boundary money.

21. Auxiliary police.

The system of boundary money is a complicated one, reminiscent of the wide range of instrumentalities through which circulating and profit-seeking capital has at all times tried to benefit and under all circumstances to insure its income. There are Polish and Jewish boundary men. The Poles smuggle the merchandise, brought by Christian suppliers to the Jews. The Jewish boundary men deliver to the Jewish smugglers on the Jewish side. The boundary men keep accounts thereby, how many tons of provisions are smuggled in, and for every kilo they get a percentage. The boundary men have their own people who watch the buying and selling and make sure they won't be cheated.

The boundary men have a hard lot. Standing on the roof means they are always in mortal danger. But what won't a Jew do to earn his bread?

Koźla Alley gives thousands of Jews their livelihood. The barrowmen who cart away vegetables and fruit and the porters live off it. Outside every smuggler shop are always a couple of porters who grab the lowered bags of flour, sacks of grain and other provisions and deliver them to their designated places. Besides their regular earnings, the porters have staked out a new claim—a package fee on every sack of food that leaves Koźla Alley.

At the corner of Franciszkańska stands Zelig the Paw, a stolid personage in a Polish-peasant hat with a lacquered visor that he wears at rakish angle, ready to spring on anyone carrying a package:

"Stop!" he hisses. "Don't be bashful, uncle, hand over fifty for a package fee."

"Me—fifty?" replies the passerby, trying to look innocent.

"Yeah, fifty and make it quick."

The other gives in. Otherwise Zelig the Paw lets him have the feel of a real paw so that he sees stars. Against such an argument all pleas are useless, so he cries and pays.

Noon Rest in Koźla Alley

At noon everything quiets down in Koźla. All the supplies of smuggled provisions have already been sold. The porters sit on the shop steps, the smugglers take a nap on the counters in the empty stores, and Koźla Alley rests, preparing itself for the afternoon smuggling, which starts at about four or five.

You never know if the afternoon prices will be the same as the morning prices. This you can tell only when they lower the supplies through the windows. In the courage of the first smuggler who carries off his bags of flour, of the porter and the boundary men, the entire alley [senses] the change on the bourse and, like a sudden wind across a wheat field on a hot summer day, a murmur gusts through the street: "Higher."

Not only the barrowmen, porters, strollers, milkmen, and boundary men live off the alley. Thousands of grocery stores live partly off it, naturally raising their prices. Last but not least, Koźla Alley supports tens of thousands of Jews who even with money in their pocket would die of hunger if the alley did not serve as their granary.

Time will tell.

Whoever will endure, whoever will survive the diseases that range in the ghetto because of the dreadful congestion, the filth and uncleanness, because of having to sell your last shirt for half a loaf of bread, whoever will be that hero, will tell the terrible story of a generation and an age when human life was reduced to the subsistence of abandoned dogs in a desolate city.

HENRYKA LAZAWERT: THE LITTLE SMUGGLER

Over the wall, through holes, and past the guard,
Through the wires, ruins, and fences,
Plucky, hungry, and determined
I sneak through, dart like a cat.

At noon, at night, at dawn,
In snowstorm, cold or heat,
A hundred times I risk my life
And put my head on the line.

Under my arm a gunny sack,
Tatters on my back,
On nimble young feet,
With endless fear in my heart.

But one must endure it all,
One must bear it all,
So that tomorrow morning
The fine folk can eat their fill.

Over the wall, through holes and bricks,
At night, at dawn, at noon,
Plucky, hungry, artful,
I move silently like a shadow.

And if the hand of destiny
Should seize me in the game,
That's a common trick of life.
You, mother, do not wait up for me.

I will return no more to you,
My voice will not be heard from afar.
The dust of the street will bury
The lost fate of a child.

And only one request
Will stiffen on my lips:
Who, mother mine, who
Will bring your bread tomorrow?

CULTURAL ACTIVITIES IN
THE VILNA GHETTO, MARCH 1942

The number of cultural events in March [1942] was exceptionally high, because all existing suitable premises in the ghetto, like the theater, gymnasium, youth club, and school quarters, were used. Every Sunday 6–7 events took place with over 2,000 participants. At the end of the month the Culture Department had to give up to the incoming out-of-town Jews a number of premises like the gymnasium, School No. 2, Kindergarten No. 2, and a part of School

No. 1.[22] This will greatly affect the work of the schools, the sports division, and also the theater, which had to take into its building the sports division and the workers' assemblies.

(1) *School Division*

A disruption in the regular school activity occurred March 24 because of the occupation of the above-mentioned part of the school premises. School No. 1 had to shift its two upper grades (6 and 7) to afternoon session. School No. 2, which occupied the upper story of the school building on 21 Niemiecka Street, also had to shift two classes (both 6th grades) to afternoon session. Kindergarten No. 2 moved into the quarters of the Children's and Youth Club. School No. 3 gave up half its quarters to School No. 2 and shifted all five high-school classes to afternoon session. All these changes are an impediment to the work of the schools, and, if at all possible, the schools should be returned to their premises as soon as possible.

At the start of the month, the schools conducted several more morning programs (see report for previous month). On March 7, School No. 3 invited all parents to a school program in the theater. School No. 1 presented a morning program on March 14 by the younger classes in its own quarters. On March 21 (Purim), special children's celebrations were held in all classes without exception. The children received a gift from the Food-supply Department—*hamantaschen.*[23] Kindergarten No. 1 and School No. 2 presented morning programs that day for the parents.

The Children's and Youth Club, beside its regular activities, organized special projects every Sunday. The History Circle presented a trial of Josephus Flavius, which was on a high scholarly level; the Literary Circle—a Yehoash[24] evening with a rich program. Besides that, the club prepared a Purim entertainment and a recitation contest. In connection with the Yehoash program, the Club set up a Yehoash exhibit, which later remained open to the public for two weeks. The older classes of the schools also visited the exhibit with their teachers.

High-school teachers have completed their work on the curriculum of the high-school classes in the ghetto.

22. The ghettos in the smaller Lithuanian towns were being liquidated. Some skilled workers who were spared were transferred to the larger ghettos. Several hundred Jews arrived in Vilna from Oszmiana, Święciany, and Michaliszki at the end of March 1943.
23. Lit. "Haman's pockets," a tricornered Purim pastry filled with poppy seeds.
24. Pen name of Solomon Bloomgarden, Yiddish poet and Bible translator (1870–1927).

On March 11 a discussion evening was held at the Ghetto Chief's on the education of the young people in the ghetto. Several dozen teachers, writers, and communal leaders were invited.

On March 12 a Sutzkever [25] evening was held at the Teachers' Association. The poet read his latest poem, "Kol Nidre." The Music School continues regularly.

(2) *Theater Division*

Two important premieres took place in the theater this month. On March 13, the symphony orchestra, under the baton of W. Durmashkin, presented its fifth program: Beethoven's Leonore No. 3; Chopin's Piano Concerto in E Minor, and Tchaikowsky's Fifth Symphony. The youthful orchestra surmounted the great difficulties of the program and the performance was satisfactory. On March 27, the opening of D. Pinski's "The Treasure" took place.[26] The play's text was significantly abridged and considerably revised by the director, I. Siegel. His conception was to turn the play into a musical comedy. Original lyrics were written by Leib Rosenthal. Musical accompaniment was by M. Wechsler. Opening night was a great success. A number of writers, teachers, and cultural leaders attended a general rehearsal (a day before the opening), of which they spoke favorably.

Because of preparations for the two openings, there were only 12 events during the month. There were 4 performances of "The Treasure," two of "The Man Under the Bridge" (for the 15th and 16th times; the play is still a success), two performances of the review "You Never Can Know" (the 19th and 20th times, a special matinee performance for residents of the Káilis blocks);[27] the program of the symphony orchestra was repeated three times, and a literary-musical evening was held once, with a mixed program. . . .

On March 30 the theater celebrated the 40th anniversary of actress Esther Lipovska's stage career. "The Treasure" was given and appropriate speeches were made. The guest of honor was awarded all receipts.

The theater's gross receipts for March totalled over 4,300 marks. Of this, the Communal Relief Committee and Winter Relief received about 2,000 marks.[28]

For April, fourteen events in the theater are planned. Because of

25. Abraham Sutzkever, a Yiddish poet of the *Yung Vilne* literary circle. He now lives in Israel, where he edits *Di goldene keyt,* a Yiddish literary journal.
26. David Pinski (1872–1959) was a major Yiddish dramatist.
27. Káilis was a factory located outside the Vilna ghetto, employing Jewish labor in fur production for the German army.
28. The Communal Relief Committee was organized by the underground political parties in the Vilna ghetto and supported by voluntary contributions. The Winter Relief Committee devoted itself mainly to the distribution of clothing.

the small number of events in March (only Saturdays and Sundays), there was no free performance. In April one free performance is being planned for the Brigadiers Council and one free concert fo the Social Welfare.

(3) *Library, Reading Room, Archives*

During the month the library lent 13,500 books (an increase of 2,800 over the previous month), 65 percent of which were for adults and 35 percent for children. In March 100 subscribers were added and by April 1 the library had 2,592 readers. On March 12, the Ghetto Chief ordered the ghetto population to return to the library all books (except textbooks and prayerbooks). By the end of the month 1,750 books had been returned. On March 25 the ghetto court tried 15 readers who had not returned books. The court sentenced them to one day conditional arrest and a fine.

An average of 206 persons visited the reading room daily (155 in February), as hitherto, a maximal number.

During the month the Archives collected 101 documents. Besides that, 124 folklore items were assembled.

(4) *Sports Division*

The Sports Division, which resumed its activity only at the beginning of February in the room at 7 Rudnicka Street, had to give up the space on March 24 and is once again without quarters. This is a great loss, because in a short time the Sports Division had attracted 415 active members, acquired considerable equipment, and developed exemplary activities. When the premises were closed, 22 groups had been organized for gymnastics, rhythmics, running and jumping games, and boxing, with 637 members (many members are registered in two or even three groups). Besides the usual program of the sports groups in March, sport competitions were held every Sunday, namely a contest of running and jumping games between the "Káilis" and the ghetto teams; a five-player team for men and a three-player game for women, and a basketball tournament.[29] In the mornings the ghetto schools held their gymnasium classes on the sports premises.

In April it is expected that Sports Division will move to the lobby of the theater. The quarters are small and the Sports Division will have very few program possibilities.

29. The Vilna ghetto sports field was made by clearing a small area of bombed buildings. Kalmanovich noted in his diary on August 21, 1942, that the place was filled with young people, especially on Sundays, when games were played: "My pious friend laments: 'So many woes, so many deaths, and here merriment and celebrations!' That's how life is. But live we must as long as God gives life. He knows best! Jewish children give themselves up to sports; may God give them strength."

(5) *Art Exhibit*

On March 29 an art exhibit of paintings, sculpture, graphics, etc., opened in the lobby of the theater. Fifteen artists are represented with a variety of works. Besides the noted Vilna artists Rachel Sutzkever (oils and watercolors), Jacob Sher (part of the album, *Vilna Ghetto*), Uma Olkenicka (graphics), and Yudel Moot (sculptures and an album of papier-maché), a number of young artists participated. N. Drezin exhibited twelve satires and caricatures of well-known ghetto figures; four members of the Plastic Plan of Vilna showed carved medallions and miniatures of the Great Synagogue, cathedral, etc. Engineering Architect F. Rom made miniatures of her own designs for office furniture; G. Sedlis exhibited three paintings (watercolors and pencil). Of special note are the works of three children in the exhibit. S. Wolmark and Z. Weiner sketched ghetto themes (gates of the ghetto, etc.). Nine-year old S. Bock is considered by the jury to be extraordinarily gifted, and the jury selected 30 of his drawings to show.

Award-winning works in the art contest (see February report) are also shown. The exhibit is extremely successful and is visited by hundreds daily. Children of the ghetto schools visited the exhibit together with their teachers. The exhibit will remain open until April 4. The Ghetto Chief intends to purchase several of the exhibited works which have ghetto themes.

(6) *Support for Writers and Artists*

During the month the Literary Association continued to submit works of its members, in order to obtain honoraria from the Ghetto Chief via the Culture Department. Dr. Gordon completed the first chapter of a philosophical work (*Apriorist Foundations of History*) and received another advance on his honorarium; Jacob Sher submitted to a jury his album, *Vilna Ghetto,* from which the jury selected ten sketches. Leib Turbowicz completed the first four chapters of a large work on the history of the Jews in Vilna, receiving a substantial honorarium (500 marks). The board of the Literary Association has strict standards for submissions and at its last meeting rejected various works of six authors. In the April budget the sum of 1,000 marks is expected to be assigned to support of writers and artists.

(7) *Workers' Assemblies*

The workers' assemblies, organized by the Brigadiers Council in cooperation with the Culture Department, are attracting ever larger audiences. In March they covered these topics: 1) Award winning writers (outside and inside the ghetto), 2) the ghetto court, 3) Itzik Manger.[30] After every lecture there is entertainment (recitations,

30. Yiddish poet (1901–1969).

singing, etc.). Last Sunday no assembly was held because the premises were taken over for sports. From April 4, the assemblies will be resumed on Sunday mornings in the ghetto theater.

Vilna Ghetto: April 2, 1943   [Signed]   *G. Jaszunski*
Director

THE POLITICAL UNDERGROUND:
A LETTER FROM THE BUND, MARCH 16, 1942

Dear friends:

After an interruption of more than a year, we again have an opportunity to let you know about us. We hope that this letter too will reach you. We will start with events in our town.[31] Benio's family [32] fares quite well here. During the past year the family strengthened its positions and enlarged its influence. But, of course, we believe that you are always aware of the changed conditions and possibilities to which one must adapt. It can be stated that we have cadres with an excellent possibility of expansion at the proper time. The organization is based upon trade-union cells and family cells.

The Jewish population has become terribly declassed. Unfortunately, illegal trade—or, rather smuggling—has become the mainstay of Jewish existence. Our people work mostly in welfare and community organizations. The family cells meet regularly, they have a family council and an executive. Life goes on the same way in Albert's family [33] and in his younger brother's family.[34] In general, the development is satisfactory, and, what is most important, they command respect in town. The specific gravity is about the same as before.

How do we adapt to the new conditions? Albert—to take an example—has some clubs, organized studies, high school courses, and is involved in a broad cultural and educational program (prop-

31. Warsaw.
32. Benio = Jewish Labor Bund.
33. Albert = *Tsukunft*, the Bund's youth organization.
34. *Skif*, children's section of the Bund.

erly fronted, of course). Albert and his younger brother continue their theatrical and choral interests. Wherever and whenever possible, the trade group takes care of its tasks. Benio and Albert engage in their literary activities, as before. Every week Benio systematically writes a short story on current events; [35] these are very popular. Once a month—a philosophical treatise.[36] In addition, monthly dissertations in Zygmunt's language,[37] very much in demand by the more refined connoisseurs, also among Zygmunt's family. Albert publishes his literary output monthly in two languages (separately): altogether a monthly output of eight works.

Saloma's enterprise [38] is active in two branches. They serve 20 percent of all the town's consumers of this product. Of course, the demand for this type of product has diminished considerably owing to prevailing conditions. The two outlets also serve a daily soup to a considerably greater number of customers. The kitchens function as before, but the food has a lower nutritional value. Despite overwhelming difficulties, Batka's firm [39] continues to produce. Nor do we neglect to help our families without breadwinners, those in transit, the refugees, the sick, and, in general, all those in need of aid. In this field, terrible conditions notwithstanding, we have succeeded in keeping our work force. At all times, we have maintained close contact with out people in the provinces, and we have given them material and moral help. . . .

Since Saloma's departure, we have received only 1,700 "little emanuels," [40] of the 7,000 that were reportedly dispatched to us through different channels. Unless the difference was recovered, someone using our name may have misappropriated those funds. Please check and examine this case thoroughly. Lately we received here in town 25,000, which amounts to 500 noodles,[41] but we do not know how much we were supposed to receive. We believe that for

35. Underground news bulletins in Yiddish.
36. Underground political review in Yiddish.
37. Polish.
38. Saloma = Central Yiddish School Organization (CYSHO), the prewar secular Yiddish school system operated jointly by the Bund and the Left Labor Zionists.
39. Batka = Medem Sanatorium, located near Warsaw, founded by the Bund as a treatment center for tubercular children, but later expanded to an all-year residential center with extensive educational and recreational facilities for poor children.
40. Dollar currency.
41. Dollars.

the future all the routes are unreliable, and also very expensive. The only possible way appears to us to be through the Delegatura here in the country.[42] But you must establish this route yourselves and obtain guarantees that we receive the sums sent by you. Until now we managed to make ends meet by borrowing against the promise of future payments.

The Jews are locked up in ghettos. The mortality due to famine and epidemics is terrifying. In 1941, our city lost ten percent of the entire Jewish population (45,000 people). The mortality rate is increasing and has lately reached fifteen percent. Deaths due to starvation edema, typhoid, and tuberculosis are widespread. Most serious for the Jews is the imminent threat of death. In many towns mass shootings of Jews take place from time to time, without regard to sex or age and without cause. A Jew is subject to the death penalty for leaving his place of domicile and the execution takes place on the spot, without a trial. Thousands of victims are sent to the forced-labor camps, and those who return home after a few months are wasted and sick.

In Pati's town [43] and its immediate vicinity, after the arrival of our hosts, their Lithuanian lackeys bestially murdered the majority of the Jewish population, without regard to age or sex. The Polish population showed much sympathy for the Jews and rendered significant help. In Pati's town, only 10,000 Jews remained. In many smaller localities all Jews were murdered. The survivors are locked up in the ghettos of three towns, where they vegetate in terrible conditions. Mass murders of Jews also took place in Polesie, Wolhynia, and Eastern Galicia. The bestiality reached its peak in the areas annexed to the Reich, as, for instance, in the Kutno region. In a number of villages the Jews were put to death by gas poisoning.[44] They were herded in a horrible way into hermetically sealed trucks transformed into gas chambers, in groups of fifty, entire families, completely nude—fifteen minutes later no one in the cars was alive. Those still alive—the next victims—were forced to bury the dead in mass trenches. To illustrate the feelings of the people awaiting death, we quote from a letter by a member of a family known to us, no longer alive now, from Żychlin, written the end of

42. The representative in Poland of the Polish Government-in-Exile, then located in London.
43. Vilna.
44. The reference is to the death camp at Chełmno.

February to their relatives here, whom we also know (and many such letters arrive):

> Dearest Bronia, my hand trembles, I cannot write. We fare terribly, our moments are numbered. God alone knows if we'll ever see you again. I write and cry, my children despair—one wants so much to stay alive. All of us say good-bye to all of you. I am not in contact with Hania and Hala, so you, my Bronia, write to them and say good-bye from us. We kiss you. Write immediately, perhaps I shall still receive your letter. If you do not hear from me soon, then we are probably no longer alive.

Efroim's place[45] is just one large concentration camp, where the Jews are hermetically isolated from the world and from the other parts of the city and where they die in terrible ways. Thousands of families are continuously being shipped out of there, and every trace of them disappears. They are being poisoned by gas. Jewish bosses rule in the ghettos with the approval of the Germans, and those people are mostly interested in their own affairs and their own groups, at the cost of the misery and suffering of the masses of the population. Corruption, extortion, and thievery are common.

Benio's and Albert's competitors show no concern for the fate of the land where they live. Borochow's friends and the youngsters from Hochar are prepared to relinquish their patrimony to the neighbor Mizrachowski.[46] In addition, in their periodic writings, they dream of leaving for Eretz.[47] They minimize the importance of Honig[48] for the future of his friends and our people. They tie their only hope to Mizrach. The remaining former competitors passively await salvation.[49] Only Benio builds hope as to the independent existence of his fatherland. As to the real Mizrachi,[50] an agency was recently established which attempts to conduct its activities under nationwide and patriotic Polish slogans. As of now, the results of their efforts in our isolation are negligible. . . .

---

45. Lodz.
46. The reference is to pro-Soviet sentiment of the Left Labor Zionists and the halutz youth.
47. Palestine.
48. Honig = the Allies.
49. Presumably a reference to the Agudat Israel, organization of Orthodox Jews.
50. Mizrachi = Communists.

Until the middle of 1941 we maintained contact with WRN and the Wolność group here.[51] This contact was loose and pretty cool, through no fault of ours. Even then differences in our respective views on a number of problems divided us; these differences deepened after the events of June 1941 and as a result of the fundamental political program then published by WRN. In the second part of 1941 we established contact with another group, which later served as the basis for the organization of the Polish Socialists.[52] You are probably familiar with their program. They are the group that has gathered all the opposition and leftist elements of the former party. Contact with the Polish Socialists became much closer since it turned out that their ideological answers to the most basic problems and relationships were very similar to our own—this they made clear in their publications. This condition prevails until now. Our relationship is close and very friendly, we help one another in many situations. We continue to meet with WRN and do not conceal from them our contacts with the P.S. We maintain contact with the Delegatura. As a result of the propaganda of the occupation forces, which finds fertile soil here, the anti-Semitic attitudes among the Polish population are fairly strong. A part of the underground press—the ONR and OZN [53] papers—conduct their anti-Semitic politics in the old style and applaud the Nazi extermination policies as a matter of principle, naturally drawing the line against their barbaric aspects. Unfortunately, other papers for the most part remain silent and do not react against this anti-Semitic policy on the part of some of the underground, a policy both inhuman and dangerous from the standpoint of national interest. The P.S. publications firmly point out and combat this policy, and so, to a smaller extent, do WRN and some democratic publications. Naturally, we for our part attempt to influence public opinion through our Polish publications. We decidedly reject any solution based on emigration, and we defend our principle of full civic, national-cultural, and social rights, retaining our goal of a free,

51. WRN = *Wolność, Równość, Niepodłegłość* (Freedom, Equality, Independence), wartime cryptonym for the Polish Socialist Party-PPS. The Wolność group was one of several leftist splinters of the PPS.
52. Wartime leftist splinter of the PPS-WRN.
53. ONR = *Obóz Narodowo-Radykalny* (National-Radical Camp), a fascist student organization. OZN = *Obóz Zjednoczenie Narodowego* (Camp of National Unity), right-wing organization which continued the political traditions of Pilsudski's authoritarian regime.

independent, and socialist Poland in a voluntary federation of a socialist republic of Europe. . . .

EVALUATING THE GHETTO:
INTERVIEWS IN WARSAW, 1941

Hillel Zeitlin

Q: Do you see any positive factors in the ghetto?
Unfortunately I see only negative ones: hunger, epidemics, mass mortality. The area of culture is precisely where something positive could be created. Within the ghetto walls a Jewish culture of our own, a Jewish life, could emerge, but Jews are a contrary people. They speak Polish with such ardor. Polish has become the holy language of the ghetto, the holy tongue of the ghetto Jews.

This is something simply paradoxical. They packed us into the ghetto so they could forcibly isolate us from other peoples, cultures, and languages. Yet we insist on speaking a foreign language and spit on our own language, our own cultural and spiritual values. We see something similar with the Sabbath. For years Jews in Poland fought against Sunday observance laws, but now that Jews in the ghetto can observe the Sabbath and do business on Sundays, they insist on doing business just on the Sabbath.

A misfortune has occurred. Assimilation has made its way from Snob Hill to the ghetto and influences the whole Jewish quarter.

Q: How do you explain the odd liberalism and tolerance with regard to converts in the ghetto?
Jews are a compassionate people. As long as the apostates were in the camp of our persecutors, we hated them. But now that they are together with us in the camp of the persecuted,[54] we pity them. "Toleration" even goes so far that the converts among us now find

---

54. The Germans regarded Jewish converts to Christianity and their children as racial Jews, in accordance with the Nuremberg Laws. These apostates lived in the ghetto and attended two Catholic churches located within ghetto boundaries. Because of expertness or high reputation in their fields, some held prestigious posts in the ghetto bureaucracy.

themselves in a privileged position. There are good public kitchens run by the ŻTOS especially for converts and the meals there are much better than those in the regular kitchens. Such is the concern for the converts. It has already come to the point that people rush to convert so as to get a better meal.

While speaking of converts, we ought to mention the deplorable role of the Kehilla, which shows favoritism to the converts, provides them the best jobs, and puts them in the forefront in our communal life in the ghetto.

Q: What is the source of this love our community leaders have for converts?

It springs from the fact that there are in the Kehilla concealed, disguised assimilationists who have contempt for Yiddish, Jewish culture, and the Jewish populace.

Q: How can you explain the decline and weakening of religious life in the ghetto? History teaches us, after all, that always when the trials of the Jews increased, religious faith increased and the people clung more firmly to their faith, to Torah.

Yes, it is unfortunately a sorrowful fact that religious life in the ghetto has declined considerably. The Sabbath is vanishing. Of the 220 families in the building where I live barely two or three observe the Sabbath. If our enemies would persecute our religion, forbid Sabbath observance, forbid Jews to pray, resistance would be strengthened and religiosity would grow. When there are no hindrances, people grow indifferent to religion.

At the start our enemies had indeed tried to persecute religion, attacking synagogues and prayerhouses. But right away they realized that these were wrong tactics because thereby they would only strengthen religiosity and consequently the spiritual resistance of the Jewish people as well. Therefore they straightaway changed their tactics.

Characteristic is the rebellion against God, against Heaven, which is noticeable among many religious Jews who no longer wish to declare that God's judgment is right.

Religious leaders in Poland regrettably did nothing before the war to strengthen religiosity among the populace. They fought for kashrut. But what was this kashrut propaganda? Did it explain just why kashrut should be observed? No, they did not explain. The Sabbath observers made scandalous scenes in the streets, fighting

with the carters. Was this "propaganda"? They explained nothing,
they did not enlighten people as to what the Sabbath was, its meaning, its significance, its sacredness.

They continue to do nothing for religious enlightenment, these
religious officials of ours. They content themselves with begging
from the Joint Distribution Committee.[55] One must admit that
unfortunately the Jews have shown themselves to be much weaker,
much less able to resist than we had supposed. The Jews have
shown themselves to be unable to withstand the least hardship, as
we saw before the war, for instance, in the struggle against prohibit-
ing ritual slaughter and on behalf of kashrut. People ate non-kosher
meat even when the difference in price was only a few pennies. We
observed this too in the struggle to keep the Sabbath as a day of
rest.

Corruption, demoralization, and thievery in the ghetto are
terrible. Their cause—the extraordinary misfortunes. Evil traits and
base instincts are now revealed in all their nakedness. But if 400,000
Gentiles were locked up in such a ghetto, who knows if the picture
would not look much worse. They would probably just slaughter
one another.

Jews in the provinces turn out to be better. The old Jewish
feeling of compassion has not yet been eradicated from them. Jews
in the provinces are self-sacrificing, renouncing a bit of food to send
packages to relatives, acquaintances, and even to strangers in
Warsaw.

It is also sad that there are no visions of the Messiah in the
ghetto, no visions of redemption, I mean redemption in the spiritual
sense. People think in purely materialistic terms, the redemption
means return to an easy life, fancy resorts, fleshpots. Perhaps there
is a perception of the travail before the Messiah's coming, but people do not want to draw the necessary conclusions and therefore
do not respond and prepare themselves for messianic redemption.

*Q: What is the outlook for the Jewish people, especially the Jewish
masses in Poland?*

Without a religious awakening, without a messianic idea, the Jews

55. The American Jewish Joint Distribution Committee—JDC, the leading
   American Jewish philanthropic organization serving needy Jews throughout
   the world.

will not be saved. Why? The political outlook is not promising. The Poles will say that the Jews made the best deal with the Germans, received autonomy from them, and Jew-baiting will continue to thrive. The optimistic hopes Jews direct toward England are also naive and ridiculous. It is clear to me as two and two make four that England will once again fool us, betray us, as she does other small and weak peoples, by not giving us Palestine. I say, therefore, that our salvation lies only in an inner religious awakening capable of working miracles. No one can rob us of Heavenly Jerusalem, the spiritual Jerusalem, and with the force of the spirit we will finally conquer also politically. . . .

Dr. Israel Milejkowski

. . . .I head up the public-health service in the program to combat epidemics and also the hospital department. Besides, I also direct the medical board here in the ghetto, where over 800 doctors are concentrated. All these activities leave me very little free time and my remarks will therefore be based on my daily practice in my own field, but I will try, as far as possible, to give my conclusions a general character. . . .

The root and source of all evil in our miserable existence at the present moment lie in the very fact that we have been locked up in a ghetto. This gives rise to degenerating and demoralizing consequences in our community life. This is the cause of our physical and moral collapse.

The ghetto and life in the ghetto have no future in themselves, because we have been locked up behind its walls against our will, because this was done by brute force which was impervious to any human feelings. We must not let ourselves be persuaded for a moment that the ghetto way of life can be adapted to our needs, that it can solve any of the vexing problems of our gloomy existence. . . .

For us the ghetto is only a temporary residence which has been forced upon us. It is a sort of roofless *sukkah*,[56] utterly unfit for human habitation, only a makeshift dwelling, a passing stage in our communal life, and the source of all our troubles and hardships at this time. The ghetto, which has hit us so murderously, is

---

56. A booth with a roof of branches and leaves which serves as a temporary residence during the festival of Sukkot.

our greatest affliction and calamity, for the generality as well as for the individual: moral insanity. All other troubles and afflictions vanish when compared with the ghetto.

The chief curse of the ghetto is that there we cannot be creative. We were creative before the ghetto, when we created cultural values for ourselves and for all mankind, for we are capable of creative work, but only under more or less free conditions. In the ghetto, however, that is impossible. Under brutal outside pressure we have lost the possibility and also the qualities of creativity.

Here in the ghetto we must now make every effort to survive this terrible period in our existence. Endurance and perseverance—this must now be our slogan in the ghetto.

From the foregoing I derive my negative attitude to the whole ghetto setup which I perceive as the most painful event in our entire history. No good will come to us out of the ghetto. Quite the contrary—the ghetto brings more demoralization and more corruption to the locked in, tightly squeezed masses.

I can explain this better by using two medical terms, endogeny and exogeny. Internally we must do everything to enable us to persevere and endure. But externally the oppressor's whip cracks over our heads, forcing us to do work beyond our weak capacities. The oppressor's attitude to us can be stated in the words of the Jewish foremen to Pharaoh: "There is no straw given unto thy servants and they say to us: "Make bricks.' " We are ordered to do many things that we are in no position to perform under ghetto conditions, precisely because of these difficult conditions themselves.

Bearing this in mind, I therefore always try to act in the area of my competence, so that "their" authoritarian orders may for a while be tempered by my instructions for their discharge and that the lash of the whip will thus be eased. Under the present terrible conditions I cannot and do not wish to be creative because this would be a wasted effort and an impossibility.

In order to get a true picture of ghetto life we cannot judge on the basis of what we see in the street. I differentiate between two strata in the ghetto. I would express it graphically as follows: The whole Jewish community in the ghetto is as if it had been thrown into a huge pot of seething water on a big fire, the fire of our afflictions. In the seething water we can distinguish an upper layer and a lower one.

The upper layer seethes and boils and many bubbles appear

on its surface. The second layer also boils, but more quietly, more slowly. The upper layer is more conspicuous, though it is not the more numerous or more important, but because it is more visibly astir. If we want to see the true face of the ghetto, we must acquaint ourselves with the lower layer.

At first glance what is most obvious is the benumbed sense of compassion among Warsaw Jews. Without any pity for the desperate plight of thousands of our brethren whom want has forced from their hovels out onto the streets, we pass almost indifferently the barely living unfortunates and the paper-covered corpses of those who died of hunger. Savagery has begun to rule our minds and, accordingly, also our actions. It is worth mentioning that "they" have condescended to note this tragic phenomenon in our lives.

The life of the first layer is not, however, the true one. That is represented by the lower layer . . . in which we find modest but very important happenings, luminous, vigorous, cheering: the sense of compassion as manifested by the work of the basic cells of organized Jewish life, the tenement committees,[57] thanks to which the true Jewish trait of compassion and of charity has been fulfilled.

In addition, there is the quiet, modest work, which has only a temporary life, being done in other areas, for example, in setting up public kitchens of various kinds, medical courses, and vocational training for Jewish adolescents. Intensive medical research on starvation and typhus is also being done. All the clinical materials, unfortunately so bizarrely voluminous, are carefully being researched and the studies are being prepared for their definitive medical conclusions.[58] This is our ambitious and prestigious undertaking!

But this is by no means an original, creative ghetto culture. Afterwards, after the cataclysm, we want to be able to show the world that even horrible persecutions could not crush us. Right now, a small scientific meeting devoted to the ghetto is being held at the hospital. Here (!) problems and scientific presentations, responses and discussions. The results of the research will be published later and I hope that they will interest a broad audience.

57. The tenement committees were a ŻTOS spinoff. Each building was organized for self-help activities and ghettowide philanthropic fund raising.
58. The study was completed October 1942 after the mass deportations from the Warsaw ghetto. It appeared in Warsaw in 1946, published by the JDC under the title, *Maladie de Famine: Recherches cliniques sur la famine executées dans le ghetto de Varsovie en 1942.*

These attempts at constructive work in the ghetto, in relation to the negative happenings, are small comfort to us, because one thing is terribly clear: the ghetto demoralizes! What is a blessing for the ghetto—smuggling, for example—is from the national standpoint a curse.

If, for a moment, we discount the utilitarian factor involved in smuggling, if we can forget that thanks to those Jewish smugglers who risk their lives to provide the ghetto with all sorts of delicacies, many Jews can supply themselves with the finest and best meals, and if we ponder instead on what sort of generation will grow out of these smugglers, good-for-nothing scamps—is the ghetto not a curse? Or take, for instance, vocational courses, medical and others. The courses will produce nothing but bunglers, though neither the teachers nor supervisors are at fault. At fault are only the harsh and abnormal conditions of the ghetto. This is not progress or advancement. This is degeneration and brutalization.

Under such harsh conditions of our communal life in the Warsaw ghetto, to return to our simile of the pot of seething water, people from the very bottom rise to the surface of our pot. Blackmailers, informers, bribe-takers of all sorts, and influence-peddlers. This layer of underworld characters, antisocial elements are always found in every society. They increase and multiply in wartime, just as if inhuman living conditions were the best subsoil for the disorderly development of these human hyenas.

I do not at all wish to deny the fact that this type of person is, in the present circumstances, to a certain extent necessary and useful for outside purposes. The authorities demand dirty work from us which, under pressure from those in power, must be done. Not everyone is capable of doing it and willy-nilly we are beholden to the underworld. In this case I realize the positive role these elements play in community life. I think that this is also the situation in the provinces.

People complain that our ghetto smells worse than any other place. This is certainly true and derives from the fact that our substance is finer, more delicate, and therefore spoils more quickly. With regard to corruption this is frightfully conspicuous. At fault, once again, are the conditions in which we live. These conditions breed corruption and the fight against corruption is a hard, hopeless one. To fight corruption means to fight the ghetto. Cursed is our vegetation within the ghetto walls, a curse hovers over the work of our leaders and officials. What is ugliest in the Diaspora comes to light in the ghetto in concentrated form. . . .

Our present educational work here in the ghetto ought to be aimed at inculcating the tradition in the hearts and minds of the young generation, that they absorb it so that it becomes part and parcel of their inner being. From this standpoint I take an altogether positive attitude to the religious values of our people. I have realized that the will to survive of the Jewish people, their stubbornness and persistence—"a stiff-necked people"—really come from the traditional religious approach to the problem of our survival. In the religious Jew I see this wholeness. He is without the self-reproachfulness and the doubts that totally consume the mind of the enlightened Jew and thus empty it of its essence.

The mind possesses a whole series of attributes among which faith occupies a prominent place. Deep faith is an antidote for the poison which comes with our daily terrible life. To close the chasm that opens up before the modern Jew's eyes and to enable him to overcome the strongest temptations, his religious feelings must be awakened. . . .

PONDERING JEWISH FATE:
FROM ZELIG KALMANOVICH'S DIARY

Sunday, October 11, [1942]. On Simhat Torah eve at the invitation of the rabbi, I went for *hakafot* in a house that had formerly been a synagogue and was now a music school. The remnants of the yeshiva students and scholars were assembled, as well as some children. There was singing and dancing. The commandant [59] and his assistants were also there. I was honored with the first *hakafa* [60]. . . . I said a few words: "Our song and dance are a form of worship. Our rejoicing is due to Him who decrees life and death. Here in the midst of this small congregation, in the poor and ruined synagogue,

59. The reference is to Jacob Gens.
60. One of seven processional circuits around the *bimah* in the synagogue, with members of the congregation carrying Torah scrolls, in celebration of the festival of Simhat Torah (Rejoicing in the Torah).

we are united with the whole house of Israel, not only with those who are here today and with the tens of thousands of the pure and saintly who have passed on to life eternal, but with all the generations of Jews who were before us. In our rejoicing today we give thanks for the previous generations, the noble generations in which life was worthwhile. We feel that with our song today we sanctify the name of Heaven just as our ancestors did. And, I, a straying Jewish soul, feel that my roots are here. And you, in your rejoicing, atone for the sins of a generation that is perishing. I know that the Jewish people will live, for it is written: 'As the days of the heaven upon the earth.' And even if we were the last generation, we should give thanks and say: 'Enough for us that we were privileged to be the children of those!' And every day that the Holy One, blessed be He, in His mercy gives us is a gift which we accept with joy and give thanks to His holy name." . . .

[*Sunday*], *October 25, [1942]*.   Today I must record. Yesterday all the policemen were assembled and the commandant gave them a summary of the terrible events of the last days.[61] Horrors, the most dreadful of all trials, but there is no way out. Praised be the God of Israel who has sent unto us this man. All our Jewish brethren in the Vilna district were gathered into one ghetto. In my town thirty out of eight hundred people remained. Our policemen were sent there with passes to be distributed among the remaining workers, and to turn over the rest of the people, "the superfluous," to the hands of the authorities to do with them what is customary these days. The young men took upon themselves this difficult task. They donned their official caps, with the "Star of David" upon them, went there and did what they were supposed to do. The result was that more than 400 people perished: the aged, the infirm, the sick, and retarded children. Thus 1,500 women and children were saved. Had outsiders, God forbid, carried out this action, 2,000 people would have perished.

The commandant said: "To be sure, our hands are stained with the blood of our brethren, but we had to take upon ourselves this

---

61. Gens briefed the Jewish police and a number of communal leaders on the participation of thirty of their ranks in the annihilation of old and sick Jews of the Vilna district, who had been assembled at Oszmiana. The minutes of this meeting are published in M. Gelbart, ed., *Sefer zikkaron lekehillat Oshmena* (Tel Aviv, 1969), pp. 407–418.

dreadful task. We are clean before the bar of history. We shall watch over the remaining. Who knows if any more victims will be demanded from us here, as they were demanded there. We shall give them only the old and the sick. Children we will not give them. They are our hope. Young women we shall not give them. There came a request for workers. I replied: 'We shall not give. We need them here.' Thereupon they went out into the street, seized a thousand Poles and sent them to Riga. Who can guarantee the future?" A heavy dread hung over the assembly while he spoke. Merciful and gracious God! Merciful and gracious God!

Sunday, November 1, [1942]. Once more, difficult and bitter days. Once more the police were asked to "arrange" matters in Świeciany. It was feared that if the action be carried out without them, then the number of victims would be much higher. This time, apparently, it was a groundless fear. But here a new difficulty arose. The commandant began to demand that he and his aides not be the only ones engaged in this activity. He does not want others to say: "Our hands are clean." Ostensibly he took the position that the entire responsibility rests upon him and that he himself would render account before the Supreme Judge. But in fact he does not want us to be merely spiritual partners with him. He wants us to be actual partners. Yesterday his former assistant [62] was arrested for refusing to go out with the police group to S. to participate in the action. The ghetto seethes like a cauldron. Conferences, meetings, consultations. He demands, it seems, that others also participate. In truth, we are indeed not innocent of Jewish blood. We have purchased our lives and our future with the deaths of tens of thousands. If we have decided that we must continue despite everything and everyone, then we must go through with it to the end. And the forgiving God will forgive us. The old rabbi [63] may serve as a model: we must save whatever can be saved. This is the situation and we cannot alter it. Of course, a noble soul cannot tolerate such deeds, but the soul's protest has only a psychological worth and not a moral one. All are guilty, or perhaps more truly: all are innocent

62. The reference is to Joseph Glazman, an active Revisionist, a popular figure in the Vilna ghetto, a leader in its underground resistance organization. He refused to direct the action at Świeciany.

63. Apparently a reference to the rabbi of Oszmiana, who, according to another entry of Kalmanovich's, had "handed down a decision to deliver the aged."

and holy, and, above all, those who actually carry it through. They must master themselves, brace themselves, and conquer the soul's sufferings. They exempt others and shield them from sorrow.

Sunday, [December] 27, [1942].   This morning I was in the children's nursery. Women who work leave their children from 7 to 6. There are 150 children between the ages of three months and two years, [one group] from two to three years, [one group] from three to six, and another group that studies reading and writing. Speeches, dramatic presentations, the children march in line. But the Jewish flavor is missing. In ghetto circumstances the order is remarkable. What vitality in this people on the brink of destruction!

Who mourns the destruction of East European Jewry? The destruction is a hard fact. Undoubtedly also those who predicted it did not envisage it in this form. Three or four years ago the central Zionist organ was writing of a Jewish center in the Diaspora parallel to the center in Palestine. But the catastrophe was nevertheless a definite thing, its contours so visible. Indeed, the innovative horror for our human consciousness is the personal destruction of human lives: old people, children, blossoming youth, weak and old men, but also those in full vigor. There is no doubt, it tears the heart. But millions of people are losing their lives in all parts of the world in the war. Not only combatants, but also infants and old people. The war has put its face on our destruction. But the destruction was certain even had there been no war. It proceeded on its way in an expansive manner. No one attempted to stem it. On the contrary, whoever attempted to convince himself and the world that he was erecting a defense, actually collapsed. The full proof came in the East [in the U.S.S.R.]. Everything was swallowed up in one great endeavor to disappear.[64] The apparent life of culture was pure nonsense, arid. When the East came here, no one as much as raised his voice. All was happiness. All found a place, a sense of belonging. Undoubtedly here and there someone thought: something is missing. Another reflected: Judaism is disappearing. But all this was glossed over by the fact of mere existence. There is no discrimination. One amounts to something, particularly something in the apparatus. One can have his say. Had the thing continued in

64. Kalmanovich was referring to the Soviet policy of forcibly assimilating the Jews and to the conformist Communist culture in Yiddish.

existence, nothing would have been left of the enemies of Israel anyway, except, of course, the youth that yearns thither [Palestine]. Could they actually have got there, they would have been saved for our people, and the people through them. But the rest? The individuals would have remained intact, but would have been lost to our people. Jewry in the East is disappearing. The final result is the same as now.

What is better? Better for whom? The individuals who are saved are saved individuals. There are two billion people in the world, two billion people + x. For our people—the Jewish people—had constructive elements in East European Jewry. Those that yearned thither, if they actually succeeded in coming there, they strengthened our people. Otherwise, our people will mourn them. Great will be the sorrow and mourning, the joy of redemption will be wrapped in black. But the same sorrow is also for the parts that disappeared through apostasy. And if you wish, the sorrow is even greater. Here the evil beast came: "Joseph is without doubt torn in pieces." But how Jacob would have wept if the first plan, God forbid, had been carried out! In that case the Jewish people would have been justified in feeling that sick, impure blood courses in our veins. No external enemy tears off our limbs. Our limbs rot and fall off by themselves. And a page of history will read: The grandchildren were not inferior to the grandfathers. Only fire and sword overcame them. A curse upon the murderer! Eternal glory to the innocent victim! But here, where comfort lures people into the camp of the mighty, it is of no interest to history. It will not condemn, but silence means condemnation. You are no longer. Like all of them—Ammon, Moab, Edom, the hundred kingdoms of Aram . . . an object for excavations and students of epigraphy. History will revere your memory, people of the ghetto. Your least utterance will be studied, your struggle for man's dignity will inspire poems, your scum and moral degradation will summon and awaken morality. Your murderers will stand in the pillory forever and ever. The human universe will regard them with fear and fear for itself and will strive to keep from sin. People will ask: "Why was it done so to this people?" The answer will be: "That is the due of the wicked who destroyed East European Jewry." Thus the holocaust will steal its way into world history. Extinction by means of a loving caress creates no sensation and means nothing to anyone.

Eventually the Jewish people itself will forget this branch that was broken off. It will have to do without it. From the healthy trunk will come forth branches and blossoms and leaves. There is still strength and life. Dried up and decayed—this happens to every tree. There are still thousands of years ahead. Lamentation for the dead, of course, that is natural, particularly if they are your own, close to you. But the Jewish people must not be confused. The mourning for close ones—some people bear their sorrow long; most find comfort. Human nature—such is the world. Whatever the earth covers up is forgotten. In the ghetto itself we see how people forget. It cannot be otherwise. It certainly is not wrong. The real motive in mourning is after all fear of one's own end. Wherein are we better than those tens of thousands? It must happen to us, too. If we only had a guarantee of survival! But that does not exist and one cannot always be fearful, then the feeling of fear is projected into mourning for the fallen, and sorrow over the destruction of Jewry. Spare yourself the sorrow! The Jewish people will not be hurt. It will, it is to be hoped, emerge fortified by the trial. This should fill the heart with joyous gratitude to the sovereign of history.

Sunday, [January] 24, [1943].   There is a vigorous cultural life in the ghetto. Last night we had the premiere of the choir, a lecture in the literary club on the subject of "Shylock and Nathan." Today a *siyum* on the completion of the tractate *Kidushin* by the Yeshiva Rabbi Chaim Ozer in Rabbi Shoulke's house of study, and in the evening in the kosher kitchen. The library is full of readers. The literary club is discussing the subject of subsidies for literary works. On the whole there is hope for salvation, although not so soon. Last week the enemy was raging again. There were victims.

Sunday, Purim, March 21 [1943].   On the first of the month there was a meeting in the house of the commandant on the problem of education. How to infuse a national spirit and if it is possible to introduce religious studies. I expressed the bitter truth that it was impossible to introduce a national spirit into the school if it was absent in the life of the community. All that exists is the will of individuals to continue their physiological existence at all cost. And this will eclipse everything. All national feeling has evaporated. When the ghetto walls will fall, all these people will scatter in disgust in all directions. The individuals, exceptions, in whom there will still remain a spark of Jewishness, will aspire to the land of their fathers. The rest—everyone will go his own way. The teachers complain, as usual. Subsidies for writers are continued. What is submitted is trash. This is readily understandable. There are no creative writers here.

Friday, [April] 30 [1943].   Passover is over. There were *sedarim* in the kosher kitchen. . . . At the second *seder* I spoke briefly.

"A year ago some intellectual circles in the ghetto searched for an answer to the question: What is a Jew or who is a Jew? Everybody was tremendously preoccupied with this question. Formerly the majority of these people had never given much thought to this question. They felt that they were Jews. Some more so, others less. Some, perhaps, did not feel so at all. And if someone suffered because of his Jewishness, he somehow found a remedy for it and, in general, occupied himself with other more substantial matters, rather than speculate about such an 'abstract' matter. Now these diverse people were herded together and imprisoned within the narrow confines of the ghetto. People of diverse languages, diverse cultures, diverse interests and beliefs, of diverse and, at times, conflicting hopes and desires were assembled together in one category: Jews. Confined as if being punished for that; that is, they committed a crime and the crime consisted in being a Jew. Many of them actually did not know what to say about the 'crime.' They did not know what it means 'to be a Jew.' To be truthful, practically nothing resulted from all these speculations and reflections. It was impossible to find a clear and definite answer to the question: Who is a Jew nowadays? For only now, in our generations, in the past 150 years, has the concept of Jew assumed so many meanings. Earlier, 'Jew' was a clear concept that had only one meaning. A Jew was one who observed Jewish law and belonged to the Jewish community. Now various kinds of people are considered and consider themselves Jews, even such as do not observe Jewish law or even respect it, or have no idea what Jewishness is. But also in this case I obtained an answer to the question 'who is a Jew' from a child in the ghetto. The truth of the verse, 'Out of the mouth of babes and sucklings has Thou found strength,' was again confirmed. A teacher of religion in the ghetto school told me the incident, from his own experience. Children attend who are totally alienated from Jews, who had never heard at home, in school, in the street, anything of the Jewish past, of Judaism. Now in the ghetto many of these children listen eagerly to the stories of ancient sacred history, of the Bible. One such child, who had once attended a Polish school and spoke Polish at home, studied with great interest the stories of the Bible. When, in the weekly portion of *Toledot*, they studied the story of Jacob and Esau, this child suddenly called out: 'Teacher, we are indeed the descendants of Jacob and they (i.e., those who do evil to us) the descendants of Esau. Isn't that so? It's good that way. For I really want to belong to Jacob and not to Esau.' I reflected on this story and discovered that I could deduce from it a method to decide who is a Jew. This is how: Man's imagination is after all free, no bonds can confine it. A ghetto person can then sometimes imagine that he has the freedom to choose: he can divest himself of his fallen and defeated Jewish identity and assume the identity of the ruler over the ghetto. Now I ask: What would he do? If he wanted to change, if he was eager to assume the identity of the ruler, we could suppose that he is not a Jew. But if by free choice he wishes to remain a Jew, then he is a Jew. Reflecting further: the Jewish child instinctively chose to be a Jew. He naturally feels at home among Jews. As for the adult who I imagine chooses freely to be a Jew, is instinctual feeling a sufficient ground or are there also rational motives?

"I think so. To be a Jew means in every instance to be on a high plane. The temporary suffering and blows that descend upon the Jew have a meaning, are not merely oppressions, and do not degrade the Jew. For a Jew is part of the sacred triad: Israel, the Torah, and the Holy One, blessed be He. That means the Jewish people, the moral law, and the Creator of the universe. This sacred triad courses through history. It is a reality that has been tested countless times. Our grandfathers clung to the triad, lived by its strength. And now too: the Jew who does not cling to this triad is to be pitied. He wanders in a world of chaos, he suffers and finds no explanation for his suffering; he can be severed from his people, that is, he can wish to change his identity. But the Jew who clings to the sacred triad needs no pity. He is in a secure association. To be sure, history rages now, a war is waged against the Jews, but the war is not only against one member of the triad but against the entire one: against the Torah and God, against the moral law and the Creator. Can anyone still doubt which side is the stronger? In a war it happens that one regiment is defeated, taken into captivity.

Let the ghetto Jews consider themselves as such prisoners of war. But let them also remember that the army as a whole is not defeated and cannot be defeated. The Passover of Egypt is a symbol of ancient victory of the sacred triad. My wish is that together we shall live to see the Passover of the future."

INTRODUCTION

THE JUDENRAT was an anomalous institution. The Germans who ordered each Jewish community to form a Judenrat regarded it as the vehicle for transmitting and executing their orders. The Jews who formed the Judenrat regarded it as successor to the kehilla, which would continue to serve the Jewish community and to defend its interests vis-à-vis the authorities.

The kehilla had traditionally maintained Jewish religious institutions (synagogues, prayer houses, religious schools and yeshivot, ritual baths, kashrut, burial), supported their functionaries (rabbis, teachers, shohetim), and cared for the community's needy, aged, and sick. The Judenrat hoped to perform these functions, too, but the Germans imposed other, still more onerous, tasks.

To begin with, by confining the Jews in ghettos, isolating them from the rest of the urban population, and cutting them off from basic municipal services, the Germans forced the Judenrat to shift its emphases from Jewish needs and objectives to general ones. The Judenrat became responsible for providing services normally within the province of a municipality—housing, utilities, food supply, police and fire protection, a judiciary system, public health and sanitation, and a host of other services. And the Germans also gave the Judenrat tasks that were to serve German ends, specifically those leading to the Final Solution. These tasks completely subverted the traditional objectives of the kehilla. For the Germans, in their systematic approach to the destruction of the Jews, demanded of the Judenrat first the money and possessions of the Jews, then their labor, and finally their lives. No Judenrat could reconcile the contradictory and antithetical German and Jewish conceptions of its role. Therein lay the tragic dilemma of the Jewish communal leaders who served in the Judenräte.

Everywhere the Judenräte were set up with the participation of prewar kehilla leaders. In Warsaw a Jewish citizens' committee of a few kehilla members was formed during the bombardment and siege of Warsaw in September 1939. Among them was Adam Czerniaków (1880–1942), an industrial engineer, who most of his life had been head of a Jewish artisan's association and its representative in both the Warsaw city council and the kehilla. Having been appointed chairman of the ad hoc Jewish citizens' committee by Warsaw's mayor, Czerniaków was made head of the Judenrat by the Germans. This man, conservative in economic and political matters, a General Zionist who had remained aloof from the ideological and cultural ferment of Warsaw Jewry, whose modest talents had enabled him to play a modest role in the prewar Jewish community, was now catapulted into the very center of responsibility for the whole of Warsaw Jewry.

Czerniaków began to keep a diary on September 6, 1939. Written in staccato, laconic prose, little more than a private shorthand, Czerniaków's diary is a guide to the day-to-day ordeals he endured in trying to perform his duties. Every day he threaded his way through the tortuous and treacherous labyrinth of the German bureaucracy in occupied Poland. His pride in having attained, even if late in life, the leadership of the Jewish community, was tempered by the humiliations he suffered at the hands of the Germans and by the inevitable failures of his hopes and efforts. He suffered constant headaches, slept fitfully, and developed a bad heart.

The excerpts from his diary have been selected to show, beside insight into his character, his daily office routine and the pressures which the Germans exerted upon the Jewish community through the Judenrat in a series of critical periods. The excerpts for 1939

*show the formation of the Judenrat from the Jewish citizens' com-
mittee, the first German threat to ghettoize the Warsaw Jews, and
the ordeals of raising money to pay the huge fines or contributions
demanded by the Germans, of ransoming hostages, freeing prisoners,
and providing forced laborers.*

*The excerpts for 1940 deal for the most part with the events
culminating in the ghettoization of the Warsaw Jews, from the
first instructions on March 29 to build a wall through the end of
October, when the ghetto had become unbelievable reality. The
few excerpts for 1941 (part of the diary for that year is missing)
bear on hunger in the ghetto, the typhus epidemic, the enormous
mortality, and the confiscation, at the end of the year, of furs which
the Germans sent to their soldiers on the Russian front.*

*The excerpts for 1942 delineate the deceitful schemes the
Germans developed in preparing to send Warsaw Jews to the
death camp at Treblinka. At the same time, in an exercise of
bizarre horror, the Germans began to shoot a film in the ghetto to
depict "Jewish degeneracy." Both sets of plans—to send the Jews to
their death and to prepare the film—advanced concurrently, and
the Germans needed Czerniaków for both. Czerniaków was fully
aware of the spuriousness of the German film production, but he
closed his eyes credulously to the deportation plans and continued to
believe, until a day before the Warsaw Jews were to be sent to
their deaths, the lying assurances of the German bureaucracy that
nothing untoward would take place in the ghetto. He even toured
the ghetto to calm the populace and rebut the disquieting reports
and rumors about mass killings. Only when the "resettlement" had
actually begun, did Czerniaków realize the full import of the situation in which he found himself. Succumbing to despair, he committed suicide.*

*During his tenure as head of the Judenrat Czerniaków was
mocked and vilified by the ghetto Jews, as the popular anonymous
song "Prexy Czerniaków" testified. His suicide redeemed him in the
eyes of many who had once censured him.*

*Lublin, in contrast to Warsaw, was a provincial capital city,
with a Jewish population of over 35,000. Its communal leaders,
representing the diversity of Jewish politics, were decent, honorable
men measuring up to the modest demands of a middle-sized kehilla.
Those who stayed on to become officers of the Judenrat, mostly
General Zionists with many lawyers among them, were confronted*

with a multitude of tasks that even men with greater resources could not have performed. The frustrations of their position must have embittered and provoked them. The minutes disclose an unattractive portrait of quarrelsome men, bureaucratic, quibbling, legalistic, formalistic, and spiritless.

The excerpts from the minute book of the Lublin Judenrat for 1940 deal primarily with forced labor and the problems of regulating the supply of Jewish workers to meet German demands. The excerpts for 1941 concern the ghettoization of the Lublin Jews, the so-called "voluntary" evacuation of nearly half the population, and the problems of administering health services in the ghetto at a time of epidemic. The minutes for 1942 depict the nightmarish drama of the factual takeover of the Judenrat by the SS. Under the whip of SS terror, the Judenrat members were forced to become instruments of the SS in calling on the ghetto Jews to report for "resettlement." The Lublin ghetto Jews were the first in the Generalgouvernement marked for liquidation; their destination was the newly completed death camp at Bełżec. But no one in Lublin then knew of mass killings.

More than half the Judenrat members were themselves deported, believing they would resume their positions of leadership in their new residence. The Germans replaced them with five men drawn from the Jewish underworld who had served as Gestapo spies. Thereafter, in the decimated ghetto, the remaining legitimate communal leaders attempted, in the only way they could conceive, to maintain standards of honor and decency. They established formal Control and Disciplinary commissions to supervise the officers and staff of the Judenrat and the Jewish police and to enforce a legally prescribed course of conduct. The bylaws for these commissions appear as a grotesque caricature, a legalistic diversion against the backdrop of the destruction of Polish Jewry.

Bialystok, too, was a provincial capital with a Jewish population barely larger than Lublin's. Its communal servants, too, were men with local reputations, accustomed to dealing with the normal problems of normal times. Bialystok, however, differed from Lublin in two respects. It had long been a textile manufacturing center whose Jews played a major role in the industry. Furthermore, the Jewish community was fortunate in having at its head Ephraim Barash (1892–1943), a man of energy and initiative. He exploited Bialystok Jewry's industrial capacity for its protection and survival under German occupation. Barash developed a strategy for making the Jews industrially indispensable to the Germans. In contrast to the attitude of the Jewish populace to the Judenräte elsewhere, Barash was widely trusted and respected in the Bialystok ghetto.

The excerpts from the minute book of the Bialystok Judenrat start with the meeting on November 2, 1941, a few months after the establishment of the ghetto, and conclude with the special meeting of October 11, 1942, when Bialystok still remained an island of relative tranquillity while most Jews in the Generalgouvernement were being consumed in the gas chambers. The first set of minutes deals with the extortionate German demand for money. The next concerns various complaints which the German authorities levelled against the ghetto.

The minutes of the general meeting on June 20, 1942, with the Jewish police present, unfolds the drama of Barash's purge of criminal elements within the police force and his successful struggle to retain control over the police apparatus. The last two sets of minutes deal primarily with questions of the ghetto's survival as predicated upon its industrial indispensability. Barash's policy was to restrain Jews from acts that might give the Germans an excuse to liquidate the ghetto. He rallied the people by calling on them for courage and strength in the hope that they would outlast the German occupation.

Ultimately, the Jews in Bialystok fared no differently from Jews elsewhere. Barash himself understood that decisions about the life or death of the Jews were not his or the Judenrat's to make. At one meeting, he said as much: "The Germans will settle things." In August 1943 the Germans liquidated the Bialystok ghetto. Barash then joined the Bialystok Jews in their last ordeal—the journey to Treblinka.

FROM ADAM CZERNIAKÓW'S DIARY, 1939–1942

X/2/1939

At the office of the Mayor, Starzyński.   (1) An announcement to the Jewish population.   (2) Armbands for community officials. (3) Food rationing.

Dead horses were buried in the courtyard of the Kehilla on Grzybowska Street 26/28. A meeting of the Jewish citizens' committee. The announcement is delivered to the printer. A meeting of the Kehilla council. A search for food. Onions are going at 1.80 zloty per kilo.

X/4/1939

The office. My wife stands in queues.

I was taken to Aleja Szucha [1] where I was informed that I must select 24 people to form a community council which I am to head.

I worked out a statistical questionnaire.

X/10/1939

In the morning in the office.

Meeting of the Ältestenrat. Choosing the list of 24 and proposals. Mr. Starczewski [2] from the city administration visited the Kehilla and demanded the cemetery rates for the German authorities. Kaminer [3] went to the cemetery with him and issued the order. At night I was called to the City Council. Trouble throughout the night.

---

1. 25 Aleja (Avenue) Szucha was the headquarters of the Security Police (SIPO) and Security Service (SD) in Warsaw
    I would like to acknowledge my indebtedness to Dr. Nachman Blumental, from whose annotations to the Hebrew editions of the documents which appear in this section I have drawn heavily.
2. Jan Starczewski headed the Health and Welfare Department of the Warsaw municipality.
3. Meshullam Kaminer, member of the Aguda, was head of the Kehilla's cemetery department.

X/13/1939

(1) SS—list of members of the Council of Elders, documents for its members.

(2) Statistical form—office of registry.

(3) The Kehilla.
Chancellery.
Welfare.
Rabbinate.
Tax department.
Accounting.
Department of education—vocational schools.
Cemetery.
Statistics.

(4) Labor brigades.

(5) Announcement on the authority of the school council. I was at the SS. They announced a visit. Batz [4] appeared at the Kehilla with a companion. They announced the opening of several departments. Meanwhile everything is sealed again.

Bonifer 45.[5]

X/15/1939

This morning at the Kehilla, at 10, a roll call of officials. From 12 to 2 in the afternoon, an SS inspection. Meanwhile a session of the Council of Elders. Then a speech by Batz to the 24. In the evening preparation for a day's session with the SS. Meetings in the afternoon. On the corner of Marszałkowska and Wspólna a house that was about to crumble was blown up. Entertainment near the Kehilla. Beards.[6]

XI/4/1939

In the morning in the office. The Kehilla. Difficulty with payments. A German official in charge of currency matters was expected at 9:30 but he didn't come. An SS soldier came demanding that we call a meeting of the Council for 3 in the afternoon. At 11:30, in

4. Dr. Rudolf Batz, SS Hauptsturmführer, SIPO.
5. SS Sturmführer Bonifer, SIPO; presumably Batz's companion. His office room number was probably 45.
6. Probably refers to the sadistic entertainment of the German occupiers in pulling or cutting the beards of pious Jews.

the name of the authorities, an SS man demanded a meeting of the Council of Elders and their alternates. Some of the Council members as well as their alternates did not appear. An SS contingent demanded that the roll be complete. We chose alternates at random.

They informed us about a restricted area of residence.[7] The alternates were removed from the hall.[8]

XI/15/1939

A cloudy morning. It is six o'clock. A downpour. I must be at the SS at 8:30. On November 30th I end my 59th year and begin the 60th. At one time I divided my life in three parts according to a theoretical scheme: (1) study and amusement,   (2) action, (3) coming to terms with God and living with myself. Fate has cancelled my account. . . .

Every evening since the curfew I get into bed at 9. Because of this I wake up at 2, then sleep in snatches until 6 a.m. In the intervals I read *Don Quixote*. Oh, what good you could have done in our time, knight errant!

My head is splitting from all the complaints I hear.

All Jews were expelled from the barracks in Annopol.[9] I am now responsible for four evacuated villages, a hospital, orphanages, Annopol, as well as the madmen now free to roam the streets. My head is whirling.

I/5/1940

Many requests now. The officials and the work pace. (A lame turtle in a funeral procession.) Attempts to create a Jewish bureaucracy. What does it matter to me? Perhaps.

A Jew remarking on a synagogue that was burned down: "It is actually God's own distress."

---

7. On the pretext of danger of a typhus epidemic, Batz told the Judenrat that within three days the Jewish population would have to move within certain specified borders. This was the first German threat to impose a ghetto upon the Jews in Warsaw. No formal ghetto was established at that time; inexplicably the SS withdrew the order. Nevertheless, the process of circumscribing the Jews within a limited area began then. For a narrative of these events, see Dawidowicz, *The War Against the Jews 1933–1945*, Chapter 10.
8. They were arrested and held as hostages to ensure the Judenrat's compliance with German orders.
9. A suburb of Warsaw, where refugees had been housed in barracks.

Today I was called to the Stadthauptmann.

I was at Daniłowiczowska 3. Kluge invited me. In Richter's name he ordered all prayer houses, synagogues, ritual baths closed.[10] Finally, when I was in the car, I received a snowball from some youths for being a *Jude*. . . .

I/22/1940

In the morning I noticed one of my pants buttons was missing. The greatest of men could become a mockery because of such a flaw.

The families of prisoners. In the evening I was called to the SS in connection with my attempts to free the doctors, etc. I learned that one hundred were shot. It was announced that more would be shot.

In the admitting rooms at the hospitals. To bed with a headache.

I/26/1940

I was called to the police (Lieutenant-Colonel Daume). The Kehilla must pay 100,000 (hundred thousand) zl. by tomorrow because a *Volksdeutsch* was beaten. Otherwise—100 Jews will be shot. I asked the Gestapo to release me from the payments, then to accept the sum in instalments, finally that they exempt me from giving them workers to clear snow, this in order to salvage something. Nothing came of it. We must pay tomorrow morning. This being the case, I began to collect money in the Kehilla. It will be necessary to borrow 100,000 and then to collect from those who owe taxes.

At the same time the police are demanding 6,100 zl. for 61 Jewish men and women who were caught without armbands.

Confronted with all this, I turned to the SS asking that I be relieved of my office, for in these abnormal circumstances I cannot lead the Kehilla. They said, in response, that they would not recommend such a step.

I received a letter to the *Reichskreditkasse* about changing bills of 500 and 100 into smaller denominations. Tomorrow another day of torment.

10. Richter was the head of the German military public-health service, but Kluge was a SIPO officer. The Germans alleged that the religious institutions were centers of contagion.

III/24/1940

This is the first day since the Germans arrived that I am at home. I am writing a memorandum for Cracow,[11] having been invited there along with council members Jaszunski, Milejkowski, Sztolcman, as well as Dr. Weichert and Bornstein (Joint).[12] Incidentally, the Kehilla is not functioning today. In the afternoon, on Jewish streets, Jews were beaten and window panes were broken. Sort of a pogrom.

III/27/1940: Cracow

I got up at 6 in the morning and prepared a speech.

THE PROGRAM

(1) Security;   (2) the Kehilla—a lecture;   (3) the legal situation and economic life—Sztolcman;   (4) the labor problem—Jaszunski;   (5) health—Mil. [Milejkowski].

In the afternoon we were received by Dr. Arlt and his assistant Heinrich. I delivered a speech on the subject of security of life and property. I related the events of a single day in the Kehilla and concluded with a call for security of life and property. I also noted that the armbands degrade the dignity of the Jews and point the way for criminals. I described the riots in Warsaw, unmatched in their violence since 1880. Finally, I outlined the financial situation of the Kehilla.

Arlt has some doubts about the armbands. The soldiers would have no way of identifying prostitutes without the armbands. He was reminded that those to whom he was referring would remove their armbands. I noted that some exceptions are being made, that it had been suggested to me that I apply to *Stadtpräsident,* for should they happen to call me—for example—during the night, I

---

11. Dr. Michal Weichert, head of ŻSS, had hoped to bring the officials of the Warsaw Judenrat into contact with Dr. Fritz Arlt, head of the General-gouvernement's Office for Population and Health Affairs, who supervised ŻSS. The idea was to provide the Judenrat with German contacts other than the SS. The SS, however, soon put an end to these efforts.

12. Josef Jaszunski, an engineer, had headed ORT, an international Jewish organization for vocational training, in prewar Poland. Dr. Israel Milejkowski headed the Judenrat's public-health and hospital departments. Abraham Sztolcman was an engineer from Włocławek, Isaac Bornstein was secretary of the Joint Distribution Committee in Warsaw.

would not be able to appear; [13] there are green bands that exempt Jews. In short, the authorities recognize the danger. Jaszunski, Sztolcman, Milejkowski spoke on forced labor, restrictions, disease.

Arlt demanded that the data pertaining to Kehilla funds, public works, and statistics on births (and miscarriages) be complete.

III/29/1940

I got up at 5 a.m. We arrived in Warsaw at 6:20. I stopped at the SS. In the Kehilla new orders—erect a ghetto wall, set up a shelter for 3,000 people evacuated from the Reich and more.

I called a council meeting for 1 in the afternoon to report on the course of the sessions in Cracow. At 3 p.m. Milejkowski will confer with Sztolcman. Many arrests and police roundups, etc.

III/30/1940

Since the morning, rumors about a ghetto. . . . Later, at Leist's,[14] I reported Richter's demands that we set up a Jewish postal service, a quarantine for the 3,000 evacuated from the Reich, also our own letter regarding the impossibility of erecting walls (as they would affect water pipes, electric wiring, telephone cables, etc.). I reported on Cracow. He answered that he is the direct authority, that we should not accept instructions from anywhere else. He gave me his card with a phone number. Mikulecki, the officer at the Discount Bank, promised a loan of 160,000 zl. (to be repaid in quarterly installments). . . .

IV/5/1940

0° *Celsius. Heavy leaden clouds.*

I have to see Herzog at Bruela Palace.[15] Is the ghetto already a reality? The consultations at Herzog's have not borne results. A copy of a letter instructing officials to leave the "ghetto" was brought to the Kehilla. The housing office asks if the Kehilla has any knowledge of this, for people are pouncing on the apartments.

Deliberations regarding the trip to Cracow (Sztolcman).

13. Subject to curfew, Jews were severely penalized for violating regulations.
14. Oberführer Ludwig Leist, Deputy District Chief for the City of Warsaw.
15. Brühl Palace was the prewar headquarters of the Polish Finance Ministry.

One of the people from Krochmalna Street died of hunger in the yard today.

VI/29/1940

6 a.m. After a stormy night, 17°C. Yesterday rumors of a more serious nature about a ghetto. I must find out today how much truth is in them. Apart from this—the financial affairs of the community. There are grounds for sorrow. In the morning I was with Heilman and Kunze[16] at Daniłowiczowska Street. Kunze directed me to the SS. I described the financial situation of the Kehilla to the secretary Żulkowska and asked that it be conveyed to Kunze. A moment later she returned, saying that 100,000–200,000 zl. would be released for the Kehilla that very day. During the meeting with Heilman we were both called to see Leist. Braun received us and announced that 300,000 [zl.] were released. I must present Kunze with a plan for liquidating workers' debts.

At the same time he indicated that Jews must show respect for the uniform of the German military corps and for officials at every rank by removing their hats; Jewish women are required to bow their heads.

I raised the question of the rabbinate and schools. He referred me to councillor Schmidt.

A car was sent from Okecie to catch work dodgers from Okęcie. 150 people were caught today, among them some who showed proof of having made payments to the Kehilla.[17]

Jewish houses, it seems, will be taken over by the K.K.O.[18] It is said that these houses bring in 4 million zl. a month. I am making every effort to have them keep the Jewish managers.

The municipality received a letter regarding the ghetto and is working up the data.

VII/8/1940

At home an afternoon of torture. My wife admits people at home who have business with the Kehilla. I sit in a small stifling room

---

16. Heilman, a Pole, supervised the Judenrat's financial affairs. He worked under Kunze, Leist's chief assistant, who also headed the German housing authority.
17. Okęcie, an airport near Warsaw, was a forced-labor site. Presumably Jews sent to work there fled. Some of those who were caught had receipts to show that they had paid for exemptions to avoid being drafted for forced labor.
18. Komunalna Kasa Oszczędności (Municipal Savings Bank).

which is like a prison. On top of this the constant grumbling of the Jews. They are unwilling to pay for the general benefit of the Kehilla, but seek intervention in personal matters, in cases of misfortune. If the intervention fails, if the matter is protracted, endless grumbling as though it all depended on me. Often the complaints are loud.

Gepner [19] asked me today how I manage to maintain such equilibrium and self-control. These qualities stem from my difficult childhood and conditions in my parents' home. I learned to suffer there.

VII/26/1940

15°C. Today seems to be a crucial day with respect to the houses. I was ordered to wait for an answer. In the city, more and more frequently furnishings are being seized from apartments.

I submitted a memorandum regarding the ban on the sale of books. Jews were forbidden to borrow books from libraries. They are forbidden to enter Ujazdowski Park.

X/1/1940

6°C. In the morning, the Gestapo. I didn't find Müller.[20] Again at 12. I described the conditions of the workers in the camps, the financial state of the Kehilla, the cóndition of the Jewish population (evictions from apartments, confiscation of furnishings), the state of Jewish buildings (management by commissioners), the matter of the hospital on Czysta about to be taken from us,[21] the matter of the ghetto. The last item has a prominent question mark.

X/10/1940

10°C. In the morning, the Kehilla. Lately the number of Jewish suicides has been mounting. Not long ago Freider and his wife took poison. Yesterday Ludwig Bergson and his wife. Ludwig Krakowski, age 85, died in prison.

They continue to work on plans for the ghetto. They seem to

---

19. Abraham Gepner (1872–1943), lifelong communal leader, head of the food-supply department of the Warsaw Judenrat.
20. Johannes Müller, SIPO commander in the Warsaw district.
21. Known as the Jewish Hospital, this venerable Jewish institution was located in an area outside the prescribed limits of the ghetto.

be matching the area statistically on the basis of 104,000 Poles = 110,000 Jews from outside the walls.

X/12/1940

I can go out a little later, this because my appearance at the Kehilla on Yom Kippur might seem like a display of atheism. But suddenly a letter arrived from the municipality that I must report to Makowski[22] on Daniłowiczowska Street at 10 a.m. The problem: 1,000 "laborers."

At 10:30 a session at Makowski's. Present: Schön,[23] Braun, Makowski, Drost. Also Czerniewski[24] and a city official.

First a German session, then one with Czerniewski and his companion, finally they asked for me.

It was announced (by Schön) that in the name of humanity, as per orders from the chief, the overall chief, the high command, a ghetto was being set up. A plan for a ghetto and a plan for a German quarter were handed to me separately. It becomes clear that those streets bordering the ghetto are intended for Poles.

I was ordered to set up a Jewish militia of 1,000 men.

Until October 31 people will have an opportunity to leave voluntarily, after that they will be compelled to leave. Furniture may not be taken out.

My objections, from a financial point of view, were answered: the militia could be composed of volunteers and, besides, the ghetto has ample material means.

At this moment (3 p.m.) municipal workers are taking apart the iron fence of the gardens at Św. Barbary and melting them down.

X/27/1940

In the morning at Mohns.[25] I described the pace of the population transfer. 5,400 apartments were exchanged with Jews, 3,200 by formal arrangement, a total of 8,600 out of the total number of 11,567 Aryan apartments in the ghetto. The 3,000 remaining apartments are: 2,500 which cannot be exchanged (the apartments of janitors, the

22. Makowski was Deputy District Chief for Housing.
23. Waldemar Schön was head of the Resettlement Division of the Warsaw district and as such in charge of ghettoizing the Warsaw Jews.
24. A Polish official in the Housing Department of the Warsaw municipality.
25. Otto Mohns was Schön's assistant.

factory crew) and 500 that can be exchanged. 58,000 Jews have moved, and 22,000 will move to the 500 + 3,200 apartments, *which leaves 55,000 Jews without a roof over their heads.*

Mohns took this issue to Schön and to the chief and was granted an extension until November 15.

After this I outlined the financial state of the Kehilla to Dr. Klein, Dr. Auerswald,[26] and Schubert. I am asking for a loan of 100,000 zl. from the Kehilla's own funds, a loan from the banks, authorization of the two codes (on immovable property and businesses), etc.

Mohns demanded that I set up an Office to grant exit permits from the ghetto to other streets. Yesterday I appointed Lt. Col. Szeryński chief of the *Ordnungsdienst* [Jewish police].[27]

VI/9/1941

In the morning the Kehilla. 3 p.m. at Auerswald's. He promised to supply the soup kitchen with 500 tons of oats within the next 3 months, 500 hundredweight of sugar and 10,000 kg. of meat a month. He will also give fat (rapeseed oil). . . .

In the afternoon, work at home, interrupted every so often by the wails of paupers under the window: "Bread, bread, I am hungry! I am starving!"

VI/27/1941

In the morning the Kehilla. Afterward at Auerswald. He ordered a list of all foreign Jews in the ghetto. I must call on Fribolin[28] (from Karlsruhe) regarding the ghetto budget. I did call on him (he is polite and nervous). Afterwards I visited Kulski, whom I asked to contact Ivánka[29] with respect to the city budget and the ghetto budget.

Auerswald exempted me and Sztolcman from wearing the armband. Finally he ordered that Milejkowski be put in harness. (It

---

26. Hans Klein was head of the Internal Administration Department of the Warsaw district. Heinz Auerswald was the German Commissioner of the Warsaw ghetto from May 15, 1941, to January 1, 1943.
27. Józef Andrzej Szeryński, formerly a colonel in the Polish police, was a convert to Catholicism.
28. Head of the Finance Department in Warsaw.
29. Alexander Ivánka, head of the Finance Department of the Warsaw municipality.

took great effort to convince him to install someone with authority in matters related to the epidemic.)

I called a consultation about combating the epidemic. I proposed that we charge the house committees, the administrators, the janitors with the responsibility for concealing the sick, the spread of lice, etc.

I received a gift from one of the students in the graphics course: a few of my sonnets with her own illustrations.

X/27/1941

In the morning the Kehilla. . . .

Worrisome rumors about the fate awaiting Warsaw's Jews in the spring.

I received the following written request from the rabbis:
> Since the epidemic rampant in our city is spreading rapidly with each passing day, we propose a religious ceremony as a countermeasure, i.e., let a wedding of a poor couple be arranged in the cemetery, immediately after Yom Kippur, and at the Kehilla's expense. This ceremony is tried and tested and will surely, with God's help, have the effect of arresting the epidemic.
>
> This decision was adopted at the meeting of the rabbis on IX/28/1941.

XII/29/1941

In the morning the Kehilla. Auerswald and Jesuiter [30] appeared to deliver a sharp rebuke: Why no report of the collection had been submitted until 9 a.m. It was explained that it had been impossible to count the enormous piles, a load which would fill 6 cars of a train.[31] They demanded that a count be made by 3. (The conversation took place at 12.)

All divisions were mobilized to count the furs.

At 3 p.m. the information was transmitted. As of 6 p.m., De-

---

30. SS Sturmführer Jesuiter, in the office of the head of the Higher SS and Police in Warsaw.

31. This refers to the furs and skins confiscated by the Germans from the Jews in the Warsaw ghetto. In the entire occupied area, the Germans seized all furs of the Jewish and Polish population to send to their soldiers on the Russian front.

cember 28, the following items were collected: 690 men's fur coats, 2,541 women's fur coats, 4,441 men's fur linings, 4,020 women's fur linings, 222 silver foxes, 258 blue foxes, 572 red foxes, 5,118 cuffs, 39,556 collars, 7,205 skins, 2,201 sheepskins, 25,569 receipts were issued. . . .

BURIALS

	1941	1940	1938
October	4,716	457	379
November	4,801	445	413
December		581	437

CASES OF TYPHUS

	1941	1940
October	3,438	16
November	2,456	23
December		17

II/2/1942

In the morning the Kehilla. −9°C.

The Economic Council met yesterday. There were expressions of dissatisfaction with the new line I wish to adopt, i.e., to take from the rich the means with which to feed the poor. On top of that a delegation came to me today with news that over twenty percent of those on relief in the refugee "locales" have starved to death.

III/8/1942

−9°C. 6 p.m. −2°C.

In the morning; the Kehilla. Last night, after serious personal happenings, a doctor was called to see me. He gave me two injections. (Heart attack?) There were deliberations in the Kehilla concerning the centralization of social welfare. The central committee should remain with me. Subordinate to it should be KOM,[32] the Welfare Department attached to the council and the food-supply section. Proposals would be referred to the committee. It would appropriate funds for aid.

The days are cold and there is no coal. Hutzinger who is the authoritative man with regard to coal does not allow Jews to have

---

32. Komitet Opieki Miejski—KOM (City Welfare Committee).

access to him personally, so that the fuel committee has no one to talk to.

III/9/1942

2°C. *In the morning the Kehilla.* Opening meeting of the religious committee and the rabbis. I made a speech about the religious spirit and the need for it. . . .

Doctor Hochsinger examined me. Enlargement of the heart and the aorta.

V/3/1942

In the morning the Kehilla. The propaganda cameramen arrived at 10 o'clock.[33] They filmed my work room, staged a crowd arriving to see me: rabbis, etc. Then they photographed the pictures and charts. They placed a menorah on my desk, with all the candles lit.

Szeryński will be transferred to the Jewish prison today or tomorrow.[34]

The Transferstelle demanded a list of all workers in the ghetto, among them the Kehilla officials. It occurs to me that this must relate to the deportation of unproductive elements from Warsaw.

V/12/1942

In the morning, the Kehilla. Avril [35] appeared with the cameramen and demanded to film a scene in the ritual bath on Dzielna Street. For this purpose 20 pious men with side locks were needed as well as 20 women of good family. There is also a circumcision scene. Dr. Milejkowski was ordered to arrange it. The candidate, unfortunately, weighs only 2 kg. There is reason to worry that he will not live that long.

V/13/1942 +12°C. −18°C.

In the morning at Brandt's with Lejkin.[36] B. reports, in answer

---

33. This and the following entries refer to a film which the Germans were making to depict "Jewish degeneracy" in the ghetto.
34. Szeryński had been arrested for dealing illegally in the confiscated Jewish furs.
35. SS Hauptsturmführer Franz Avril of the SD in Warsaw.
36. SS Obersturmführer Karl Georg Brandt was assistant to the Warsaw head of

to my question, that the Commander does not agree to free Szeryński. He will be transferred to the Jewish prison. At the end of the conversation he added that even if Szeryński is freed, he will no longer be in charge of the Jewish police, but, at best, will be an adviser.

Yesterday they took pictures in the ritual bath. The women they brought had to be replaced, because one of them refused to undress.

They demanded that the circumcision not take place in a clinic, but in a private home.

I questioned B. and the Commissioner about the subjects being filmed. I asked why no pictures were taken of the school, etc.

V/15/1942   14°C.

In the morning the Kehilla. At home the film crew is expected at 8:30. I asked that a man and some women be hired to act the roles for the camera.

They arrived at 8:45 and filmed until 12:30. They hung a sign on the door with an address. They brought two women and a "lover" to the apartment. Also an old Jew. They filmed a scene.

There is more talk in the city about a deportation. They talk in terms of tens of thousands. The ability to work in such conditions, to follow through on a plan, is to be commended. Still, we do our everyday tasks. Tears will not help us. Again, in the words of Dickens: "You cannot wind the clock with tears." . . .

V/21/1942

In the morning the Kehilla. Air raid drill at 10. We all went down to the archives. Auerswald ordered that the group of 400 required to leave for the camp be supplemented, perhaps by some German and Czech Jews.

There is the possibility of releasing a few youths, under 17,

---

the Reich Security Main Office (RSHA) section dealing with Jews (IV B 4). Jakob Lejkin, a lawyer, succeeded Szeryński as head of the Jewish police. He distinguished himself by his bestiality during the deportations of the summer of 1942. On October 29, 1942, he was executed by the Jewish Combat Organization.

and, in addition, a few hundred adults. I am making every effort in this direction. . . .

In the afternoon a hall was made ready for the cameramen. A dance is to take place there tomorrow at 8:30 with champagne, etc.

Someone appeared from the Jewish police and announced that Avril was expecting me to serve as the host at the dance the following day. I answered that at 8:30 I was due, together with Lejkin, at Brandt's. He answered that he would try to release me from the appointment with Brandt so I could present myself for the filming.

I phoned Auerswald who told me: I forbid you to appear. He ordered me to be at the Kehilla at 7:30. Maybe, still and all, something will change. The matter was, obviously, not settled. Will I have the strength to maintain myself on a level of honor?

Toward evening I see flowers being carted from the cemetery on a hearse, for the dance.

VII/1/1942

In the morning at 8, with Lejkin at Auerswald's. I presented a request for the release of 10 employees of the Jewish police (death penalty).[37] A. said he would refer the request to the German police. I noted that three of them had been arrested on the street as hostages for three others who had been ordered to appear but had slipped away. Apart from this, there were some individuals on the list who had no connection with smuggling.

A. stopped the printing of the notice about the execution of 100 prisoners as well as the 10 members of the Jewish police and announced that the copy would be changed.

In the afternoon he informed me that I was mistaken, for the [German] police had proved the guilt of all the imprisoned Jewish policemen. . . .

I imagine they will be executed tonight, or toward morning. . . . I raised the matter of the probable execution with Brandt as well. He made no promise of help.

I talked with his superior, Böhme,[38] about Szeryński. He promised to submit a plea for pardon.

37. The Germans had taken 110 hostages (90 men, 10 women, and 10 Jewish policemen) from Jews being held in Pawiak prison on minor charges. The Germans shot them in an act of reprisal for violations by the Jewish populace of police regulations and for police insubordination in enforcing regulations.
38. Böhme headed the Warsaw SD section dealing with Jews.

Today, in the street, Jews were seized for labor. Very few appear willingly. Panic in the [Jewish] quarter. Since yesterday there were rumors about deporting 70,000 Jews from the quarter. The rumors are unfounded. (At least for the present.)

VII/8/1942

Many people are complaining because I arrange plays for children, festive openings of nurseries with orchestras playing, etc.[39] I am reminded of a movie: a sinking ship—the captain orders the jazz band to play to lift the passengers' spirits. I have decided to imitate this captain.

VII/18/1942

In the morning with Lejkin to Brandt and Mende. A day filled with dire forebodings. Rumors that on Monday the evacuation will begin. (Of everybody?!) I asked the Commissioner if he has any information about this. He answered no, adding that he doesn't believe it. In the meanwhile, there is panic throughout the quarter. Some speak of evacuation, others of pogroms.

Today and tomorrow we are expected to clear the synagogue: refugees are to be accommodated there.

VII/19/1942

In the morning the Kehilla. The city is filled with unimaginable panic. Kohn, Heller, Ehrlich [40] are spreading terrifying rumors. The whole thing gives the impression of phoney propaganda. Let us hope this is the case. On the other hand there is talk of 40 cars, ready and waiting. It turns out there are 20 ordered by the SS, for 720 workers scheduled to set out for the camp tomorrow.

Kohn claims that at six p.m. tomorrow, the deportation of 30,-000 Jews from the small ghetto (Śliska Street?) will begin. He himself, with his family, slipped away to Otwock. Others have done the same.

39. A playground had just been dedicated on a bombed-out area cleared of its rubble and debris. Three children's choirs performed and Czerniaków and other communal officials spoke.
40. Kohn and Heller, a Jewish business firm engaged in transportation, were involved in dealings with the SS and German police. Józef Ehrlich, a Jewish underworld character, was a Gestapo agent and a confidant of the head of the German criminal police in Warsaw.

Because of the panic I toured the entire quarter in a car today. I was in three kindergartens. I don't know if I succeeded in calming the population. But I did what I should. I try to encourage the delegations that come to me. No one sees what this costs me.

Today I took two drugs for headaches, valerian and cybalgin. Still, my head is splitting. I try to keep the smile on my face.

VII/20/1942

In the morning at 7:30 at the Gestapo. I asked Mende [41] how much truth was in the rumors. He answered that he had heard nothing. I then turned to Brandt. He said he knew of no such plan. To the question, could such a thing, nonetheless, happen, he answered that he knows nothing. I left him feeling uncertain. I went to his superior, Commissioner Böhme. He answered that this was not his department, that perhaps Holenmann would have some information about the background of these rumors. I commented that according to the rumors the evacuation would begin today at 19:30. He answered that he would surely know something if this was so.

There being no other way, I turned to the assistant director of Section III, Scherer. [42] He expressed surprise about the rumor and also claimed that he knew nothing about it.

Finally, I asked if I could inform the population that there was no cause for fear. He answered that I could, that what was being said was "rubbish" and "nonsense."

I ordered Lejkin to make this announcement in the local precincts.

I went to see Auerswald. He informed me that he had told the SS Police Leader everything.

Meanwhile, First [43] saw Jesuiter and Schleterer who expressed indignation at the rumors and said there would soon be an investigation to discover their source.

VII/22/1940 [42]

At 7:30 a.m. in the Kehilla. The boundaries of the small ghetto are guarded by a special unit, in addition to the regular one.

41. Gerhardt Mende worked under Brandt in the Warsaw RSHA IV B 4.
42. SS Obersturmführer Rudolf Scherer of the SD in Warsaw.
43. Israel First, director of the Judenrat's Economics Department, presumably a go-between of the Judenrat and the Gestapo. He was executed by the Jewish Combat Organization, November 1942.

At 10, Sturmbannführer Höfle [44] appeared with his men. We disconnected the telephone line. The children were cleared out of the kindergarten across the way.

It was announced that Jews, without distinction of age or sex, apart from specific exceptions, will be deported to the East. Today by 4 o'clock, 6,000 souls must be produced. The same quota (at least) will be expected every day.

There was an order to clear the building at 103 Żelazna Street for the needs of the German functionaries in charge of carrying out the evacuation.

Furnishings were left in place.

Since Council [Judenrat] officials as well as their wives and children were exempted from the deportation, I requested that the exemption be extended to include workers in the ŻSS, the association of workers removing the garbage, and I received approval for this.

I asked for the release of Gepner, Rozen, Sztolcman, Drybiński, Winter, Kobryner [45]—the request was granted.

At 3:45, all of them, except Rozen, are already in the ghetto.

In the afternoon Lejkin ordered that I be informed that glass was apparently thrown at a police car. He threatened that should such a thing reoccur, our hostages would be shot.

The most tragic problem is that of the children in the orphanage, etc. I raised this question—I may be able to accomplish something.

At 5:30, Forwort(?),[46] one of the functionaries, arrived and demanded that Jozef Ehrlich be made Lejkin's assistant. He already boasts 3 stars.

Sturmbannführer Höfle (who is directing the evacuation) called me to the study and informed me that my wife is free—for the time being—but should the evacuation fail, she would be the first to be shot as a hostage.

---

44. Hanz Höfle, in charge of the deportations from the Warsaw ghetto, with the title Commissioner for the Resettlement of the Warsaw Ghetto.
45. Six of the forty or so officers and staff of the Judenrat whom the Germans had taken hostage the previous day to ensure the Judenrat's compliance with their orders.
46. Probably Worthoff, mentioned in Czerniaków's next entry and likely the same SS Obersturmführer Josef Worthoff referred to in footnote 54.

VII/23/1942

In the morning the Kehilla. Worthoff, of the team in charge of the evacuation, appeared. We discussed a number of matters. He exempted trade-school students from the evacuation. Also, husbands of working women. As for the orphans, he instructed me to take this up with Höfle. He also instructed me to discuss the matter of artisans. As for the question how many days a week will the action take place, the answer received was seven days a week.

In the city a great push to set up workshops. A sewing machine could save a man's life.

It is 3 p.m. At the moment there are 4,000 ready to go. By 4 there must be—as per orders—9,000.

Some official or other appeared at the post office and ordered all incoming letters and packages forwarded to Pawiak.

[end of journal]

PREXY CZERNIAKÓW

Prexy Czerniaków, the fat pot,
Eats his chicken soup hot.
How so? Just dough!
Money is a dandy thing.

Mme. Czerniaków likes to get her hair done.
She drinks her tea with sugar and bun.
How so? Just dough!
Money is a dandy thing.

The Jewish policeman is a ruffian thug,
Goes out in the street and hauls you off to the jug.
How so? Just dough!
Money is a dandy thing.

FROM THE MINUTE BOOK OF THE LUBLIN JUDENRAT

MINUTES NO. 32

Plenary session of the Jewish Council of Lublin

June 20, 1940

The deliberations were devoted to the reorganization of the Department of Forced Labor for Men and to the matter of monthly payments for substitutes.[47]

During the discussion, in which all present participated, the following proposals were made:

Councilman Tenenbaum: to secure a guarantee of respite for persons paying the fee for a substitute.

Councilman Kestenberg: Setting a fixed price for a work substitute, ranging from 50–100 zl. a month.

Councilman Halbershtat: Favors preserving the sliding scale of payments for substitutes, so that the lowest rate would be 25 zl. a month.

Councilman Lewinsohn: Favors raising the present payments by 10 zl. on a monthly basis.

Councilman Kantor: Supports Councilman Halbershtat and adds that a few divisions should be opened to receive these payments.

Councilman Edelstein: A single equal sum for anyone requesting a substitute.

In the voting, the proposals of Councilmen Kestenberg, Halbershtat, Kantor, and Edelstein regarding fees for substitutes were defeated, whereas the proposal of Councilman Lewinsohn to raise the present fee by 10 zl. was accepted.

47. Like all Judenräte, the Judenrat in Lublin maintained a labor registry from which the specified number of forced laborers demanded by the Germans was drawn. A person eligible for forced labor could pay for a substitute. These payments were used by the Judenrat to feed the forced laborers (the Germans did not provide food) and for other communal needs. Despite this system, the Germans often arbitrarily seized Jews off the ghetto streets and took them for forced labor, even though they had already served their terms or had paid for substitutes.

Also the proposals of Councilmen Tenenbaum and Kantor were accepted as desirable.

It was also decided to tax any exemption from additional excused days at the rate of 50 groszy per day, and it was noted that this source of income would be available to the Jewish Welfare Committee for the exclusive benefit of the sick and indigent in the hospital.

Chairman:	[Signed]	*Eng. H. Becker*
Recording Secretary:	[Signed]	*D. Hochgemain*

MINUTES NO. 61

Plenary session of the Jewish Council of Lublin

December 28, 1940

(1)   In the name of the entire Jewish Council, the chairman extended a warm welcome to Councilman Kelner, who returned to work after a prolonged illness.

(2)   The chairman read a letter from the Stadthauptmann in Lublin, dated December 17, 1940, approving Dr. Josef Siegfried, the newly elected Councilman. (2) An invitation from the Jewish public kitchen for black coffee on December 29, 1940, in celebration of Hanukkah.

(3)   Councilman Hochgemain reported on activities of the fiscal section. It was decided to apply sanctions against those failing to pay the advance toward the Kehilla tax for the second half of 1940.

(4)   It was decided to require a monthly fee, beginning January 1941, from every Lublin Jew, 16 years of age and over, for expenses entailed in carrying out official orders pertaining to the labor obligations of the Jewish population. These fees will be collected by specially designated individuals. The Labor Commission is to be responsible for carrying out this decision.

(5)   The chairman announced: (1)   the opening of an Arbeitsamt penal work camp at Browarna St.[48] (2)   As for the failure to open gardening courses according to plan, only one applicant appeared.[49]

48. Established by the German occupation authorities for those Jews who evaded forced labor without paying for substitutes.
49. Gardening courses in the urban ghettos were intended to help the Jewish population grow herbs and vegetables to supplement their inadequate food rations.

(6)   Councilman Schlaf reported on activities of the School Commission. He explained that efforts are directed for the moment toward acquiring adequate housing.

Chairman:	[Signed]	*Eng. H. Becker*
Councilman, Secretary:	[Signed]	*D. Hochgemain*

APPENDIX I

NOTICE

In the matter of fixing fees for male labor.

The Jewish Council of Lublin announced to the Jewish population of Lublin:

(1)   In order to cover expenses entailed in carrying out the orders of the authorities relating to the labor requirement of the Jewish population, every Jew in Lublin, over the age of 16, beginning January 1, 1941, will be required to pay a monthly sum, a "work fee" at a rate to be determined by the Labor Commission.

(2)   Collection of this fee will be carried out by specially designated persons who will appear monthly in the home of every payer.

(3)   Beginning January 1, until further notice, the obligation to appear for forced labor at the square at 2 Narutowicz Street is no longer in effect. On the other hand, the obligation that all unemployed males of registration age—between 12 and 60—appear once a week for a check at the German Labor Office, 3 Królewska St., remains in effect.

(4)   Those paying work fees may, just as they have done thus far, continue to fulfill the obligation to appear for a check—as outlined in paragraph 3—through the Labor Commission functioning in the premises at 10 Lubartowska St.

(5)   The Labor Commission receives the public every day, except Saturday, from 9 to 14 o'clock, on matters connected with the new fee as well as matters relating to cancelling debts for work.

The collection of debts will be pursued rigorously. New fees will be expected on time. Otherwise the Council will take measures at its disposal. It is in the best interests of the payers to settle their debts as early as possible and to pay further fees for work as they become due.

Jewish Council of Lublin   Lublin: 1940

MINUTES NO. 10–14 (71–75)

Plenary sessions of the Jewish Council of Lublin

March 23, 24, 25, 26, and 27, 1941 [50]

All 24 Councilmen were present.

At these meetings the problem of furnishings and other property in storage was considered in detail. The meeting heard a report by the Housing Division on the project to provide housing connected with the establishment of the ghetto; the order of the head of the Lublin district, dated March 24, 1941, on the establishment of a Jewish residential quarter (ghetto) was read and in connection therewith a detailed discussion of the Council's work plan directed toward execution of this order. Chairman Becker reported on distribution by the authorities of flour for matzot for the Jewish population and in this connection the Matzo Commission was asked to make the necessary technical arrangements. Dr. Alten reported on efforts to influence the *Stadthauptmannschaft* as well as the *Treuhandstelle* [51] with regard to opening the closed stores; in the matter of the disposal of the Jewish houses in the ghetto and their management a committee of Councilmen Edelstein and Hufnagel was appointed.

Chairman:	[Signed]	*H. Becker*
Councilman-Secretary:	[Signed]	*Hochgemain*

MINUTES NO. 15 (76)

Plenary session of the Jewish Council of Lublin

March 29, 1941

(1)   Council Chairman Eng. Becker announced that the authorities have agreed to grant travel permits as well as the right to take belongings to those leaving Lublin voluntarily on the dates specified in the District head's order. Thus far, the authorities have

50. On March 24, 1941, the German governor of the Lublin district decreed that a ghetto would be established by April 15 to accommodate no more than 20,-000 Jews. Consequently, 15,000 Jews had to leave the city "voluntarily." Though the evacuees were permitted to take their belongings, the lack of transport forced them to leave behind most of their goods and furnishings. The Germans gave the Judenrat responsibility for this property.

51. The *Treuhandstelle* was the German agency in charge of immovable property.

granted permits for settlement in the districts of Radzyń, Chełm, Krasnystaw, and Janów. In this connection the Council Chairman proposed acceptance of the principle that those leaving Lublin be required to pay debts owed the Kehilla for 1940 as well as for the first quarter of 1941.

Various Councilmen participated in a discussion of this proposal; Edelstein suggested setting up an evacuation fund from fees to be levied on all Jews remaining in Lublin; Tenenbaum proposed that the authorities be asked to entrust the Kehilla with responsibility for the transfer operation; Siegfried is opposed in principle to taxing those who leave, but should they, nonetheless, be taxed, these funds should be earmarked solely for expenses involved in the transfer.

There was further discussion by Councilmen Kantor, Davidsohn, Hochgemain, Waiselfish, Kelner, Kershman, Schlaf, and Alten.

After discussion the Council decided to require those leaving to pay their debts to the Kehilla for 1940 as well as the first quarter of 1941 and, otherwise, to deny [exit] permits.

The Financial Division was put in charge of carrying out this decision.

(2)   Chairman Eng. Becker reported on activities undertaken thus far by the Housing Division. He began his remarks by reading a letter of resignation from Councilman Rechtman, chairman of the Housing Division. The Housing Division is not making any further allocation of apartments until final arrangements are made regarding the apartment houses on Grodzka Street for Jews employed in German institutions; at present the buildings in the Jewish quarter are being measured to exploit fully its space, voluntary agreements are being accepted which will be approved, applications are being registered from candidates for apartments in the Jewish quarter.

As Chairman he nominates Councilman Siegfried for internal organizational work in the Housing Department.

Councilmen participated in the ensuing debate as follows:

Waiselfish proposed that a committee of 7 Councilmen be set up to head the Housing Division. He later proposed that apartments be allocated without delay and the fees therefor be collected.

Goldsobel proposed 2 more members to the Housing Committee in addition to Councilman Siegfried.

Burstein proposed that the resignation of Councilman Rechtman not be accepted. To appoint a committee of 3 to 5 Councilmen who would head the Housing Division.

Kershman opposes a broader housing commission. He nominates Councilmen Goldsobel, Siegfried, and Rechtman for this committee.

Hufnagel suggests that negotiations with the *Wohnungsamt* [Housing Office] in the name of the Jewish Council be entrusted to a Councilman rather than to Wiener, head of the Housing Division.

Tenenbaum appealed to the committee that when subleasing quarters where tenants are already in residence, they should give consideration in the choice of subtenants because these people will have to live together and a suitable selection should be made.

Schlaf opposed expansion of the Housing Committee.

Kantor recommends that voluntary agreements be excluded from the competency of the Housing Division and referred to a special committee. He favors a committee of five. He presses for quick action to extend the area of the ghetto.

Rechtman also is for a committee of three Councilmen.

Davidsohn moves not to accept Rechtman's resignation; favors the referral of voluntary agreements to another committee as well as allocation of apartments in order to collect fees.

Alten expresses the opinion that the Housing Division should be headed by Councilmen Rechtman and Goldsobel as well as by the officials Wiener and Altman. As for Councilman Siegried, he proposes that he organize the entire machinery and participate in meetings on fundamental matters. He favors excluding voluntary agreements from the competency of the committee.

In the election which took place, the proposal for a 5-man committee received 7 votes, a 4-man committee received 5 votes, a 3-man committee received 9 votes. Councilmen Rechtman, Goldsobel, and Levi were chosen to serve on the committee. Councilman Siegfried was elected to coordinate and organize the work of the committee. Councilman Levi declared that he considers the election coerced.

(3)   Councilman Kelner was chosen chairman of the Division for Registration, Information, and Emigration.

(4)   Councilman Waiselfish was chosen to replace Councilman Levi on the Matzo Committee.

Council Chairman: [Signed]   *Eng. Becker*
Councilman, Recording Secretary: [Signed]   *Hochgemain*

MINUTES NO. 47 (108)

Plenary session of the Jewish Council of Lublin

October 6, 1941

The chairman opened the meeting, explaining that it would be a continuation of the one that was interrupted on the 4th of the month and would be devoted to continued debate on the subject of improving the management of the Jewish Hospital in Lublin. His actual proposal was that the General Hospital be consolidated with the Hospital for Contagious Diseases.

Councilman Tenenbaum proposes that the administration of the General Hospital become subordinate to the Health Department, in a set-up similar to that of the Hospital for Contagious Diseases.

Councilman Kantor maintains that his motion concerning the immediate dismissal of Mendel Horowich from the post of administrative director of the hospital should be dealt with before considering any further business.

Councilman Hufnagel proposes that the question of possible changes in the management of the hospital be referred to the Health Department.

Councilman Davidsohn maintains that the debate is straying from its proper course, that the goal of today's meeting was to consider how the hospital should be administered in the event Mendel Horowich is relieved of his position.

Councilman Tenenbaum emphasizes that one should distinguish between the two questions, improving future relationships inside the Jewish Hospital and the issue of Horowich.

Vice-chairman Kestenberg proposes the establishment of a committee consisting of Mr. Horowich and two other Councilmen to conduct the hospital administration.

Vice-chairman Alten supports the proposal of Councilman Tenenbaum and, in the matter of Horowich, supports the motion of the presiding officers presented to the Jewish Council on September 21.[52]

Councilman Siegfried declares that he will vote for the motion of the presiding officers and that this proposal adequately reflects a lack of confidence in Horowich.

Councilman Kantor withdraws the motion he presented at the Jewish Council meeting of September 13 to relieve Horowich of his duties. Justifying his position, he maintains that though he is deeply convinced of its justice, he sees no possibility that his motion would be passed.

A vote was held in which the Council decided (1) unanimously to transfer administrative management of the Jewish Hospital of

52. That motion was to dismiss Horowich for mismanagemest of hospital affairs.

Lublin to the Lublin Health Department; along with this a decision to enact suitable changes in the bylaws of the Jewish Hospital of Lublin; a recommendation to Councilmen who are also members of the hospital board to carry out these suggestions.

(2) By a vote of 12 to 4, with the rest abstaining, it was decided: on the basis of the investigation undertaken by the board of supervisors and the examination of books and certification of the Jewish Hospital of Lublin for the period April 1, 1939–January 31, 1941, the Jewish Council has concluded that the organizational and supervisory management and accounting of the Jewish Hospital during the aforementioned period were conducted in a most slovenly and defective manner, that those in charge did not live up to their task and made it possible for fraud to be perpetrated. Hence this expression of censure toward those responsible for the hospital administration and especially its management, and Mendel Horowich, administrative director, for this unfortunate situation.

Chairman: [Signed]   *Eng. H. Becker*
Secretary-Councilman: [Signed]   *D. Hochgemain*

MINUTES NO. 53 (114)

Plenary session of the Jewish Council of Lublin

November 23, 1941

[Besides the Councilmen a] delegation of doctors also participated in the meeting: Dr. Tenenbaum, Dr. Goldwag, and Dr. Susser.

The chairman announced that today's meeting was called to consider a strategy to combat the typhus epidemic. The chairman also announced that during the past week Dr. Wolberg, a representative of the ŻSS, spent some time in Lublin, during which period the Chairman and the Health Commission consulted with him on this matter.

After a debate in which the doctors and nearly all members of the Council participated, it was decided: (a) that the kitchen situated on the ground floor of the Hospital for Contagious Diseases should be transferred to another building to make that space available for the needs of the hospital, and in two days' time the sick now located throughout the city for lack of hospital space are to be transferred to this area; (b) to begin work immediately to make the second floor of the Peretz building available to the hospital; (c) to entrust a committee consisting of Councilmen Eng. Becker, Levi, Kelner, and Lerner with carrying out these two decisions; (d) to call on all members of the Jewish Council to conclude the collection of contributions for the benefit of the Hospital for Contagious Diseases during the current week; (e) to issue an appeal to the Jewish population for voluntary contributions of linen for the Hospital for Contagious Diseases.

Chairman: [Signed] Eng. H. Becker
Councilman-Secretary: [Signed] D. Hochgemain

MINUTES NO. 16 (140)

Plenary session of the Jewish Council of Lublin

March 31, 1942

In conjunction with an order received from the authorities conducting the evacuation action, the following members of the Jewish Council met at 14 o'clock: Dr. Alten, Becker, Burstein, Zimmerman, Davidsohn, Goldsobel, Halbershtat, Hochgemain, Hufnagel, Kantor, Kershman, Kershenblum, Kelner, Levi, Lewinsohn, Lerner, Siegfried, Tenenbaum, Waiselfish.

Absent Councilmen: Kestenberg and Edelstein (detained in prison yesterday),[53] also Rechtman.

A number of nonmembers of the Council were also invited today and they are: Isaac Brodt, Daniel Kupferminz, Joseph Rotrubin, Sholem Taykef, Boleslaw Tenenbaum, Wolf Wiener.

After the arrival of representatives of the authorities—SS-Obersturmführer Josef Worthoff, SS-Untersturmführer Walter, SS- Untersturmführer Dr. Sturm, SS-Unterscharführer Knitzky[54]—Messrs. Worthoff and Dr. Sturm made the following announcement:

53. Kestenberg and Edelstein had, with the consent of the Judenrat board, assembled an immense ransom to offer the Germans in an effort to halt the deportation. But the Germans, having taken the money and jewels, arrested them. Neither man was seen again.
54. Worthoff was the expert on Jewish affairs in the Lublin district office of the RSHA, IV B 4, and the superior of Walter and Knitzky. After completing the deportation of the Jews from Lublin, he was assigned to the deportation of the Jews from Warsaw. Sturm was the expert on racial purity in the Lublin SD.

Deportation (evacuation) of the Jewish population will continue in the future with the difference that the conclusive document, entitling one to remain in Lublin, will no longer be the SIPO stamp on the work certificate, but the J-identity card.[55] Those who have J-identity cards may remain in Lublin. All others will be deported.

The Jewish population must be informed that all those who have the J-identity card must watch out that no one without a J-identity card is hidden in their ghetto apartments which were and will be checked. Otherwise, those with the identity cards will also be deported.

Since those remaining in Lublin will be of an insignificant proportion of the former Jewish population, the Jewish Council will be reduced from 24 to 12 members.

The authorities appointed the following as members of the Jewish Council:

From its previous roster: (1) Dr. Mark Alten, (2) Isaac Kershman, (3) Davoid Hochgemain, (4) Leon Hufnagel, (5) Jacob Kelner, (6) Nachman Lerner, and (7) former Council official Wolf Wiener; besides those on the roster of the previous Council, the following temporaries: (8) Isaac Brodt, (9) Daniel Kupferminz, (10) Joseph Rotrubin, (11) Sholem Taykef, (12) Boleslaw Tenenbaum.

Those former Councilmen who were not included in the body as constituted today will be deported along with their families and will leave Lublin today with the first transport.

Those former Councilmen who reside outside the ghetto will be accompanied to their apartments by SIPO officials and after they take out the necessary things for deportation, their apartments will be sealed.

Former Councilmen Eng. Becker and Dr. Siegfried, by virtue of experience in this area, will assume administrative functions in the Jewish Council and the ŻSS in their new residence.[56]

When the former Councilmen left the room, Dr. Sturm made this announcement:

Dr. Alten has been appointed chairman of the Jewish Council. Kershman has been appointed Vice Chairman.

---

55. J = *Jude*, Jew.
56. The new "residence"—the death camp at Bełzec—had no Jewish organizations. The "assignment" was intended to deceive the Judenrat officials about the destination of the deportees, themselves included.

Alten, Kershman and Kupferminz were appointed to the prae-
sidium.

The assignment of functions among Councilmen, with the possibility that changes will be suggested, should be carried out in the
following manner:

Councilman Kupferminz will be in charge of provisioning the
ghetto.

Councilman Tenenbaum will be in charge of police affairs, disinfection, delousing, housing sanitation.

Stokfish will assist him. Beginning today the Office of Disinfection
and Delousing will be attached to the Jewish Council and become
part of it. As Commandant of the Jewish police, Mendel Goldfarb
remains executive officer.

Councilman Brodt takes over affairs of labor;

Councilman Wiener takes over affairs of housing;

Councilman Hochgemain takes over affairs of finances;

Councilman Hufnagel takes over affairs of social welfare;

Councilman Rotrubin takes over affairs of public health;

Councilman Kelner takes over affairs of records and information;

Councilman Taykef takes over affairs of collecting taxes together
with Councilman Hochgemain.

Dr. Alten is appointed to represent the Council in appearances
before the authorities, but he has the right to delegate his authority
to the heads of other divisions.

Councilmen are required to carry out the recommendations of
Council chairman Dr. Alten.

Any additional proposals for issuing J-identity cards will not be
considered.

The Jewish police is required to call for a voluntary deportation; therefore, 1,600 persons will be deported voluntarily today.

[Signed]   *for Alten*
[Signed]   *D. Hochgemain*

MINUTES NO. 17 (141)

Meeting of the Jewish Council of Lublin

March 31, 1942 [57]

Present: Alten, Kershman, Kupferminz, Hochgemain, Hufnagel,
Taykef, Lerner, Kelner, Rotrubin, Brodt, Tenenbaum.

57. A continuation of the previous meeting, with the new roster of members
selected by the Germans.

Absent: Wiener (sick).

SS-Untersturmführer Dr. Sturm participated in the meeting.

(1)   It was resolved to announce publicly that all those who submitted requests for the J-identity card and filled out yellow questionnaires should appear immediately to receive them; otherwise they will be deported.

(2)   As for the 12 Council officials who have thus far not received the J-identity card, Dr. Sturm ordered that until they receive the J-identity card, these officials, along with their families, shall move to the building at 13 Grodzka Street and thus they will be excluded from the deportation action.

(3)   In accordance with Dr. Sturm's orders, it was decided that in addition to the 12 officials mentioned above, these conditions apply also to cemetery workers (the precise number to be determined with the Police Chief), 2 messengers, 3 mail clerks.

(4)   Dr. Sturm announced that 35 of the 113 active members of the Jewish police will be deported in the course of the present action. Of the remaining 78, 35 will be accepted by the Jewish police on a permanent basis after the action is terminated.

(5)   It was resolved to transfer all food supplies remaining in the empty apartments to one warehouse.

(6)   In accordance with Dr. Sturm's order, it was decided: (1) to issue a call to the population advising them to appear voluntarily for the evacuation, informing them that those hiding in attics, etc., will be shot, that 10 people were shot today who had been hiding in an attic at 10 Grodzka Street; (2)   to send the Council officials, escorted by Jewish police officers, to inform the population of this order.

[Signed]   *D. Hochgemain*

[Signed]   *Dr. Alten*

MINUTES NO. 51 (175)

Second plenary session of the Jewish Council of Lublin

August 26, 1942 [58]

(1)   The bylaws of the Control Commission were discussed. The Council Vice-Chairman Kershman reported on this proposal. After

---

58. The first meeting that day took up the question of a Volunteer Fire Brigade and adopted a set of bylaws governing its composition, functions, and conditions of work.

discussion, the following bylaws of the Control Commission were unanimously adopted.

Bylaws of the Control Commission of the Jewish Council of Lublin

I To provide continuing control over the administration of all of the agencies of the Jewish Council of Lublin a Control Commission shall be set up.

II The Commission shall be chosen by the entire body of the Jewish Council for a year's term.

III The Commission will consist of 4 (four) Council members, one of whom is a presiding officer.

IV The Commission will check the activities of all institutions of the Jewish Council and report the results of its supervision quarterly to the entire body of the Council.

The election of members to the Control Commission was put off to the following meeting.

(2) The proposed Bylaws of the Disciplinary Commission of the Jewish Council were discussed. The Council Vice-Chairman Kershman reported on this proposal. After discussion, the bylaws of the Disciplinary Commission were adopted in the version which follows, along with a note authorizing the chairman Dr. Alten, after receiving a copy of the plan as adopted and after a detailed study of its contents, to present recommendations for revisions to the next session.

Bylaws of the Disciplinary Commission of the Jewish Council of Lublin

§ 1 Members of the Jewish Council, employees of the Jewish Council, including members of the Jewish police, who fail to live up to their positions through any act, evasion, or negligence, and also by their conduct at work or away from it, demean the authority, seriousness, or trust of their position, shall be held responsible and incur disciplinary action.

§ 2 Those actions which incur penalties of a disciplinary nature fall into the categories of misdemeanors and felonies in the line of duty.

§ 3 a. A misdemeanor in the line of duty is a violation of an obligation in the line of duty and is not in the character of a felony in the line of duty.

b. A felony in the line of duty is a violation of official duty which brings injury both to the interests of the service and to the interests of the individual, or to the interests and reputation of the Council, or its institutions. A felony in the line of duty includes a number of misdemeanors or frequent recurrence of misdemeanors in the line of duty which give rise to especially grave consequences.

§ 4   Misdemeanors are punishable according to rules: namely: 1) oral warning; 2) written warning; 3) a fine from 5 to 50 zl. These penalties are to be administered by the Councilman heading the relevant department or by the Commandant of the Jewish police if the offense is committed by a member of that service. If the offense is committed by a Councilman, the Council chairman will administer the penalty.

§ 5   In the case of a penalty administered by a Councilman, a department head, it may be appealed before the Council Chairman. A penalty administered by the Council Chairman may be appealed before the entire membership of the Council. The decision of the Council Chairman is final in the latter case.

The disciplinary punishments are: 1) a warning; 2) censure; 3) suspension of rights and duties for a period from one to three months. (The Disciplinary Commission may impose an additional penalty by withholding salary for this period); and 4) dismissal from service (for Councilmen this means recommending to the authorities that the Councilman be deprived of his position).

§ 6   The warning penalty may not be appealed. Other disciplinary penalties may be brought before a plenary session of the Council within 7 days from the time they are served, along with a written explanation.

§ 7   To preserve the quality of service impaired by defection in the line of duty, the full body of the council elects a disciplinary advocate and an assistant. The disciplinary advocate must have legal training.

§ 8   The Disciplinary Commission will make no decision without first hearing the disciplinary advocate. During the consultations and deliberations of the adjudicative staff, the disciplinary advocate may not be present.

§ 9   The duties of the disciplinary advocate are: 1) to participate in all the meetings of the Disciplinary Commission; 2) to initiate procedures either in accordance with a motion by the Chairman of the Council or as a result of information received from other sources, after contacting the Council Chairman; 3) to present proposals to summon witnesses in case of need; 4) to safeguard the secrecy of all information to which he has access by virtue of his position.

§ 10   The Disciplinary Commission consists of three persons: if the defendant is a Council employee or a member of the Jewish police— two Councilmen and one employee or member of the Jewish police; if the defendant is a Council member—three Council members. The chairman of the Disciplinary Commission or one of its members must have legal training. The judges' decisions are determined by a majority. The chairman casts the final vote. Abstentions are not permitted.

§ 11   In connection with legal action the Council Chairman may suspend the defendant from his position, but he must, within three days, receive authorization from the Disciplinary Commission.

§ 12   In disciplinary proceedings, the defendant may choose a Council member, a Council employee, or a member of the Jewish police to act as his defense. At the defendant's request, the Council Chairman may provide an official counsel for the defense in place of one chosen. The defense counsel may, during office hours, check those documents of his client's dossier which pertain to the disciplinary proceedings. A member of the Disciplinary Commission must be present while the defense counsel studies these documents.

§ 13   Members of the Disciplinary Commission must guarantee the confidentiality of all information received in the line of duty.

Election of members to the Disciplinary Commission was put off for the following week.

Chairman of the Jewish Council:
Council Vice Chairman:
[Signed]   *Kershman*

FROM THE MINUTE BOOK OF
THE BIALYSTOK JUDENRAT

November 2, 1941
Assembly of Judenrat staff with the Judenrat

Chairman Rabbi Dr. Rosenman opens the meeting with the statement that the meeting has been called so as to communicate with the whole ghetto. The Jewish dictum "Hear, O Israel!" refers to the responsibility of the individual for the community and of the community for the individual. We must have 5 million for taxes—head taxes and housing taxes. Everyone, without exception, must pay. But we must look at the future with hope. It is a time of woe unto Israel, but out of it shall we be saved.

Eng. Barash takes the floor.

Honored assembly: For the past four months there was nothing like this. What has been done by us, history will narrate. There was not one tranquil moment: men,[59] contribution, ghetto, articles, evacuation, demand for 10 million. As much as possible, mitigation of the demands was achieved: instead of 25 kg. of gold—6 kg., instead of 5 million—$2\frac{1}{2}$ million. Instead of a ghetto in the quarter of Chanajkes [60]—today's ghetto. The order for 10 million was annulled. No more than 4,500 persons were evacuated to Prużana.[61] The order to submit lists of the intelligentsia was revoked. All this succeeded after much difficult effort, thanks to our good relations with the authorities.

The Judenrat serves as bulwark and protects the ghetto from evil. But the relations of the ghetto to the Judenrat are not as they should be. It's not a matter of gratitude; we do everything because of the goad of conscience. But we have not deserved curses and abuse in any case. The mistakes which happen we try to correct.

Then Mr. Barash reports that on demand of the City Commissioner the Judenrat must pay 700–800,000 rubles every three days, starting Thursday, the 6th of this month. If a deadline is missed, we will be liable to the "ruthless means of the Gestapo." After explaining the situation, Mr. Barash concludes: "If we comply with the demands for work and taxes, we will be sure of our life—otherwise, we are not responsible for the life of the ghetto. God grant that we all meet again, and that no one of us will be missing."

Mr. Subotnik reports on the state of the finances in all regards. Mr. Subotnik remarks that also those burnt out, the poor, those who work outside the ghetto who don't get their wages, and officials who are on our conscience because they work without pay—all will have to pay both the taxes and for electricity and water.

Since all this will not cover even half the demands (they de-

59. Presumably men seized for forced labor.
60. A run-down outlying district of Bialystok.
61. On September 13, 1941, the Germans ordered the evacuation of a large number of "nonproductive" Jews to Prużana, a nearby town.

mand for 48,000 residents, even though 35,000 in all are left), a special tax on the well-to-do will have to be levied.

We will exercise the strictest sanctions against recalcitrants, like arrest, excommunication, etc.

Mr. Subotnik appeals to those present to take into consideration the gravity of the situation and to pass the word on.

Mr. Goldberg relates that only the poor responded to the first appeal; the well-to-do did not. Now there are trades that do good business: wagoners and dealers; we must get after these upstarts.

Mr. I. Lifschitz: For the past 20 years till now I protected Jewish property; now Jewish life must be protected. We must put an end to luxury. All the money must be given away. In a war it is enough to save one's life. We must renounce everything as long as life is saved. . . .

Chairman Rabbi Dr. Rosenman appeals to the Jewish women [62] who often rescued the Jewish people in past times of peril; in a time of good will, we shall, with God's help, conclude this matter.

January 31, 1942

Eng. Barash reports on the purpose of the meeting:

(1)   The Germans are dissatisfied with our workers, they turn up too late for work, they work feebly, and this is considered sabotage. Dr. Kennewig says that he cannot accomplish anything with the Jewish workers, and the Kirchhof firm tried to set up a labor camp where the workers are kept several days on end. The result will be that they will establish such concentration camps for the workers, if the situation will not improve.

(2)   The Gestapo charges that the Jews spread false news about the war and all Israel is responsible for one another. Politics should not be discussed especially with non-Jews; they often pass it on in distorted form.

(3)   There are charges that Jews have bought Russian money, which is a crime in the present situation.

The matter of the two ghettos, continues Eng. Barash, has not yet been nullified. It has now been reopened. One consolation, we hope to keep putting it off. The development of industry in the ghetto is

---

62. Women apparently served as voluntary collectors, going from door to door, house to house, for the money or the objects which the Germans demanded of the Judenrat.

our salvation. Today the City Commissioner and Deputy Commissioner of Ghetto Industry visited our industry. . . .

A. Marcus raises the question of cases of return from Pružana.

Following an exchange of opinion with the participation of Goldberg, Fetsiner, Subotnik, Eng. Barash, Puniansky, Schvif, it is resolved:

(1)   Criminals (thieves) will be sent back.

(2)   Evacuees will not be registered.

(3)   Confiscate the bread ration cards of tenants who permit evacuees to stay with them.[63]

June 20, 1942

Meeting of Jewish Police

The hall is filled with policemen, among whom there are also civilians. Members of the Judenrat are seated on the dais.

Rabbi Dr. Rosenman opens the meeting at a quarter to one with a brief talk, in which he says: Today, after the cleaning-out action, which had to be done, we called this meeting so that I can demonstrate the importance of the duties which are your obligation to carry out for the benefit of the ghetto. You are engaged in the service of order and security. It is a difficult service. Day and night you are vigilant for the security of the population and for the satisfaction of the authorities, to keep order in the life of the ghetto, individual and communal. The ghetto, this miniature state, requires especially great vigilance. Today's meeting, therefore, has great significance. We wish to turn to you with an appeal that you inspire yourself with the deep importance of your office and cherish it honestly and loyally, with great honor.

Eng. Barash takes the floor: I have long sought an opportunity to talk with you about our difficult questions and concerns, which have great significance, especially for your department. But between us stood a wall, an obstacle which made it impossible to communicate. In that situation words were not useful, deeds were required.

Only now has the time come when we can say that evil elements infiltrated you. We ourselves are to blame for this, because at first

63. Blumental, in his notes, asserts that the Germans demanded that the Judenrat do so, but that in fact the Judenrat never carried out the order.

we did not understand the importance of your duties. The whole 35,000-man ghetto is like an organism which has various organs, like a brain, heart, etc. The police—they are the hands for carrying out various decrees, for bringing protection and security to the ghetto. All this is theoretical; actually, however, instead of defense, there was defenselessness; instead of security, lawlessness.

I am far from accusing the entire body of the police, but certain elements like Zelikowicz,[64] Fenigstein, the Fifth and their sympathizers exploited our terrible situation in the ghetto to blackmail and put the 35,000 Jews at the mercy of criminals. As soon as they discovered that someone had merchandise or gold, they noted it and made a house-search, regardless if the man had been taken away on Saturday, or even shot! Like the Chicago gangsters, like the well-known Al Capone, the bandit Zelikowicz prepared lists of places for house-searches, but he won't live to make them. In certain backroom bars and saloons, some members of the police caroused on this expectation.

Such tremendous fortunes were confiscated from this crook Zelikowicz that I am embarrassed when the matter is discussed with me outside the ghetto. There were all kinds of goods, perfumes, liqueurs, champagne, gold, jewels, dollars. The search is not yet finished. Unfortunate people gave him the last they had, just to avoid his threat about a certain place.[65]

And then there were the imitators, who continually extorted, beginning with Prużana, that dreadful disaster and overwhelming terror which struck our ghetto—and so on all occasions—they blackmailed and did other ugly deeds.

A net of go-betweens came into being which ensnared the population as in a cobweb. We have recorded a whole set of facts about their harmful acts, which are too painful for me to discuss now. They also entangled in their net the black market, which is a separate blot on our life. In peacetime we were not obliged to supervise the other fellow's business, but in the ghetto, here everyone is responsible for the deeds of individuals. Even if the thieves are non-Jews, it's all right to shoot ten Jews for the theft.

The ringleader of the black market was Zelikowicz, with his

---

64. Grisha Zelikowicz and sixteen other members of the Jewish police were dropped from the force, five of them sent to a labor camp.
65. Presumably the Gestapo.

agents. This lasted too long, but finally the time came and he and his helpers were removed. And now we give you a warning: if anyone among you will try to continue on this path, we will deal with him mercilessly!

On this occasion I cannot omit mentioning also the criminal acts at the [ghetto] gates. It is a dreadful scene, when 7,000 people return home after a hard day's work, try to bring something through, it is taken from them, and the members of the Jewish police who are at the scene buy it up. Later they sell the confiscated products in their own places. They are, it appears, interested in having the products confiscated, so that they themselves can steal the wretched belongings of poor working people. These we will deal with without mercy!

Now the discussion among the police is whether the recent purge raised or lowered their prestige and authority. Gentlemen! The statistics show that among you 10 percent were criminals—I had expected worse—a full 90 percent of you are honest officials! The gangrene had to be cut out, and that doubtlessly raised your prestige.

If among the populace there are people who interpret it otherwise, then we will use our means to compel them to treat you with the respect which you deserve, and all means will be proper to punish those who insult the police.

Our situation in the ghetto is clear. Until now, for nearly a year, we succeeded in creating the necessary conditions for avoiding the fate of other cities. But to preserve ourselves further, one thing is necessary, which must be understood by everyone, from watchman to official—he must do his job 100 percent. For us there is only one goal! To bring Jews through the Bialystok ghetto and out of it. Now is no time for careers! If we exert all our strength, we must set up such an order! I know that it is very hard for you to manage to make a living, but I cannot give you any assurances. We are a state without finances, without budgets, without gold reserves. The Executive Board will try to meet your needs, within our poor means, so that you can bring your sacred historical obligation to a successful conclusion. (heavy applause)

The newly appointed Vice-Commandant Mr. Moshe Berman gets the floor: Honored colleagues: With the consent of our Commandant Marcus, I accepted the post of Vice-Commandant and I hope my association may add spirit to our organization. I am not a mere nobody, nor a bureaucrat. I will cooperate with Commandant Marcus and we will be pleased to find a common language. I am not one of those people who plays politics, who says "no" just because the other fellow says "yes." My collaboration with Marcus is a guarantee; we both have a Jewish heart, a ghetto heart. First of all must come the interests of the community, our private matters must be thrust aside. He is really committed to the community; my outlook is also the same—why shouldn't we be able to work together?

Recent events have eliminated the group which was convicted by public opinion. Didn't we ourselves talk about a needed clean-up? Weren't we aware of the stigma upon us? But we weren't sure if we could wash it out. Now that this thing is finished, we are satisfied, because the few days cost us no small heartache.

Those who continue to wear the uniform should be pleased. I am happy and cannot imagine but that this will serve as a lesson.

We are intelligent people and let us hope that the Judenrat will succeed in eradicating wrongdoing.

But I want to stress that the ghetto affords opportunities for abuses, not just among us but in various offices. I appeal to you to use the same tough broom to sweep out the dirt everywhere (applause), not to stop with the police, which is not a spoiled child and not a stepchild—we are all one family; the dirt must be cleaned out.

The ghetto is not forever. A time will come when we will meet our brothers without the uniform; all officials must remain unsullied. . . .

What is the meaning of honest work? My personal view is that we are all engaged in communal work. We must have military discipline, but essentially—clean hands. There is no place here for dirty hands.

I swear that I will continue to be as honest as I have been until now! I appeal to you: follow in my footsteps! Walk the ways of honest men! Let us do our jobs and demand what is coming to us!

Commandant Marcus has a saying that the coin has two sides. Let us talk about the other side of the coin: existence; our bellies, my friends. Under ghetto conditions the chance of being satisfied is limited, but I will run to rooms #1, #10, and #16,[66] I will demand respect, recognition, and I have no doubt there there will be a

66. These were the Judenrat offices for Administration, Finance, and Food Supply.

response. What Eng. Barash said is a sacred pledge. Our minimal livelihood must be granted.

We approach our task with the sole intent that when the walls will fall, when a new life will open before us, we shall be able to look our brothers in the face, and I hope that if some day a monograph of the ghetto will be written, we will be mentioned favorably. (applause)

Mr. Marcus (speaks Polish) first tells the history of how the police was established, and concludes on the need to serve honestly and loyally.

Rabbi Rosenman closes the meeting with a short speech.

August 15, 1942

Chairman Rabbi Dr. Rosenman opens the meeting. The minutes of the previous meeting of June 20 are read and approved without comment.

Eng. Barash takes the floor for a report.

The most important events in the ghetto lately have been the visits to our enterprises, and generally to the ghetto. They are important for our fate, our being or nonbeing hangs on these visits, says Eng. Barash, and passes on to the most important visits in order.

(1)   A visit from the Party District Leader to the enterprises, with good results.

(2)   A visit to the enterprises by the press with the participation of 60 correspondents. The impressions which they carried away are evident in the article in the press, which was favorable to us.

(3)   We also had visits from the Director of the Ministry of Economy accompanied by Mayor Schwendavius.

(4)   By the Director of the Ministry of the Interior and other representatives of the authorities.

(5)   Two delegations from the Gauleiter, from whom we heard the opinion that they have not encountered such well-organized work in the whole of East Prussia.

(6)   On behalf of the authorities films were made of the ghetto, all favorable. They photographed the exhibit with many details; at the suggestion of Eng. Barash, they also filmed scenes of Jewish poverty.

(7)   The President of the Red Cross with women doctors of the Wehrmacht also visited us.

(8)   Last Friday Gestapo leaders—old and new personnel—from Berlin visited us. They said about our production: "It's amazing."

(9)   Friday afternoon the Oberpräsident of East Prussia visited us.[67] He had no time and originally planned to visit only two factories. Naturally, the rumors circulated in connection with this visit are baseless.

The opinions which we heard both from them and their escorts prove that our way—to make the ghetto useful to the authorities—is the correct one.

The scope of the enterprises is unbelievable. They employ 1,700 persons. In knitwear the number of women at work has doubled. The new factories which we had planned to set in operation—of barrels and horseshoes—are already long at work. The new tailoring factory would have been many times larger by now, but the German instructors who were assigned here made difficulties. They have a different system of organization from ours.

Large orders were placed with our enterprises, for instance, for 100,000 hats, 40,000 pairs of gloves. The Wehrmacht puts pressure on the tempo of production, consequently this affects the development of our enterprises.

Eng. Barash proposes that members of the Judenrat set a date to visit all the enterprises. The visit is set for Saturday, August 22, 10 a.m. Mr. Barash reports further: There are a number of serious matters.

(1)   The most important and the saddest question is that of the refugees; from the conflagration all around us, Jews are fleeing to Bialystok. We are obligated to submit reports about the arrivals to three agencies, and this can have bad results. They come from two opposite directions: Slonim and Warsaw.[68] They have again started to come from Pružana, and that is still worse. First of all, things in Pružana are not so bad; it is a crime to endanger our city unnecessarily. Secondly, as is known, this is regarded as sabotage, and the people from Pružana themselves face the greatest danger.

(2)   As is known, the Gestapo gave the order to confiscate our

67. Erich Koch, Gauleiter and Oberpräsident of East Prussia, was also Reich Commissioner of the occupied Ukraine.
68. The refugees from Warsaw were probably escapees from the trains en route to Treblinka, which lay about halfway between Warsaw and Bialystok. The deportations from Warsaw were then in full swing.

electrical appliances and furs. In this situation unfortunately it is hard to say if it pays to try [to hold back] and—succeed. As one of the authorities put it: "Life is dearer than a fur coat." . . .

About our fate? Everyone would gladly hear our opinions. In the ghetto people often spread different false rumors. That comes no doubt from the great fear which seizes the populace, and sometimes they may possibly be circulated with malice aforethought; perhaps someone wants to create panic among the Jews. Eng. Barash asserts that the rumors [presumably about imminent deportations] are complete and utter lies. [In matters that we fear, the Oberpräsident says he would be the first to know.] [69]

What is Bialystok's situation? I am convinced that our path is the only correct one. True, there have been such signals before, that the Bialystok ghetto is too large, too many Jews are here. This view is expressed especially by the new faces, just arrived, but the regularly stationed Germans here are for the ghetto, the local authorities appreciate us. And as long as there is no general decree from above, no peril awaits us.

Mr. Puniansky: Until now the number of residents in the ghetto has not changed, registrations check with removals. Now child refugees are arriving, a new stream of refugees can be expected. They ask for aid, housing; what's to be done in these cases? . . .

Mr. Marcus: The Judenrat is obligated to protect Bialystok Jewry. We must register all arrivals—only on their own responsibility. At the same time, we should organize them into labor brigades.

Mr. Subotnik remarks that despite all the proposed means the ghetto will still become larger.

Rabbi Dr. Rosenman: Since workers from other towns are being sent to Bialystok, and labor camps are being organized for them, perhaps the German Labor Office would agree to organize labor camps outside the ghetto for the new arrivals, which would then not burden the ghetto.

Mr. Polansky informs us that all who arrive are put to work.

Mr. Fetsiner: Perhaps the authorities would agree to enlarge the ghetto with skilled workers?

Eng. Barash: The matter is difficult. The decisions will not after all be made by the Judenrat, nor by the Executive Board. The

69. Crossed out in the original.

Germans will settle things. I knew this beforehand, but I considered it necessary to call it to the attention of the Judenrat. . . .

October 11, 1942

SPECIAL ASSEMBLY

Invited: Judenrat, directors and vice-directors of the enterprises, building superintendents, police and fire commissioners, and others.

The hall is jam-packed. On the dais the Judenrat.

At 12:30 Rabbi Dr. Rosenman opens the meeting.

Today's assembly, he says, was called especially for propaganda purposes, in connection with the disorderliness which has lately swept through the ghetto; not to obey ordinances, to evade the obligation of [forced] labor and to hide those called up for labor, arousing strong dissatisfaction on the part of the authorities, and instead of Bialystok's being a model, in which we took pride, conditions have now changed.

But the labor front is your own accomplishment, and you must try to establish normal relations; and then we can have hope in the future for the possibilities of existence.

Engineer Barash gets the floor. Today, he says, we invited to the assembly all those who with us bear the burden of the ghetto, to lay out our present situation without mincing words. Lately, concrete dangers threaten the district of Bialystok and the city of Bialystok, which we must find means of warding off or postponing, or at least diminishing in scope. Unfortunately, our Bialystok has become the second largest ghetto after Lodz, and therein lies a great danger. The enemy has trained his sights on us, and there have to be special reasons if the misfortune is to pass us by. The conflagration is raging on the east and on the west and has almost reached our region, from the east up to Dereczyn and from the west up to Małkinia. To prevent the conflagration from spreading, everyone, and first of all Bialystok, must use extraordinary means. But our ghetto is doing just the opposite, exactly as though it deliberately desired to provoke catastrophe; our ghetto has lately become reckless, demoralized. If only 14,000 out of 35,000 inhabitants are working, then even well-meaning authorities ask: Where are the rest of the people? True, there are all sorts of reasons, but among those not working are some employables, especially women. After all, you do know where the annihilation begins; precisely with those who don't work. Besides those who hide behind false papers, there are 6,000 non-working women.

Look what happened: a couple of weeks ago the German Labor Office requisitioned 200 women for work, but out of the 6,000 the required 200 could not be found. The German Labor Office transferred the matter to the commander of the Security Police, who sent us an order to assemble all the unemployed in one spot on one morning! Only after this threat did the ghetto yield these first 200 women! And what went on then! How the ghetto conducted itself! There were scenes, people hid those who were called up. As if it were a struggle between the Judenrat and the populace. When they were being taken away, people ran after the truck and screamed, "Hear O Israel!" Hopefully this misconceived "Hear O Israel" will not bring closer that day when the true "Hear O Israel" will be uttered.

When our policemen have to carry out their police duties on the street, they appear to the populace just like the "child snatchers" of old.[70] Instead of being helped, they are hindered! Often I think: Are these people crazy? Don't they understand what's happening? The psychology of the masses must be reversed, otherwise things will be very bad. The ghetto believes *we* are enacting these wicked orders! They come to me with requests about mothers who must stay with their children, and the like. Of course children should be with their mothers in normal times; but now there is a still greater danger—that mothers together with their children will be destroyed.

Even physicians—I speak of the honest ones—have a psychological attitude as in normal times. They certify that anyone with tuberculosis is unable to work. Certainly! But the danger is that the person will die not from tuberculosis, but from not working!

All these illusions that we live in normal times must come to an end. Anyone who can wiggle a finger must go to work and increase our security. The ratio of a labor force of 14,000 workers out of 35,000 ghetto residents—that is where the danger lies—even if no demand for work comes from the authorities, we must make every effort so to insinuate ourselves in the economy, that they will spare

70. A reference to the period of 1825–1855, under Nicholas I, when Jewish children were kidnapped by agents of the Kehilla and sent away to serve a 25-year term of military duty in the Tsarist army.

us, for if they would destroy us, there would be a hole in the economy. Then we can hope, but not wait for their pity, as I said not once before, especially if they demand daily and we do not fulfil the demand! What the consequences of this can be, you can imagine for yourselves!

What scenes took place when the girls were taken out to dig potatoes! It was simply beyond comprehension! Everyone knows after all what happened in Warsaw, Słonim; today it is already time to count the cities where the catastrophes did not occur! Where is the sense of self-preservation? Why don't they understand that it is better to be sent to Wołkowysk than to Treblinka! It is time to pass from words to deeds! I am not an adherent of propaganda. We will have to adopt practical methods. Men will have to leave their offices and go to work and their places will be taken by women. It has anyway already been pointed out to us that we have too many officials. We will have to organize a large women's brigade, which will always be ready for work, not like now, when instead of 100, 20 are sent out. If this is still not enough, we will have to take the bigger children from school. A whole series of steps will have to be taken, and I call on you, as helpers and leaders of various divisions.

A reorganization of the police will have to be carried out. One clean-up was already made. Certain elements will be eliminated and we now have a very decent leadership. But some stayed who should not have stayed and they hurt the name of the others. Consequently, our orders are not carried out 100 percent, not even 50 percent. There are rumors of bribery. The fact is that some of the police must leave and be replaced by others. We have even tried to appeal to our officials in whom we have confidence to join the police, but they refused. Such a situation should not exist, it is impermissible and we won't tolerate it any longer.

We must also start a tough fight against favoritism. The Judenrat is still a young government, but ancient flaws have already become entrenched in it. No action can be undertaken because of the pieces of paper. We must put an end to this. The pieces of paper should be torn up, even those from me—although I err less than everyone else in this respect. We have not yet taken up the question in the Executive Board, but anyone who dodges work by any illegal means should know that a blacklist of such elements will be compiled, and be at hand. And if the peril will come sometimes, these folk will be the first victims.

These are all issues that are very important.

The second item of exceptional seriousness is the factories. They have really created something colossal. Our enemies must give them their due. If there are any hopes that Bialystok will avoid the terrible danger, it is only because of the factories. But the factories themselves can bring us great danger, if they are not in order. We just had the case in our tailor shop, where slipshod work was delivered.

In this connection the speaker reads a letter from the City Commissioner.[71]

It is easy to imagine what was involved and what is still involved. It is also easy to understand what looms if things continue as till now. It took a lot of effort so that for the time being things are tranquil, that they should not react. But if, God forbid, such a thing recurs, we will no longer stand here. Once more I must mention the psychological attitude. The Judenrat is not building factories, today we are not at that point. The worker must not regard the Judenrat as an antagonist, as he once regarded the manufacturer. He must bear in mind that he is working first of all for himself, his wife, and children. If there really were sabotage, the workers in the factory would be the first to be shot. I request the labor-brigadiers to pass this on to the workers, especially the shoemakers; because people say that the shoemakers are an ignorant element—I don't believe that—but still let them know that work is their only defense.

At this opportunity, I wish also to send a warning to the smugglers, particularly of livestock. It has reached the point where we are accused of eating their [the Germans'] meat. The police ought not to hesitate to hand them over. Such scoundrels may be handed over to the authorities!

We are making exceptional efforts to push back the peril threatening the city and district of Bialystok. The Wehrmacht has

71. A Yiddish translation of the letter, dated October 1, 1942, addressed to the Judenrat, was appended to the minutes. The Commissioner complained about the poor quality of quilted winter apparel produced in the ghetto factories. The Military Apparel Office in Königsberg, Prussia, in its report of receipt, September 21, 1942, had pointed to defects of such seriousness that sabotage was suspected. The City Commissioner stated that he had already personally warned the Judenrat and that he would hold it solely responsible for all future incidents. He concluded with a threat: "Besides the most severe penalties, the Jews will have only themselves to blame for their irresponsible acts if, as a result, other consequences of a more serious character ensue."

an interest in maintaining us.[72] They want to open three factories outside the ghetto, where Jewish craftsmen will work: one in Trilling's factory, the second in the former bread bakery, and the third is still kept secret. One will be an auto-repair shop, the second of optical instruments, and of the third I cannot say. The factories will be opened only if there is a sufficient number of skilled workers. They did not want to put the plan in the works until they know definitely that there will be enough workers. They waited for my answer, and I promised without consulting anyone. If Bialystok won't have enough workers, we'll look for them in the district, and it's everyone's duty to let us know if he knows of a skilled worker and not make liars of us. In this way our counterpressure on the enemies becomes still stronger, because they will not waste the machinery that was assigned—we must carry out our promise.

In closing, if there are threatening signs, we should not give up and lose heart. On the contrary, because there are threats, because there is danger, our efforts must be more energetic. We are experiencing great events, a terrible time that demands strong people. Strong is what we must be. Let us fulfil our obligations 200 percent.

Let us be strong! (applause)

Rabbi Rosenman closes the meeting:

You have heard reports about the situation, mainly from Eng. Barash, and at the end I want to add: We always entreat and pray: "Stop the mouths of our enemies and detractors." But we ourselves, by our own behavior, open their mouths. We must conduct ourselves rightly, so they should not say that Jews are a gang of liars, parasites, loafers; we must prove that we are fit to work and honest people, and thereby we will be saved.

---

72. Barash's estimate of the situation was correct. The Wehrmacht had an interest in maintaining Bialystok's industrial production and tried to delay the liquidation of the ghetto by the SS.

8 CONFRONTING DEATH:
THE ORDEALS OF DEPORTATION

INTRODUCTION

APPREHENSION, anxiety, and foreboding gripped the Jews who were to be "resettled" and no less those who remained behind in their prison ghettos. In a short time the apprehension turned into overpowering terror, when it seemed that the Jews who were taken away had been engulfed in a void. They had disappeared from the face of the earth. That the Germans were transporting the Jews from the ghettos of Poland to some mysterious location just in order to murder them was an idea altogether too monstrous to be credible, too bizarre for plausibility.

The first reports of systematic murder came from the underground Bundist and Zionist organizations, and were disseminated through their clandestine press. The Jewish underground had obtained its information from Jews who had escaped from the death camps, from networks of underground informants and party couriers, and through contacts with the Polish underground. The underground press, the only source of authentic news in the ghettos about German plans for annihilation, provided the Jews of Poland with the truth of their intended fate.

The Jewish underground party leaders realized that the shock of such news could traumatize the ghetto populace and induce total despair. Yet they hoped that the news might also galvanize the Jews into some form of passive or even active resistance. Fearing precisely this possibility and hoping to forestall it, the Gestapo undertook a program of intensive surveillance against the underground press in Warsaw and elsewhere. On April 17, 1942, the Gestapo in Warsaw located and seized about fifty Jews, most engaged in writing for and printing the illegal newspapers. All were shot dead in the street, and the Gestapo and their underworld Jewish henchmen spread the rumor that they had been engaged in illegal political activities. To dispute this claim, the underground Bundist weekly, Der veker, of April 30, 1942, in its thirty-seventh issue to appear clandestinely in the Warsaw ghetto, published a front-page editorial, "The Bloody Night." Written by Maurycy Orzech (ca. 1892–1943), then the ranking Bundist leader in the ghetto, the editorial showed the spuriousness of the German argument by giving facts and figures about the annihilation of the Jews throughout Poland. The killings in the ghetto on the bloody night of April 17, the editorial concluded, were "only one small link in the great chain of the bestial murders of the Jews by Hitler."

Like people everywhere and anywhere, the Jews in the ghettos found it hard to confront the thought of their death. Many succumbed to wishful thinking, believed the German promises about resettlement and fantasized about some distant place where, however wretched their circumstances, they might continue to live with their families. The denial of unacceptable truth was the one means available to ghetto Jews to make their situation bearable. Many, however, unblinkingly did confront the fact and the face of their own death, resignedly, or bitterly. Some hoped their survivors would exact vengeance; others wanted only to be remembered. Such a one was Israel Lichtenstein (1904–1942), a teacher in a Yiddish school, associated in the ghetto with Oneg Shabbat, the clandestine archives. On July 31, 1942, on the eleventh day of the "resettlement" of the Warsaw Jews, having already written an account of the first ten days of desperation, Lichtenstein composed his last will and testament. Early in August, in the midst of the consuming conflagration, when it appeared that all Warsaw Jewry was doomed, Lichtenstein buried large quantities of Oneg Shabbat ghetto materials, his own testament among them, in the hope that they would be found after the war.

(Most were in fact recovered.) In his testament, he squarely faced the imminence of his death and that of his wife and child. Without mentioning the Germans, without hate or rancor, Lichtenstein asked only that he, his wife, and their child be remembered.

On August 12, 1942, in Będzin, during the second stage of "resettlement," about 10,000 Jews were taken away to Auschwitz. That day an adolescent whose parents had been sent to their death composed a song. It expressed the pathos of the young and able-bodied, spared by the Germans for slave labor, who were left without homes and parents. The song was sung in the Będzin ghetto and the nearby labor camps.

No contemporaneous document matches the horror and despair of Josef Zelkowicz's account, "Days of Nightmare," which describes the Lodz ghetto in September 1942, when the Germans deported the aged, the children, and the sick. Zelkowicz (1897–1944), a Yiddish journalist and essayist, then a staff member of the Lodz archives operating within the Judenrat administration, wrote many graphic descriptions of Lodz ghetto life which now serve as sources of social history. The most powerful writing of his career, however, is contained in the account of the September deportations, a time when most of the ghetto already knew the fate of those to be "resettled." Historically authentic in its merest detail, psychologically perceptive, Zelkowicz's eyewitness recital of the harrowing events is without parallel in the documentation of the Holocaust.

The Jews in the ghettos were helpless against German force and terror. In desperate efforts to rescue the Jewish population of Poland, the leaders of the Jewish parties sent urgent appeals to the Allied governments and to world Jewish organizations, demanding acts of reprisal against the Germans. In May 1942 the Jewish Labor Bund in Poland sent through clandestine channels a report to the Polish Government-in-Exile. Concluding that Hitler had indeed undertaken the total destruction of the European Jews, the Bund called upon the Polish Government immediately to take necessary steps to prevent the further annihilation of Polish Jewry, and specifically asked that the Allied Powers apply a policy of retribution against German citizens and German fifth columnists in their countries. Seven months later, December 17, 1942, when most Polish Jews had already been killed, the Allied governments issued, simultaneously from London, Moscow, and Washington, a joint declaration citing reports that the Germans were "now carrying into effect

Hitler's oft-repeated intention to exterminate the Jewish people in Europe." Condemning "in the strongest possible terms this bestial policy of cold-blooded extermination," the declaration strangely made no reference to the death camps and the gassing installations. It concluded with a reaffirmation of the Allies' "solemn resolution to ensure that those responsible for these crimes shall not escape retribution."

At the same time the Jews in Lublin were being sent to the gas chambers in Bełżec, the Jews of Slovakia were being deported to the gas chambers at Auschwitz. A committee of Jewish communal leaders in Bratislava undertook to try an old Jewish strategy for rescue: they planned to bribe local Slovakian officials and Germans operating in Slovakia to induce them to halt the deportations. When the group learned that the Germans were killing all European Jews, it expanded its fantastic idea, now calling it the Europa Plan, to embrace the rescue of all remaining Jews. One of the initiators of the Europa Plan was Michael Dov Weissmandel (1904?–1957), an eminent rabbi who had headed the renowned yeshiva at Nitra, near Bratislava. The committee made contact with Dieter Wisliceny, one of Eichmann's deputies, who indicated his willingness and that of his principals to engage in negotiations to "ransom" the Jews. To raise the astronomical sums demanded and to obtain political clearance, Weissmandel and his colleagues corresponded clandestinely with world Jewish organizations through their representatives located in Switzerland. Officials of the Jewish Agency for Palestine, the Joint Distribution Committee, the World Jewish Congress, and the Vaad Hatzala, an Orthodox organization for relief and rescue of Jews, received copies of Weissmandel's importunate letters. One, May 11, 1943, excoriated the Jews abroad for having failed to come to the aid of European Jews. Another letter, May 31, 1944, dealt with the deportation of the Jews from Hungary to Auschwitz, at a time when Allied governments and Jewish leaders throughout the world knew what Auschwitz meant. Describing the plan and progress of the deportations, Weissmandel then gave an account of the negotiations under way, dissecting the motives of the Germans and the alternatives available. The letter concluded with a demand for the destruction of all roads from Hungary through Poland to Auschwitz and set forth a series of other proposals to help save the Jews.

Neither Auschwitz nor the rail lines leading to it were bombed. Weissmandel's pleas in 1944, like the earlier urgent appeals from the Jewish political leaders in Warsaw to the Polish Government-in-Exile and world Jewish leaders, went unfulfilled. On September 1, 1944, an undersecretary in the British Foreign Office responded as follows to Chaim Weizmann's request to Foreign Secretary Anthony Eden that Auschwitz and the rail lines to it be bombed: "The matter received the most careful consideration of the Air Staff, but I am sorry to have to tell you that, in view of the very great technical difficulties involved, we have no option but to refrain from pursuing the proposal in present circumstances." [1]

1. Eichmann Trial, Jerusalem, Proceedings, May 30, 1961, Session 57.

In this connection, it is interesting to consider the radio message sent to the Chief Government Delegate in Poland (then Jan Stanislaw Jankowski) from London on August 28, 1943, by Władysław Banaczyk (code name: Orkan), then Minister for Home Affairs of the Polish Government-in-Exile, London:

> The English Staff expresses its readiness to bomb Auschwitz, especially the synthetic rubber and synthetic gasoline factories, as also similar factories of this sort in Silesia. We, for our part, wish to combine this with a mass liberation of the prisoners in Auschwitz. It is necessary to have your substantial cooperation in liberating them right after the air attack and to give them help. Besides, you must also help us classify the targets according to their importance and direct the planes correctly to the targets, in order to avoid losses among Poles. Inform us what you think about this and what you want of us in this matter. Can you also prepare the prisoners for this in advance? The operation is planned during the time of the longest nights.

FACING FACTS: THE BLOODY NIGHT
APRIL 17, 1942

The Fascist beast bared its teeth and let loose. On Friday night into Saturday (April 17th into 18th), arrests according to lists were carried out in the Warsaw ghetto by Gestapo officers. Forty-eight of the arrested were shot right away in the yards or side streets by other Gestapo men who were waiting for the victims.

On Saturday, after Friday's bloody night, the ghetto was silent. Shrouded in deep sorrow, heads bowed before the dead bodies of the bestially murdered martyrs, the Jewish population of Warsaw asked what the next night would bring. What is being prepared, what is the bloody executioner devising for us?

On Sunday strange rumors began to spread through the ghetto. The Germans had indeed murdered Jews, but not just so, without cause. They shot Jews who "were engaged in matters that were not their business." The Jews they shot had busied themselves with *"politics,"* had published *illegal* newspapers. It was *Socialists* who were shot. They are the ones who bring misfortune to the ghetto.

This filthy, disgusting stream of reports began to flood the ghetto. All those who live high and mighty under the bloody rule of Hitler's regime, all those fine Jews who rejoice in the "autonomy" bestowed upon us in the form of this cursed ghetto, they all began whispering and murmuring, dropping names, judging and condemning. They, the filthy scum of our time, have become the judges and the dunners for the "injury" which the "politicals," the "Socialists" brought on the Warsaw ghetto!

But was that the cause of the bloody night? Let the facts speak.

Beginning in mid-February until the end of March, the following events took place in *Tarnów*. Every day Gestapo and SS men entered the Jewish residential quarter, killing innocent Jews whom they encountered by chance on the streets, in the yards, and in their homes. In *Radom*, in March, in one night 70 Jews of various strata of the population were arrested. That same night 24 of the arrested were murdered right away and the rest were sent off to Oświęcim [Auschwitz]. In *Cracow* at the beginning of April, over 50 Jews were arrested from lists and were murdered in the same bestial way as in Warsaw.

And what about *Lublin,* where from March 15 until April 10, 25,000 Jews were sent out in sealed trains in an "unknown direction"? During this action all the children of the Jewish orphanage, all the old people in the old-age home, and all the sick in both Jewish hospitals were murderously, outrageously shot. Besides that, *over 2,000 Jews were shot* in the streets and in their homes. That happened—we emphasize this—at the end of March, the beginning of April 1942.

Need we mention the terrible poison-gassing in Chełmno, where 5,000 Jews from the Koło district and 35,000 Jews from the *Lodz ghetto* were put to death?

These are all facts of the last 3–4 months. But we must not forget what happened in the fall of 1941 in *Vilna,* where 50,000 Jews were murdered, and in the entire Vilna district and in the Kovno area of Lithuania, where altogether 300,000 Jews were slaughtered. And what about *Słonim* with 9,000 murdered Jews; what about *Równe* with 17,000 Jews shot? What of the whole of Eastern Galicia where there is not a single townlet of which at least half of its Jewish population has not been murdered?

Then let the dogs be silent who dare to bark on the graves of those who fell during the bloody Friday night in Warsaw. Let them not dishonor the peace of the martyrs. Let them not try to argue that it was Socialists who brought on the misfortune. That Friday night in the Warsaw ghetto was only one *small* link in the *great* chain of the bestial murders of the Jews by Hitler.

Yes, we know well enough that the Jewish leeches, the vampires who, under the protection of Hitler's wings, suck out the last bit of strength of the Jewish populace, really want the ghetto to appear as one cemetery, that deathly stillness should reign here, which will not disturb them while they do the work of jackals and hyenas.

ISRAEL LICHTENSTEIN'S LAST TESTAMENT

With zeal and zest I threw myself into the work to help assemble archive materials. I was entrusted to be the custodian, I hid the material. Besides me, no one knew. I confided only in my friend Hersh Wasser, my superior.

It is well hidden. Please God that it be preserved. That will be the finest and best that we achieved in the present gruesome time.

I know that we will not endure. To survive and remain alive [after] such horrible murders and massacres is impossible. Therefore I write this testament of mine. Perhaps I am not worthy of being remembered, but just for my grit in working with the society Oneg Shabbat and for being the most endangered because I hid the entire material. It would be a small thing to give my own head. I risk the head of my dear wife Gele Seckstein and my treasure, my little daughter, Margalit.

I don't want any gratitude, any monument, any praise. I want only a remembrance, so that my family, brother and sister abroad, may know what has become of my remains.

I want my wife to be remembered. Gele Seckstein, artist, dozens of works, talented, didn't manage to exhibit, did not show in public. During the three years of war worked among children as educator, teacher, made stage sets, costumes for the children's productions, received awards. Now together with me, we are preparing to receive death.

I want my little daughter to be remembered. Margalit, 20 months old today. Has mastered Yiddish perfectly, speaks a pure Yiddish, At 9 months began to speak Yiddish clearly. In intelligence she is on a par with 3- or 4-year-old children. I don't want to brag about her. Witnesses to this, who tell me about it, are the teaching staff of the school at Nowolipki 68. . . .

I am not sorry about my life and that of my wife. But I am sorry for the gifted little girl. She deserves to be remembered also.

May we be the redeemers for all the rest of the Jews in the whole world. I believe in the survival of our people. Jews will not be annihilated. We, the Jews of Poland, Czechoslovakia, Lithuania, Latvia, are the scapegoat for all Israel in all the other lands.

July 31, 1942
The eleventh day of the
so-called "resettlement action."
In reality, an annihilation action.

HOMELESS

Without a home, without a roof—
We tramped the whole night through,
Not knowing whereto
Or what our end would be.

At the station we were jammed in a pack
And held in leash by the SS police;
How much longer will our pain last?
Hell-fire surely can't be worse!

Without a home, without a roof . . .

No bread, no water did we get
They kept us there a day, a night,
Children torn from their mothers' arms
And dragged off who knows where.

Without a home, without a roof . . .

They hound us, they harass us,
They torment and torture us,
This is how they draw our blood.
Alas, our blood! Alas, our blood!

For without a home, without a roof . . .

To that staging area they drove us
And selected us like sheep;

Torn away from our parents
We the young were herded to the camps.

　　Without a home, without a roof,
　　We tramped the whole night through—
　　Not knowing whereto
　　Or what our end would be.

JOSEF ZELKOWICZ: DAYS OF NIGHTMARE

Friday, September 4, 1942

The deportation of children and old people is a fact.

This morning the ghetto received a horrifying shock: What seemed improbable and incredible news yesterday has now become a dreadful fact. Children up to the age of ten are to be torn away from their parents, brothers and sisters, and deported. Old people over 65 are being robbed of their last life-saving plank, which they have been clutching with their last bits of strength—their four walls and their beds. They are being sent away like useless ballast.

If only they were really being "sent away," if only there were the slightest ray of hope that these "deportees" were being taken somewhere! That they were being settled and kept alive, even under the worst conditions, then the tragedy would not be so enormous. After all, every Jew has always been ready to migrate; Jewish life has always been based on a capacity for adjusting to the worst conditions; every Jew has always been prepared to fold up his tent at command, to leave his home and country, and all the more so here in the ghetto, where there's no wealth, no property, no peace of mind, and where he is not attached to anything. Jewish life has always relied only on faith in the ancient Jewish God, who, the Jew feels, has never abandoned him. "Somehow or other, everything will turn out all right. Somehow or other, we'll manage to survive, with our last bit of wretched life."

If there were the slightest assurance, the slightest ray of hope they were being sent somewhere, then the ghetto would not be in such a turmoil over this new and unwonted evil decree. There have already been so many new and unwonted evil decrees and we have had to put up with them and, whether or not we wanted to, we had to go on living, so that we might somehow or other swallow this one too. But the fact is that no one has the least doubt, we are all certain that the people now being deported from the ghetto are not being "sent" anywhere. They are being taken to nowhere, at least the old people. They are going to the scrap heap, as we say in the ghetto. How, then, can we be expected to make peace with this new evil decree? How can we be expected to go on living whether or not we want to?

There is simply no word, no power, no art able to transmit the moods, the laments, and the turmoil prevailing in the ghetto since early this morning.

To say that today the ghetto is swimming in tears would not be mere rhetoric. It would be simply a gross understatement, an inadequate utterance about the things you can see and hear in the ghetto of Litzmannstadt, no matter where you go or look or listen.

There is no house, no home, no family which is not affected by this dreadful edict. One person has a child, another an old father, a third an old mother. No one has patience, no one can remain at home with arms folded awaiting destiny. At home you feel forlorn, wretched, alone with your devouring cares. Just run into the street. Out there you don't feel so blind, you don't feel so abandoned. Animals, too, when they feel some sorrow, supposedly cling together, animals having mute tongues which cannot talk away their sorrows and their grief. How much more so human beings.

All hearts are icy, all hands are wrung, all eyes filled with despair. All faces are twisted, all heads bowed to the ground, all blood weeps.

Tears flow by themselves. They can't be held back. People know these tears are useless. Those who can help it refuse to see them, and those who see them—and they too shed useless tears— can't help themselves either. Worst of all, these tears bring no relief whatsoever. On the contrary. It's as though they were falling on, rather than from, our hearts. They only make our hearts heavier. Our hearts writhe and struggle in these tears like fish in poisoned waters. Our hearts drown in their own tears. But no one can help us in any way, no one can save us.

No one at all? No one in the whole ghetto who wants to, who can save us? Could there be someone after all? There must be someone who wants to, who's able to! Perhaps we still don't know who that someone is? Perhaps he's hiding somewhere, because he can't help everyone, he can't save everyone!

Maybe that's why people are scurrying all over the ghetto like poisoned mice. They're looking for that "someone." Maybe that's why the ghetto Jews are clutching at straws, maybe this straw is the "someone" they're looking for. Maybe that's him over here, maybe that's him over there. Everyone is looking to revive old acquaintanceship with those who can help, everyone is looking for pull. Perhaps God will help.

And the little children who don't yet understand, the little children who have no way of knowing about the Damoclean sword hanging over their innocent heads, perhaps subconsciously sense the enormous threat hovering over them, and their tiny hands cling tighter to the scrawny and shrunken breasts of their fathers and mothers.

Son of man, go out in the street. Look at all this, soak in the subconscious terror of the infants about to be slaughtered. And be strong and don't weep! Be strong and don't let your heart break, so that later on you can give a thoughtful and orderly description of just the barest essentials of what took place in the ghetto during the first few days of September in the year 1942.

Mothers run through the streets, one shoe on, one shoe off, their hair half combed, their shawls trailing on the ground. They are still holding on to their children. They can clasp them now tighter and closer to their emaciated breasts. They can still cover their bright little faces and eyes with kisses. But what will happen tomorrow, later on, in an hour?

People say: The children are to be taken from their parents as early as today. People say: The children are to be sent away as early as Monday. They are to be sent away—where?

To be sent away on Monday, to be taken away today. Meanwhile, for the moment, every mother clings to her child. Now she can still give her child everything, the very best thing in her possession—the last morsel of bread, all her love, the dearest and the best! Today the child doesn't have to wait for hours on end and cry until his father or mother figures out how much to give him from the half-pound of bread. Today they ask the child: "Darling, would you like a piece of bread now?" And today the piece of bread that the child gets isn't dry and tasteless like always. If there's just a bit of margarine left, they spread it on. If there's any sugar left, they sprinkle it on. The ghetto lives recklessly today. No one weighs or measures. No one hoards sugar or margarine to stretch it for a whole ten days until the next ration. Today in the ghetto no one lives for the future. Today one lives for the moment and now, for the moment, every mother still has her child with her; and wouldn't she, if she could, give it her own heart, her own soul? . . .

There are children who do indeed understand. In the ghetto, ten-year-old children are mature adults. They already know and understand what is in store for them. They may not as yet know why they are being torn away from their parents—they may not as yet have been told. For the moment it's enough for them to know that they are being torn away from their devoted guardians, their fathers and their loving and anxious mothers. It's hard to keep such children in one's arms or to take them by the hand. Such children go out into the streets on their own. Such children weep on their own, with their own tears. Their tears are so sharp and piercing that they fall upon all hearts like poisoned arrows. But hearts in the ghetto have turned to stone. They would rather burst but they can't, and this is probably the greatest, the harshest curse. . . .

The sorrow becomes greater, and the torture more senseless, when one tries to think rationally. Well, an old man is an old man. If he's lived his 65 years, he can convince himself, or others convince him, that he should utter something like: "Well, thank God, I've had my share of living, in joy and sorrow, weal and woe. That's life. Probably that's fate. And anyway, you don't live forever. So what's the difference if it's a few days, a few weeks, or even a few months sooner? Sooner or later, you've got to die, sooner or later, everything's over. That's life."

Maybe they can talk the old man into telling himself these things, maybe they can talk his family into telling themselves. But what about children who have only just been hatched, children who have only seen God's world in the ghetto, for whom a cow or a chicken is just a legendary creature, who have never in their lives so much as inhaled the fragrance of a flower, laid eyes upon an orange, tasted an apple or a pear, and who are now doomed to die? . . .

The sky above the ghetto, like yesterday and the day before, is unclouded. Like yesterday and the day before, the early autumn sun shines. It shines and smiles at our Jewish grief and agony, as though someone were merely stepping on vermin, as though someone had written a death-sentence for bedbugs, a Day of Judgment for rats which must be exterminated and wiped off the face of the earth.

There are nevertheless still enough people in the ghetto who doubt, still enough people in the ghetto who continue to live with faith. There are even those who reason logically:

"This ghetto, where eighty percent of the population performs useful work, is not one of your provincial towns which could have been made *Judenrein,* free of Jews, in half an hour. Here people are necessary, are needed for work. It's not possible that they would take people from here and send them away."

And those who cannot argue rationally, who are just full of faith, they simply believe in miracles:

"Things like this have happened before. All through history, Jews have been threatened with bitter decrees, and deliverance has come at the last minute. There just was an air raid on Lodz for the first time since the war began. So maybe they'll withdraw the evil decree. Who can tell?". . .

The files of the vital statistics records were sealed last night.

No one knows who did the sealing. The German authorities? No. They were sealed by the Jewish Resettlement Commission,[2] sealed so that none of the dates of birth could be falsified. The child is not to make himself older or the old man younger. And therefore the decree, in its full severity, remains in force. No miracles take place today; perhaps they did in the past, but the past is so old that none of the ghetto Jews remembers it. No miracle ever happened to a ghetto Jew. No ghetto Jew ever heard of a good rumor coming true. Always the other way around, the bad is always the brutal actuality. People also have been saying in the factories: "The Resettlement Commission has already been formed."

There are people in the ghetto who, compulsorily or merely of

2. The Resettlement Commission included leading officials of the Lodz ghetto administration: the head of the office of vital statistics (Naftalin), the Jewish police commandant (Leon Rosenblat), the prison commandant, the director of penal administration, the head of the office of investigations, and the chairman of the ghetto courts (Jakobson).

their own free will, have taken it upon themselves to act as a Great Sanhedrin and issue death sentences. A commission has been formed with Jakobson, Blemer, Rosenblat, Naftalin, and Greenberg, and they will be in charge of deporting the 20,000 old people and children. They are the ones who will have to sever living limbs from living bodies. They are the ones who will be halving Jewish families.

Certainly they've been charged, probably by the Chairman, to take care of this matter. Certainly there has to be such a body in charge of even a matter as halving Jewish families. But still no person with conscience would undertake to issue death sentences.

This commission and a whole staff of officials involved with them have been working all night long. They have drawn up a list of the population by streets and buildings.

The commission is operating in the Office of Vital Statistics at 4 Kościelna Street, the focal point where all eyes of the ghetto are turned. This is where people come to plead and weep for those near and dear to them. But so much chaos and turmoil are here, so much disorganization and confusion that none of the aforementioned gentlemen on the commission knew what was being asked of him, what his assignment was, or if he could do anything for anyone. None of the gentlemen on the commission knew anything definite about the substance and nature of the decree.

One of them said that the age in question was from one to ten years, so that children under one year would not be included, and another one claimed that the edict was inclusive, that it applied to children from one minute to nine years and 365 days old. The commission likewise had differences of opinion about old people. They didn't know whether the age limit began with people who were already past 65 or whether it applied to those who were still in their 65th year. . . .

It was rumored during the day that the deportations would take place without the involvement of the German authorities. The edict will be carried out by the Resettlement Commission with the help of the Jewish police, the Jewish fire department, and the like. As a reward for their efficient and loyal performance, they have been promised that their own families, i.e. their children and parents, will be exempt from the edict. The police will thus be able to "work" with untroubled heads and calm spirit. They will do a fine job—you can rely on them. They've already passed the test a few times.[3] The same deal obviously was promised to exempt the families of all the heads of the factories or offices. The reason is the same—so they can work with untroubled minds.

But the question is: At whose expense have they been privileged? If all the old people and children without exception amount to only 13,000 souls, and now, if they are going to make exceptions and exempt several thousand people in the families of the police, the fire department, and higher officials, then who will be deported in their place? . . .

At a quarter to five, accompanied by David Varshavsky[4] and S. Jakobson, the Chairman showed up. No one could fail to notice the tremendous change he underwent in the past few days or hours. His head was bowed as though he couldn't keep it on his shoulders, his eyes dull and lifeless. We were looking at an old man barely able to totter on his feet. He was an old man like all the old men who gathered on the square. Only his face was fuller and less emaciated than theirs. Only his body was garbed in fine and fancy wear instead of rags and patches like theirs. In the tangle of his white hair you could tell how fearfully he had lived through these last hours. In the spasms of his lips you could tell he had no word of comfort for the people gathered here, that there would be no cheerfulness today.

The Chairman barely dragged himself up to the platform and announced that Varshavsky had the floor. He's not much of a speaker, and he probably can't manage a personal conversation either. But then who wants to drink gall from a beautiful goblet? Poison from an ugly cup is as effective as from a beautiful cup. No one came today to hear and admire any feats or oratorical talents. Everyone came to hear the truth, and David Varshavsky told the truth in all its bitterness, in bitter and crude words:

"Yesterday the Chairman received an order to resettle some 20,000 people from among the children and the aged. How strange is human fate! We all know the Chairman. We all know how many years of his life, how much energy, how much work and effort he

---

3. The ironic reference is to the role of the Jewish police during the deportations from Lodz in the first half of 1942.
4. David Varshavsky was head of the tailoring enterprises in the Lodz ghetto.

devoted to rearing the Jewish child. Now precisely from his hands is the sacrifice being demanded. Precisely from him who has reared more children than the present edict covers! But there's nothing we can do. This is a decree that cannot be annulled. They are asking for sacrifices and the sacrifices have to be offered. We understand and we feel the anguish. There is no place to hide it and there is nothing to hide from you. All children up to the age of ten and all old people have to be handed over. The decree cannot be annulled. We can only soften it perhaps by carrying it out quietly and peacefully. Also in Warsaw there was a similar decree. We all know how that was carried out, it's no secret. And it happened that way because the German authorities were in charge, not the Jewish community. We undertook to carry out the decree ourselves because we do not want, we cannot allow the execution of the decree to assume catastrophic proportions. Can I comfort you, set your minds at ease? Regrettably, I cannot. But there is one thing I can tell you, perhaps it will set your minds at ease, perhaps it will bring you some comfort. It seems, according to all probabilities, that after this decree we will be permitted to remain undisturbed. There is a war going on. Air-raid alarms are frequent. We often have to flee. At such time, children and old people are only a hindrance. They must, therefore, be sent away.". . .

The next to speak was the lawyer Jakobson.

"Residents of the ghetto! Yesterday an order arrived to deport over twenty thousand people from the ghetto; they are to come from among the children, the aged, and the sick who have no chance of recovery. None of the previous resettlement decrees has been as difficult to carry out as this one. The present edict has been rendered even more difficult by our lack of means or possibilities to heal or even ease the wounds.

"We have had to assume this heavy duty and this great responsibility to carry out this edict ourselves. We have had to take it upon ourselves, because other cities have shown us what happens when the edicts are carried out by strangers and not by our own hands." (Loud weeping in the audience.)

"Weeping and wailing unfortunately won't help us. There were hints like: 'If you don't carry out the order yourselves, then we will carry it out.' There's nothing more to say. We already understand everything and much too much.

"The resettlement will involve some three thousand people

daily. The responsibility for complying with the edict has fallen upon the entire community. The whole ghetto is responsible that it be carried out.". . .

Neither speaker made anyone feel any easier. Both David Varshavsky and Jakobson explicitly pointed out there is nothing anyone can do. Varshavsky explicitly said he had no comfort to offer, and Jakobson explicitly said he had no means at his disposal for healing or even easing the wounds. The two speakers had only one virtue. Everyone learned the truth from them, the truth about the number to be sent away, about the categories to be sent away, and about the pedestrian embargo.[5] As bitter as these truths may be and as desperate, they are still ever so much better than the unuttered truths, the rumors, and various speculations. But everyone felt that not everything had been fully said. Everyone felt that the Chairman still had something to say. The crowd waited in great suspense and with bated breath in order better to hear the Chairman's words.

The Chairman wept.

This proud Jew, who till now had governed his realm high-handedly and with total despotism, this man who had never heeded anyone and always did everything on his own responsibility and his own authority, this same man stood before the crowd a shattered man. He could not control his tears. The Chairman wept like a child. We could see how stricken he was by the common woe, how deeply afflicted by the decree, even though he himself was neither directly nor indirectly subject to it. These were no artificial tears. These were Jewish tears flowing from a Jewish heart. These tears helped to score a great deal with the crowd.

As soon as he mastered himself, he began with the following words:

"The ghetto has been afflicted with a great sorrow. We are being asked to give up the best that we possess—children and old people. I was not privileged to have a child of my own, and so I

5. In order to carry out the deportations with a minimum of resistance, the Germans ordered Rumkowski to declare a general embargo on pedestrian traffic in the ghetto, beginning Saturday, September 5, 1942, at 5 a.m. Persons who wanted a pedestrian permit had to apply to Jewish police headquarters. All building concierges were held responsible to see that only bona-fide tenants of their buildings were domiciled there. The notice which Rumkowski issued about the pedestrian embargo warned that all unauthorized persons on the ghetto streets would be evacuated.

devoted the best years of my life for the sake of the child. I have lived and breathed with the child. I would never have imagined that my hands would deliver the sacrifice to the altar. In my old age I must stretch forth my arms and beg: Brothers and sisters, yield them to me! Fathers and mothers, yield me your children." (Enormous and fearful weeping among the crowd.)

"I had a premonition that something threatened us. I was expecting something and I stood always like a sentry on guard to prevent this something from happening. But I couldn't, because I didn't know what was in store for us, I didn't know what awaited us.

"The removal of the sick from the hospitals was something I never expected at all. You have the best proof. I had my own nearest and dearest there and I could do nothing for them. I thought that with that it would stop. I thought that with that they would leave us in peace. But it turns out that instead of this peace which I crave so strongly, for which I have always worked and striven, something else is destined for us. That is, after all, the fate of Jews— always to suffer more and worse, especially in wartime.

"Yesterday afternoon, I was given an order to deport some 20,-000 Jews from the ghetto. If not: 'We will do it.' And the question arose: Should we have taken it over and do it ourselves or leave it for others to carry out? Being guided by the thought not of how many would be going to their destruction, but rather of how many we could save, we, that is, I and my closest colleagues, concluded that however difficult it would be for us, we would have to take over the responsibility for carrying out the decree ourselves. I have to carry out this difficult and bloody operation. I have to cut off limbs in order to save the body! I have to take children, because otherwise—God forbid—others will be taken." (Terrible wails.)

"I have not come to comfort you. Nor have I come to set your hearts at ease, but to uncover your full grief and woe. I have come like a thief to take your dearest possession from your hearts. I left no stone unturned in my efforts to get the order annulled. But when this was impossible, I tried to mitigate it. I then gave orders for a registration of all nine-year-old children. I wanted at least to rescue all those aged nine to ten. But I could not get them to assent. I did succeed in one thing—saving all children past the age of ten. Let this be a comfort in our great sorrow.

"In the ghetto, we have a great number of tuberculars who have only a few days, perhaps a few weeks, left to live. I don't know,

perhaps this plan is devilish, perhaps not, but I cannot hold back
from uttering it: 'Give me these sick and in their place we can
rescue the healthy.' I know how dearly each family, especially among
Jews, cherishes its sick. But with such an edict, we have to weigh
and measure: Who should, can, and may be saved? Common sense
dictates that we should save those capable of being saved, those who
have prospects of survival, and not those who can't be saved anyway.

"We live, after all, in the ghetto. Our life is so austere that we
don't even have enough for the healthy, much less for the sick. Each
of us keeps the sick man alive at the price of our own health. We
give the sick man our bread. We give him our bit of sugar, our piece
of meat, and the consequence is that not only does the sick man not
become well, but we become sick. Naturally, such sacrifices are noble.
But at a time when we must choose either to sacrifice the sick man,
who not only has no chance of becoming well but is even likely to
make others sick, or to rescue a well man. I could not mull over this
problem for long, and I was forced to decide in favor of the well
man. I have therefore given orders to the doctors and they will be
compelled to turn over all the incurably ill in order to rescue in
their stead all those who are well and who want, and are able, to
live." (Terrible weeping.)

"I understand you, mothers, I see your tears. I can also feel
your hearts, fathers, who, tomorrow, after your children have been
taken from you, will be going to work, when just yesterday you had
been playing with your dear little children. I know all this and I
sympathize with it. Since 4 p.m. yesterday, upon hearing the decree,
I have utterly collapsed. I live with your grief, and your sorrow
torments me, and I don't know how and with what strength I can
live through it. I must tell you a secret. They demanded 24,000
victims, 3,000 persons a day, for eight days, but I succeeded in
getting them to reduce the number to 20,000, and perhaps even
fewer than 20,000, but only on condition that these will be children
to the age of ten. Children over ten are safe. Since children and old
people add up only to 13,000, we will have to meet the quota by
adding the sick as well.

"It is hard for me to speak. I have no strength. I will only
utter the appeal I make to you: Help me carry out the action! I
tremble. I am frightened at the thought that others, God forbid,
might take it into their own hands.

"You see before you a broken man. Don't envy me. This is the most difficult order that I have ever had to carry out. I extend to you failing and trembling hands and I beg you: Give into my hands the victims, thereby to ensure against further victims, thereby to protect a community of a hundred thousand Jews.". . .

Saturday, September 5, 1942. . . .

It has begun.

It's only a few minutes after 7 a.m. now. All the people, practically the entire ghetto, are on the street. Whose nerves don't drive them out? Who can sit home? Who has peace of mind? Who can just sit with his arms folded? No one! . . .

Consequently, from early morning the streets of the ghetto are busier than ever. And what a strange busyness. A silent, lifeless busyness, if one can put it that way. People don't talk to one another, as though everyone had left his tongue at home or had forgotten how to speak. Acquaintances don't greet each other, as though they feel ashamed. Everyone is rigid in motion, rigid standing in the long lines at the distribution places and rigid in the enormous lines at the vegetable places, A dead silence dominates the ghetto. No one so much as sighs or moans. Today huge, heavy stones weigh on the hearts of the ghetto residents.

People run through the ghetto streets like transmigrant spirits, perhaps like sinful souls wandering through the world of chaos. With that same stubborn silence on their clenched lips, with that same dread in their eyes—that's the way those spirits must look. People stand in line, perhaps like prisoners condemned to death, standing and waiting until their turn comes to go to the gallows. Rigidity, terror, collapse, fear, dread—there is no word to describe all the feelings that swell and grow in these petrified hearts that can't even weep, can't even scream. There is no ear that can catch the silent scream that deafens with its rigidity and that rigidifies with its deafening silence.

They run over the three ghetto bridges, like a host of hundred-headed serpents surging back and forth. The host of serpents extends forward and back. These are people hurrying and hastening. The air is pregnant with oppressiveness. Macabre tidings are in its density. The sky keeps swelling, billowing, and will soon burst, and out of the void will tumble the full horror and the full reality.

It has begun!

No one knows what, no one knows where, no one knows how. Supposing that everyone keeps silent, supposing that no one looks at anyone else, supposing that everyone avoids everyone else the way the thief avoids his pursuer, then who was the first to utter these dreadful words: "It has begun!". . .

No one. No one spoke them. No one uttered these macabre tidings. Only the heavens burst and its spilled guts dropped those words: "It has begun!". . .

Where has it begun? People say: "They're already taking out all the residents of the old-age home on Dworska Street."

People say: "On Rybna Street there's already a truck, and they're loading it with old people and children."

Alas, all the stories are true: They're taking them from here, from there, from everywhere, and they're already loading on Rybna Street.

It has begun.

The Jewish police made the first start. They began as if they wanted to practice their work along the line of least resistance— the old-age home. There it was as easy as pie—they were just ready to be taken. And the people there are being taken wholesale, there's no selecting and rejecting. They're all old, and so all of them are to go to the scrap heap. It's really the line of least resistance. Who is going to speak up for them, who's going to waste words for these old people who have been living on the good graces of the community for weeks and months now? . . . They are being loaded on the trucks like lambs for slaughter and driven to the staging area. There they may get the condemned man's last meal consisting, supposedly, of a soup with lots of potatoes, cooked with horse bones, and later they'll be taken away from this staging area—

To the scrap heap. . . .

Over on Rybna Street the police have to take them out of apartments. There they are encountering resistance. There they have to cut living, palpitating limbs from bodies. There they wrench infants from their mothers' breasts. There they pull healthy molars out of mouths. On Rybna Street they tear grown children from under their parents' wings. They separate husband from wife, wife from husband, people who've been together for forty or fifty years, who've lived in sorrow and in joy, who've had children to-gether, who've reared them together and lost them together. They've been with one another for forty or fifty years and become practically one body. . . .

The sick, too, are being taken there, sick people who at great risk escaped from the hospital, whom mortal terror gave the strength and courage to leap over barriers, sick people who were given someone's last crust of bread, last bit of sugar, last potato just to keep them alive one more day, one more week, one more month, because the war might end and then they could perhaps get back on their feet. Also the sick are being taken.

Living limbs are cut off. Healthy molars are extracted. Palpitating bodies are halved. The anguish is great. Let someone try to describe it, he won't be able to! Let someone try to depict it, he'll only collapse! Is it any wonder that people scream? . . .

People scream. And their screams are terrible and fearful and senseless, as terrible and fearful and senseless as the actions causing them. The ghetto is no longer rigid; it is now writhing in convulsions. The whole ghetto is one enormous spasm. The whole ghetto jumps out of its own skin and plunges back within its own barbed wires. Ah, if only a fire would come and consume everything! If only a bolt from heaven would strike and destroy us altogether! There is hardly anyone in the ghetto who hasn't gasped such a wish from his feeble lips, whether he is affected directly, indirectly, or altogether uninvolved in the events which were staged before his very eyes and ears. Everyone is ready to die; already now, at the very start, at this very moment, it is impossible to endure the terror and the horror. Already at this moment it is impossible to endure the screams of hundreds of thousands of bound cattle slaughtered but not yet killed; impossible to endure the twitching of the pierced but unsevered throats, which let them neither die nor live.

What has happened to the Jewish police, who undertook to do that piece of work? Have their brains atrophied? Have their hearts been torn out and replaced with stones? It's hard, very hard, to answer these questions. One thing is certain—they are not to be envied. And there are also all sorts of executioners. There is an executioner who for a worthless traitor's pay would raise his hand against his brother; another, besides getting his traitor's pay, also has to be gotten drunk, otherwise his ignoble hand will fumble.

And there are executioners who do their bloody work for the sake of an idea. They were told: "So-and-so is not only useless to society, he's actually detrimental, he's got to be cleaned out." So they act for the good of society, they do the cleaning out.

The Jewish police have been bought. They have been intoxicated. They were given hashish—their children have been exempted from the order. They've been given three pounds of bread a day for their bloody bit of work—bread to gorge themselves on and an extra portion of sausage and sugar. They work for the sake of an idea, the Jewish police do. Thus our own hands, Jewish hands, extract the molars, cut off the limbs, slice up the bodies. . . .

No, they are not to be envied at all, the Jewish police!

The bloody page of this history should be inscribed with black letters for the so-called "White Guard," the porters of Balut Market and of the Food Supply Office. This rabble, fearful of losing their soup during pedestrian embargo, volunteered to help in the action on condition that they get the same as had been promised the police —bread, sausage, and sugar, and the exemption of their families. Their offer was accepted. They participated voluntarily in the action.

The bloody page of this history should be inscribed with black letters for all those officials who petitioned to have some role in this action, only in order to get bread and sausage rations instead of the soup they wouldn't have gotten sitting at home. . . .

The Seizures

O God, Jewish God, how defenseless Jewish blood has become!

Oh, God, God of all mankind, how defenseless human blood has become!

Blood flows in the streets. Blood flows over the yards. Blood flows in the buildings. Blood flows in the apartments. Not red, healthy blood. That doesn't exist in the ghetto. Three years of war, two and a half years of ghetto have devoured the red corpuscles. All the ghetto has is pus and streaming gall, that drips, flows, and gushes from the eyes, and inundates streets, yards, houses, apartments.

How can such blood satisfy the appetites of the beasts? It can only whet their appetites, nothing more!

It is no longer just a rumor, not just gossip; it is an established fact. The head of the ghetto administration, Biebow,[6] the man most interested in the ghetto's existence, in its survival, has put himself in charge of the action. He himself directs the "resettlement."

People are being seized. The Jewish police are seizing them with mercy, according to orders: children under ten, old people over 65, and the sick whom doctors have diagnosed as incurable. . . .

The Jewish police have addresses. The Jewish police have Jewish concierges, and the concierges have house registers. The addresses inform that in such and such an apartment is a child who was born on such and such a date. The addresses inform that in such and such an apartment is an old man who was born so and so many years ago. A doctor comes into every apartment. He examines the occupants. He observes who is in good health and who just pretends to good health. He's had so much practice in the ghetto that a mere glance distinguishes the well from the mortally ill.

Nor does it avail the child to cling to its mother's neck with both little hands. Nor does it avail the mother to throw herself on the threshold and bellow like a slaughtered cow: "Only over my dead body will you take my child!" It does not avail the old man to clutch the cold walls with his bony fingers and plead: "Let me die here in peace." It does not avail the old woman to fall on her knees, kiss their boots, and plead: "I've already got grown-up grandchildren." It does not avail the sick man to bury his feverish head in the damp, sweaty pillow, and moan, and shed perhaps his last tears.

Nothing avails. The police have to supply their quota. They have to seize people. They cannot show pity. But when the Jewish police take people, they do so punctiliously. When they take people, they help them weep, they help them moan. When they take people, they try to comfort them with hoarse voices, to express their anguish. . . .

It's totally different when others come! [7]

They enter a yard and first off is a reckless shot of a revolver. Everyone loses courage. All blood stops coursing. All throats are stopped with hot lead. The lead freezes the gasps and sobs in the throat. You tremble. No! To tremble you have to have flowing

6. Hans Biebow was the German chief of the ghetto administration of Litzmannstadt. He was tried for war crimes in Poland, condemned to death, and executed in 1947.

7. The reference is to the SS, which had in fact taken over the deportations because the Jewish police had not proved sufficiently competent for the task.

blood, but your blood refuses to circulate. It has curdled, it is rigid like water in a frost. The Jews wait, benumbed, paralyzed, helpless. They wait for what happens next.

Next comes a harsh, terse, draconic order, yelled out, and then repeated by the Jewish police. "In two minutes everyone downstairs! No one is permitted to stay inside. All doors must be left open!"

Who can describe, depict the crazed and wild stampede on stairways and landings, the rigid and inanimate figures who hasten to obey the order on time? No one.

Old, rheumatic, twisted sclerotic legs stumble over crooked stairs and angular stones. Young, buoyant, deer legs fly with bird-like speed. The heavy and clumsy legs of the sick heaved from their beds are bent and bowed. Swollen legs of starvelings tap blindly along. All scurry, hurry, rush out into the courtyard.

Woe to the latecomer. He will never finish that last walk. He will have to swim in his own blood. Woe to him who stumbles and falls. He will never stand up again. He will slip and fall again in his own blood. Woe to the child who is so terrified that all he can do is scream "Mama!" He will never get past the first syllable. A reckless gunshot will sever the word in his throat. The second syllable will tumble down into his heart like a bird shot down in mid-flight. The experience of the last few hours proved this in its stark reality.

When the Jewish police take people, they take whomever they can, whoever is there. If someone has hidden and can't be taken, then he remains hidden. But when *they* come to take people, they take those who are there and those who are not there. If someone is not located, they take another in his place. If the missing man is found, he will not be seized; he will have to be carried out.

The Jewish police, further, can be bought. Not with ghetto marks of course, but with more valuable items. As long as it's hush-hush and no one can see or hear, then anyone who's got something can ransom his way out. But when *they* come to take you, you can buy your way out only with your rarest and most precious posses-sion—your life. You can take the choice of not wishing to go, and you'll never have to go anywhere again. . . .

The sun sets bloodily in the west. All the west is bathed in blood. Ridiculous and grandiloquent to speak of the heavens reflecting the blood that was spilled in the ghetto today. The heavens are too far from earth. The screams and the shouts from the ghetto did not carry up there, not even an echo of their echo. The screaming was of no avail; the tears were shed for nothing and were lost. No one saw them; no one heard them.

To say that "the sun sets bloodily in the west" is therefore merely a datum that symbolizes today's bloody ghetto day. To say that "all the west is bathed in blood" is a datum that symbolizes this evening. But the day still strives with the evening. The day is not yet over, as if this day were not long enough. The measure is not yet full. The last tidings of Job have not yet been heard.

What iron strength this day has! It stretches as long as the Jewish Exile. It is as heavy as Jewish woe. What dark strength the ghetto people have! After three years of hunger, after three years of wretched enslavement, they can still endure such days as this day. . . .

Sunday, September 6, 1942

The clock says 12 noon. It is a full-blown summer's day. It's impossible to stay indoors. No one can stay at home. Perhaps because you must stay inside, perhaps because you're surrounded by your family and you have nothing to say to them. You yourself are indeed young. You yourself have your work certificate proving you're a useful citizen of the ghetto. Your wife is young too, and her papers are fully in order. Younger than both of you is your fourteen-year-old son, who already works. He is tall and slender and handsome, a fine figure of a lad. You have no reasons to be afraid, not for yourself, not for your wife, and not for your son. But you sit at home, listening to the sighs and shouts and screams of your neighbors, from whom pieces of flesh were torn away yesterday. You sit at home and hear yet another scream every minute from another neighbor, or mute sobs from people sick with sorrow. You sit at home and constantly hear yet another scream from a neighbor who, in his great despair over the children who were seized from him, tries to end his broken existence with a knife or by leaping from a high window. You sit at home, devoured by your own sorrow, your wife's sorrow, your son's sorrow, and the sufferings of all your neighbors and all Jews. Sitting at home like this, on and on, every time you glance at the mirror and it reflects a yellowed, sunken, confused contenance: "You, too, are a candidate for the scrap heap!" Sitting at home, casting furtive glances at your wife who has aged dozens of years in these last two days, then looking at your beautiful son, seeing his dark hollow face and the mortal fear lurking in his deep black eyes, then all the terror around you makes you fear for yourself, makes you fear for your wife, makes you fear for your trembling child. All of you are candidates!

THE BUND APPEALS TO
THE POLISH GOVERNMENT-IN-EXILE, MAY 1942

From the day the Russo-German war broke out, the Germans undertook the physical extermination of the Jewish population on Polish territory, using for that purpose Ukrainians and Lithuanian Šiauliai.[8] It began first of all in Eastern Galicia in the summer months of 1941. Their method everywhere was as follows: Men from 14 to 60 were rounded up in one place—a square or cemetery—where they were slaughtered, machine-gunned, or killed by hand grenades. They had to dig their own graves first. Children in orphanages, inmates of old-age homes, and the hospitalized sick were shot, women were killed on the streets. In many towns Jews were taken away to an "unknown destination," and executed in the nearby woods. 30,000 Jews were murdered in Lwów, 15,000 in Stanisławów, 5,000 in Tarnopol, 2,000 in Złoczów, 4,000 in Brzeżany (the town had 18,000 Jews, now has 1,700). The same happened in Zborów, Kołomyja, Stryj, Sambor, Drohobycz, Zbaraż, Przemyślany, Kuty, Śniatyń, Zaleszczyki, Brody, Przemyśl, Rawa Ruska, and other places.

The extermination actions in those towns recurred repeatedly in many towns; they are still going on—Lwów.

In October and November the same thing began to happen in Vilna, the Vilna area, and Lithuanian Kovno. In Vilna 50,000 Jews were murdered during November. There are now 12,000 Jews in Vilna. According to various estimates, the number of Jews bestially murdered in the Vilna regions and Lithuanian Kovno is put at 300,000.

In September, the murder of the Jews started in the environs of Słonim. Nearly all Jews were murdered in Żyrowice, Lachowicze, Mir, Kosów and other places in the area. The action in Słonim be-

8. Members of a paramilitary fascist police organization.

gan October 15. More than 9,000 Jews were killed. In Równe, the destruction of the Jews began in the early days of November. In the course of three days and three nights over 15,000 people—men, women, and children—were shot. 6,000 Jews were shot in Hance-wicze, near Baranowicze. The annihilation action embraced all Polish territory beyond the San and Bug rivers. We have mentioned only a few places where it occurred.

In November and December, the annihilation action was begun in the Polish territory incorporated into the Reich, i.e., *Warthegau*. The annihilation was carried out by means of gassing, which took place in the village of Chełmno, 12 km. from Koło. A special van (gas chambers) was used, in which 90 people were loaded. The victims were buried in special graves in a clearing in the Lubard Forest. The graves were dug by the victims themselves. On average, 1,000 people were gassed daily. Between November 1941 and March 1942, the Jewish inhabitants of Koło, Dąbie, Bugaj, and Izbica Kujawska—all in all, 5,000 persons, 35,000 Jews from the Lodz ghetto, as well as a certain number of Gypsies were gassed in Chełmno.

In February 1942, the annihilation of Jews in the territory which is called the Generalgouvernement was started. The beginning: Tarnów and Radom, where Gestapo and SS men began visiting the Jewish districts daily, systematically killing Jews in the streets, courtyards, and houses. In March, a mass action began in Lublin of deporting all Jews from the city. Children and old people, in the orphanages and old-age homes and also the patients in the general hospital and the hospital for contagious diseases, were bestially put to death, and also many people were killed in the streets and in their homes. The total number of victims was over 2,000. Some 25,000 Jews were taken away from Lublin in sealed railroad cars to an "unknown destination," after which every trace of them has disappeared. Some 3,000 Jews were confined in barracks in Majdanek Tatarowy, a suburb of Lublin. Not a single Jew is left in Lublin today. In the last days of March in Cracow, fifty Jews were rounded up, from a list prepared beforehand, and were shot in the yards in front of their homes. In Warsaw, in the night of April 17–18, the Gestapo organized a blood bath in the ghetto. According to a prepared list, they dragged out more than fifty Jews, men and women, from their homes and murdered them in front of their buildings. Many were not found at home. Starting with April 18, even in broad daylight, they kill a few Jews a day in their homes and on the streets. This action is conducted with prepared lists, comprising all strata of Jews in the Warsaw ghetto. There is talk of bloody nights to come. To date the Germans have murdered an estimated 700,000 Polish Jews.

The above facts confirm irrefutably that the criminal German government has undertaken to carry out Hitler's prophecy that five minutes before the war ends, however it ends, he would annihilate all the Jews in Europe. We firmly believe that Hitler's Germans will at the proper time be presented with an appropriate reckoning for their atrocities and bestialities. For the Jewish population, which now endures an inconceivable hell, this is not consolation enough. Millions of Polish citizens of Jewish nationality are threatened with imminent extermination.

We, therefore, turn to the Government of Poland, as custodian and representative of the whole population living on Polish soil, immediately to take the necessary steps to prevent the annihilation of Polish Jewry. To that end, the Government of Poland should bring all its influence to bear on the governments of the Allied Powers and on all authoritative circles in those countries so that they will, without delay, apply a policy of retribution against German citizens and the fifth columnists living in the countries of the Allied Powers. The Government of Poland and the governments of the Allied Powers should notify the German government as to the application of retribution. It should be made aware that Germans in the United States and in other countries will even now be answering for the bestial annihilation of the Jewish population.

We realize that we are asking the Government of Poland to take extraordinary measures. This is the only possibility of rescuing millions of Jews from certain annihilation.

MICHAEL DOV WEISSMANDEL:
LETTERS FROM THE DEPTHS

Tuesday, May 11, 1943

Greetings:

. . . As for the massive task of rescuing all of Europe's Jews from deportation, we have already stated in earlier letters that it is our grave responsibility to begin to negotiate; we must begin the negotiations, and if our adversaries accept our terms, or if they demand more, as is common in negotiations, it is our duty to meet their conditions, regardless. One can hardly imagine the outcome should we fail to do this. If, God forbid, this should be the case, the fate of the surviving remnant will of course deteriorate, from bad to worse.

You have written us recommending that we continue the talks—which we have done—and now the adviser [9] says that he is authorized by his superiors to grant what we ask: to suspend deportations throughout Europe for 2 to 3 thousand dollars.[10] When he says 2 to 3, in my humble opinion, we should figure 3—a sum which is not subject to further negotiation, as it was arrived at after much discussion and approved by his superiors.

He expects an advance payment of 1,000, to be delivered between June 10 and 20. Deportations will then be cancelled for a period of about two months. During these two months there will be further directives regarding the manner and timing by which the balance is to be paid.

Thus far, in that forsaken land,[11] more than three million have been killed. The surviving remnant is wandering through caverns and forests, awaiting death in walled camps. Under discussion was the question whether there is any hope of salvation for them; but this is, according to him, a chapter in itself. He will bring an answer after consulting his superiors, at the end of the week.

The situation is as follows:

(1)   It is impossible to stop the deportations in other countries for the aforementioned sum.

(2)   It may be possible to stop the massacre in the forsaken land for an as yet undetermined sum.

Pertaining to paragraph 1, which is at present a firmly established fact: stopping the deportations means an end to the massacre. This requires no explication. The deportations could, God forbid, involve more than a million in Europe—and the price is 2 or 3 bills to rescue a single Jewish soul after so many thousands and tens of thousands have already been massacred, many of whom could, indeed, have been saved with money.

9. Presumably Dieter Wisliceny.
10. Per person.
11. Poland.

These words are not addressed to you, readers of this letter—for we are well aware of your good will—but to communities of Jews residing in lands of peace and tranquility and to their leaders, none of whom, by God's grace, even given the imagination of a madman, could picture the fate of Jews in these blood-filled lands. We impose on them a grave oath, written in the blood of millions of pure and holy martyrs spilled on Israel's altar and in the surging blood of millions being prepared for sacrifice to the Moloch—for it is still possible to rescue them and their posterity:

If you are worthy, if you provide the money without discussion, without delay, even a moment's delay, then you will have atoned in some measure for the spilled blood. If, God forbid, you lose time in deliberation, talk, meetings, in doubts, negotiation, argument, consultations and proposals, then there will be an unprecedented slaughter by Israel's own hand.

We know these are harsh words, that we indict the innocent, that there is no Jew in the world who would not give all his wealth to save a single soul, all the more so an entire community. Still, we must tell the truth as it is. For if, God help us, and I even hesitate to mention this, should we not have the money in our hand by mid-June, the thousand demanded as an advance, if it is not in our power to say that the Jewish community abroad is ready and willing to provide the required sum, according to the prescribed conditions, then our words will have been damaging. For, rather than canceling the evil decree, having failed to salvage the lives of the surviving remnant, we will have, God forbid, actually hastened their end, with the cruelty of a miser, sitting on his money.

Bitter is our soul to utter such harsh words, but the past gives us a right to speak of the future in this fashion. We know that if the community there had not asked for such an advance accounting from the community here and if there had not been such a delay in payment, had pockets been opened, if there had been an ample supply of money, money and more money flowing to the community here, to those very people who are in a position to determine for themselves what the need is, though they are not the people in charge, but they are involved in terms of time and place; if in response to vague hints sent abroad, money, money and more money had been made available, to the utmost capacity of our brethren in the land, indeed the lands, of tranquility, granting those here the absolute right to do with that money whatsoever they deem right—

then we know clearly that thousands and tens of thousands, entire communities and countless smaller groups would still be alive. And it was not a vague hint we dispatched, but piercing screams. Yet many weeks and months passed. We received letters setting forth conditions. Those actions, which any group would surely have undertaken, finding itself in a secure position while others of its own faith were trampled by murderers, were not initiated by our brothers, by our own people, a fact before which we are incredulous. For neither a lover of Israel nor an enemy could believe it.

Now the time has come—a singular opportunity for rescue. Please, I beg of you, do this deed immediately, without delay.

Regarding the surviving remant in lands where the evil decree applies, there is one plan at the moment: to smuggle individuals from there to here, from here to Hungary and perhaps from Hungary to Palestine. It costs about 20,000, in our money, to smuggle a single person. Each day they come. At the moment there are fifty souls waiting at the border of a particular village and we can not help them for lack of funds. For this purpose alone it is the sacred obligation of all Jews abroad to provide unlimited sums on our account, for which we will be responsible. This is the sole means of rescue for the surviving remnant there. Many hundreds, perhaps even thousands, can be saved, only through money. Who, if not you, can we ask to provide it? We, therefore, request that you allocate a large sum for this rescue operation, explicitly for this, and transmit it to us unconditionally, without delay and in the manner known to you, which is tried and tested.

We pray that the good Lord will see fit to end the trials of His people, that His holy nation Israel will no longer have to beg a fellow man for its life, that He in His mercy will save us with the rest of Israel and bless you dear and beloved folk who are sacrificing yourselves for the general good, with every sort of blessing and salvation. As you have responded to the trouble of your beseeching brothers, so may you live to see them saved and to hear their jubilant voices soon. . . .

Wednesday, May 31, 1944

Greetings:

. . . Though we wrote some weeks ago, we have not to date received any indication that the letter was received and are concerned about this. If you did receive the letter, we ask that you send a telegram to Weiss Mano, Bratislava, Hotel Central, with the message "Let us know how you are. . . ." If you have not received the letter, send a telegram to that same address saying "We are worried about you."

Now for the facts.

Since May 15, 13,000 Jews have been evacuated from the area east of the Tisza River, Carpatho-Russia, and the general district of Košice. These transports proceed via Košice-Prešov-Orlova-Nowy Sącz-Cracow to Auschwitz-Birkenau.

As of yesterday, that is, May 30, 190,446 Jews have gone this route. We know this to be a fact from incontestable documents. For example, on May 29th five transports were sent off:

(1)   23 cars carrying 860 persons
(2)   45 cars carrying 3,299 persons
(3)   49 cars carrying 3,382 persons
(4)   45 cars carrying 3,305 persons
(5)   43 cars carrying 3,066 persons
A total of 13,912 persons.

On the 30th day of this month 4 transports were sent off:

(1)   45 cars carrying 3,475 persons
(2)   46 cars carrying 3,203 persons
(3)   45 cars carrying 3,268 persons
(4)   46 cars carrying 3,230 persons
A total of 13,246 persons.[12]

From these figures the daily average number appears to be 13,000, the average number in each car being 75–80.

In this initial stage 320,000 persons were deported in an orderly fashion and without any interference, at the appointed hour and minute, aided by your monstrous neglect and that of the Allied Powers. This operation will undoubtedly be concluded on the eighth or ninth day of June.

And what will follow?

In Budapest there is a noted personage, Eich, who, along with his assistant Willi [13] and other officials, has been negotiating with Jewish leaders in terms of the old Europa Plan with which you are all familiar. They have promised that if the Jews fulfill their side of the

---

12. The figures actually add up to 13,176. These statistics were written in Hebrew letters; the letter *ayin*, whose numerical value is 70, may have been inadvertently omitted.

13. Eichmann and Wisliceny.

bargain, they will content themselves with the deportation of 320,000 and that those remaining will not be deported.

If the Jews are unwilling to accept or fulfill these terms, then everyone will be deported. They go even further, saying that if these terms are met, they will permit a great exodus from this country toward the neutral sea through Germany-France-Spain. They claim that those already deported are living in Germany and are being kept as hostages until the Jews meet their terms. (This, of course, is an outright lie.)

Their terms are:

(1)   Twice 1,000,000 dollars.

(2)   Supplies. They demand various supplies that can be obtained and others that are difficult or impossible to obtain, such as trucks, for example, and these in large numbers.

For this purpose Brand was sent with great dispatch to Turkey.[14] He went by air and has been there almost two weeks. This entire matter, of course, must be a guarded secret from friends and enemies alike.

It is now essential to consider the matter. To this end certain facts must be known:

(1)   All those transports are heading for Auschwitz-Birkenau.

(2)   Auschwitz is a huge murder factory. They are all gassed there and cremated, except for a very tiny portion. Two or three percent are spared to perform necessary labor (lead the victims to the gas chambers, cremate them, check and sort their clothes) and these, too, when their strength dwindles, are exterminated and replaced by others. Details are contained in the enclosed eyewitness testimony.[15]

(3)   Though the capacity of the four gas chambers in Birkenau is only 6,000, we know from responsible sources that the facilities there have been expanded to this end (for Hungary's Jews). Apart from this, they have repaired the death camp mentioned on an earlier page, which is in Birkenwald. (We know this from a survivor who arrived here today, a Hungarian who was taken there and escaped miraculously.)

(4)   3,000 letters from "Waldsee" have reached Budapest, writ-

14. Joel Brand, an active member of a Zionist relief and rescue committee in Budapest, was delegated by Jewish communal leaders to conduct the negotiations of "blood for trucks." He was accompanied to Istanbul by Bandi Grosz, a Gestapo agent.
15. This was the Vrba-Weczler report about Auschwitz, which appears in Section 4.

ten by Hungarian deportees. They write that the conditions of their life are adequate, that everyone works at his trade.

(5)   You will see from the enclosed evidence that the victims are forced to write these letters to which later dates are attached.

In conclusion: the essence of the above information, particularly the tales of the Hungarian refugee who escaped from there, is that they all go to Auschwitz (with the exception of a small portion and this may be a device to mask what they are doing); that at least 95 percent have already been killed or are being killed; that they are led to the transports through various ruses (they are told they will be taken to another part of Hungary, for example to Hortobagy) and the entire operation is carried out through the slyest trickery and by gravely misleading tactics.

These are the real facts:
In addition it is known to us that Hitler's Foreign Minister (R) [16] has declared: "Hungary is a Jewish stronghold. We will exterminate them." He has said this in secret to a few confidants.

There is an entirely other line of facts leading up to this negotiation.

(1)   In October 1942 we presented the Europa Plan through Willi to his superior, the man Eich.

(2)   A few weeks later we received an affirmative answer.

(3)   Your approach in this regard, the politics, the comings and goings, empty-handed, are of course familiar to you.

(4)   In the summer of 1943 Willi presented an agreement to suspend the deportations for one or two months ("closed season" to use his term), during which period we would be required to begin payment. As you know, this was not within our power.

(5)   At the end of the summer of 1943, W. suddenly brought a message from his superior that he was not, just then, responsive to our proposals.

In connection with this, one must note that the Gestapo and the SS, as we all know, are two systems working toward a single goal. Still, they are independent of each other and actually function autonomously, in many cases in opposition to each other. They do, however, have Himmler as a common head.[17] Apart from this, each unit goes its own way.

16. Joachim von Ribbentrop.
17. Weissmandel's perception was correct. The Gestapo had originally been part of the state apparatus, while the SS was a Nazi party institution. Himmler became head of both in 1936, but the internal rivalries between the two bureaucracies continued.

(1)   Unfortunately, our people in Turkey chose a German courier, which was unnecessary. This occurred in the summer of 1943. He showed our correspondence with Turkey to his superior. (We know this with absolute certainty.)

(2)   At this very time the head of the Gestapo (Schmidt) began negotiating with Brand and his people in Budapest and proposed the Europa Plan, on his own.

(3)   So that the Europa Plan proceeded in two separate directions: via W. and his superior on the one hand, through the SS on the second, and via Schmidt and his superior through the Gestapo.

(4)   Eichmann's negative answer transmitted by Willi is consistent with the beginning of new negotiations by Schmidt just this month. It is possible that Eich. was in a tight spot because of what was said and needed to prove himself through new massacres.

(5)   You will see from the enclosed testimony that July 1943 really was a month of respite.

From the above one can speculate that for the moment the two have arrived at some compromise and will prove themselves to the Führer by further murders of 320,000 in this last blood center of Jews, arguing that those to the west are already assimilated and no longer such a menace. There were articles to this effect in *Der Grenzbote* as well as in other German periodicals.

If so, we have Premise No. 1:

(1)   Despite their dreadful murders and vile treachery, the German proposal is sincere. Certain decisive heads, those that determine Himmler's opinions, perhaps, or at least influence him, believe that the burden of the past can be heaped on Hitler and Himmler and intend to credit themselves with the present and the future, guaranteeing for themselves a portion in heaven.

This possibility must be accepted, and whether it appears near or far from the truth is irrelevant. It is obvious that negotiations must be concluded without delay or negligence, that our side must accede.

a. We must immediately give substance, not merely with words, but in real terms; more money perhaps, and fewer supplies. If we were to give something, it would be possible to offer excuses, but excuses alone are inadequate.

b. We must come to terms with each party separately.

c. We cannot overstate our confidence that though there certainly are more than enough reasons for distrust, we must accept the premise in theory and in practice, that their intentions are honest in this matter and conclude negotiations in the manner most acceptable to them. The events of the summer of 1943 must not, under any circumstances, be allowed to recur.

Premise No. 2:

(2)   Possibly, even almost certainly, all this is a plot, a maneuver, a gesture of camouflage which they have undertaken to win our confidence, to undermine our already meager and paltry power to resist them. They are negotiating in order to divert every means of moral pressure and resistance such as the radio and the press. If negotiations are in process, then those Jews who affect public opinion will undoubtedly suppress all opposition to their thinking.

Though we must in our posture and money operate on the basis of premise No. 1, we must also in theory and in practice confront premise No. 2. To this end we demand, absolutely, and in the strongest terms:

a. The destruction of all roads leading from Hungary to Poland or Germany, in particular the following roads: (1) Košice-Kysak-Prešov-Orlova; (2) Legene-Laborce, Čadca-Žilina.

b. This destruction must occur close to the highway exits to obstruct attempts to divert the traffic to other roads.

c. This must be undertaken as a regular and systematic operation.

d. The fact that these roads are already burdened by heavy traffic from all directions must be considered.

e. In terms of morale on his home front, the dictator cannot conceivably allow himself publicly and openly, in the very midst of the country, to commit 13,000 murders a day. It is only by the devious and hidden means of Auschwitz that this is possible and he could not otherwise accomplish this.

f. Destruction of the highway exits, would, in itself, prevent these murders.

Now we ask: how can you eat, sleep, live? How guilty will you feel in your hearts if you fail to move heaven and earth to help us in the only ways that are available to our own people and as quickly as possible? Consider that every day 13,000 of your brothers and sisters, old and young, women and children, are destroyed. Do you not fear the day of judgment and reckoning in this world and in the world to come?

Should you say you did what you could, we say this is not so. For had you done what you could, you would surely have arrived at some action. Since you have not acted, we know this is not true.

For God's sake, do something now and quickly. This course would be effective, considering how burdened they are by their oppressive state of war, as well as the grave condition of their roads and transportation facilities. This course is most expedient, most secure, most speedy, and most simple. And it is eminently possible to pursue. But it must be done immediately, without delay.

And there is no reason to declare the purpose of this destruction over the radio. God forbid. This must be a guarded secret.

On the other hand, heads of government and radio must announce what was done to our people in the slaughter houses of Bełżec, Małkinia,[18] Sobibór, and Auschwitz. Till now six times a million Jews from Europe and Russia have been destroyed.

The Pope must be moved to protest these massacres vigorously in a voice that will resound to heaven and earth.

Heads of governments and peoples under Hitler's rule must be warned of their forthcoming punishment. . . .

An awesome and holy responsibility devolves on you. You will be fortunate if you understand and confront it, but woe unto you in the contrary case. The Lord is granting you the privilege to be agents of mercy on behalf of the surviving remnant who are being killed, murdered, choked, burned every day in sanctification of His name. . . .

---

18. The reference is to Treblinka. Małkinia was the nearby railroad station.

9 RESISTANCE:
THE ORDEAL OF DESPERATION

INTRODUCTION

*R*ESISTANCE IN THE GHETTOS *of Eastern Europe was born out of the desperate knowledge that the Germans had embarked on the destruction of all the Jews. The impulse to organize armed resistance originated with the Bundist and left Zionist parties operating underground in the ghettos and especially with their youth affiliates. Nearly half a century before, these parties had created Jewish self-defense* (zelbshuts) *organizations to protect the Jews against pogromists in Tsarist Russia. That spirit of defiance which the parties nurtured in their members remained alive in the ghettos, but was inhibited by the exercise of self-discipline and restraint in view of the relentless policy which the Germans pursued of exacting collective retribution from the Jewish community for the acts of individual Jews. Hoping to survive both the war and the German occupation, the Jewish parties at first abstained from outright provocation of the Germans. Yet once they realized that hope for Jewish survival was but a snare and a delusion, they began to organize for an ultimate armed struggle against the Germans, however unequal their resources, strength, and opportunities. They* *never envisioned their purpose as military, for they knew that they could not change the course of the war. Resistance for the Jews was purely affective—to exact vengeance from the Germans and to die fighting, to die, as they liked to phrase it, "with honor."*

The first resistance organization to be formed was in the Vilna ghetto. For a half-year since the German invasion in June 1941, the Vilna Jews had been subjected to random mass killings and then to systematic depopulation by mass shootings. Ponary, a desolate village about ten kilometers away, the site of these killings, became a by-name of horror. The Jewish population of Vilna, once over 60,000, was reduced to 12,000. After December 21, 1941, the first stage of killings came to a halt. The surviving Jews began to rebuild their shattered community. Out of the wreckage of their institutions young Zionists decided to create an organization for self-defense. At a clandestine meeting on January 1, 1942, held in a public kitchen, with about 150 young people present, Abba Kovner, a Hashomer Hatzair activist and Hebrew poet, then twenty-three years old (now a well-known poet in Israel), read a proclamation he had composed, "Let us not be led like sheep to the slaughter!" Evoking the phrases and values that had animated the left Zionist movement for a half century, Kovner concluded his appeals "Better to fall in the fight for human dignity than to live at the mercy of the murderer!"

Mounting an armed-resistance movement against the Germans demanded more than rhetoric and passion. Political stability, maturity, and responsibility were prerequisite, if the underground parties were to muster wide-ranging support from the Jews within the ghetto as well as from the non-Jewish underground movement outside the ghetto. All over Europe resistance groups turned for material aid and moral support to either England or Russia. In Vilna, for instance, the young Jews who organized the resistance movement turned to the Lithuanian and Russian Communists for assistance and instructions and, through them, to the Soviet partisan movement which was directed by the Red Army. In the General-gouvernement the Jewish resistance movement turned to the Polish underground, the Polish Home Army, and the Delegatura, the representative in Poland of the Polish Government-in-Exile.

In the first stage of the German occupation, before "resettle-

ment," each Jewish underground political party operated on its own, jealously guarding its autonomy and integrity and, just as important, its security. But once the parties recognized that the Jews were living in a period of extreme crisis, that the situation demanded emergency measures, the Bund and the several Zionist bodies agreed to coordinate their efforts and to set up a joint organization for armed resistance against the Germans.

Negotiations for coordinated action had begun in the spring of 1942 in Warsaw, when the underground Jewish political leaders were first assimilating the reports about the German annihilation of Jews. During the mass "resettlement" of Warsaw Jewry in the summer of 1942, while terror and death stalked the streets of the Warsaw ghetto, all efforts for joint action collapsed. In October, when the Germans suspended the murder operations for a time, negotiations among the Jews were resumed. At the same time, delegates from the Jewish parties contacted the Polish underground to explore the possibilities of arms aid. To warrant assistance from the Polish government, the Jewish parties had to show a common front that was widely representative of the whole Jewish population and that evidenced political maturity and responsibility.

To meet these requirements and also to preserve the parties' independence of political action, a Coordinating Committee was established, consisting of two bodies—the Jewish Labor Bund and the Jewish National Committee, an association of the Zionist parties. The Coordinating Committee, representing the Jewish community at large, was the politically responsible body which directed the operations of the Jewish Combat Organization. Bylaws of these newly created agencies were prepared for submission to the representative of the underground Polish government and transmitted through Wacław, party name for Henryk Wolinski, then in charge of Jewish affairs of the Polish Home Army's Chief Command.

The Coordinating Committee and the Jewish Combat Organization, commonly called by its Polish acronym ŻOB (Żydowska Organizacja Bojowa), at first operated in Warsaw only, but through its network of couriers and other underground contacts, it expanded its activity to encompass most of the area of Poland to which access could be obtained. The Zionist youth groups, for instance, deployed their activists to resistance groups in Cracow, Bialystok, Będzin, and Częstochowa. The resistance group in Cracow, a relatively small company of Zionist pioneer (halutz) youth, isolated from their own political leadership, took instructions for diversionary and sabotage operations from the Polish Communist underground. The young Jewish resisters were, for the most part, naive and idealistic, imbued with romantic conceptions of resistance. One of them, Gusta Dawidsohn Draenger (1918–1943), whose underground name was Justina, kept a secret record while imprisoned by the Gestapo. An extract from her account describes the moods of the Zionist youth after the deportation, in October 1942, of 7,000 Jews from the Cracow ghetto to the death camp at Bełżec.

The Zionist underground in Warsaw assigned Mordecai Tenenbaum (1916–1943), an activist in the halutz movement, as organizer of the resistance movement in Bialystok. Tenenbaum's cohorts were largely idealistic Zionist youth torn between their loyalties to the Jews in the ghetto, their commitment to making a last desperate stand, and the attraction of setting up or joining partisan units in the woods. On February 27, 1943, the members of Dror, Tenenbaum's own group, discussed these alternatives; the minutes were kept by Tenenbaum himself.

The resistance organizations in Vilna, Cracow, and Bialystok, whose members were predominantly untested youth, failed to win the support of the Jewish ghetto as a whole. In Warsaw, however, the organized underground was broadly representative and it achieved legitimacy as the authentic leadership of Warsaw Jewry. This legitimacy and authority were won through the effective use of two weapons: the mimeograph machine and the gun. Through their leaflets and proclamations ŻOB and the Coordinating Committee maintained contact with the ghetto populace, gave them news about German plans and intentions, outlined the direction of coming events, interpreted their political meaning, and provided the cues for appropriate responses. By carrying out death sentences against Jewish informers and collaborators, ŻOB became the protector of the ghetto Jews, assuming the leadership vacated by the impotent Judenrat. Three ŻOB leaflets—October 30, 1942; December 4, 1942; March 3, 1943—depict the accelerating struggle which the resistance movement conducted against the ghetto's internal enemies and against the lying propaganda of the Germans.

After an abortive military action in January 1943 against a German attempt to "resettle" the remaining Warsaw Jews, ŻOB began to prepare in earnest for the ultimate ordeal of final liquidation. That day came on April 19, 1943, when the battle of the Warsaw ghetto began. A few hundred young Jews with a pitifully small arsenal of weapons stood up against the military might of the SS, the Waffen-SS, and their helpers. On April 23, 1943, on the fifth day of battle, ŻOB issued a proclamation to the Polish population on the other side of the ghetto walls: "Let it be known that every threshold in the ghetto has been and will continue to be a fortress, that we may all perish in this struggle, but we will not surrender."

After the Germans destroyed the Warsaw ghetto, a few survivors of ŻOB and of the Coordinating Committee and its constituent bodies continued their clandestine activities on the "Aryan" side of Warsaw. There, in March 1944, Yitzhak Zuckerman (b. 1915, now living in Israel), halutz activist and one of ŻOB's initiators, wrote an account of ŻOB's origins and development. That report, together with letters and other documents, was forwarded through underground channels to London. It was the death chant of Warsaw Jewry.

A SUMMONS TO RESISTANCE IN
THE VILNA GHETTO, JANUARY 1942

Let us not be led like sheep to the slaughter!
Jewish youth!
In a time of unparalleled national misfortune we appeal to you!
We do not yet have the words to express the whole tragic struggle which transpires before our eyes. Our language has no words to
probe the depths to which our life has fallen nor to vociferate the
anguish which strangles us.

It is still too hard to find the proper definition for the state in
which we find ourselves, for the extraordinary cruelty with which
the annihilation of the local Jewish population has been carried out.

The community of Jerusalem of Lithuania [1] numbered 75,000.
On entering the ghetto, 25,000 were already missing, and today only
12,000 remain. All the others have been killed! Death strolls in our
streets; in our tents—powerlessness. But the anguish at this huge misfortune is much greater in the light of the ignoble conduct of the
Jews at the present time. Never in its long history of martyrdom has
the Jewish people shown such abjectness, such a lack of human
dignity, national pride, and unity, such communal inertia and
submissiveness to the murderers.

The heart aches even more at the conduct of Jewish youth,
reared for twenty years in the ideals of upbuilding and halutz
defense, which now is apathetic, lost, and does not respond to the
tragic struggle.

There are, however, occasions in the life of a people, of a
collective, as in the life of an individual, which seize you by the hair
of your head, shake you up, and force you to gird up all your
strength to keep alive. We are now experiencing such an occasion.

With what can we defend ourselves? We are helpless, we have
no possibilities of organizing any defense of our existence. Even if
we are deprived of the possibility of an armed defense in this un-

---

1. Vilna was called "the Jerusalem of Lithuania," an epithet attributed to
Napoleon, when he passed there in 1815 in the retreat from Moscow.

equal contest of strength, we nevertheless can still defend ourselves. Defend ourselves with all means—and moral defense above all— is the command of the hour.

Jewish youth!

On none but you rests the national duty to be the pillar of the communal defense of the Jewish collective which stands on the brink of annihilation!

I   *Let us defend ourselves during a deportation!*

For several months now, day and night, thousands and tens of thousands have been torn away from our midst, men, the aged, women, and children, led away like cattle—and we, the remainder, are numbed. The illusion still lives within us that they are still alive somewhere, in an undisclosed concentration camp, in a ghetto.

You believe and hope to see your mother, your father, your brother who was seized and has disappeared.

In the face of the next day which arrives with the horror of deportation and murder, the hour has struck to dispel the illusion: There is no way out of the ghetto, except the way to death!

No illusion greater than that our dear ones are alive.

No illusion more harmful than that. It deadens our feelings, shatters our national unity in the moments before death.

Before our eyes they led away our mother, our father, our sisters— enough!

We will not go!

Comrades! Uphold this awareness and impart to your families, to the remnants of the Jerusalem of Lithuania.

—Do not surrender into the hands of the kidnappers!

—Do not hand over any other Jews!

—If you are caught, you have nothing to lose!

—Let us defend ourselves, and not go!

Better to fall with honor in the ghetto than to be led like sheep to Ponary!

II   *On guard over national honor and dignity*

We work for Germans and Lithuanians. Everyday we come face to face with our employers, the murderers of our brothers. Great the shame and pain, observing the conduct of Jews, stripped of the awareness of human dignity.

Comrades!

—Don't give the foe the chance to ridicule you!

—When a German ridicules a Jew—don't help him laugh!

—Don't play up to your murderers!

—Denounce the bootlickers at work!

—Denounce the girls who flirt with Gestapo men!

—Work slowly, don't speed!

—Show solidarity! If misfortune befalls one of you—don't be vile egotists—all of you help him. Be united in work and misfortunes!

—Jewish agents of the Gestapo and informers of all sorts walk the streets. If you get hold of one such, sentence him—to be beaten until death!

III   *In the presence of the German soldier*

Instead of submissiveness and repulsive bootlicking, you are given the possibility in daily encounters with German soldiers to perform an important national deed. Not every German soldier is a sworn enemy of the Jews, not every German soldier is a sworn Hitlerite. But many have false ideas about Jews. We, the youth, by our conduct, in word and deed, can create in the mind of the German soldier another image of a Jew, a productive one, a Jew who has national and human dignity.

Comrades, show the Jews with whom you work and live togther that this is the approach to the German soldier.

IV   *To the Jewish police*

Most tragic is the role of the Jewish police—to be a blind tool in the hands of our murderers. But you, Jewish policemen, have at least a chance to demonstrate your personal integrity and national responsibility!

—Any act which threatens Jewish life should not be performed!

—No actions of mass deportation should be carried out!

—Refuse to carry out the orders which bring death to Jews and their families! . . .

—Do not let service in the police be turned into national disgrace for you!

—Jewish policeman, sooner risk your own life than dozens of Jewish lives!

Comrades!

Convey your hatred of the foe in every place and at every moment!

Never lose the awareness that you are working for your murderers!

Better to fall in the fight for human dignity than to live at the mercy of the murderer!

Let us defend ourselves! Defend ourselves until the last minute!

THE STRUCTURE OF
JEWISH RESISTANCE IN POLAND, 1942

*Bylaws of the Coordinating Commission
and the Jewish Combat Organization*

In order to organize the Jewish population of Warsaw against the annihilation drive by the occupant and in order to protect the Jewish population of Warsaw against traitors and police agents who collaborate with the occupant, a Coordinating Commission [2] is created which includes the Bund and the Jewish National Committee whose composition is made up of the following parties: the Zionist Organization, Right Labor Zionists, Left Labor Zionists, the Revisionist Party, Hehalutz, Hashomer Hatzair, Dror.[3]

The activities of the Coordinating Commission are based on the following bylaws:

COORDINATING COMMISSION

(1)   On the basis of the agreement concluded between the Jewish National Committee and the Bund, a Coordinating Commission has been established in Warsaw.

(2)   The purpose of the Coordinating Commission is:

a. To organize the defense of the ghetto in case of a further deportation action.

b. To protect the Jewish masses of the ghetto against the hirelings and flunkies of the occupant.

(3)   The Coordinating Commission summons into being a combat organization, sets the guidelines for its activities, and supervises it.

(4)   The Coordinating Commission is composed of one delegate of each political party.

2. In later documents this body is designated as the Coordinating Committee, not Commission.

3. At the time these bylaws were prepared, the Revisionists had agreed to join both the Combat Organization and the Jewish National Committee. Subsequently, breaches of security by the Revisionists and differences between them and the other parties about arms supplies created tension and open conflict. After a short while, relations were severed and the Revisionists later formed their own combat organization. As for the Communists (PPR), informal coordination between their fighting units and the Jewish Combat Organization was regularly maintained.

COMBAT ORGANIZATION

I   *Structure*

(1)   The basic unit is a combat "sixth," with a commander of the "sixth" at its head.

(2)   The "sixths" are organized according to workshops. At the head of each workshop is a command post consisting of a commander and two deputies.

(3)   At the head of the Combat Organization is the Chief Commandant and a five-man high command.

(4)   The "sixths" are to be set up along organizational lines, that is, according to membership in the organization. Wherever that is impossible, mixed "sixths" are to be set up and in accordance with the development of the action, the unorganized are to be drawn in as well.

(5)   In deciding on the leadership, the qualifications of the candidates should be the exclusive consideration.

II   *Arms supply*

(1)   Counted as arms are: firearms, axes, knives, brass knuckles, caustic substances, incendiary materials, and others.

(2)   Every member of a "sixth" is to be armed.

(3)   Every area is to be provided with arms and the necessary means for a general action.

III   *General guidelines for combat action*

(1)   In case of a further deportation action the resistance will be conducted under the watchword: "We will not yield a single Jew."

(2)   A terrorist campaign with regard to the Jewish police, the Jewish Community Council, and the *Werkschutz*.[4]

(3)   Active fight against the workshop directors, gangsters, open and secret Gestapo agents, in the name of protecting the Jewish masses.

IV   *Next undertakings*

(1)   Setting up the "sixths" and the leadership.

(2)   Arming the "sixths" and the workshops.

(3)   Securing financial means.

(4)   The workshop commands will prepare:

a. a precise map of the area (supplies, treasury, Werkschutz, management),

b. a list of the harmful elements,

c. precise plan of action in the area of respective workshops.

---

4. Special detachments of police, sometimes Jewish, but also Polish or Ukrainian, who were assigned to guard the property of the workshops and to supervise movement in and out of the workshops.

(5)   The High Command will prepare an overall plan of action: sabotage and terrorist acts.

(6)   Propaganda for resistance and struggle in the community.

NAMES

(1)   The combat organization takes the name Żydowska Organizacja Bojowa [Jewish Combat Organization].

(2)   In order to maintain close contact between both bodies, i.e., between the Combat Organization and the Coordinating Commission, the Commandant of the Combat Organization will participate in the meetings of the Coordinating Commission.

In relation to the military authorities, the Coordinating Commission is to be represented by the delegate of the Jewish National Committee who is known under the pseudonym Jurek and by the delegate of the Bund who is known under the pseudonym Mikolaj.[5]

Warsaw: XII/2/42

Memorandum to the Polish Government-in-Exile regarding the Jewish Combat Organization

On December 2, 1942, I contacted the delegate of the Bund, Mikolaj, with the delegate of the J.N.C., Jurek. At the meeting Jurek presented me with the enclosed bylaws of the Coordinating Commission and of the Combat Org., which is the representative of the Jewish public in Warsaw.[6] These bylaws were adopted by the C.C. in the ghetto during the night of December 1–2, 1942.

All doubts which Mikolaj had hitherto raised about the right of the J.N.C. to represent the Jews vis-à-vis the Polish authorities were clarified, and from now on both delegates—Mikolaj and Jurek—will in concert represent the C.C., in accordance with the authorization contained in the bylaws.

As for the organizational activity of the Jews in the areas outside Warsaw, that will continue to be conducted on the initiative of the J.N.C.

---

5. Mikolaj was the party name of Leon Feiner (1886–1945), also known as Berezowski, chairman of the wartime underground Central Committee of the Bund in Poland. Jurek was the party name of Israel Chaim Wilner (1917–1943), also known as Aryeh, a leading member of Hashomer Hatzair.

6. Negotiations between the Jewish National Committee and the Bund, especially with regard to autonomy in political matters, began October 1942 and continued until early December. At this time, the Bund agreed to coordinated activity only in Warsaw; by April 1943, the Bund extended the terms of the agreement to include operations in all of Poland.

Both delegates of the C.C. (Jurek and Mikolaj) stressed the immediate necessity of providing the J. Comb. Org. with arms, for they have no doubt that the liquidation action in Warsaw is by no means completed and it can begin at any moment (lately shooting on a large scale was again carried out in the streets and workshops). The liquidation of various workshops and the recent complete cutting off of Többens' shop [7] from the rest of the ghetto indicate that as a matter of fact the annihilation action continues without pause. An intensification of the action is anticipated in connection with the fact that a large number of beggars have appeared (the work in the shops is unpaid, just for sustenence: 10–20 decagrams of bread and soup; those who have nothing left to sell "wriggle" out of the shops to beg for a few hours).

In these conditions Mikolaj and Jurek request:

(1)   a larger supply of arms, for the 10 pieces received do not suffice to organize an armed resistance or any other action of a collective and non-individual character.

(2)   enabling and organizing the purchase of arms; they, for their part, will investigate the ways of mobilizing funds for this purpose (my opinion: the purchase ought to go through us with regard to control).

(3)   instruction and instructors. The combat element has been partly trained within the framework of the Polish military training. There is a shortage of instructors here, because the people who have the necessary qualifications fulfill various functions in the police and do not possess the indispensable trust of the C.O.

With regard to point 1, I would like the supply of arms at the least to meet the "dozen or so" pieces repeatedly referred to.

I request a prompt decision.

3.XII.42   Wacław

FROM JUSTINA'S DIARY:
RESISTANCE IN CRACOW

They were free. Their last links with everyday life were broken. Thus, after this "action," those who had still hesitated to leave be-

---

7. Walter C. Többens, a German, had become the owner of the largest factory in the Warsaw ghetto, employing about 8,000 Jews.

hind a younger brother, an only sister, aging parents, suddenly felt free to plunge into the maelstrom of [underground] work; it was a feeling of freedom which sprouted out of the rubble of shattered family life. That itself proved difficult for those who embraced the cause only after all feeling was gone. For questions arose, questions that pierced like pangs of conscience: Why was I not willing to commit myself sooner? Why was death necessary before I could feel free to act? These questions penetrated deeper and deeper into the hearts of many and whenever one or another found himself behind prison walls, he spent long hours searching for the answers.

Now, however, thrown into the whirlpool of work, they could not worry about it for long: there was no time for contemplation. But pain gnawed at the hearts with such intensity that people demanded work as a last resort. One after another, they volunteered, and there were assignments for all, without delay.

It was the end of October. The fall season was exceptionally beautiful. The leaves retained their fresh greenness for a long time. The sun gilded the earth, its rays warmed the air. But these were only days of grace. At any moment the sky could turn gray and heavy rain start pounding the ground. Rainy, muddy autumn loomed just ahead. One had to expect a change in weather at any moment. After two difficult experiences in the woods, they knew that this was not the time to seek a new field of operations: it was too late in the year. Spring was the time for a new start. Now it was autumn, with winter to follow, which would undoubtedly thwart their newly-started efforts.

A new concept was born. Here they were stuck in the capital. Surely targets for their activity could be found nearby. Without building a large secret organization in the forests, they could operate right where they were. Even their smallest act would reach the nerve center of the authorities. To damage the essential cogs of the machine—this was to become their goal. There, in the woods, partisan actions could only be carried out with larger detachments; a mere handful would hardly be effective. Here, however, every act carried out singly or in pairs would cause the authorities to feel uneasy, more than uneasy. It was important to shake them up by daring self-assurance; to make them realize that they did not exercise their bestial rule over a soulless mass, that the downtrodden people had awakened, had suffered enough, and that the long awaited springtime of nations was coming.

Here and there voices of reason argued that the vigilance of the rulers must not be aroused, that it was more important to muster one's strength and create the impression that nothing was happening, that every suspicious sign must be suppressed at the roots. Yet such behavior was not for them. How could they be certain that they would live to see the spring? They brushed against death every day. They could never know whether they might escape its reach. Thus they were forced to act, so as to make the enemy feel their rebellion. They decided to transfer their activities to Cracow and later to the other larger cities.

Even within the district so much needed to be done! Within the ghetto the traitors had to be dealt with—those who for a few pieces of silver or for a self-serving promise of survival would sell their own brothers. Among them were those who had the murder of hundreds of Jews on their conscience. For an entire year the populace had dreaded the mass arrests conducted at night, when the police went from house to house and collected innocent people, according to perfidiously drawn lists, people who were killed off within a few days. They promised themselves to get first the head, and then his helpers.

They decided to leave one base of operations within the ghetto, another on the outside. Contact points were established in all larger cities along the Cracow-Lemberg lines. Cracow itself was surrounded with a network of suburban apartments. The leadership was slowly moving out of Cracow. It was high time: their names were abroad in the entire district. The news that it was they who dispatched people to the forests was being spread from person to person. Their names were almost invariably spoken with reverence, with charged emotion, because their names became the expression of a new idea of freedom to which people clung with all their hearts. But at the same time their names had reached the ears of the wrong people as well. They became quite well known to the Jewish police which really served the authorities better than it did its own people. . . .

The leadership was again complete. The operations continued at full speed. People had strictly defined tasks which they pursued from morning till night—intelligence gathering, liaison work, technical matters, or specific assignments. Everyone was always totally absorbed by this effort. And so, exhausted, pursued, they rushed home late in the evening, crossing the threshold with joy in their hearts. It was the last home of their lives, the last place in which all human sentiments rose once again like a tall bright flame. Such was their need for mutual love, such was the constant longing for the warmth of life together that whenever one hearth was extinguished, they immediately kindled another, even more potent than the one they had lost. The storms of war kept blowing out their fires, but time and again their old desire to stay together would be awakened. . . .

The leadership suddenly became swamped with work which pinned them in place. They worked without stopping; one assignment followed another. Even though all stood ready to work, they were still shorthanded. They operated simultaneously in different places. They believed that the tactic of parallel concurrent strikes in different sections had a shattering effect on the authorities. The greater the shock, the greater their zeal to continue. These were truly unusual times for them.

But the shreds of personal feelings were never fully extinguished. There was always an ember left in one's heart, a small flame of feeling remained in the depths of one's soul. When they reassembled after a difficult assignment, this small flame burned stronger and higher; a new fire of brotherly togetherness was lit. Young people remained alone, without parents or family, with few belongings, usually in a sparsely furnished one-room apartment. The remaining belongings of the deported parents had to be sold or otherwise disposed of when one got ready to leave.

Someone had an idea: to establish a "liquidation place"—that was what it was called. It was organized in the apartment of Szymek, whose parents had been deported.[8] Here the young people brought everything they possessed: linens, clothing, shoes, valuables —all that could be useful to others or that could be sold for the common good. After all items were assembled and sorted, the "liquidation" process began. Every one registered his needs and received the items he required. Thus people's personal belongings became communal property. . . . A joint treasury was established, and a communal kitchen soon followed. Slowly the feeling of homelessness began to disappear. The missing warmth of the parental home was

---

8. Szymon Draenger (d. 1943), Justina's husband. This apartment was located at 13 Józefińska Street and was dubbed No. 13. For security reasons, Justina was then living in the suburbs.

replaced by a new warmth, one based, not on bonds of blood, but on bonds of the spirit.

They gathered at mealtimes, and those were the most joyful times of the day. The next step came when they all moved in together into a small two-room apartment, and this became their home. It was on the ground floor, entered by way of a large, long anteroom. Even before one reached the door, the cheerful sound of youthful voices within could be heard. One opened the door and was immediately in the warm circle of happy laughter and animated talk. Elsa invariably stood busy at the kitchen stove. She was forever cooking, washing, ordering people about, complaining. She was like a worried mother whose chores were never finished—coal bricks to be cut, water to be fetched, the fire refused to burn—and the children, always giving trouble. And all the while the children circled the stove in a tight group, hands on their hips, and scoffed at their angry mother. . . . She devoted her entire being to that kitchen. . . . She liked neatness above all. She swept, scrubbed the floor, cleaned incessantly. People always upset her work, but she was never angry. She did not know how to be angry. Abashed, she only smiled and rather than scold, she shyly asked, "Clean your shoes before you enter the room. Please understand." Then she grabbed the broom and swept the floor again. She kept busy at it all day long.

Szymek played an important part here. First of all, he was the official tenant of the place. He rather liked this role; he looked into every corner observing everybody at work, hands in his pockets. Having surveyed all the activities, he would move away dissatisfied, saying "What a mess it is here! What a horrible mess!" Szymek and Noli were in charge of the supplies. They reigned over the wardrobes and fitted out the people with whatever was needed. They had a lot of fun with it. Various old-fashioned pieces of apparel, relics of an older age, which found their way to the "liquidation place," caused much merriment and laughter.

The life of the entire movement was concentrated here. Whoever came to Cracow made certain to visit the district so as to come to No. 13 and meet people, no matter what the difficulties. . . . The residents and the visitors, those who had been together for years and those who for years had longed for one another, met here. How did these oppressed people generate so much joy? Perhaps it was that they felt that once they left this place at No. 13, their last family nest would be gone. Or they may have felt that this environment was not only their last home, but also the last focal point of national life, the last assemblage of their own people, among whom they could be themselves.

So they tried to absorb all national values, revive old traditions; they tried to live in the specific atmosphere of traditional Jewish life. Dolek [9] visited frequently. The whole crowd would gather around him, and that evening a more solemn, more profound mood would prevail. There was an unexplained beauty in the room. These unusual evenings, festive and charged with emotion, were indelibly impressed on the memories of all those who experienced them.

The apartment became more and more crowded. More people came, and though many left for new assignments, still more arrived to take their place. During the day the door was in constant motion. At night it was difficult to find space for all. Two beds would be placed side by side, and people slept crosswise, six or seven together. Sleeping places were improvised on the floor, on chairs; every nook and cranny would be used for sleeping. Living conditions were poor, the most primitive comforts were lacking, but no one would willingly part with these hardships, which were dearer to them than the greatest luxuries, the most affluent life.

At that time the apartment at No. 13 was the base for all underground activities. Toward evening, groups of two or three left stealthily, some to take action against traitors and informers within the ghetto, others to seek arms on the outside. A minute before the curfew they returned, out of breath, at times triumphant, at times mortified at having failed, though they had so nearly succeeded. Frequently they miraculously eluded the police. At times it seemed the bullets passed right over their heads, that only a timely turn of the head had saved them.

One of the most beautiful evenings was arranged in Anka's honor. It was the ushering in of the Sabbath. The preparations for the celebration lasted fully two days. All were waiting for it impatiently: it was to start at dusk on Friday and last until daybreak the following morning. This tradition has been maintained in the movement for many years. From the grayness of a weekday one is suddenly plunged into a festive mood. In religious concentration

9. Party name of Aaron Liebeskind (1912–1942), top leader of Akiva halutz movement.

one anticipates the moment when the candles will flame into light in the festively decorated room. The girls in white blouses, the boys in white wide-collared shirts took their places around the table, covered with a white cloth. First a moment of silence, then a strong burst of song, greeting the Sabbath. Eyes gleamed in the candlelight. Strong emotions were reflected in those wide-open black pupils. Another spirit animated them, purer and better. This is the way it had always been, for years and years. In a quiet village, in the noisy city, high up in the mountains, among the factory smokestacks, they had come to greet the Sabbath with the same song, with the same emotions. And today it was the last time together. They had no presentiment of disaster. They were so happy! Song followed song, the ringing notes binding them more tightly and strongly together! In the midst of this happiness that filled them to overflowing, from out of somewhere came its epithet: it was *our* last supper. The name caught on, it was remembered. Thenceforth that evening was never referred to otherwise.

Dolek sat at the end of the table and around him were all the dear faces, radiant, friendly, brave, and so very, very close. They sat crowded together. The room had been filled long since, and new guests kept arriving. Room had to be made for all. In a corner, Martusia, wide-eyed, staring at Dolek, at the radiant faces, at the flaming candles. This was her first Sabbath away from home. She left Tomaszów a few days ago, when the "action" had already started, aware that she might never again see her parents. They were so young in spirit! Her father, saying good-bye to her, told her, "Too bad I am not a few years younger. I would certainly have gone with you!" Marta took those words along and kept them in her heart, her dearest memento of her father. Now she kept thinking of them all the time.

Her home was no more! There the "action" most likely caught her father, her mother, her younger sister. She is alone, all alone in the world. Only seventeen, her eyes wide, she scans the room. She does not feel pain, she does not long for her lost home, for her childhood, for that carefree girlhood which has gone forever. Here is her place, among this youthful company. She feels happy in the crowded room. It is so good to listen to Dolek's words. She has known him for a long time. She feels that today he speaks in quite a different way from the past. Power used to resonate in his words, creative force which summoned faith in life and love of it. Tonight his words forebode the inevitable end which they must confront with dignity.

It was as if he felt death approaching, because he spoke frequently about it. He did not believe that they could survive and he did not want others to believe it. He did not want to delude himself. He wanted all those who undertook the underground work to realize that the end was near. Even now he dropped his hard words into the festive mood:

"There is no return from our journey. We march along the road to death, remember that! Whoever desires to live, let him not seek life among us. We are at the end. But our end is not the dusk. Our end is death, which a strong man steps forward to confront. I feel that this is our last communal ushering in of the Sabbath. We will have to leave the ghetto. There is too much commotion around us. This week we will start dismantling our cozy center at No. 13. Another phase of our life will be over. But we must not regret anything. This is the way it must be."

The windows were gray with dawn, when this, our last supper came to an end.

FACING DEATH IN
THE BIALYSTOK GHETTO, FEBRUARY 1943

Mordecai: Good that at least the mood is good. Unfortunately, the meeting won't be very cheerful; this meeting is historic or tragic, as you prefer, but definitely it is sad. The few people sitting here are the last halutzim in Poland. Around us the very dead. You know what has happened in Warsaw; no one is left. The same also in Będzin and Częstochowa, and probably everywhere else. We are the last. It's not a particularly pleasant feeling to be the last; it implies a special responsibility. We have to decide today what to do tomorrow. There is no point in sitting together in the cozy atmosphere of memories! Nor in awaiting death together, collectively. What do we do?

We can do two things: decide that with the first Jew to be deported now from Bialystok, we start our counteraction, that from tomorrow on nobody goes to the factories, that nobody is allowed to hide during the action.

Everybody will be mobilized. We can see to it that not one German leaves the ghetto, that not one factory will remain intact. It's not out of the question that after we have finished our task, some may perchance still be alive.

But combat to the finish, till we fall. We can go out into the woods. The possibilities should be considered realistically. Two members left today to make a place ready; in any event, after the meeting, military discipline will be instituted. We must decide now; our parents won't take care of us. This is an orphanage. One prerequisite: our approach must be ideological, our thinking—ideas of the movement. Whoever wishes, or imagines or thinks that he has a real chance, to stay alive, and wants to make use of it—fine, we'll help him in whatever way we can. Let each one decide himself about his own life or death. But together we have to find a collective answer to the common question. Not wishing to impose my opinion on anybody, I will refrain for the time being from expressing myself on the fundamental question.

Isaac: We're considering two different means of death. Attack means certain death. The other way—that is death two or three days later.

We ought to analyze both ways; perhaps something can be done. Because I'm unfamiliar with the exact details, I should like to hear more details from better informed comrades.

If comrades think that they could remain living, we ought to think about it.

Hershl: It's premature to strike a balance on everything we've lived through in the past year and a half. But in the light of the fateful decision confronting us, we must make a reckoning of what has been experienced. Hundreds of thousands of Jews were murdered in the last year; with great sophistication the enemy managed to deceive us and lead us like cattle to the slaughterhouses of Ponary, Chełmno, Bełżec, and Treblinka. The story of the annihilation of the Jewish communities of Poland will be not only the most tragic but also the ugliest chapter in Jewish history, a chapter of Jewish impotence and cowardice. Even our movement did not always stand on the desirable moral level. Instead of giving the signal for desperate resistance, we have everywhere temporized. Even in Warsaw the resistance would have looked different, if it had been started not at the end but at the beginning of the liquidation. Here in Bialystok we are destined to live through the last act of the bloody tragedy. What can and what should we do? The way I see it, this is the objective situation. The preponderant majority of the ghetto and also of our family are doomed to death. We are condemned. We have never looked to the forest as a place in which to hide; we have seen the forest as a base for combat and vengeance.

But the dozens of young people who are now going to the woods are not seeking a battlefield; most of them are living a beggar's life there and will probably find a beggar's death there.

In our present conditions our present fate is associated with the same beggar's and vagrant's fate.

Only one thing remains for us: to organize collective resistance in the ghetto, at any cost; to consider the ghetto our Musa Dagh, to write into history a proud chapter of Jewish Bialystok and of our movement.

I can imagine the natural reaction of all other peoples, if their families had been subjected to what ours have been. The commonest gentile would have spat on his own life and stuck a knife into the guilty one. The only emotion dominating him would have been the thirst for revenge.

Our way is clear: with the first Jew to be deported, we must begin our counteraction. If anyone succeeds in taking weapons from the murderer and going into the woods—fine. A young armed person can find his place in the woods. We still have time to prepare the woods as a place for combat and revenge.

I have lost everything, all those close to me; and still, subconsciously, one wants to live. But there is no choice. If I thought that not only individuals could save themselves, but fifty or sixty percent of the ghetto Jews, then I would say that our movement's approach should be to remain alive at any cost. But we are condemned to death.

Sarah: Comrades! If it is a question of honor, we have long since lost it. In most Jewish communities the actions were carried out smoothly, without counteraction. It is better to remain living than to kill five Germans. In a counteraction we will all die, without any doubt. On the other hand, in the woods forty or fifty percent of our members can be saved. That will be our honor and that will be our history. We are still needed; we shall yet be of use. Since in any event we no longer have honor, let our task be to remain alive.

Enoch: No illusions! We have nothing to expect but liquidation to the last Jew. We have before us two possibilities of death. The woods are no rescue and certainly not the operation in the ghetto. We are left only with the option to die—with honor. The prospects for our resistance are poor. I don't know whether we have adequate means for combat. It's the fault of all of us that our means are so small, but that's that—we'll have to make do with what we have. Bialystok will be liquidated completely, like all the other Jewish cities.

In the first action the factories were exempted,[10] but no one can believe that this time they will be spared. Obviously the woods offer greater opportunities for revenge, but we must not go there to live on the mercy of the peasant, to buy our food and lives for money. Going to the woods means joining the active partisan movement. That requires the appropriate weapons.

The weapons we have aren't suited to the woods. If we have time left, we should acquire arms and go to the woods.

But if the action happens before, we must respond with the first Jew taken.

Chaim: Already now, there are no Jews left, only remnants. There is no more movement, only remnants. There is no point in talking about honor; if we can, we must save ourselves. It's not important how we'll be judged. We must hide in the woods. [Constant interjections of the part of commrades.]

Mordecai: If we wish hard enough and see it as our task, then we can protect our members to the end, as long as any Jews remain in Bialystok. I put an extreme question: do the comrades who are for the woods propose that we should hide and not react at the next action, so that we can escape into the woods later?

[Voices from all sides: No, No!]

There are two opinions, one represented by Sarah and Chaim, and the other by Hershl and Enoch. Make your choice. One thing is sure—we won't go to the factories and pray to God that the people

10. Between February 5 and 12, 1943, the Germans deported about 10,000 Jews from the Bialystok ghetto. The SS had promised Barash, head of the Judenrat, that only nonworking Jews would be taken, that the action would be limited. The underground—informed by Barash—consequently decided not to jeopardize the remaining Jews in the ghetto and to offer no resistance at that time.

who have hidden in the bunkers will be seized so that we can be saved. And we won't watch passively from our factory windows when comrades from another factory are taken away.

We can have a vote: Hershl or Chaim.

Fanya (Branch): I agree with Enoch. We have to choose between one big action here or a series of much smaller acts, which in sum will mean much more—that is the route to the woods. Because we don't have the opportunity to go straight to the woods, and because the situation is very tense, we must emphasize counteraction here on the spot and with the first Jew seized, we must attack with all our determination.

But if the quiet spell lasts a few weeks, we must make every effort to leave.

Eliezer Suchanitzky (Branch): Comrades! I think we should not go in two directions at the same time. Taking to the woods is an attractive idea; it gives us some chance to remain alive. But at the present moment, when the action is so imminent, it is an illusion. Even if we have another three or four weeks, we won't manage to assemble all the necessary materials and take it with us into the woods. I think there is only one option left to us: to answer an action with our counteraction. I think we should work only along this line, so that with the feeble means at our disposal we can give an appropriate response.

Jochebed: Why is there all this talk about death? It's unnatural. A soldier at the front or a partisan in the woods thinks, in the greatest danger, only about life.

We know what the situation looks like, but why frighten everybody with death? Let's go into the woods if we should, or start the counteraction here. That doesn't mean that we must be killed. Everything we've been saying here is contrary to the most elemental life instinct within us.

Ch.: [disagrees with Jochebed.] We must be consistent, we should not give anyone the moral dispensation to flee. This is not piece work. When we fight, it will have to be to the last. To fight means to be killed. I think we would be accomplishing more if we remained alive, by going into the woods.

[Proposes setting up a hideout outside the ghetto, from which to continue acts of sabotage even after the action.]

Moshe: Let's start with the main thing, the counteraction. If possible, preparing for the woods. Absolutely everyone here should speak his mind, because the lives of all the comrades depend on this meeting. Even if the meeting should last until morning.

Chaim: You are forcing everybody to speak so the meeting should decide against. [Protests.]

Dorke: (Branch): I think our stand must be the stand of party people, of people with full consciousness of what they're doing, who know what has happened to our closest ones.

We will die an honorable death. The chances for vengeance are greater in the woods, but we cannot go there as vagrants, only as active partisans. Making the necessary preparations for the woods is impossible now. Therefore we must devote all our energy to the counteraction.

Zipporah: It's hard to say anything, it's hard to choose a death for yourself. I feel a conflict within me, a conflict between life and death. It's not important for me whether I or somebody else will remain alive. After what we have lived through and witnessed with our own eyes, we can treat life recklessly. But I am pondering more deeply the question of our movement.

We're proud of the fact that our movement lived through the most difficult period in the history of the Jewish settlement in Poland. I and many others were brought here from Vilna. There were certainly more important people to save. Neither you nor I were brought here, but the movement was. Now the question is: will the movement altogether perish? Does it have the right to? We are a movement of the Jewish people; we must, and we do in fact, share all the sorrows and afflictions of our people.

As for the right to stay alive, I say yes, we have every right. Perhaps our movement may have to be the only one to speak up, when needed. Take the example of Warsaw. An honorable, humanly beautiful death, but not the deed of a movement. The deed of a movement will command: Survive!

Survival not for its own sake, but survival for further work, for continuing the chain that was not even for one second broken off even in the darkest days.

Options are few, minimal, but if we devote all our strength to the effort, we can succeed.

Shmulik: The first time in my life—a meeting about death. We are undertaking our counteraction not to write history, but to die an honorable death, as young Jews in our times should. And if someone will write our history, it will be different from the history of the Spanish Jews, who leaped into the flames with "Hear, O Israel!" on their lips.

Now as to the action. All our experience teaches us that we can't trust the Germans, despite all their assurances that the workshops will be protected, that only the unemployed will be sent away, and so on. Only by deception and dupe did they succeed in driving thousands of Jews to the slaughter. Still, despite everything, we have a chance to come out of the impending action safely. Everyone is counting on time, and so should we. In the short time that remains, we can work and increase our weapons, which are poor and few in number.

We should also do what we can about the woods, where we can fulfill a dual task.

I don't want to be misunderstood and to have the proposal of hiding during the action interpreted as cowardice. No, no, no!

Man's instinct for life is so great, and here we must be selfish. I don't care if others will go in our stead. We have a greater claim on life than others—and rightly.

We have set ourselves to an aim in life—to survive at any cost! We were brought here from Vilna because there liquidation was in the air, and living witnesses had to remain. We must therefore exert every effort, if there will be no liquidation now, to wait and gain time.

But if the liquidation is now imminent, then let it be all of us together in the counteraction, and "let me die with the Philistines."

Sarah: I want the comrades to know that I will do whatever is decided. But I'm amazed by the calmness with which we talk about this.

Whenever I see a German, everything in me trembles. I don't know whether the comrades, and especially the girls, have enough strength for this. I said what I said before because I don't have any faith in my own strength.

Ezekiel: [Disagrees with Sarah.] In the face of death you can become weak and impotent. Or you can become very strong, when there's nothing to lose. I agree with Shmulik that we should begin our counteraction only in the event of a final liquidation.

Ethel: Specifically to this matter: if an action occurs in the next few days then the only option left to us is to begin a counteraction; but if we will have more time at our disposition, we should work along the lines of going into the woods.

I pray I can be equal to the duties that will be imposed on us.

Perhaps in the course of events I should be strengthened. In any case, I am resolved to do everything that needs to be done.

Hershl spoke rightly. We are going to perform a desperate act, whether or not we want to. Our fate is sealed. There remains for us only to choose between one kind of death and another. I am calm and cool.

Mordecai: The position of the comrades is clear. We will do everything to take out as many members as possible to join the partisan combat in the woods. Everyone of us who is in the ghetto during the action must respond with the first Jew seized. We are not the ones with whom to haggle about life; we must understand objective conditions.

The most important thing is to maintain until the very end the character and pride of the movement.

THREE COMMUNIQUÉS OF
THE JEWISH COMBAT ORGANIZATION

This is to inform the public that after the Jewish police in Warsaw, its officers and men, were found guilty, as reported in a communiqué on August 17, the sentence against Jacob Lejkin, assistant Jewish police chief, was carried out on October 29, at 6:10 p.m.

Further reprisals will be taken, with the full strictness of law.

Also, this is to inform the public that the following were found guilty:

(1)   The Judenrat in Warsaw and its leadership for cooperation with the occupier and for signing the deportation order.[11]

(2)   The managers of the factory shops and their officials who oppress and exploit the workers.

(3)   Squad leaders and officials of the Werkschutz for their cruel treatment of the workers and the Jewish population without appropriate work permits.

Reprisals will be taken, with the full strictness of law.

Warsaw: October 30, 1942

11. See Section 7, footnote 43.

Uncertainty about the next day poisons every moment of the bitter slave existence of the Jewish community in Warsaw. Every day brings various "sure" news, gossip, rumors, deadlines affecting the fate of the Warsaw ghetto. We are being "granted" two weeks, three weeks, three months, four months, to live. Our quivering nerves tremble; our spent spirits see-saw between hope and resigned despair.

Have we still learned nothing from our dreadful experience? Will we still allow ourselves to be lulled by good words from one or another German murderer, by one or another lie spread by Jewish Gestapo agents, venal traitors or trusting souls?

Without doubt Hitlerism aims to destroy all Jews. But it is done gradually, in stages. The chief aim of its tactics is to fool and trap the Jewish populace. Hitlerism plunges the knife deep into its victim's throat and meanwhile throws a bone to the next victim before slaughtering him.

Let us therefore bravely look the truth straight in the face.

We do not believe in any "stabilization action." [12]

We remember all the lies, starting with "resettlement to the East," and ending with the numbers, mass permits, selections, and registrations.

We all know the truth about the gigantic slaughterhouse in Treblinka, where hundreds of thousands of our fathers and mothers, brothers and sisters, sons and daughters were so inhumanly murdered with bestial sophistication.

Therefore we don't believe at all in the "new" decree about creating [new] Jewish ghettos. This is a trap in which at any moment the door between life and death can be slammed shut.

The *Umschlag* [13] has been liquidated, the "illegal Jews" [14] have been given amnesty, all Jews will be "employed" and "provisioned"—what cynical mockery! The murderer plays a while with

12. Van Sammern-Frankenegg and Auerswald had "guaranteed" a delegation of the Judenrat that the situation in the ghetto was stabilized, that no harm would came to the Jews if they continued to work industriously.
13. Called the *Umschlagplatz*, a square near a railroad siding at the outskirts of the ghetto, where the Jews were assembled and loaded on freight trains going to Treblinka.
14. Those who did not have permits identifying them as workers in one of the German enterprises. To avoid "resettlement," they hid in bunkers during the roundups.

the defenseless victim before bringing down the bloodied axe on his head.

Jews, citizens of the Warsaw ghetto, be alert, do not believe a single word or act of the SS bandits. Deathly danger threatens. Remember the last "action"—seizing Jews to send them "for work" to Lublin. They needed "tailors," but seized old people, children. People were seized for "work," and taken away just as they were, in their bare rags. The old story repeats itself once again: messages arrive and letters saying that they were indeed sent to Lublin. We remind you of the "letters," the "reliable" messages from Brest-Litovsk, Minsk, Bialystok, which the Germans fabricated. We remind you that Bełżec is located in the Lublin district, where tens of thousands of Jews have been murdered according to the Treblinka method.

Let's not fool ourselves.

The Lublin "action" of November 10 and 11 teaches us also something else.

Once more the Germans have found helpers and agents among the Jews themselves. Once again they have found scoundrels who have, with their own hands, delivered their brothers to the slaughter, the price for saving their own vile, despicable lives. The gangrene which the Jewish police and Judenrat members has let loose in Warsaw has infected the circles of the workshop managements, often run by the meanest scoundrels, ready for any infamy.

Do not believe the Jewish "big wheels," the directors of the workshops, the foremen—they are your enemies. Do not let yourselves be fooled by them.

Do not delude yourselves, and do not let yourselves be deluded, that the better craftsmen, the senior workers who have numbered tickets, are safe, and so let the weaker ones, the unprotected be delivered [to the Germans].

All are endangered.

Let nobody dare lend a hand, nor help—actively or passively—to deliver into the hands of the executioner his brother, his comrade, his neighbor, or his coworker.

Let us not act like scum, like vermin, in the face of destruction. Help one another.

The vile traitors who help the enemy must be spewed out of our camp.

Do not let yourselves be destroyed like sheep.

Prepare yourselves to defend your lives.

Remember that also you—the civilian Jewish population—are at the front in the fight for freedom and humanity.

The enemy has already been severely hurt. Let us bravely and nobly defend our honor.

Long live freedom!

December 4, 1942

WARNING

The passive and active resistance of the Jewish masses during the memorable days of January 18–22, 1943, took the Hitler bandits by surprise and convinced them that the Jews will no longer go like sheep to the slaughter. The deportation action was marked by an interruption which was forced upon the German thugs. The bloody occupant has convinced himself that he will not wipe out the remnants of Warsaw Jewry with the means hitherto used.

But, unfortunately, the meanest scoundrels of society have come to his aid.

With their aid the occupant wishes to uncover and destroy the centers of armed resistance; they provide information about hiding places; their degenerate minds offer up to the beasts the plan of liquidating the Warsaw Jews with the method of Poniatowa or Lublin.[15]

After the shooting of the Gestapo agent Arek Weintraub on February 21, a document was found confirming that he and his "colleagues" had suggested to the Germans the plan of a "voluntary" and "peaceful" resettlement of the Jews to Poniatowa.

Shot February 22, the Gestapo agent Nossig,[16] who provided

15. The SS had established a labor camp at Poniatowa, a village near Lublin. "Resettlement" for work at Poniatowa was often given as the pretext for deportation to Treblinka. A similar argument was given in Lublin when the Jews there were sent to Majdanek.

16. Alfred Nossig (1864–1943), had played a leading role in the intellectual and political life of his native Lemberg (Lwów) before the First World War and also in Berlin and Vienna. When the Second World War broke out, he turned up in Warsaw as a refugee. He held various posts in the Warsaw Judenrat, but was regarded with suspicion by most of his colleagues, largely for his independent contacts with the Gestapo. Bernard Goldstein, Bundist leader, in his memoirs about the Warsaw ghetto, *The Stars Bear Witness* (New York, 1949), disclosed that the Jewish underground searched Nossig's apartment and found an identity card showing he had served the Gestapo since 1933.

the Germans with information about Jewish bunkers in attics and cellars.

Shot February 26, the chief loader at the Umschlagplatz, Brzeziński, who behaved provocatively toward the demands of the Combat Organization, and put secret agents on the trail of its representatives.

Shot February 28, the well-known Gestapo agent Bobi Nebel, who engaged in spying on the circles of Jewish political life.

Shot February 28, the editor of the traitorous Gestapo sheet *Żagiew*, Adash Schein, who engaged in informing on and in demoralizing Jewish political life.

The Combat Organization is in possession of a complete list of all those who, remaining in the service of the Germans, have forgotten that they are Jews and human beings.

THE COMBAT ORGANIZATION WARNS ALL THESE SCOUNDRELS THAT UNLESS THEY IMMEDIATELY CEASE THEIR CONTEMPTIBLE ACTIONS, THEY WILL ALL BE SHOT!

We warn all officers and functionaries of the Jewish police not to interfere with the activity of the units of the Combat Organization. Let them also remember that no protection against the bullet of the resisters can be found with the chief executioner Brandt,[17] in concealment or in flight to the so-called Aryan side.

We warn all directors of the workshops, inside and outside the ghetto, not to agitate for nor to urge upon the workers voluntary evacuation of Jews!

The German villains will not let you alone for long. Therefore, we summon you to gather around the banners of struggle and resistance. Hide your wives and children and enlist—with whatever you can—in the struggle against the Hitlerite bandits. The Jewish Combat Organization is counting on your complete moral and material support.

Warsaw Ghetto   *High Command of the*
March 3, 1943   *Combat Organization*

17. Karl Brandt, see Section 7, footnote 36.

FOR YOUR FREEDOM AND OURS

Warsaw Ghetto: April 23, 1943

Poles, citizens, freedom fighters!

From out of the roar of the cannon with which the German Army is battering our homes, the dwellings of our mothers, children, and wives;

From out of the reports of machine-guns which we have captured from the cowardly police and SS men;

From out of the smoke of fires and the blood of the murdered Warsaw ghetto, we—imprisoned in the ghetto—send you our heartful fraternal greetings. We know that you watch with pain and compassionate tears, with admiration and alarm, the outcome of this war which we have been waging for many days with the cruel occupant.

Let it be known that every threshold in the ghetto has been and will continue to be a fortress, that we may all perish in this struggle, but we will not surrender; that, like you, we breathe with desire for revenge for all the crimes of our common foe.

A battle is being waged for your freedom as well as ours.

For your and our human, civic, and national honor and dignity.

We shall avenge the crimes of Auschwitz, Treblinka, Bełżec, Majdanek!

Long live the brotherhood of arms and blood of fighting Poland!

Long live freedom!

Death to the hangmen and torturers!

Long live the struggle for life and death against the occupant.

Jewish Combat Organization

YITZHAK ZUCKERMAN:

THE CREATION AND DEVELOPMENT OF ŻOB

Assuming that you are generally familiar with the process of the liquidation of Polish Jewry and the defense of the ghettos, we wish to give you in this review details which, for the sake of truth, must not be lost without trace and which will help you understand the struggle of the Jews from the day the Germans began murdering them—to which we responded with defense action, creating a Jewish combat organization.

As the Germans crossed into the territories east of the Bug River, a new chapter in the history of the Jews under German occupation began—the total destruction of Jewish settlements. It started with Vilna and the Vilna area. Tens of thousands of Jews were shot in the woods of Ponary, while the survivors had not yet learned that Ponary meant death.

The Jews in the Generalgouvernement had by then been almost hermetically locked in ghettos for over a year. The only link between the ghettos were smugglers and the couriers of illegal Jewish underground groups. News was disseminated by the clandestine Jewish press. However, the events in the northern provinces were totally unknown. At the end of October 1941, a courier of the Hehalutz was sent to the areas of Bialystok, Vilna, and Lithuania to establish contact with the movement there. He returned in the middle of November with the incredible news that the Germans were murdering the Jews and that tens of thousands had already perished. The courier had been an eyewitness to the mass deportation of all the Jews from Troki [18] and its surrounding area to an island on Troki Lake, where they were killed by machine-gun fire and buried in a mass grave. Shortly thereafter a delegation of a Jewish group from Vilna reached Warsaw: Mordecai Tenenbaum (Tamaroff—later commandant of the heroic Jewish combat organization in Bialystok), Tema Schneiderman, Chayka, Edek, and Solomon [Entin].[19] They came to Warsaw to obtain weapons and funds. The delegation submitted a report during a large conference attended by prominent communal leaders: more than 50,000 unsuspecting Jews had been transported to Ponary. In Vilna, outside the ghetto walls, a larger group of Jews engaged in passive resistance,

18. A small town about twenty kms. from Vilna, with a prewar Jewish population of about 450.
19. Tamaroff was Tenenbaum's underground appellation. Tema Schneiderman (1917–1943), a leading member of Hehalutz, served as a courier. Chayke Grossman, now in Israel, and Edek Buraks (1918–1943) were members of Hashomer Hatzair. Solomon Entin (1916–1942) was a leader of Hanoar Hazioni, General Zionist youth organization.

refusing deportation and demanding to be shot on the spot. The Germans did not open fire. They were still concealing their destructive intent from public opinion. They brought the Jews back to the ghetto and there forced them into vans and shipped them to Ponary.

The Hehalutz representatives expressed their belief that the actions in Vilna were the beginning of the liquidation of Polish Jewry and that preparations for an active defense should be undertaken. A few conference participants felt that the extermination work of the Germans was an act of vengeance against Jews residing in territories previously occupied by the Soviets, that such events could not take place in the Generalgouvernement and especially not in Warsaw, situated in the heart of Europe. Hehalutz did not agree with this appraisal and began organizing combat units. Thus the first groups of Hehalutz, Dror, and Hashomer Hatzair came into being.

In January 1942 Frumka Plotnicka [20] succeeded in reaching the province of Wołyń; she found out that in all the towns and villages the Jews had been killed, and that only Kowel still remained the site of a larger Jewish settlement.

Also in January a few Jewish refugees from the Reich arrived in Warsaw; they said they had escaped from Chełmno and that there the Germans were transporting all Jews into nearby forests on special trucks. They were gassed in those trucks, and the bodies buried in the woods. Thousands of Jews had already perished, but even in the neighboring towns people refused to believe that Chełmno meant death.

The area all around the Generalgouvernement was in flames. In the Generalgouvernement itself calm still reigned. In the middle of March Hehalutz, after due preparation, convened a preliminary conference of political parties. Attending were: Leizer Lewin and Sholem Grajek (Right Labor Zionists), Melech Fainkind and Hersh Berlinski (Left Labor Zionists), Orzech and Abrasha Blum (Bund), Yitzhak Zuckerman representing Hehalutz. After submitting the latest reports on the events in the eastern and western areas and analyzing the situation as the first step toward the annihilation of Polish Jews, the Hehalutz representative made the following concrete proposals:

20. An intrepid courier, she was a leading member of the halutz movement in Poland. She was killed during the resistance in Będzin in August 1943.

(1)   To establish a general Jewish combat organization.

(2)   To create a joint body of all Jewish political parties and Jewish youth organizations to serve as a representative vis-à-vis the civil authorities of the Polish underground and a delegation of the combat organization similarly with regard to the Polish military underground.

(3)   To organize on the Aryan side an apparatus to procure arms and to establish shops in the ghetto to manufacture arms.

These proposals were supported by both Right and Left Labor Zionists. Orzech, representing the Bund, stated that it was premature to talk of a joint combat organization. Each organization or party should, instead, build its own combat units. A joint representation does not come into consideration. The Bund is committed to a Socialist policy, not to a pan-Jewish policy.

The meeting yielded no positive results.

At about this time, at the initiative of the Left Labor Zionists, an understanding was worked out among all the anti-fascist, labor, and youth organizations and factions except for the Bund.[21] This bloc set itself the following tasks:

(1)   To organize a joint political and propaganda force against fascism and the reactionary forces inside the ghetto.

(2)   To create anti-fascist combat units.

(3)   To organize help for the victims in the anti-fascist struggle.

Among the bloc's leaders were: Shachne Zagan, Joseph Lewartowski, Joseph Sack, Zivia Lubetkin and Mordecai Anielewicz.[22] The bloc began publishing a joint periodical called *Der Ruf*. Within a short

21. Known as the Anti-Fascist Bloc, this group was probably initiated by the Communists who operated in German-occupied Poland under the name *Polska Partja Robotnicza* (PPR). The Anti-Fascist Bloc collapsed early in June, after two PPR activists were caught by the Gestapo. In a letter of March 29, 1974, to the present author, Zuckerman confessed that for the sake of harmony he had acceded to Adolf Berman's insistence that prominence be given to the Anti-Fascist Bloc in this report. Berman was then—in 1944—a top officer of the Coordinating Committee and of the Jewish National Committee. Zuckerman himself did not then—and does not now—share Berman's evaluation of that group.

22. Zagan (189?–1942) was one of the leaders of the Left Labor Zionists in Poland. Joseph Lewartowski (1896–1942) was a member of the Central Committee of the Communist Party in prewar Poland and a PPR leader in the Warsaw ghetto. Joseph Sack (b. 1899) was a leader of the Right Labor Zionists. Zivia Lubetkin, now living in Israel, represented Hehalutz and Dror, the Right Labor Zionist halutz organization. Mordecai Anielewicz (1919–1943), active in Hashomer Hatzair, became commandant of the Jewish Combat Organization.

time, a broad network of combat "fives" sprang up. A few hundred young people and workers belonged to these units. Despite the lack of arms, the combat "fives" underwent military training. . . . The Anti-Fascist Bloc created the first large-scale fighting cadres, which— despite arrests of its leaders and the destruction of its apparatus— became the keystone of the Jewish Combat Organization, created later.

During Passover 1942 the liquidation of the Jews in the General-gouvernement got underway. The Jews in Lublin became the first victims, followed soon after by the Jews of the entire Lublin district. They were deported to Bełżec and there put to death in newly erected gas chambers. The Jewish underground press carried extensive reports about these mass murders. But Warsaw did not believe. Simple common-sense refused to accept the possibility of the mass destruction of tens and hundreds of thousands of Jews. It was argued that the Jews were being transported to the newly-occupied Russian territories for farm work! Views were voiced that the Germans had started to convert the Jewish lower class to higher productivity! The Jewish press was decried for panic-mongering, even though the descriptions of the deportation actions were strictly true. The news about the German crimes was received with incredulity and mistrust —not only abroad. Even here, in the immediate vicinity of Ponary and Chełmno, Bełżec and Treblinka, these reports found no credence. Unfounded optimism went hand in hand with ignorance; to those isolated from the outside world, the present situation proved their point: for two and a half years many deportations had been staged by the Germans—from Cracow, Lublin, the Warsaw region, from the Reich—and there was no lack in victims and blood. But total destruction?

There were those who did believe the truth about Ponary and Chełmno but they said, "This is only a whim of the local author-ities." For, after all, until death levelled all the Jews in the General-gouvernement, the German authorities had no uniform approach to the ghettos in the cities and towns. In many a place people responded to the news about German murders which we had disseminated by saying, "Nothing like that could happen here."

Of course this optimistic mood was fostered by the Germans. For two and a half years the total extinction of three and a half million Polish Jews was being prepared with German thoroughness.

By means of murder, oppression, hunger; by means of ghettos and deportations, the Jewish masses were being prepared for inaction. Years of continuous experimentation brought about refinement in the German methods of meting out death. In Vilna a few days were required to murder a thousand Jews, in Chełmno half an hour sufficed to kill one hundred. In Treblinka ten thousand people were put to death every day.

Hundreds of thousands of Jews went without resistance. (If one does not believe in death, why should one offer resistance?) Indeed, many volunteered for "resettlement." Where to? Letters arrived from Bessarabia, Smolensk, Minsk, with reports that the new settlers had arrived safely and were satisfied. This, of course, was a German hoax. And thus—with heavy hearts, to be sure—Jews said farewell to their old settlements and went to "foreign places—for farm work." They were forced by the hopelessness, by the lack of prospects, by hunger. In Warsaw alone, during 1941, 6,000 Jews died monthly of starvation and contagious diseases; during the period of the "resettlements," the price of bread in Warsaw jumped from 7 zlotys a kilo to 80.

The ghetto walls split an organism of three and a half million into thousands of cells, sunk into terrible destitution. The ghetto walls separated the Jews from the outside world and also from themselves. In the days of destruction, every community confronted its fate on its own.

In the cities where the Germans carried out their destructive efforts, they divided the Jewish population into "productive" and "nonproductive" groups—those subject to deportation and those who were to remain. Thus with devilish perfidy they succeeded in thwarting at the source any possibility of unified resistance: every Jew stood by himself, while the entire German machinery of destruction was against him.

The liquidation of the Warsaw ghetto was preceded by two acts of mass terror on the part of the Germans. They murdered 110 Jewish prisoners "for offering resistance to the German authorities" [23] and in the night of April 17, 1942, they dragged out from their homes 49 Jews, from all walks of life and political groupings (among them the economist Linder),[24] murdered them in the streets,

---

23. Cf. Section 7, footnote 37.
24. Menachem Linder (1911–1942) was an economist, active in the Yiddish Scientific Institute—YIVO, and a founder of *Yikor*, a Yiddishist culture organization in the Warsaw ghetto.

left their bodies wherever the murder took place. By applying the principle of "collective responsibility," they sought to destroy all opposition. If resistance was weak during this first liquidation action, it was not because of fear—the fighters had enough firm determination and faith, but their hands were empty.

On Wednesday, July 22, the liquidation of the Warsaw ghetto began. Immediately a communal council was convened to consider the situation and take appropriate measures. Participating in the deliberations were: L. Bloch, Samuel [Braslaw], Dr. A. Berman, Yitzhak Zuckerman, Zisha Friedman, Finkelstein-Lewartowski, D. Guzik, Isaac Giterman, Joseph Kaplan, Menachem Kirshenbaum, Alexander Landau, M. Orzech, Dr. Emanuel Ringelblum, Josef Sack, Shachne Zagan, and Dr. Ignacy Schipper.[25] Opinions were divided. The representatives of the leftist Zionist groups, of Hehalutz, as well as several other political leaders, demanded decisive action. The majority, however, was for waiting. How long? Until the situation became clarified. Reports were circulating that 50–70,000 Jews would be deported from Warsaw, and with that the action would be ended. All others would remain. Consequently, the more active elements, the leftist factions in the Anti-Fascist Bloc, jointly with the Bund, formed a united labor committee which was to assume responsibility for the fate and honor of the ghetto. By that time the action had been in full swing for five days, with unprecedented, indescribable horror. Every heedless step meant death. Crossing a street was like crossing the frontier of two belligerent states on the front-lines. In those circumstances, it is easy to understand the difficulties in maintaining contact and communication as well as coordinating action.

25. L. Bloch (1889–1944?), a General Zionist, was active in ŻTOS. Samuel Braslaw (1920–1942), a member of Hashomer Hatzair, worked in ŻTOS. Adolf Berman, now living in Israel, was a ranking leader of the Left Labor Zionists and engaged in child-care activities in the Warsaw ghetto. Rabbi Zisha Friedman (1889–1943) was a leader of the Aguda. David Guzik (1890–1946) was one of the directors of the JDC in Poland. Isaac Giterman (1889–1943) was the executive head of the JDC in Poland. Joseph Kaplan (1913–1942) represented Hashomer Hatzair. Menachem Kirshenbaum (1893–1943) was a member of the Central Committee of the General Zionist Organization of Poland and a ŻTOS leader. Alexander Landau (d. 1944?) was an engineer and owner of a furniture factory in Warsaw which the Germans took over and operated as *Ostdeutsche Bautischlerei Werkstatte*, where he worked in a managerial capacity. He was close to the Left Labor Zionists and Hashomer Hatzair. Ignacy Schipper (1884–1943) was a noted Jewish historian and lifelong Labor Zionist.

The members of the labor committee were: Braslaw, Zuckerman, Finkelstein-Lewartowski, Kaplan, Orzech, Sack, and Zagan. But even this group proved unequal to the task, for the reasons cited above. Moreover, only a few days after its emergence, its complement was diminished: Zagan was slain, Orzech left the ghetto.

On July 28, 1942, a conference was called of Hehalutz and the youth groups associated with it: Hashomer Hatzair, Dror, and Akiva. It was decided to create the Żydowska Organizacja Bojowa, Jewish Combat Organization, whose Polish-language appeals were signed with the initials ŻOB. The High Command comprised: Braslaw, Zuckerman, Zivia Lubetkin, and Mordecai Tenenbaum. A delegation . . . was sent to the Aryan side to establish contact with the Polish underground movement and obtain weapons.

A combat organization was created, but the total arsenal of the entire ghetto was one single pistol.

We were witness to a heroic stance of Jews who resisted the Germans on numerous occasions. They are the unknown who appear in the files as "5,394, shot," reported in the official German accounts of the "resettlement" action. Yet what could be accomplished by a combat organization operating with hundreds of young boys and girls prepared for every contingency, but totally unarmed (except for that single pistol) against the Germans, Ukrainians, Latvians, and Lithuanians who were armed to the teeth? Impatiently we awaited the first transport of arms from the Aryan side. Meanwhile we decided:

1. To issue a proclamation to the Jewish population, explaining that "resettlement" meant Treblinka and that Treblinka meant death; suggesting that Jewish men hide their wives and children and then resist German orders.

2. To forge German "life cards" and distribute them among those not fortunate enough to find work in the German shops and hence regarded as "nonproductive" elements. (Many thousands of such factory cards were distributed.)

3. Owing to the fact that the Jewish police as well as the Judenrat—like the Ukrainians and the Letts—became the executors of German orders, they were to be actively opposed in their dastardly work. The commandant of the Jewish police, Josef Szeryński, was condemned to death.

To our amazement and bitterness this proclamation did not, at the time, find acceptance. People were still incredulous. The Jews were being led to their death, and the Jewish postal service in the ghetto was active. "Greetings" from the deported Jews arrived and the news spread through the ghetto with lightning speed. Thousands of people, driven by hunger and despair, volunteered day after day for "resettlement." At the staging area *(Umschlagplatz)*, the Nazis "mercifully" distributed three kilograms of bread and one kilogram of marmalade to the volunteers.

After the evacuation of entire streets and districts, we set fire to several dozen empty houses to prevent Jewish belongings from falling into German hands. The fires reached their greatest intensity the night of August 20. On that day also ŻOB fired its first shot: Israel Kanal seriously wounded Josef Szeryński with two bullets. The attempt on the life of Szmerling, an officer of the Jewish police, failed.

The following day we received from our comrades on the Aryan side five pistols and eight hand grenades. In our circumstances, a real treasure! Meantime, since the action was interrupted—the German "Resettlement Commando" or the Annihilation Commando, as the Germans themselves called these monsters, moved elsewhere in the Warsaw district to do their work and only a very few Germans were on the ghetto streets—we decided that day to attack the Germans and Ukrainians entering on Smocza Street, in the sector between Nowolipie and Dzielna Streets.

But bad luck seemed to jinx our activities. A group of comrades, whom we had previously dispatched to the Hrubieszów forest to organize partisan action, perished. (We had sufficient forces, but lacked arms!) A similar fate met the detachment we sent into the Międzyrzec woods. On September 3, 1942, the Gestapo arrested Joseph Kaplan. A few hours later, Samuel Braslaw was murdered in the street by the Germans and in the evening our pitiful arsenal of arms and ammunition fell into their hands. Thus all our efforts to defend the honor and dignity of the Warsaw Jews were aborted from the start.

On September 5, the Germans renewed their action and it took forms that went beyond past events. On September 12, the day the action was declared completed, not many more than 50,000 Jews were left in the ghetto. These were crowded into four small ghettos:

    I   From the corner of Karmelicka and Leszno streets—only even-numbered houses on Leszno, from 34 to 80 (corner of Żelazna), one side of Żelazna up to Nowolipie, part of Smocza to Nowolipki, the odd-numbered side of Nowolipki up to Karmelicka, odd numbers of Karmelicka as far as Leszno—the productive ghetto, in which were the establishments belonging to the Germans—Többens, Schultz, G. K. Schulze, Röhrich, Hoffmann, Hallmann, and Schilling.

II   Gęsia, even numbers until Smocza; Smocza to Parysowski Square, Szczęśliwa, Stawki, Pokorna, Muranowski Square between Pokorna and Nalewki streets, Franciszkańska even numbers to Boni-fraterska—the so-called Central Ghetto, in which were the Judenrat and its institutions as well as the *Werterfassung*, an SS unit charged with appropriating all remaining Jewish property. The "unproduc-tive" elements lived here, except for a block of buildings near the even-numbered side of Nalewki, the site of the factories of the German firm Brauer and the lodgings for its Jewish employees.

III   The area between Franciszkańska odd numbers, Wałowa even numbers, Świętojerska even numbers, and Bonifraterska—the brush workshops, producing for the German Army employment ad-ministration, and the ghetto for their Jewish workers.

IV   The area comprised by Pańska, Żelazna, Waliców, Prosta, Ciepła and Twarda—a branch of the Többens workshops and the ghetto for its workers.

The area between Ghetto I and Ghetto II was a "neutral zone," where nobody lived. The area between Ghetto I and Ghetto IV was part of the Aryan district.

One felt ashamed to be alive! Many comrades argued that the ghetto ought to be set on fire, that one ought to attack the Germans with bare fists and die. Others advised taking advantage of the lull beween the first liquidation and the next one to build up the combat organization and to acquire quantities of arms. This latter course was taken. Hehalutz adopted the following resolutions:

(1)   To dispatch couriers to all cities to mobilize the remaining ghettos. To Bialystok we delegated Mordecai Tenenbaum (Tamaroff), later ŻOB commander in the Bialystok region. Zvi Brandes and Frumka Plotnicka went to Będzin and Baruch Gaftek was named ŻOB commandant there. In Cracow Leib Leibowicz (Laban) was appointed commander. Dolek Liebeskind and Draenger later became his adju-tants. Rivka Glanz and Yehuda Glikstein went to Częstochowa; Abba Kovner to Vilna.[26]

26. Zvi Brandes (1917–1943) was a Hashomer Hatzair activist. Baruch Gaftek (d. 1943) was active in Hehalutz, especially in its self-defense training pro-gram. Abraham Leib Leibowicz was a leading figure in the halutz movement in Cracow. Rivka Glanz (1915–1943) and Yehuda Glikstein (d. 1943) were both active in the halutz movement.

(2)   To strengthen cooperation with all political and community groups; the right- and left-wing factions of the Labor Zionist party
immediately offered cooperation. Negotiations with the Bund dragged
on. The Bund agreed to enter ŻOB and take joint action only in
Warsaw (at this time about two million Jews still lived in Poland),
but did not agree to participate in a joint representation. To enable
and to expedite the cooperative effort, Hehalutz, Dror, Hashomer
Hatzair, Gordonia, Right Labor Zionists-Hitachdut, Left Labor Zionists, and General Zionists decided to form the Żydowski Komitet
Narodowy—ŻKN (Jewish National Committee). Coordination with the
Bund was made possible by creating the Żydowski Komitet Koordin-
acyjny—ŻKK (Jewish Coordinating Committee), with representatives
of the above-mentioned groups as well as those of the Bund. ŻOB was
recognized as the military arm of the ŻKK. . . .[27]

During the three months of relative quiet in the ghetto, we succeeded in partially arming the combat units of Dror and Hashomer
Hatzair; other groups were still in their organizational and training
stages at that time.

The first ŻOB armed action took place in Cracow. On December
24, 1942, ŻOB's Cracow branch carried out an act of vengeance
against the Germans. A few coffee houses frequented by the Germans
were attacked with hand grenades, and a few higher Gestapo officers
were shot. The Germans announced twenty as the number of killed
and wounded. This action, however, was also the end of ŻOB activities in Cracow. A few days later, the Cracow organization, including Laban, its heroic leader, fell into German hands.

On January 18, 1943, strong detachments of German gendarmes,
SS, and military surrounded the Warsaw ghetto. In the two preceding days the Nazis had undertaken a series of large-scale raids on the
Aryan side and carried out mass arrests, and the Jews in the ghetto
least expected a German action at that time. At daybreak, the Germans took control of all streets and entries to the ghetto. Workers
going to the factories were taken to the Umschlagplatz, without
having their "productivity" checked. Others managed to take cover.
Volunteers for "resettlement" no longer showed up. During the past
three months hiding places had been prepared in attics and cellars;
rooms were walled in, double ceilings were built. Only a few
[resistance] groups remained outside the shelters, trained as best

27. For more on the formation and political character of these bodies, see
Dawidowicz, *The War Against the Jews 1933–1945*, Chapter 15.

they could. Some of the armed units in the Central Ghetto under the command of Mordecai Anielewicz deliberately allowed themselves to be seized together with a few hundred other Jews. When they reached the corner of Zamenhof and Niska, they opened fire on the Germans. The Jews being led to death scattered, and the Germans panicked and fled. Soon, however, overcoming their first fright, the Germans returned with reinforcements. There were losses on both sides. The ranks of the Jews began to thin out. . . . After an hour's battle, the entire group perished with the exception of the commander, who miraculously got away.

Other groups . . . waged partisan warfare within the buildings. . . . The results of this battle exceeded our greatest expectations. The Germans were panic-stricken before entering buildings and they discontinued the action on the third day.

In the area of the workshops, Israel Kanal headed a small group of heroic fighters. As a result of these battles, we seized more than a dozen guns and pistols, and we killed or wounded fifty Germans.

Beginning in February, the Germans proceeded with the further partial liquidation of the ghetto in Częstochowa. There a small group of Jewish combatants, armed with a few pistols delivered to them by the Warsaw ŻOB, actively fought the Germans. It was an indescribably tragic picture: old rusted pistols jammed and failed. The fighters attacked the Germans with their bare fists and all perished by German bullets. This mute heroism elicited astonishment and admiration even from the Germans.

The passive resistance of the civilian populace as well as the combat of the ŻOB units forced the Germans to discontinue the liquidation action in Warsaw. The populace hid in shelters; when caught, they broke the sides of the freight cars and jumped off the trains running at full speed. A few Jews even managed to escape from Treblinka. The repercussion of the shooting and exploding hand grenades electrified the population. Everywhere the fighters were greeted as saviors. The population supported them as best they could: bakers made gifts of bread, leather workers made holsters. The Combat Organization grew in numbers and strength from day to day.

Since the funds provided by the Citizens' Committee could not meet the budget, which ran into millions, the Combat Organization levied higher taxes upon the wealthier elements of the Jewish population. Strong methods applied against shirkers resulted in regular tax payments. Tax delinquents were arrested. The Jewish workshop managers, the Jewish police, and all those who had business dealings with the Germans were heavily fined. The Judenrat and its institutions were requested to contribute about one million zlotys. This contribution was paid within three days. . . .

ŻOB could call on twenty-two fighting groups, eleven units of the youth groups within the Hehalutz organization (Dror—5, Hashomer Hatzair—4, Akiva—1, Gordonia—1); of the rest: Bund—4, Right Labor Zionists—1, Left Labor Zionists—1, Hanoar Hazioni —1 and the left-wing trade unions—4. . . .[28] Nine of the groups were billeted in the Central Ghetto, eight in the area of the Többens-Schultz workshops, and five in the brushworks ghetto.

The mainstay of the ŻOB arms supply was a larger arms transport delivered by the Polish military authorities. It consisted of pistols, hand grenades and explosives. Further, with the funds raised, we bought a few hundred more pistols and ammunition. For a Visa or Parabellum [29] we paid between ten and fifteen thousand zlotys!

For long weeks we dug tunnels all the way to the gates of the ghetto where the German sentries were posted, and we laid mines. In accordance with the viewpoint that ŻOB could offer effective resistance if it could count on the total and unquestioned support of the Jewish community, we started a relentless and ruthless fight against all traitors, those who collaborated with the Germans or who demoralized the ghetto by their immoral attitudes. Those who did not escape to the Aryan side were executed by ŻOB. Among those executed after he was condemned to death was Dr. Alfred Nossig.

The atmosphere was cleared! The remnants of Warsaw Jewry, purged in the most monstrous trials of fire and blood, breathed more freely. During the January actions, the Warsaw ghetto evidenced the change in mind and conduct of the surviving Jews. The Germans also had to take account of this. But obviously neither the populace's brave posture nor the fierce resistance put up by the Combat Organization could influence the ghetto's fate, which was already sealed. The Germans, however, did not want to suffer losses

---

28. A circumlocution for the PPR. This report was destined to be read by members of the Polish Government-in-Exile in London, many of whom anyway charged the Jews with being Communists.
29. Automatic revolvers.

and they decided to finish the Warsaw ghetto in a "peaceful" manner, having in mind two goals:

(1)   To make use of those "fit to work" for war production, obviously only for as long as they were needed;

(2)   By separating those "fit to work" from the "nonproductive" (for the most part, those able to work, but shunning employment in German enterprises), to weaken the ghetto and destroy it morally by arousing hatred and jealousy between those Jews marked "to stay alive" and those whose death was only a matter of days.

At the beginning of February 1943, the owners of German enterprises began a broadly conceived effort to induce the shop workers to register for voluntary evacuation. "Warsaw will be cleansed of Jews," they proclaimed at specially convened workers' meetings; only those who would leave for Poniatowa and Trawniki, where the shops would be relocated, would be sure of bread and of "lasting through the war." Designated as master of ceremonies of their propaganda was Többens's partner, a degenerate named Stehman, who had earlier gained popularity among the Jewish workers for his alleged friendliness toward them, as evidenced by his joviality and clowning. At the same time, he was a big shot in various Nazi party formations, and he may well have been one of the best informed regarding the decisions about the liquidation of the Jews taken by the SS authorities in Berlin. In his rhetorical speeches, he painted for his listeners a paradisaic existence in beautiful bucolic surroundings, a life rich in magnificent amusements in leisure hours and days. He babbled nonsense about nonexistent beaches, pools, concerts, theatrical performances, excellent food, visions of cleanliness, schools, care centers, etc.

To emphasize the "civilian" character of the resettlement, the industrialist Többens, rather than an SS representative, was named to head the resettlement effort.

The first enterprises chosen to be liquidated were the Hallmann carpentry factory and the brush shops. ŻOB began an immediate counteraction in word and deed. During the night preceding the evacuation set for the Hallmann factory, a unit of the Combat Organization got inside the factory and completely burned the buildings, all the raw materials, and the machinery already packed. The Germans in the factory area fled in panic. The ŻOB unit withdrew without casualties. Next day, only 25 of the 1,000 workers showed up for evacuation, while not one of the 3,500 workers in the brushworks turned up. A group of sixty Jews imprisoned at the Schultz shops was freed by ŻOB in plain view of the German guards. The authority of ŻOB grew not only among the Jewish population, but the Germans also had to regard it very seriously. On March 14, ŻOB posted a proclamation calling for resistance to the German decrees and emphasizing that the "voluntary" resettlement was nothing but the inevitable annihilation of the ghetto. Next to our proclamations Többens affixed his own notices on March 20 (most of which ŻOB confiscated when it learned they were printed). Its text was as follows:

> *To the Jewish munitions workers in the Jewish district:*
> The night of March 14 the command of the Combat Organization posted a proclamation to which I wish to reply. I state categorically that:
>
> (1)   There is no question of any resettlement action;
>
> (2)   No one forced Mr. Schultz or me at gunpoint to undertake this action;
>
> (3)   I categorically state that the last transport did not perish. Regrettably, Mr. Schultz's munition workers did not follow his well-meant advice. I regret that I was forced to relocate one of the workshops, to take advantage of the availability of transportation then. An order was issued that the names of the workers who arrived at Trawniki be immediately determined and that their belongings be transferred with them at the same time. To maintain that the convoy of the second transport, from Prosta to Poniatowa, did not know what had happened to the [earlier] transport is a dastardly instigation of the munition workers and a most vulgar lie. The convoy members all remained on the spot, dispatched the train, and also meanwhile came here back and forth in trucks together with the workers from Poniatowa to transport the machinery, etc. The luggage did not leave Prosta Street and remains under the care of a Jew, Engineer Lifshitz, who is prepared at any time to provide information about this. The luggage will leave with the next transport to Poniatowa.
>
> In Trawniki as well as in Poniatowa every worker received and keeps all his baggage, his personal belongings.
>
> Jewish munitions workers! Don't believe those who wish to mislead you. They want to incite you to bring about unavoidable results. The hideouts do not offer any security, and there is no chance to keep alive there or in the Aryan district. The uncertainty itself and inactivity will morally destroy munitions workers who are used to working. I

ask you, why do wealthy Jews from the Aryan district come to me to beg to be admitted to work? They have enough funds to live in the Aryan district, but they are unable to stand the strain. I can advise you in complete sincerity: go to Trawniki, go to Poniatowa, for there you have a chance to live and there you will survive the war. The Command of Combat Organization cannot help you; they offer only empty promises. They sell you space in the hideouts for exorbitant sums of money, and then they will chase you into the street again and abandon you to your fate. You have already had enough experience with deceitful tricks. Believe only the German shop directors who remain together with you to continue production in Poniatowa and Trawniki.

Take along your wives and children, for they will also be taken care of!

Walter C. Többens—Plenipotentiary
for the Relocation of Enterprises in
the Jewish District of Warsaw

The German shop owners did not lag far behind their SS compatriots in treachery. In addition, Mr. Többens had the audacity, through the intermediary of some of his Jewish stooges, to invite the Combat Organization to a conference on the subject! But the German propaganda bore no fruit. No one believed in it. If a few hundred workers volunteered for evacuation, hunger drove them and primarily the hopeless morrow. Consequently, the Germans realized that they would have to use force, which, however, did not fit their plans. On the one hand, it would show up their real intentions; on the other, the results would be meager. The Jews began to hide themselves. Apparently the final liquidation of the ghetto did not yet fit into German plans and they considered it premature. They then turned to the Judenrat, requesting it to carry out the action. Through Dr. Schipper as intermediary, the Judenrat asked the Combat Organization for a conference. This invitation was, of course, rejected with contempt, after which the Judenrat chairman, the discredited Eng. Mark Lichtenbaum, gave the Germans the following characteristic answer: "I have no power in the ghetto. Another authority rules here."

The German plans dissolved in complete fiasco. This time they did not succeed in dividing the strength of the remaining handful. If the Germans issued a death sentence upon the entire Jewish community—then, let us die in battle! That was ŻOB's decision.

The night of April 18 the final act of the tragedy of the Warsaw ghetto began. It was intended as a birthday gift for the Führer.

ŻOB rose to fight. At 2 a.m. the Germans posted patrols, 25 meters apart, composed of Germans, Letts, and Ukrainians, around the walls of the ghetto. Singly, by twos, and threes, the Germans entered the uninhabited part of the ghetto, aiming to surprise the fighters and the populace. At 2:30 a.m. the first dispatches from our outpost sentries signalled the concentration of large military units within the ghetto. At 4:00 a.m. all combat groups were at their assigned positions. They were ready to receive the entering enemy properly. At 6:00 a.m. a contingent of 2,000 heavily armed SS men entered the Central Ghetto, with tanks, rapid-fire guns, three trailers loaded with ammunition, and ambulances. Waffen SS units were accompanied by the entire "Resettlement" staff, among them these Gestapo and SS officers: Michelson, Handtke, Höfle, Mireczko, Berteczko, Brandt, and Mende. The Jewish populace was nowhere to be seen; all were hidden in underground bunkers or other hiding places. Only ŻOB was on the alert above ground. The fighters were located at three ghetto key points, which controlled access to the main ghetto streets. The first engagement took place at Nalewki, where two barricaded combat groups defended the street. The first battle ended with victory for the fighters. The Germans retreated, leaving many dead. At the same time, the main onslaught took place at the corner of Zamenhof and Miła. The fighters, barricaded at all four corners of the intersection, attacked the main German column entering the ghetto. After the first machine-gun salvo and well-aimed grenades tossed against the SS in marching formation, the street emptied. Green uniforms were nowhere to be seen. They hid in stores and entries of nearby buildings. Single shots were exchanged. Fifteen minutes later tanks passed through the checkpoint and moved hard against the very positions of the fighters. Incendiary bottles aimed carefully and calmly hit a tank. The flames spread unexpectedly fast. An explosion erupted. The tank was immobilized. Its crew was burned alive. The remaining two small tanks retreated immediately, followed by the hastily retreating Germans, who were being picked off by accurate fire and grenades. The Germans lost some 200 killed and wounded. Our losses: one fighter.

Two hours later, the Germans moved their guns into the inter-ghetto area and began to harass our positions. Their access seemed clear, our position taken. Suddenly from the windows on the opposite side of the street (Zamenhof 29), grenades showered down on the Germans. One of our groups, which had hitherto held its fire so as not to disclose its existence, attacked the Germans once again on the same spot. Our group withdrew without losses. At 5:00 p.m. the Germans were no longer within the ghetto. They had withdrawn into the uninhabited areas. We had the upper hand, having taken them by surprise and by our swiftness from well-camouflaged positions.

The second day of the action began with the concentration of larger SS detachments in the interghetto area and on the Aryan side. The main force, however, did not enter the inhabited section. About 3:00 p.m., a group of 300 SS men approached the gate of the brushworks area. They stopped only for a while, but this sufficed for our fighters to explode an electrically-operated mine under the SS men's feet. The Germans fled, leaving 80–100 dead and wounded. Two hours later they returned to the area, cautiously, in single file, battle-ready. The fighters waited for them in their own positions. Thirty Germans entered, but only two got out. They were attacked with grenades and incendiary bottles. Those who were not killed by the grenades were burned alive. Only then did the Germans call in their artillery. The block was placed under the fire from four sides. At the same time, two higher SS officers appeared on the scene and requested the fighters to lay down their arms, proposing to halt operations for fifteen minutes. Otherwise the entire area would be bombed. The reply consisted of a few shots. On the opposite side of the block, from Franciszkańska Street, another SS detachment entered, but they did not get far. They were scared off by a few rounds of rifle fire. Once again, the area was clear of Germans. This was the second total victory for the fighters.

On the same day, voluntary conscription for labor camps was announced in the area of the Többens and Schultz shops. But there were no volunteers, nobody came forward. Here, as in the Central Ghetto, all inhabitants were in underground shelters. The shop management kept extending the deadline for voluntary resettlement every few hours, but without success. After an announcement that the same methods used in the Central Ghetto would perforce have to be applied here, fighting groups billeted in these areas attacked an SS detachment on the Aryan side with bombs and grenades, leaving forty killed and many wounded, and also attacked other units on Smocza and Nowolipie, marching toward the Central

Ghetto. On orders of the Police Leader Globocnik,[30] brought especially for the duration of the action from Lublin, the Germans started setting fire to the ghetto on the second day of the action. The first buildings set afire were those houses and blocks where resistance was encountered: at 33, 35, 37 Nalewki; 28 and 19 Miła; 28 Zamenhof; then the entire block of the brushworks (this was the first gigantic conflagration). In response to this, the fighters set fire to all the Werterfassung warehouses as well as the shop stores, worth several tens of millions of zlotys.

The action continued. The Germans began a search for the hideouts. Their task was made easier because the insufferable heat forced some people to leave the shelters at night; their telltale traces led to the hideouts. Listening devices and police dogs proved very helpful to the Germans. At this time the fighters shifted from offensive to defensive tactics. They attempted, as far as possible, to rescue the people in the shelters. A reshuffling of the forces took place. Many combat groups were assigned to shelters. On the sixth day of the action, defensive battles in the Többens and Schultz areas began. The fighters took positions inside the buildings and in the attics, barring the Germans from the shelters. Every day the fighters defended the populace in the shelters in different places. Particularly sharp engagements were fought in 41 Nowolipki; 78, 76, 74 Leszno; 67, 69 Nowolipie. The combat groups also undertook offensive action. Whenever the Germans tried to force their way into the ghetto, heroic resistance forced their retreat, leaving hundreds of dead on the battlefield. Ashamed of their continued defeats, they started a rumor that the defense of the ghetto was led by German deserters. But they had to take the ghetto. Artillery was brought in and heavy batteries were placed on Krasiński Square, Muranowski Square, and Świętojerska and Bonifraterska streets.

The outright siege of the ghetto began. Flame throwers spread death among the populace. Planes cruising overhead dropped explosive and incendiary bombs. The entire district, set on fire on all sides, was in flames, causing thousands of deaths. In their desperation Jews would jump from the highest floors of the buildings. Those who managed to leave the buildings alive perished by German bullets. The combat groups, driven from their postions by the raging flames, turned to new tactics. They organized a guerrilla

30. See Section 4, footnote 16.

struggle among the ruins, where they lay in ambush for the German units. The battles went on without interruption day and night. The Germans were forced to fight for every street, for every house. The situation, nevertheless, became increasingly intolerable. The fighters had almost no losses, but, exhausted by the continuous struggle, they had no place to rest, for the entire ghetto was aflame. The pavement became a sticky pulp of tar because of the intense heat. The food reserves went up in flames. The wells, which had been dug with such effort, became filled with rubble from the crashing buildings. Worst of all, the supplies of ammunition ran out. The fighters now moved through the streets in small groups, dressed in German uniforms and helmets, their feet covered with rags so as to deaden the sound of their footsteps. They attacked Germans marching past in decreasing numbers. The flames instead did the fighting for the Germans, as well as the planes and the artillery stationed behind the ghetto walls.

After a thorough examination of the situation, the ŻOB Command decided to send a delegation to the Aryan district to establish contact with the ŻOB representative there. (On the eve of the action, Yitzhak Zuckerman had been sent out in this capacity, replacing Aryeh Wilner. Wilner, who had been caught by the Germans, managed to escape from the Pawiak prison and had to return to the ghetto.) We mustered our forces to organize a rescue action. During the night of May 8, Simcha Rathauser, the ghetto emissary, returned to the ghetto to help evacuate some people.[31] But it was too late.

With the help of special listening instruments and police dogs, the Germans began to uncover the underground Jewish shelters. On May 8, the Germans surrounded the main bunker of the Combat Organization and closed all its five entries. In this helpless situation, Aryeh Wilner addressed the fighters and summoned all to commit suicide, lest they fall into German hands alive. Lutek Rotblat was the first, shooting his mother, then himself. In this shelter most members of the Combat Organization met their deaths, including its commandant, Mordecai Anielewicz. We rescued from the ghetto some eighty people, most of whom, however, later perished on the Aryan side or in the forests. The groups of Josef Farber and Zacharias Artzstein, with whom contact could not be made, continued

---

31. Born in 1924, Rathauser, who now lives in Israel, was active in the halutz movement.

fighting in the ghetto for long weeks, after which all trace of them was lost.

After the heroic defense of the Warsaw ghetto, the liquidation and defense of the ghettos in Częstochowa, Bialystok, Będzin and other cities took place. The most tenacious and heroic was the struggle fought by the Bialystok ŻOB. Thanks to the help of the vice-president of the Bialystok Jewish Council, Barash, who made explosive experts and raw materials available to ŻOB, grenades and various acids useful in defense were manufactured within the ghetto itself. Mordecai Tenenbaum was in command of ŻOB fighting units. The first skirmish took place on Fabryczna Street, while the fiercest battles were fought on Białostoczańska Street, where a Jewish machine-gun was emplaced. As in Warsaw, the Germans brought in armor and heavy field artillery. The bitter fighting lasted eight days. Acts of armed resistance on the part of the Jews lasted for a long time—more than a month. The Jews killed or heavily wounded a few hundred Germans and Ukrainians. They fought with extraordinary determination, and were admired by the population of the entire city and district. To break the fighters' resistance the Germans set fire to the ghetto, as they did in Warsaw, and the ghetto was burned to the ground. The entire sector of the railroad tracks between Bialystok and Małkinia and Treblinka was covered with the bodies of escapees who had jumped from the trains. From the roofs of the freight cars the Ukrainians incessantly fired machine guns at the escaping Jews. Only a handful of Jews succeeded in escaping and hiding in the villages and forests. The destruction of the murder chambers of two large death camps, Treblinka and Sobibór, by Jewish inmates will be inscribed in golden letters in the chronicles of Jewish resistance. The battle in Treblinka has been described by a participant in the authentic report, *A Year in Treblinka*,[32] which we enclose. The struggle in Sobibór, near Chełm Lubelski, took place in the following circumstances: some 600 surviving Jewish prisoners in this death camp organized into combat fives and, at a prearranged time, started an armed action. On October 14, 1943, the Jews killed all the German and Ukrainian camp wardens and set fire to the crematorium, gas chambers, clothing stores, and

32. It was written by Yankiel Wiernik and published in an English translation by the Jewish Labor Bund in New York in the 1940s.

barracks, cut the barbed wire, and escaped to the neighboring woods. While crossing the mined area surrounding the fences, some 200 people were killed; and the following day close to sixty were caught by the Germans during a roundup and shot on the spot. The rest hid in the forests and villages.

Thanks to the help provided by the Warsaw ŻOB, the combat organizations in Częstochowa, . . . Będzin, and Trawniki offered resistance during the German liquidation of these centers, fighting to the last bullet. A handful of Częstochowa ŻOB members managed to escape, and they remain in the forests.

In spite of the most difficult conditions in which we live, and despite the numerous sacrifices which we have been forced to make as members of a conspiratorial movement and as Jews, the Jewish Combat Organization continues its activities, preparing the young in the remaining Jewish centers for the hopeless battles which will undoubtedly take place.

APPENDIX

ESTIMATED NUMBER OF JEWS KILLED
IN THE FINAL SOLUTION

Country	Estimated pre-final solution population	Estimated Jewish population annihilated Number	Percent
Poland	3,300,000	3,000,000	90
Baltic countries	253,000	228,000	90
Germany/Austria	240,000	210,000	90
Protectorate	90,000	80,000	89
Slovakia	90,000	75,000	83
Greece	70,000	54,000	77
The Netherlands	140,000	105,000	75
Hungary	650,000	450,000	70
SSR White Russia	375,000	245,000	65
SSR Ukraine *	1,500,000	900,000	60
Yugoslavia	43,000	26,000	60
Belgium	65,000	40,000	60
Rumania	600,000	300,000	50
Norway	1,800	900	50
France	350,000	90,000	26
Bulgaria	64,000	14,000	22
Italy	40,000	8,000	20
Luxembourg	5,000	1,000	20
Russia (RSFSR) *	975,000	107,000	11
Finland	2,000	——	——
Denmark	8,000	——	——
TOTAL	8,861,800	5,933,900	67

* The Germans did not occupy all the territory of this republic.

SUGGESTIONS FOR FURTHER READING

The War Against the Jews 1933–1945 by the present author may serve as a companion text to this reader.

The following suggestions for further reading represent a selection of the soundest works available in English, culled from an enormous quantity of books. New works are constantly appearing. Those who wish to explore Holocaust printed sources—historical, memoiristic, and literary—in greater depth will profit from the twelve-volume Bibliographical Series issued jointly by the Yad Vashem Martyrs' and Heroes' Memorial Authority in Jerusalem and the YIVO Institute for Jewish Research in New York. The first volume, *Guide to Jewish History Under Nazi Impact* (1960), edited by Jacob Robinson and Philip Friedman, is an authoritative guide to all sources for this subject. Four subsequent volumes are devoted to works in Yiddish, five to works in Hebrew, and one to the fate of the Jews in Hungary. The latest volume (1973), edited by Jacob Robinson with the assistance of Mrs. Philip Friedman, is *The Holocaust and After: Sources and Literature in English.*

For a variety of valuable studies and articles, the student is advised to consult the volumes in three series: *Yad Vashem Studies, YIVO Annual of Jewish Social Science,* and the *Year Books* issued by the Leo Baeck Institute.

THE ORIGINS OF NATIONAL SOCIALISM

Arendt, Hannah, *The Origins of Totalitarianism* (New York:Meridian, 1958).

Cohn, Norman, *Warrant for Genocide: The Myth of the Jewish World-Conspiracy and the Protocols of the Elders of Zion* (New York: Harper and Row, 1969).

Massing, Paul, *Rehearsal for Destruction: A Study of Political Anti-Semitism in Imperial Germany* (New York: Harper, 1949).

Mosse, George L., *The Crisis of German Ideology: Intellectual Origins of the Third Reich* (New York: Grosset and Dunlap, 1964).

Pinson, Koppel S., ed., *Essays on Antisemitism* (New York: Conference on Jewish Relations, 1946).

Pulzer, Peter, G. J., *The Rise of Political Anti-Semitism in Germany and Austria* (New York: John Wiley, 1964).

Stern, Fritz, *The Politics of Cultural Despair: A Study of the Rise of the Germanic Ideology* (Berkeley and Los Angeles, Calif.: University of California Press, 1961).

HITLER AND THE THIRD REICH

Bracher, Karl Dietrich, *The German Dictatorship: The Origins, Structure, and Effects of National Socialism* (New York: Praeger, 1971).

Bullock, Alan, *Hitler: A Study in Tyranny* (New York: Harper, 1964).

Dallin, Alexander, *German Rule in Russia, 1941–1945: A Study of Occupation Policies* (New York: St. Martin's Press, 1957).

Fest, Joachim, *Adolf Hitler* (New York: Harcourt Brace Jovanovich, 1974).

Heiden, Konrad, *Der Fuehrer: Hitler's Rise to Power* (Boston: Beacon, 1969).

Hitler, Adolf, *Mein Kampf* (Boston: Houghton Mifflin, 1948).

Jäckel, Eberhard, *Hitler's Weltanschauung: A Blueprint for Power* (Middletown, Conn.: Wesleyan University Press, 1972).

Smith, Bradley F., *Adolf Hitler: His Family, Childhood, and Youth* (Stanford, Calif.: Stanford University Press, 1967).

Trevor-Roper, H. R., *The Last Days of Hitler* (New York: Collier Books, 1966).

THE SS AND THE DEATH CAMPS

Buchheim, Hans, et al., *Anatomy of the SS State* (New York: Walker, 1968).

Friedländer, Saul, *Kurt Gerstein: The Ambiguity of Good* (New York: Knopf, 1969).

Hoess, Rudolf, *Commandant of Auschwitz* (New York: Popular Library, 1961).

Höhne, Heinz, *The Order of the Death's Head: The Story of Hitler's SS* (New York: Coward-McCann, 1970).

Naumann, Bernd, *Auschwitz* (New York: Praeger, 1966).

Smith, Bradley F., *Heinrich Himmler: A Nazi in the Making 1900–1926* (Stanford, Calif.: Stanford University Press, 1971).

THE FINAL SOLUTION

Braham, Randolph, *The Destruction of Hungarian Jewry: A Documentary Account* (New York: World Federation of Hungarian Jews, 1963), 2 vols.

Chary, Frederick B., *The Bulgarian Jews and the Final Solution, 1940–1944* (Pittsburgh: University of Pittsburgh Press, 1972).

Hilberg, Raul, *The Destruction of the European Jews* (Chicago: Quadrangle, 1967).

——, *Documents of Destruction: Germany and Jewry, 1933–1945* (Chicago: Quadrangle, 1971).

Levy, Claude and Paul Tillard, *Betrayal at the Vel d'Hiv* (New York: Hill and Wang, 1969).

Presser, Jacob, *The Destruction of the Dutch Jews* (New York: Dutton, 1969).

Reitlinger, Gerald, *The Final Solution: The Attempt to Exterminate the Jews of Europe, 1939–1945* (New York: Yoséloff, 1968).

Yahil, Leni, *The Rescue of Danish Jewry* (Philadelphia: Jewish Publication Society of America, 1969).

THE EICHMANN TRIAL

Arendt, Hannah, *Eichmann in Jerusalem: A Report on the "Banality of Evil"* (New York: Viking, 1964).

Hausner, Gideon, *Justice in Jerusalem* (New York: Harper and Row, 1966).

Robinson, Jacob, *And the Crooked Shall Be Made Straight* (New York: Macmillan, 1965).

THE JEWS IN EASTERN EUROPE

Friedman, Philip, ed., *Martyrs and Fighters: The Epic of the Warsaw Ghetto* (New York: Praeger, 1954).

Trunk, Isaiah, *Judenrat: The Jewish Councils in Eastern Europe under Nazi Occupation* (New York: Macmillan, 1972).

Zuckerman, Yitzhak, ed., *The Fighting Ghettos* (Philadelphia: Lippincott, 1962).

DIARIES AND SURVIVOR ACCOUNTS

Borzykowski, Tuvia, *Between Falling Walls* (Israel: Ghetto Fighters House, 1972).

Donat, Alexander, *The Holocaust Kingdom: A Memoir* (New York: Holt, Rinehart and Winston, 1965).

Flinker, Moshe, *Moshe's Diary* (New York and Jerusalem: Jewish Education Press and Yad Vashem, 1972).

Frank, Anne, *Diary of a Young Girl* (New York: Pocket Books, 1965).

Goldstein, Bernard, *The Stars Bear Witness* (New York: Viking, 1949).

Kaplan, Chaim A., *Scroll of Agony* (New York: Macmillan, 1965).

Meed, Vladka, *On Both Sides of the Wall: Memoirs from the Warsaw Ghetto* (Israel: Ghetto Fighters House, 1972).

Ringelblum, Emanuel, *Notes from the Warsaw Ghetto* (New York: McGraw-Hill, 1958).

Rosen, Donia, *The Forest, My Friend* (New York: World Federation of Bergen-Belsen Associations, 1971).

Rudashevski, Yitzhok, *The Diary of the Vilna Ghetto: June 1941–April 1943* (Israel: Ghetto Fighters House, 1972).

Wells, Leon Weliczker, *The Janowska Road* (New York: Macmillan, 1963).

Wiesel, Elie, *Night* (New York: Avon Books, 1969).

ART, FICTION, AND POETRY

Bor, Josef, *The Terezin Requiem* (New York: Knopf, 1963).

Green, Gerald, *The Artists of Terezin* (New York: Hawthorn, 1969).

Habe, Hans, *The Mission* (New York: Coward-McCann, 1966).

Hersey, John, *The Wall* (New York: Knopf, 1950).

Kantor, Alfred, *The Book of Alfred Kantor* (New York: McGraw-Hill, 1971).

Karmel, Ilona, *An Estate of Memory* (Boston: Houghton Mifflin, 1969).

Karmel-Wolfe, Henia, *The Baders of Jacob Street* (Philadelphia: Lippincott, 1970).

Kovner, Abba, and Nelly Sachs, *Selected Poems* (London: Penguin Books, 1971).

Kuznetsov, Anatoly, *Babi Yar* (New York: Dial, 1967).

Langfus, Anna, *The Whole Land Brimstone* (New York: Pantheon Books, 1962).

Sachs, Nelly, *O the Chimneys* (New York: Farrar, Straus and Giroux, 1967).

Schwarz-Bart, André, *The Last of the Just* (New York: Bantam Books, 1961).

Sperber, Manès, . . . *than a Tear in the Sea* (New York: World Federation of Bergen-Belsen Associations, 1967).

Wiesel, Elie, *The Gates of the Forest* (New York: Holt, Rinehart and Winston, 1966).

———, *The Town Beyond the Wall* (New York: Atheneum, 1964).

Wouk, Herman, *The Winds of War* (Boston: Little, Brown, 1971).

Anti-Semites' Petition, 1880: Ernst Reventlow, *Judas Kampf und Nieder-lage in Deutschland: 150 Jahre Judenfrage* (Berlin, 1937), pp. 342–344. Translated from the German by George Salomon.

Hitler's letter to Adolf Gemlich, September 16, 1919: Ernst Deuerlein, "Hitlers Eintritt in die Politik und die Reichswehr," *Vierteljahrshefte für Zeitgeschichte,* VII (1959), 203–205. Extract translated from the German by the editor.

Hitler's speech "Why Are We Anti-Semites?": Reginald H. Phelps, "Hitlers 'Grundlegende' Rede über den Antisemitismus," *Vierteljahrshefte für Zeitgeschichte,* XVI (1968), 400–420. Extract translated from the German by the editor.

Hitler's speech, April 12, 1922: Adolf Hitler, *My New Order,* ed. Raoul de Roussy de Sales (New York, 1941), pp. 14–27.

Adolf Hitler, *Mein Kampf* (Boston, 1943), pp. 65, 651, 661, 662, 679. Translated by Ralph Manheim from the German for that volume.

Hitler's memorandum on the Four Year Plan: *Documents on German Foreign Policy 1918–1945,* Series C (1933–1937), vol. 5 (Washington, D.C., n.d.), pp. 853–862.

Hitler's speeches, January 30, 1939, and November 8, 1942: Max Domarus, ed., *Hitler: Reden und Proklamationen, 1932–1945,* I (Würzburg, 1962), pp. 1058, 1937. Excerpts translated from the German by the editor.

Hitler's political testament: Office of the United States Chief of Counsel for the Prosecution of Axis Criminality, *Nazi Conspiracy and Aggression,* VI (Washington, D.C., 1946), 258–263.

Laws and decrees of the German government 1933–1938: *Die Gesetzgebung des Kabinetts Hitler: Die Gesetze in Reich und Preussen,* ed. Werner Hoche (Berlin, 1933–1938), I, 113–118, 200–201, 118–119; II, 365–366, 368–370; XV, 49–51, 51–53; XXVI, 523–524; XXVII, 321; XXVIII, 86–87. Translated from the German by George Salomon.

Decree on a penalty payment, November 12, 1938: Helmut Genschel, *Die Verdrängung der Juden aus der Wirtschaft im Dritten Reich* (Göttingen, 1966), p. 300. Translated from the German by the editor.

Reinhard Heydrich, Instructions to chiefs of all Einsatzgruppen, September 21, 1939; *YIVO-Bleter,* XXX (1947), 163–168. Translated from the German by George Salomon.

Decrees issued by Governor Hans Frank in the Generalgouvernement:

Verordnungsblatt für das Generalgouvernement, No. 1 (1939), 6–7, 61, 72–73; No. 99 (1941), 2. Translated from the German by George Salomon.

Secret order by Field Marshal Keitel, March 13, 1941: International Military Tribunal, *Trial of the Major War Criminals Before the International Military Tribunal: Official Text*, XXVI, 53–58. Translated from the German by George Salomon.

Order by Field Marshal Walter von Reichenau, October 10, 1941: *Trial of the Major War Criminals . . .* , XXXV, 81–86. Translated from the German by George Salomon.

Göring's commission to Heydrich, July 31, 1941: *Trial of the Major War Criminals . . .* , XXVI, 266–267. Translated from the German by George Salomon.

Minutes of the Wannsee Conference, January 20, 1942: Robert M. W. Kempner, *Eichmann und Komplizen* (Zurich, 1961), pp. 133–147. Translated from the German by George Salomon.

Operations situation report, U.S.S.R. No. 106, October 7, 1941: Nuernberg Military Tribunals, *Trials of the War Ciminals before the Nuernberg Military Tribunals under Control Council Law, No. 10, IV: The Einsatzgruppen Case* (Nuernberg, October 1946–April 1949), 146–149.

Round-up report of Einsatzgruppe A to October 15, 1941: *Trial of the Major War Criminals . . .* , XXXVII, 670–673. Translated from the German by the editor.

Himmler's order, July 19, 1942; "Resettlement" order for the Warsaw ghetto, July 22, 1942; General Gienanth to General Jodl, September 18, 1942: T. Berenstein et al., eds., *Eksterminacja Żydów na Ziemiach Polskich w Okresie Ocupacji Hitlerowskiej: Żbiór Dokumentów* (Warsaw, 1957), pp. 295–296, 300–302, 241–243. Translated from the German by George Salomon.

Himmler's circular memorandum, October 9, 1942: NO-1611, Office of the Chief of Counsel for War Crimes, courtesy of the National Archives. Translated from the German by George Salomon.

Kurt Gerstein's deposition, April 26, 1945: *Le Monde Juif*, XIX (January–March 1964), 4–12. Translated from the French by Rose Feitelson, with minor additions and emendations by the editor in accordance with Gerstein's German text of May 4, 1945; *Vierteljahrshefte für Zeitgeschichte*, I (April 1953), 185–193.

Auschwitz observed, report by Alfred Weczler and Rudolf Vrba: United States War Refugee Board, "German Extermination Camps—Auschwitz and Birkenau" (November 1944).

General Stroop's Report, May 16, 1943: International Military Tribunal, *Trial of the Major War Criminals . . .* , XXVI, 628–698 (Part I omitted). Translated from the German by George Salomon.

Himmler's summation, October 4, 1943: *Trial of the Major War Criminals* . . . , XXIX, 110–173. Translated from the German by George Salomon.

"Wear the Yellow Badge with Pride!": *The Dynamics of Emancipation* ed. Nahum N. Glatzer (Boston, 1965), pp. 104–108. Translated from the German for that volume by Harry Zohn.

Memoranda of the Zionist Federation for Germany, June 21, 1933, and of the Reichsvertretung, January 1934: *In Zwei Welten: Siegfried Moses zum Fünfundsiebzigsten Geburtstag*, ed. Hans Tramer (Tel Aviv, 1962), pp. 114–127. Translated from the German by George Salomon.

Martin Buber on education and adult education: Martin Buber, *Die Stunde und die Erkenntnis: Reden und Aufsätze 1933–1935* (Berlin, 1936), pp. 111–112, 128–130. Translated from the German by George Salomon.

The Reichsvertretung program, September 1935: *C-V Zeitung*, September 26, 1935. Translated from the German by George Salomon.

The Central-Verein Balance Sheet, 1935: *Jüdischer Central-Verein E.V.: Aufgaben/Satzung/Organisation* (Berlin, 1935), 12 pp. Translated from the German by George Salomon.

Song of the Chełm ghetto: *Yizkor-bukh khelem*, ed. Melech Bakalchuk-Felin (Johannesburg, 1954), cols. 589–590. Translated from the Yiddish.

Song of the Bialystok ghetto: Original in the Ghetto Folksong Collection of the YIVO Archives. Translated from the Yiddish.

ŻTOS report on refugees care in the Warsaw ghetto: Original in the Wasser Collection of the YIVO Archives. Translated from the Yiddish by Adah B. Fogel.

Reports of the health and social-welfare departments of the Vilna ghetto Judenrat: Original documents in the Sutzkever-Kaczerginski Collection of the YIVO Archives. Translated from the Yiddish by Adah B. Fogel.

Janusz Korczak's appeals: L. Bursztyn, "Odezwy Janusza Korczaka z Lat Okupacji," *Biuletyn Żydowskiego Instytutu Historycznego*, No. 45/46 (1963), pp. 263–266. Translated from the Polish by Szymon Dawidowicz and the editor.

Rabbinical Decree of the Lodz ghetto: Original in the Zonabend Collection of the YIVO Archives. Translated from the Yiddish by the editor.

Peretz Opoczynski, Smuggling in the Warsaw Ghetto: Peretz Opoczynski, *Reportazhn fun varshever geto* (Warsaw, 1954), pp. 62–74. Translated from the Yiddish by Adah B. Fogel.

Henryka Lazawert, The Little Smuggler: Emanuel Ringelblum, "Stosunki polsko-żydowskie w Czasie II wojny światowej," *Biuletyn Żydowskiego Instytutu Historycznego*, No. 29 (January–March 1959), pp. 36–37. Translated from the Polish by Ted Hudes.

Report of the culture department of the Vilna ghetto Judenrat: Original in the Sutzkever-Kaczerginski Collection of the YIVO Archives. Translated from the Yiddish by Adah B. Fogel.

A letter from the Bund, March 16, 1942: A copy of the original in the YIVO Archives. Translated from the Polish by Ted Hudes and Mark Nowogrodzki.

Interviews with Hillel Zeitlin and Dr. Israel Milejkowski in the Warsaw ghetto: *Bleter far geshikhte*, I, 2 (April–June, 1948), 111–114, and 3–4 (August–December 1948), 189–194. Translated from the Yiddish by David L. Gold.

From Zelig Kalmanovich's diary: *YIVO Annual of Jewish Social Science*, VIII (New York, 1953), 9–81, with alterations by the editor according to the Yiddish text in *Yivo-bleter*, XXXV (1951), pp. 18–92.

From Adam Czerniaków's diary: Adam Czerniaków, *Yoman geto varsha 6.9.39–23.7.42*, eds. Nachman Blumental, Nathan Eck, Joseph Kermish, Aryeh Tartakower (Jerusalem, 1968), pp. 8–9, 11, 12, 15, 20–21, 23–24, 43, 49, 50, 71, 72, 74, 77, 108–109, 113, 119, 148, 151–152, 157, 194, 199–200, 239, 254–255, 264, 276, 293, 296, 297–298, 300, 316, 320, 324–328. Translated from the Hebrew version by Zeva Shapiro and edited in accordance with the Polish original by Szymon Dawidowicz.

Prexy Czerniaków: Original in the Ghetto Folksong Collection of the YIVO Archives. Translated from the Yiddish.

From the minute book of the Lublin Judenrat: *Teudot migeto lublin*, ed. Nachman Blumental (Jerusalem, 1967), pp. 164–165, 207–209, 226–229, 273–275, 283, 314–320, 365–368. Translated from the Hebrew version by Zeva Shapiro and edited in accordance with the Polish original by Szymon Dawidowicz.

From the minute book of the Bialystok Judenrat: *Darko shel yudenrat: teudot migeto bialystok*, ed. Nachman Blumental (Jerusalem, 1962), pp. 33–35, 121–123, 195–201, 229–235, 253–265. Translated from the Yiddish original by Adah B. Fogel.

The bloody night: *Der Veker*, April 30, 1942, original in the Franz Kursky Archives of the Jewish Labor Bund. Translated from the Yiddish by the editor.

Israel Lichtenstein's last will and testament: A copy of the original in the Wasser Collection of the YIVO Archives. Translated from the Yiddish by the editor.

Homeless: *Pinkes bendin*, ed. A. S. Stein (Tel Aviv, 1959), p. 199. Translated from the Yiddish by the editor.

Josef Zelkowicz, Days of nightmare: The original document in the Zonabend Collection of the YIVO Archives. Translated from the Yiddish by Joachim Neugroschel.

The Bund's appeal to the Polish government-in-exile, May 1942: A copy of the original in the YIVO Archives. Translated from the Polish by Szymon Dawidowicz and the editor.

Michael Dov Weissmandel's letters: Michael Dov Weissmandel, *Min hametzar* (New York, 1960), pp. 162–165, 182–193. Translated from the Hebrew by Zeva Shapiro.

A summons to resistance in the Vilna ghetto: Original in the Sutzkever-Kaczerginski Collection of the YIVO Archives. Translated from the Yiddish by the editor.

Bylaws of the Coordinating Commission and the Jewish Combat Organization, with covering memorandum to the Polish government-in-exile, December 3, 1942: "Statut Żydowskiej Organizacji Bojowa," ed. Bernard Mark, *Biuletyn Żydowskiego Instytutu Historycznego*, No. 39 (July–September 1961), pp. 58–60. Translated from the Polish by Szymon Dawidowicz and the editor.

From Justina's diary: Gusta Dawidsohn-Draenger, *Pamiętnik Justyny* (Cracow, 1946), pp. 86–101, Translated from the Polish by Ted Hudes and Mark Nowogrodzki.

Facing death in the Bialystok ghetto, February 1943: *Khurbn vilne,* ed. S. Kaczerginski (New York, 1947), pp. 315–322. Translated from the Yiddish by Milton Himmelfarb in *Commentary*, VIII (February 1949), 105–109, with alterations by the editor.

Communiqués of the Jewish Combat Organization, October 30, 1942, and December 4, 1942: *Oyfshtand in varshever geto: naye dergentste oyflage un dokumentn-zamlung,* ed. Bernard Mark (Warsaw, 1963), pp. 188, 197–200. Translated from the Yiddish by Adah B. Fogel.

Communiqué of the Jewish Combat Organization, March 3, 1943: "Statut Żydowskiej Organizacji Bojowa", ed. Bernard Mark, *Biuletyn Żydowskiego Instytutu Historycznego,* No. 39 (July–September 1961), pp. 61–62. Translated from the Polish by Szymon Dawidowicz and the editor.

For your freedom and ours, April 23, 1943: A copy of the original in the YIVO Archives. Translated from the Polish by Szymon Dawidowicz and the editor.

Yitzhak Zuckerman, The creation and development of ŻOB: A copy of the original in the YIVO Archives. Translated from the Polish by Ted Hudes and Mark Nowogrodzki.